SUFFER
THE CHILDREN

SUFFER THE CHILDREN

Growing Up in Italy During
World War II

DONATO DE SIMONE

Copyright © 2007 by Donato De Simone.
Revised Edition

Photo credits:
Imperial War Museum, London
Commissione Giovanni Palatucci (Rome)

The cover—The beautiful, placid and serene seascape reproduced on the front of this book is the pride and joy of my native town of Fossacesia, province of Chieti, Abruzzo, Italy. It is the NE corner of its territorial extension. But, it is also something else: on December 1st, 1943, I saw eleven American bombers shot down over these waters by German antiaircraft batteries. Each downed airplane carried as many as ten American airmen to their deaths. These, then, are hallowed waters to me. Someday, I hope to be able to erect a modest memorial by the seashore in memory of those gallant airmen who died that day in an effort to liberate us from Nazi oppression.

(Photo by my two daughters Maria Pia and Rosanne)

Library of Congress Control Number:		2007900120
ISBN:	Hardcover	978-1-4257-2093-3
	Softcover	978-1-4257-2092-6

This book was printed in the United States of America.

Cover design by Dominic Roberti, Prof. Emeritus, St. Joseph University

To order additional copies of this book, contact:
Xlibris Corporation
1-888-795-4274
www.Xlibris.com
Orders@Xlibris.com
34636

CONTENTS

DEDICATION

A TRIBUTE TO INNOCENCE

This book
is also intended as
a tribute to children all
over the world and throughout history
who languished, suffered and died only
because the adults in their midst failed to control
their passion for waging war against one another. I wish,
particularly, to honor the memory of my fellow Italians, Marco
and Tito Grauer, 4 and 2 years of age respectively, born on Italian soil
of Polish Jewish parents and killed at Auschwitz on February 6, 1944, Marco's
fourth birthday. Tito's second birthday had occurred two days earlier aboard that infamous
death train designated as #6 that left the Milano station on January 30. After traveling for seven
days under the most horrible conditions, the boys were killed immediately upon reaching destination.
No one knows what became of their parents. It's easy to blame it all on the Nazi's, but there comes a time in
every man's life when he must accept responsibility for his own actions. We, Italians, must accept our share of
culpability for a crime against humanity that has no parallel in the history of the human race. NEVER AGAIN!

DDS

ACKNOWLEDGMENTS

My eternal gratitude goes to the following people whose counsel, encouragement or even financial assistance made this book possible.

Concetta Sorgini Berardelli
Maria Pia De Simone
Dominic and Carol Roberti
Alfredo Tozzi (Fossacesia)
Rose Peduto

A special thanks goes to Dr. Vincent Sollimo and his wife Patricia, and to Donna Farsaci-Sanna, whose friendship transcends the commonplace and whose invaluable contribution to the realization of this book has been simply priceless.

And to my grandson, Anthony Chiaravalloti, who helped me coordinate the photographs.

EPIGRAPH

Rhetorical question to John Vader, British war correspondent who, in December 1943, wrote an article about the crossing of the Sangro River, Region of Abruzzo, Italy, by Marshall Montgomery's 8th Army:

"Excuse me, Sir, but one who reads your article does not become aware of the presence of children, women, the elderly, or infirmed in the battle area. What did you do, send them all on vacation before starting hostilities?"

INTRODUCTION

In the Gospel of Saint Mark we read that the Lord Jesus Christ had a special predilection for children. Parents, in His time, recognized this and brought their children to the Lord Jesus to have Him bless them. When the disciples tried to interfere, Jesus said to them: "Suffer the children to come to me and do not hinder them. It is to just such as these that the Kingdom of God belongs." (Mk 10:14)

Unfortunately, the Lord's concern for children is not always shared by people of little faith who live among us and who shape the events of history.

In *Suffer the Children: Growing Up in Italy during World War II*, Donato De Simone (Danny to us, his long time friends), has given us an account of events during World War II in the Abruzzo Region of Italy from the perspective of an eleven-year-old boy. His narrative is most interesting and disturbing at the same time as we realize that so many innocent people, especially the children, were caught in the middle of such insane violence. Danny describes vividly how so many children were able to survive it all despite the rigors of modern warfare.

After the war, Danny and his family came to America where his father lived. He was admitted to West Catholic High School for Boys, and accepted in the 10th grade. The transition from trying to survive the war to coping with academic and social pressures in American schools makes for some very interesting reading.

Scarcely a year after settling in Norristown, Pa. tragedy struck again. After surviving innumerable bombings during the war, Maria Sorgini De Simone, his courageous mother, died of complications from childbirth. Now, Danny and his younger brother Philip had to help rear the child who was born at that time. Despite this setback, he continued his studies and eventually became a much respected high school and university professor.

As comfortable as he was in America, Danny could not forget Italy and the Italian culture he had brought with him. His hometown beckoned and he returned there in 1956 and married his childhood neighbor, Anna Maria. While Danny is fully American, the events that color *Suffer the Children*, are such that they are forever in his mind.

This is a book for all to read, especially the young, from junior high school to college. I especially recommend it to Americans of Italian roots who share with Danny their bi-cultural heritage. As we read, our thoughts and prayers will be directed to so many of God's children who, even today, are caught in the middle of violence. May the Lord Jesus, who blessed the children of his day, bless and protect children everywhere.

Most Rev. Louis A. De Simone, D. D.
Aux. Bishop of Philadelphia, Emeritus

FOREWORD

"Looking back, something I did all my life in order to make sense of it all, I concluded that Ninni's family was probably from Rome," writes Donato De Simone of the Jewish refugees lodged in his house in Fossacesia, a town on the Adriatic coast in the region of Abruzzo, during the Nazi occupation of Italy. By "looking back . . . in order to make sense of it all," De Simone joins the ranks of Italian writers and filmmakers who grew up under Mussolini and who now, in their 70s and 80s, feel the urgent need to bear witness to the ravages of Fascism and war. As the last generation to have directly *lived* the convulsive experiences of Nazi occupation and Allied liberation, Italy's septuagenarians and octogenarians have precious lessons to impart to us—lessons that official history overlooks in its obsession with the generals, kings, and dictators who operate from "on high," oblivious to the suffering they cause "on the ground." In this memoir, De Simone does a superb job personalizing the historical record, for his account teaches us what it means to suffer the concrete effects of the abstract decisions made by the generals and dictators and kings—what it means to be the family member whose home is bombed, to be the farmer whose field is mined, to be the child who has seen too much death. Like Ettore Scola's *Concorrenza sleale* (Unfair Competition), the Taviani brothers' *Night of the Shooting Stars*, or Rosetta Loy's *La parola ebrea* (First Words: A Childhood in Fascist Italy), De Simone's book tells two concurrent stories. At the literal level it tells of an extraordinary child caught up in an extraordinary series of dramatic events, but on another level, it tells of the adult's attempt to understand that story within the context of the history that nearly swallowed it up. The child's perspective is fragmentary, uncomprehending, enchanted, and it is the adult's task to assemble those pieces into a coherent whole, capable of testifying to a public trauma of the greatest possible magnitude and consequence. The result is a riveting document of the utmost cognitive and moral urgency in a time when the memory of Fascism and war is weakening, and the pendulum is swinging dangerously toward a more benign view of a vicious historical chapter.

My own interest in De Simone's testimonial project is two-fold. As a scholar of contemporary Italian culture, I have been struck by the recent outpouring of books and films on the subject of the Italian Holocaust, and as the holder of the Mariano DiVito Professorship at the University of Pennsylvania from 1998-2005, I became intrigued by the Abruzzese origin of my benefactor. That the Holocaust could reach this remote, mountainous region came as no shock to me, nor was I surprised to learn of the Abruzzesi's courage and hospitality in hiding Jews (and others in need of sanctuary), given the reputation of this populace for its courage, hardiness, and most important, its hospitality—virtues which appear everywhere in the pages of De Simone's memoir. The "four splendid blond girls" who resided briefly in the author's boyhood home, followed by the above-mentioned threesome of Ninni, his mother and grandmother, were among the 214 Jewish refugees lodged with the families of Fossacesia, putting their hosts at the greatest possible risk of Nazi recriminations. But it took very little to convince De Simone's mother to take in such perilous guests—Monsignor Tozzi merely had to invoke the ancient, pious belief that the visitor might be a divine Personage in human guise in order to win her compliance. After the battle front passed the Sangro and then stalled at Ortona, a steady parade of refugees would share the make-shift shelters and meager food stuffs of the De Simone's, including downed British pilot Joseph Campbell and later, in freedom, the Canadian Herb Speedie.

Needless to say, De Simone's memoir is a veritable gallery of human portraiture (including that of Anna Maria Fantini, fellow war-time resident of Fossacesia) endowed with the doubleness of perspective that made each encounter a magical childhood adventure and a mature reflection on its meaning and aftermath (Campbell was to die in Normandy, Speedie would prosper in Toronto, Anna Maria would become the author's wife, and De Simone himself would become an English teacher at the high school and college level). But by all measures the most vivid portrait to emerge from this memoir is that of De Simone's mother, a woman whose strength, resourcefulness and devotion may remind the reader of Moravia's Cesira (*La Ciociara*) but whose intellect and foresight far surpassed that of her literary counterpart. With her husband away in the U.S., Maria Sorgini De Simone was alone responsible for the welfare of her two sons—Donato (age 8-13 during the war) and his younger brother Filippo. This woman's remarkable grasp of military strategy and her ability to second-guess the Germans meant constantly moving from hideout to hideout trying to spare her family the dangers of proximity to the front. De Simone does not shy away from the threat that Maria's superior tactical understanding posed to older male members of the extended family unit. "My mother's brain worked like a fine Swiss watch while the rest of the family remained in a state of deep fog," De Simone writes in a memorable passage. "She could see things that others couldn't and this always caused a clash of personalities and ideas."

Though nowhere explicitly stated, this towering maternal figure is the undisputed heroine of De Simone's memoir, and it is therefore with the greatest regret that the reader learns of her death in 1948 from complications of childbirth after finally joining her husband in the New World. In writing this book, De Simone has offered a poignant tribute to the woman who gave him life, who saved his life, and who has come to personify, in my own mind, the humanity, resourcefulness, and generosity of the *popolo italiano* at its very best.

Millicent Marcus
Yale University

PROLOGUE

The Battle of the Sangro River was one of the most important battles of the Italian campaign during World War II. It took place at the end of November, 1943. It was the last great battle in which the British 8th Army was engaged in Italy under the command of General Bernard Montgomery. Shortly afterward, "Monty" was recalled home to plan the Invasion of Normandy. Significantly, the title of the General's memoirs is, *From El Alamein to the Sangro River.*

The Sangro flows totally in the Abruzzo Region, nearly all within the province of Chieti, in the central east coast of Italy. It runs for 73 miles in a northeasterly direction from the Majella (pronounced Ma-yel-la) range of the Apennine Mountains. It empties into the Adriatic Sea between my hometown of Fossacesia to the north and the town of Torino di Sangro to the south, about half way up the Italian boot's eastern coast. The terrain on its southern bank for the last five miles of its course begins to rise almost immediately to form a high ridge upon which the town of Torino Di Sangro is located. The left bank, on the north side, features a fairly large extension of very fertile flatlands, appropriately called "the plains," before the terrain begins to rise toward a northern ridge upon which sits Fossacesia. The town's population is about 6,000 in the winter, distributed in two sites, the town itself with about 5,000 residents, and the beach area with 1,000. Being a sea resort, however, during the summer its population rises to about 20,000, with traffic to match. For the benefit of the purists among us, its global coordinates are 12° 14' 42" x 18° 28' 47".

On December 3, 1943, Captain John Vader wrote an article describing the battle of the Sangro River for a military magazine. Like all articles that describe any of the myriad battles disputed by warring factions at any time in history, it read like the account of a football or soccer game fought on a playing field completely devoid of any obstructions or people. In reading it, one is duped into believing that the civilian population was not there at all. Of course, they were there, including children, women, the elderly, the sick and the infirmed. When the war arrived, most of the disabled people could not be moved, and some were killed right in their own beds. My wife, Anna Maria, and I, twelve and eleven and a half years old respectively and neighbors at the time, were there, too. We were first chased out of town on October 12, 1943, by the first air raid we had ever experienced. Then on October 25th Fossacesia and twenty-two other neighboring towns were ordered evacuated by the Germans. Finally, in late November and early December the entire region was pummeled by swarms of American bombers which, with reckless abandon, dropped five-hundred-pound bombs by the thousands over our heads ("carpet bombing" was the military term for it). I suppose murder is less biting and easy on our consciences if done from a distance. Ironically, both Anna Maria and I were American citizens, since our respective fathers had been naturalized United States citizens when we were born. My father, Nick De Simone, along with my grandfather, Filippo Sorgini and his son, my Uncle Nick (yes, there were two Nicks in the family), still lived in Norristown, Pa., although we had not been able to correspond with them during the previous three years. Those bombers, then, were our bombers. Perhaps, my father, who lived in Norristown but worked in Philadelphia, might have even helped in making the bombs in the plant where my mother knew he worked.

Furthermore, during the months of October and November, German oppressors were everywhere dispensing terror as only they knew how. With colossal arrogance, the Third Reich considered Italians expendable, so it mattered but little if we lived or died. The only thing Italian they liked was Italian art. Of course, the people they disliked even more were the Jews. At age eleven I didn't know this, but in Abruzzo we had many Jews, both foreign and domestic who were running for their lives. Since in those days we lived in a mostly homogeneous area, we wouldn't have known a Jew from a juniper. We simply called those people "refugees." The Catholic Church was deeply involved in protecting them, and our pastor, Monsignor Tommaso Tozzi, asked the people in town who owned large houses to give them hospitality. In our own beautiful house we gave lodging to two families consecutively, with all the danger it entailed, because until the very last minute of the war, the Germans, in their blind, despotic belief in "the final solution," made a bullheaded effort to destroy them all.

The following narrative represents my memories of the first fifteen and a half years of my life, the most crucial years for any developing young man. Regrettably, World War II snaked its way into my experience and its effects have impacted the rest of my life (and my wife's, too, who at twelve years of age had to witness the death of her dog, unceremoniously shot by two Nazi soldiers). Most of the stories herein contained are events that I witnessed personally. However, since at eleven years of age I could not possibly have witnessed all that I narrate, especially the stories that took place in remote battlefields, I have added some details I was able to construe from my research. In any case, all of my narration is based on true stories. People who never experienced the horrors of war couldn't even begin to imagine all that I tell in this book, let alone describe it. One had to be there.

This book will also show that war has the rare virtue of inspiring men and women to rise above their personal little world and perform heroic deeds on behalf of a suffering humanity. Sadly, however, it will also show that war has the uncanny ability to bring out the nastiest, most wicked and shameful side of Man's character: his willingness to inflict harm on his fellow human being, without mitigation and often without remorse.

I suppose most readers will assume I'm talking about the Nazis; and I am! But, I'm also talking about the British, other members of the British Commonwealth nations, the Italians, possibly the members of all other nations, and yes, the Americans as well. Fortunately, not many, but some! War has a strange pull on the human psyche.

Many young people today are confused as to the relationship the Italian people had with the Nazis during WWII. And, how could it be otherwise? Well over sixty years have passed since that terrible conflict came to an end. It's ancient history to them. Many think the Italian people, being allied with Germany, were enamored of the Nazi ideals and objectives. Nothing could be further from the truth.

The problem with the Italian people goes back to the end of the Roman Empire. It must be remembered that the seat of the Roman Empire wasn't just the city of Rome. The entire Italian peninsula constituted "Rome and its provinces." Proof of this is that two of ancient Rome's greatest poets, Ovid and Virgil, were not born in the city of Rome. Ovid was from Sulmona, in my own region of Abruzzo, a hundred miles east of Rome, and Virgil saw the light of day at Mantova, in Lombardy, three hundred miles or so north of the city.

When the Roman Empire fell and its last emperor, Romolo Augusto, nicknamed Augustolo, after two years of trying to keep afloat a sinking ship, simply quit his post in A.D. 473, the city and the entire peninsula were left without guidance or protection, open to invasions by barbarian hordes and other marauding looters during the Middle Ages. After the 14th century, the more sophisticated British, French, Spanish, and even the Austrians did their best to trample all over what they called "the garden of Europe." As a result, after the fall of the Empire, the peninsula became a kaleidoscope of city states each of which had to provide for its own welfare and protection. As a result, Italy, as a nation, never materialized, and the Italian people were never able to develop a national consciousness like the English, French and Spanish people did. Over the centuries, many patriots dreamed of seeing a reunification of the duchies, grand duchies, and seignories into a single sovereign State, beginning with Dante in the late 13th and early 14th century. Ironically, the great poet actually envisioned what is now a reality, a union of European nations under the Holy Roman Emperor (at that time, anyway).

Finally, the revolutionary movements of the 19th century concluded with the Expedition of the Thousand under the command of Giuseppe Garibaldi. *I Mille*. The One Thousand Volunteers started in Sicily and fought their way up the boot and past Naples. It was just outside the city of Teano, in the province of Caserta, that Garibaldi met up with King Victor Emanuel II, presented to him the southern regions of Italy and proclaimed, *"Ecco il Re d'Italia"* (Behold the King of Italy). Italy, as a nation, was thus born that day. It was the 26th of October, 1860. That's what is meant when historians refer to Italy as a young nation. The land is ancient and its history replete with events great and not so great, superb works of art and ignominious intrigues, saints and rogues, Lorenzo il Magnifico and Mussolini, the Renaissance and the Mafia. But, the country as a single political entity did not become a reality until 1860. Rome became the capital of Italy only in 1871 after the *Bersaglieri* troops breeched the city walls at Porta Pia.

Mistakes were made from the very beginning, however. Camillo Benso, Count of Cavour, the diplomat negotiator of the revolutionary group which included Giuseppe Mazzini, gave away the regions of Nice and Savoy to the French. Garibaldi resented that, because he had risked his very life to "make Italy," and now Cavour gave away his very hometown of Nice. In my opinion, another early mistake was made by Garibaldi himself when he proclaimed Victor Emanuel II, Re d'Italia. Had he proclaimed Italy as a Republic, perhaps based on the American model, Italian history would have been very different, indeed. Garibaldi, after all, had lived in Staten

Island, N.Y. for a number of years, in the very home of Antonio Meucci, the real inventor of the telephone (Really! The Supreme Court of New York so decreed, in 1888. By then, however, Antonio Meucci was ill and died shortly afterward, so nothing came of it. But that's another story). Giuseppe Garibaldi was even offered a commission in the Union Army by President Lincoln. He turned it down because he had to go and "make Italy." With that kind of experience in the United States, he should have made a republican Italy and given the power to the people. But, he didn't and the new nation, set up as a constitutional monarchy, was placed in the hands of the Savoy family. By the time World War I started, Italy as a united nation was only 55 years old and was still trying to get on its young feet with the steadiness and assurance of a new-born calf. Eighty-five years later, the nation lay prostrate and in ruins. The Italian people had little to with any of it, especially the people of the southern regions.

Even before the unification, the leaders of the revolutionary forces got involved in wars, thinking, perhaps, that in order to be a great nation you needed a few great victories. Italy, as the State of Piedmont, participated in the Crimean War (1854-55). After the unification, they got involved in Libya (1911), and then World War I. Throughout it all, the people remained agricultural and pastoral. Italians are not warriors.

In response to the ignominious and disappointing treatment Italy received at the Treaty of Paris of 1919, Mussolini managed to emerge as the Head of State and his Fascist Party regaled the nation with twenty years of political propaganda typical of a dictatorial style of government. Many people believed in him, however, including many Italian Jews in high positions, simply because the Italian people needed to believe in a new era. There were a number of improvements in their way of life and so the Italians kept on believing that he was the salvation of Italy. They still were not warriors, and many families were still smarting from the loss of their loved ones killed in battle up in the Alps in World War I. In that conflict, the Italian people, mostly farmers and sheep herders, wanted to remain neutral, but the decisions were always made somewhere else. The nation, even then, was divided into two sections, the poor, rural, uneducated south, and the industrialized, not so poor, better educated north. They even spoke different languages. The invaders of the north, the Austrians, at least promoted education, and the people north of the Po Valley learned how to read and write. The invaders of the southern regions, that is the Spanish, the French and the English, kept our people poor, barefoot and ignorant. So, during World War I, when millions of Italians were gathered for the first time as soldiers all in one place, they might as well have been foreigners to one another. They spoke different dialects and many of them couldn't read or write.

The causes of World War I are so vague that it's easy to understand why a farmer from Calabria or a shepherd from the mountain areas of Abruzzo was reluctant to pick up arms and go to the Alpine regions to kill people. So the government's propaganda swelled their heads with the cause for Trento and Trieste. Gotta save Trent and Trieste! And so, reluctantly, they went. Six-hundred thousand men never made it home.

When World War II erupted, the people wanted to stay out of it again. Again they were reluctant to leave their fields and their herds to go to kill someone. I can attest to this personally, because I remember the night of June 10, 1940, very well. It was the night when Mussolini announced that the declaration of war against France and England had taken place that day. There was a pall in my house. We were supposed to go to rejoin my father in the United States, but with the nation at war against the British and the French, and on the side of Germany, my mother wondered if we would ever be able to go to America. The entire country, especially the southern section, had family in the United States, and war was the last thing they wanted. Within my extended family, two of my aunts had lost their husbands in WWI. They hated the Germans. The pact with Hitler, the "Axis Rome-Berlin," at the vigil of the war was made by one man only—Benito Mussolini, who then reported it to the King and the Joint Chiefs of Staff as a *fait accompli*, and they didn't have the political leverage to stop it. The people were completely in the dark as to what was happening. They were not pleased that our nation was now going to war again, and on the side of our former enemy, Germany. The Italian people found themselves in that situation completely against their will.

Recently, I came across a book about war in Abruzzo written by a young Italian journalist, Max Franceschelli, *La guerra in casa*—(War in our very homes)—Édicola Editrice, Chieti, 2006, who, based on interviews he conducted in our area, tried to reconstruct the tragedy that crashed upon our people at the time. He writes that when World War II began to raise its evil head, the people "participated in the event without having the slightest idea of what was going on or what its consequences would be." And I can attest to the fact that until we in Fossacesia heard that first bomb explode in our town, at 10:30 A.M., Tuesday, October 12th, 1943, our people were peacefully going about their business, hoping against hope that the war would be soon over. That first explosion woke everybody up, but fast!

Finally, a word about the title, *Suffer the Children*. It is a Biblical quotation, of course, that has been used by everybody in a myriad of circumstances throughout history. I'm using it because it fits my story to perfection. The word "suffer" is being used here in an ironic sense because in the quote it means, "to allow, to permit." But here, I mean "suffer" literally, because the children are always the ones who suffer the most when adults shed each other's blood to resolve real or imaginary disputes over wrongs that may or may not have been committed. I offer as an example the story of Marco and Tito Grauer, respectively four and two years of age, found on page 82. It is for such as they that the Kingdom of God must be reserved. It is the only way justice can possibly be served.

AN AFTERNOON AT THE OPERA

It was the fourth day of the month of December, 1993. My wife Anna Maria and I were in a van driving to the Lincoln Center in New York City to see an opera at the New York City Opera. With us was my brother Philip with his wife, Arlene, and our Uncle Nick (Maestro Cavaliere Nicola Sorgini), whose seventy-fifth birthday we were celebrating somewhat ahead of time. Phil was driving. Just as we entered the Pennsylvania Turnpike at Norristown, I said to him:

"Hey, Phil, do you know what day this past Wednesday was?"

"Yes, December 1st, 1993! I had a root canal done. Why do you ask?"

"No, no, I don't mean that."

Knowing that he does not really remember much of what went on during World War II in our native town in Abruzzo, I volunteered the information. He was barely 8 years of age at the time, while I was almost twelve.

"It was the fiftieth anniversary of the day that almost was our last day on earth."

"Oh, yea, when an errant shell hit that almond tree in front of Aunt Angela's house!"

"Exactly!"

This conversation aroused the curiosity of both my uncle and my sister-in-law. They wanted to know more, so not being a man who shies away from a chance to tell a story, I began.

Maestro Cavaliere Nicola Sorgini

This is my Uncle Nick. He was mamma's toy bear before I arrived on the scene. Under her tutelage, he managed to become a clarinet player, making his debut at age 8 in 1927. On the evening of the very day he arrived in Norristown, July 16, 1936, feast of Our Lady of Mount Carmel, my father took him to the concert of the Verdi Band. He introduced him to Maestro Loreto Marsella, the band's director. The maestro asked him to go home and get his clarinet. He did and became an instant member of the band. Eventually he became the band's conductor. Mamma never considered music for me, however. She wanted me to be the doctor I, myself, wanted to be, but never was. Instead, I became a reluctant language teacher and University professor. But, I think my mother would be proud of my accomplishments anyway, modest as they are. (The Maestro died on his 88th birthday, February 21, 2007.)

A CLOSE CALL (brought forward from page 231)

It was the 1st of December, 1943. We had been liberated from German occupation the evening before. The town clock at Fossacesia had just rung the 9:00 A.M. hour tolling nine times on the larger of its two bells. As the women gathered our few belongings and prepared to depart for home (they had to bathe and dress our one-month-old cousin Pina), Phil and I, enjoying the first day of freedom, ventured outside the stable door and, leaning against its wall, we cautiously considered the new situation, delighting in the unusually warm December sun. It was a hazy, lazy sun that shone upon us that morning. A very thin layer of high clouds filtered its rays, rendering them soft and pleasant. Leaning against the outer wall of Aunt Angela's little stable, which had given us hospitality for the past three weeks, we were somewhat bewildered by the new reality. Not knowing how to handle this new phase of our adventure, we simply basked in the delight of the beauty of a fall day lived in freedom. Our mother objected to our being outside, saying that we were still under war conditions, and that it was dangerous to be out there. "Oh, ma," we demurred, "war is over—relax." She relented, but not without some apprehension and one last admonition about the ever-present possibility of another disaster. As it turned out, it was almost as if she had a direct line to a divine source of information, because not ten minutes had passed when something did happen that came uncomfortably close to proving her right. From the area of Fossacesia, scarcely two miles to the southwest, a line of small caliber guns had begun to fire round after round as the front continued its march northward toward the port city of Ortona. From the sound of their report, we could tell they were small-caliber cannons, like mortars. We could hear the report of the cannons as the shells were fired, and within a few seconds we would hear the explosion when the projectiles fell on their targets. We had become experts on things military. They sounded pretty far away, so we felt safe.

A few minutes later, however, we all came within a prayer of losing our lives. We heard those little cannons fire their rounds, but instead of a pause followed by the explosion somewhere in the distance, we heard a deafening whistle followed by a tremendous roar, and we were suddenly surrounded by a shower of tree limbs falling all around us. It was fortunate that we had been leaning against the wall which protected us from shrapnel and falling tree limbs, some of which were fairly large. One of the cannons had misfired and its shell went berserk, heading straight for the front door of Aunt Angela's house (our little stable was on the east side of the house, and to the rear, while her front door faced south). About thirty feet from her front door, almost directly ahead, there was a large almond tree. That shell headed straight for that tree's crown and exploded, covering the entire area with a million toothpicks. It was ironic that, after going through nearly two months of heavy bombardment and surviving it, on the first day of freedom we nearly lost our lives all because of a shell that went astray. We thanked the almond tree for being there and absorbing the destructive power of that shell! We thanked God, too, for saving our lives once again. Needless to say, both Phil and I had to take much harassment from our mother, along with an endless barrage of "I told you so's." But everyone was safe, so after a while mamma turned her attention to other things. By then the anticipation that we would soon be back to our own home had raised the excitement to fever pitch, even though we had already heard that Fossacesia had been 90% destroyed.

"Wow! That's amazing," my sister-in-law said. "You guys were in a real war, weren't you? Phil never talks about those days."

"Well, Arlene, it was not exactly a picnic. I have written a few things about it. As soon as I complete the narrative I'll let you read it, and then you'll know the extent to which adult insanity of war impacts on the lives of the innocent, especially the young."

I was going to reminisce some more, but the demands of driving on the New Jersey Turnpike were such that I couldn't continue telling the stories of World War II without distracting my brother as he drove, so our conversation was derailed onto other, more immediate concerns. Among other things, I had to explain the story of Verdi's *La Traviata* to the group, even though they had all seen it at least once before. I promised everybody that within a year I would finish my book, and they could read all about our war. Well, it took me a lot longer than I thought, but I finally completed it.

Here it is.

THE STORY

FOSSACESIA, WHAT A BEAUTIFUL TOWN!

These are the words with which Judge Sebastian Natale, of happy memory, describes Fossacesia. He was Judge of the Dauphin County Court of Common Pleas, Commonwealth of Pennsylvania, between 1985 until his retirement in 1994. He died in November, 2002.

Judge Natale, too, was born in Fossacesia, in 1924. His father brought the entire family to America in 1929, when he was just five years old. In a similar twist of events, his mother, like mine, died shortly after the family had settled in Harrisburg. In 1978, Judge Natale and his family returned to Fossacesia for the first time since he had left it. He was duly impressed with the beauty of his hometown. Shortly after his election to the judgeship, he wrote an autobiographical booklet entitled *From Ellis Island to the Bench.* I never met Judge Natale, although I spoke to him on the telephone in the early 90's. I would have loved to have been with him when he arrived at Fossacesia. I could have shown him the odyssey of war which the inhabitants endured in those days, including the spot where a cruel German soldier murdered his cousin, Tommaso Natale.

THE DE SIMONE'S

We were a family of emigrants. Like the Natale family, we were supposed to come to America during the 30's. Technically, we were old "Americans," since both my nonno's (that's "grandpop" in Italian—nonna means grandmother), papà's father, the first Donato De Simone, for whom I was named, and our mother's father, Filippo Sorgini, for whom Philip was named, had migrated to America in the 1890's. Their intention, like that of thousands of Italians, was not to expatriate entirely, but to go there to work a few years just to earn some money. Upon returning to Italy they would hope to purchase a home in which to live and a piece of land from which to eke out a living, and that would be the end of the adventure. Once a man crossed the ocean, however, it was not so easy to escape the lure of the land of the free and the home of the brave. America seemed to have a hold on everyone.

In 1896, Nonno Donato emigrated to Norristown, Pa., since one of his cousins had gone there to work a few years before. They both worked for the Norristown Water Company (digging ditches, of course!). He never moved anywhere else. His pattern was a five-year cycle: four years working like crazy in America "eating bread and onions,"(but, accompanied by a good glass of wine, of course!), as he used to say, and then return to Italy for a year. During his American period he worked hard, bearing upon his bent back the pains of a growing America. He, like all immigrants, was grateful for the opportunity to have a job, and he repaid his adopted country with a sterling loyalty and unalloyed devotion. Still, he didn't think the rest of the family would make it in America, so he made no attempt to settle in. Granted, life in America was no picnic for the immigrants. There were in Norristown, Pa. numerous families with as many as ten, twelve children. It was tough for a working man to feed and shelter such a family. As soon as each child was old enough to be able to earn some money he was put to work. My friend, Harry Billela used to tell me that he began shining shoes downtown every Friday and Saturday beginning at age seven. He was the seventh of ten children. His sister Josephine once told me that throughout the school year, the children's day began at 4:30 in the morning when their father would awaken each one. The three girls would help their mother with the household chores traditionally reserved for the female of the species such as doing laundry, making *"sugo"* that is gravy for the pasta (or is it sauce?), preparing fruit and vegetables for canning, and the like. The boys, especially during the winter months, had to leave the house by 5:00 A.M. armed with two buckets each and walk a half a mile to the railroad tracks, and then walk along the tracks for a mile in each direction to pick up anthracite nuggets that dropped from the coal cars of dozens of trains as they made their nightly runs from Reading, Pa., to Philadelphia. They would return home with the buckets full of anthracite nuggets. The railroad companies didn't mind because it saved them from having to hire workers to do the job of keeping the tracks relatively clean, and the families would benefit as they could heat their homes free. After returning home, each of the boys would wash up, grab a meager breakfast, and walk to school in time for the first bell. Our family wouldn't have had that kind of problem, but life was difficult in general among immigrants, and we would have had our own hardships to contend with.

Nonno Donato was tall, good looking, and possessed a sparkling sense of humor, a distinguishing quality of most of the De Simone's. He was not very good at decision making, however, and this flaw caused my mother untold hardships while she lived in his house.

In 1920, he brought his oldest son, Nicola, my father, to America so that he could earn money and contribute to the general welfare of the family. My father, hereafter referred to as papà, was fourteen at the time. As recently as the 1980s, there was one venerable personage in my circle of friends in Norristown, Pa., Mr. Gioacchino Tomasello, a gentleman of unimpeachable qualities, who remembered my father from the time when he worked alongside him the first week after he had arrived from Italy. Papà had just turned fourteen shortly before he had left his home. According to Mr. Tomasello, everybody thought papà was seventeen or eighteen, since he worked alongside the very best of the full-grown men and was able to keep up with them, shovelful by shovelful. Like Nonno Donato, he settled in Norristown, and never moved anywhere else. He was an indefatigable worker and an exceedingly honest man. He had grown up pretty much on his own, without any guidance or advice, from his early teens. Except for three trips home, each lasting no more than five months, he practically grew up in Norristown, where he died in 1989, age of 83.

In 1926, Nonno Donato returned home, and papà accompanied him. With the money they had raised jointly, nonno purchased a beautiful piece of land in the choicest rural spot in town. He decided not to return to America, so papà had to make the return trip alone. In the next few years, nonno built a small summer home on the property and proceeded to cultivate the land for a living. According to one of my aunts, "that piece of land produced pure gold!" Of course, it had to be worked all year round. The entire family pitched in, including my mother, after her marriage to papà in February, 1931. The smart thing would have been for both my parents to return to the United States together, but my father's thinking was geared to the town's tradition: marrying, taking your bride to live in your family's household, and returning to America to support the family. My mother, Maria Sorgini De Simone, hereafter referred to as mamma, didn't see it that way, but for several years she waited patiently, hoping against hope to join him in America. Meanwhile, throughout the 1930s, she wrote innumerable and extensive letters to him, every one of which he kept. These letters, now in my possession, are nothing short of encyclopedic. They are loaded with detailed information about everything that happened in the family. Papà, however, never got the message.

After the wedding, it didn't take papà long to start a family, but by the time I was born, on January 16, 1932, he had already returned to America. He did provide the necessary cash flow, but it was intended to sustain the entire family, so he sent the money to his father rather than to my mother. This practice was one of the reasons papà never had enough money to bring his own family to America. When it came to making decisions, my father was like his own father, only worse: he always made the wrong decision. That's another reason that my brother and I, instead of coming to America as children, had to wait until after the war was over. This caused us many problems, but there was a positive side to the problem. In Italy, young as I was, I was able to acquire a cultural dimension that would not have been possible had I gone to America as a child, or young boy. I'm not insinuating that I would not have been able to acquire a cultural dimension in America, but it would have been different. I might even have had the opportunity to become the doctor I wanted to be, who knows? But in Italy, I absorbed the spirit of the Renaissance with my mother's milk. The rest, I had to do it on my own despite the war.

In November, 1934, papà returned to Fossacesia. That was the only time I ever saw him. I remember his arrival that fall, but that's all. I was two months shy of my 3rd birthday. One would think that he had made arrangements to bring mamma and me back to America with him at that time, but no, he claimed that with the Great Depression in full swing, it would have been difficult for us to survive in America. Before sailing westward once again, he made arrangements for the birth of my brother Filippo. Once again, by the time the new baby was born, he had returned to America, and he never again set foot on Italian soil. It seems to me that, instead of spending money on a round trip to Italy for himself, he should have sent the money home and had the family join him in America.

My mother was an extremely intelligent person whose fourth grade education belied the vast culture she had acquired on her own and the wisdom she had developed to go along with it. She had a vivid imagination, an insatiable intellectual curiosity, and the rare ability to work at fine needlework, and she was considered one of the best-educated women in town. My biggest regret is that she didn't have the chance to come to the United States when she was young. With her talent, she might have become a fashion tycoon. Instead, she was condemned to a life of anxiety and tribulation. Living in the same house with several of my aunts, whose education ranged from an unimaginative fifth grade to total illiteracy, she experienced life as a living hell. Nonno Donato's ability to handle women was not particularly good, either, so mamma had to contend with petty quarrels every day, further making her life miserable. Such was the atmosphere in which I grew up until I was six and a half years old. Meanwhile, mamma continued to hope that papà would send her the necessary money for us to join him in America, but to no avail. The money never arrived. The war came, instead.

My Grandfather Donato and my eighteen-year-old father in Norristown, Pa. ca. 1924

There is an obvious story here. It appears that the suits they're wearing were purchased from the Jewish merchants on South Street, Philadelphia. The merchants had learned the necessary phrases in Italian to attract the Italian immigrant. They always asked for a higher price and allowed the customer to talk them into selling the item at a "bargain price." The bartering was part and parcel of the ritual of the buy-and-sell mystique in those days. Nonno Donato probably purchased the suits soon after they arrived in America, in 1920, undoubtedly for about 10 or 12 dollars each. My father was then 14. Four years later he had grown several inches, so his pants were now several inches too short, as one can plainly see.

THE SORGINI'S

If Nonno Donato's personality, though pleasant enough, lacked the fiery spark I would have expected in such a revered personage, Nonno Filippo Sorgini's personality more than made up for it. He, too, was tall, handsome in a rugged way, and a respected man in town. Unlike Nonno De Simone, however, Nonno Sorgini was a man of quick decisions. Unfortunately, he was a rover. Nonna Concetta, his wife (Grandmother Concetta), who didn't mince words in describing him, used to quip: "He has pepper up his ass!" He was never happy in one place for too long at a time.

Nonno Filippo's most unusual characteristic was his love of politics. He fought in World War I in the Italian Army as an artillery corporal major. At the time he was already forty years old, but he was needed because he was "educated," having completed the third grade. After the war, he got into politics and became an activist in Filippo Turati's Italian Socialist Party, the party of Benito Mussolini. At the end of the war, however, that party underwent a triple split: one group stayed with Turati, while another drifted to the right and followed Mussolini as he founded the PNF (Partito Nazionale Fascista—National Fascist Party), and the third group went completely to the left and adhered to Lenin's Communist ideologies. This latter group soon blended into the PCI (Italian Communist Party). At the local level, in our little town, Nonno Filippo didn't want to compromise his position with the American Immigration Authorities, as he was hoping to be able to return to the United States, so he remained with Turati. An elementary school teacher named Adriano Saraceni, the elder, who lived in the corner house at one end of his street also stayed in the Turati organization. Nonno Filippo's brother, Cola, went fascist and became the bugler of the local section of the PNF. Another of his friends, Giovanni Natale, who lived in the corner house at the other end of his street, went communist.

On October 28, 1922, Mussolini marched on Rome and became prime minister. I read somewhere that when Mussolini's wife, Donna Rachele Mussolini, received the message that her husband had been asked by King Victor Emanuel III to form a new government, she turned to some of her friends and said: *"Mio marito è il nuovo Capo dello Stato. Roba da matti!"* It is best translated as: "My husband is Italy's new Head of State. Is that crazy, or what?"

During the year that followed, the PNF consolidated its position in Rome, picking up many adherents. It was inevitable that the ensuing turmoil would cause new problems. Some young fascists began to form squads of hoodlums and they began roaming around the neighborhoods of Italian cities causing trouble. They forced non-fascists to swallow a pint of castor oil, thus putting them out of commission for a few days while they solidified their position. Instead of going after the lives of their political opponents, as the Germans would do ten years later, the fascist hoods went after their dignity. For four or five days, the victims were confined to their homes and toilets, if they had one. I don't think Nonno Filippo was ever given castor oil, though. At least, no one in my family ever talked about it.

In Fossacesia, on the evening of December 26, 1923, a year and two months after Mussolini had taken over the government, a squad of fascist rogues, after a drinking binge that had lasted all afternoon, decided to stage a home invasion at the house of all three "renegades," as they called them, "to teach them a lesson." They began at the Natale family household, being the first house they came to when they arrived. Forcing the front door, they went in and ransacked every room in the house. Inside they found Giovanni Natale's mother, Rosa, and a cousin who was visiting the family from Canada. They roughed them up a little bit. No one was killed in this incident, nor did the fascists engage in other wanton acts, but they did cause some heavy physical damage to the inside and outside of the house. Giovanni had left the house earlier that evening to go to a secret political meeting in another town, so he was unaware of what was going on in his home during his absence. The attack lasted about a half hour, during which the neighborhood was filled with the dreadful noises typical of a home invasion—shouts, blasphemies, pieces of furniture snapping, clanging of kitchen utensils being strewn all over the floor. After it was over, the Canadian cousin, passport in hand, went to the police station to file with the Carabinieri the appropriate complaint as a Canadian citizen. However, nothing came of it. The Carabinieri were probably aware of the incident and either sympathized with the gang or were ordered by the PNF not to interfere. So they appeased her anger the best they could but did nothing about it. Livid, disappointed, and scared, she decided to shorten her vacation, sailing for home in January, instead of March as originally planned, and she never returned to her native Italy, again.

After they left the Natale household, at the northern end of the street, the pack of wolves made its way up the street, stopping in front of my grandfather Filippo's door. His house at that time was a low, single-story ancient structure in the middle of the block; he had not yet built the new home where I lived before the war arrived. At the time my mother was sixteen years old, and my Uncle Nick only three. Weeping in fear, they sought refuge under the bed, which provided for them only the illusion of protection and no more. The punks outside kept making insulting remarks, touting my grandfather's dubious parentage as well as my grandmother's alleged lascivious profession, as can be imagined. The moment was serious and replete with danger. Suddenly, a bugle was heard in the distance, calling all "combatants for liberty," as they called themselves, to assemble for new orders. Immediately they all gathered around the trumpeter, who was none other than my Great-Uncle Cola, short for Nicola (the first Nick in the family), and Nonno Filippo's brother. He did not wait for the gang to go to him, however. Instead he ran to nonno's house, placed his unusually large frame in front of it (according to my Uncle Nick, Uncle Cola was 6'7"), and announced, "Boys, this is my brother's house—it's off limits. Nobody touches it! You'll have to kill me first." And so the "boys" left the area with some reluctance, but meekly. And a good thing they did, too, because unbeknown even to Great-Uncle Cola, Nonno Filippo was behind the door armed with his Colt 45 revolver. The gun had "seven bullets in it—six in the cylinder and one in the chamber," or so my mother used to describe it. Nonno Filippo had brought it back to Italy from America in one of his frequent escapades to the land of the Stars and Stripes. As for its size, to me it looked like an artillery piece, or at least that's the impression the weapon made on a very young boy. When I was seven or eight, knowing where it was hidden, I used to sneak a peak at it when nobody was looking. I knew that it was not loaded, but it was so heavy that I could hardly lift it. I suppose one had to be the size of John Wayne to be able to handle one of those "artillery pieces." After the war started, that gun disappeared. I think mamma and nonna buried it somewhere. The Germans had issued a "notice" in the spring of '43, pasting it on the door of the town hall. Signed by the German Command, it required that all weapons in the possession of any citizen had to be turned in to the German MP's under severe penalty of the law. Whose law they were talking about was not made clear. I don't think Nonna Concetta turned it in, however, probably fearing that the gun, being a distinctively American weapon, might have caused us even more problems than the threatened reprisals for possessing a gun. They probably took it with them one day to the field we owned just outside of town and buried it there, probably under an olive tree as a marker.

Behind Nonno Filippo that night was Nonna Concetta brandishing an ax, while my teenaged mother, hiding under the bed, petrified as she was, tried to comfort her baby brother. Had those "gentlemen" attempted to break down the door, there would have been in our narrow street that night a massacre of draconian proportions which might well have changed the course of history but for the fortuitous presence within the squad of vandals of my bugler Great-Uncle Cola. The group obeyed his request without comment, remaining in the area milling around for awhile and eventually dispersing altogether. The net effect of the fascist raid was that it stirred the anger of Giovanni Natale, the nineteen-year-old head of the vandalized house, who eventually became dean of the local branch of the Communist Party. In 1944, he even served a brief stint as mayor of Fossacesia. Before he died in 1992, he told me several stories related to that attack. He told me he knew exactly who those "gentlemen" were and as mayor, 22 years later, he was in a position to retaliate on a personal basis, but he chose not to. I considered that a noble act. He was my neighbor, and I knew him to be a wise and benevolent old gentleman, despite his visceral commitment to the Marxist ideals.

After the incident, Nonno Filippo was left alone by the Fascists. As Mussolini solidified his dictatorial position, he discouraged hoodlum tactics, and for more than a decade all was quiet on the political front in our street. During that time, Nonno Filippo built a brand new and beautiful house on the same lot as his family's ancient dwelling which he had inherited from his father, my great nonno, Nonno Giovanni. The family occupied the new house in the winter of 1930, in preparation for my parents' wedding.

Late in 1934, however, according to the stories I heard around the house as I was growing up, a new "secretary" of the PNF was assigned to our town hall. It must be remembered that during the twenty years of the Fascist regime the Secretary of the PNF was the real power behind governmental organizations at all levels. Nobody messed with the secretary of the party. To make matters worse, this character who came to town from somewhere up the mountains hated "Americans." He began to harass all the Americans in town, and there were lots of us in Fossacesia. By Americans, I mean all the men who had been in the United States at one time or another and their families, including the families of many men who were working in America at that particular time—families such as our own. In concert with the postmaster who worked on the first floor of the municipal building and with whom he was often seen having lunch at a local *trattoria*, he began to withhold the letters that arrived from America. Many of them contained money orders for the families' subsistence. He didn't steal anything because it would have been a crime against the State to open someone else's mail, let alone steal its contents, but with one excuse or another, he held some of the mail for a week or two, simply to make life difficult for them. Withholding mail was a crime, but any law that cannot be enforced, might as well not be in the books. At one point in 1934, my father wrote several letters to Nonno Filippo from America in anticipation of Nonno Filippo's imminent return to America. The letters were rather substantial in content because he was sending some important documents that Nonno Filippo had requested of my father.

The Secretary took umbrage to that. Not only did he withhold two of the letters, but he called my grandfather to his office and demanded that he open them right in front of him and submit their contents to his inspection and approval. Nonno Filippo refused to open his letters in front of anyone and threatened the secretary with *a "denuncia,"* (an official citation) to the tribunals in Lanciano for his illegal withholding of mails, which, if convicted, carried severe penalties plus the loss of his job. The "job" was a political appointment and was protected by the fascist party, but that protection could not supersede the laws of the State. The secretary knew that Filippo Sorgini was not one to be messed with, so he backed off. Later, however, my grandfather began to receive various "visits" from "unknown elements." One night, coming home from working his fields out of town, Nonno Filippo was assaulted by three thugs. He held his own, beating all three pretty well, but he was beaten, too, and was confined to his house for several days. As a result, he began to return home earlier than usual from his farm, especially if the field was far out of town, to make sure that it was still daylight when he got home, for fear of being ambushed again. He also began to carry a *"bastone,"* a cane with bolts embedded in its business end. As far as I know, he never had to use it.

In the summer of 1935, he began to receive anonymous letters with threats to his life and similar terroristic warnings. My mother, who was petrified by it all, talked him into going back to America and placing himself under the protection of the Stars and Stripes. The family concurred, and on July 9, 1936, he sailed aboard the famed transatlantic liner Rex and returned to the United States, taking with him my Uncle Nick, who was seventeen at the time and of draft age. That was the official excuse for his departure from town. I believe that once they reached America, a further decision was going to be made with regards to the rest of the family finally migrating to America, especially since we were all American citizens.

Once nonno arrived in his old environs in Norristown, Pa., he was faced with a series of difficult tasks that required immediate attention. First he had to find a family with whom to "board" as was the custom all over America in those days. Since he had lived in Norristown before, however, he had many friends there, and so this didn't take very long. More urgent, however, was the task of finding a job for himself and for his seventeen year old son, my Uncle Nick who didn't speak English, yet. I don't know if nonno found a job for himself. It was depression times, and I suspect he made do with day jobs. Uncle Nick, however, after a few months of inactivity, lucked out. There was a shipyard in Chester, Pa. that had a band which greeted the workers with martial music each morning as they reported for work. When Uncle Nick applied for a job as a general worker, he happened to mention that he played the clarinet. He was hired on the spot.

Still, for one reason or another, Nonno Filippo and papà took their good old time about deciding what to do with the rest of the family, so nothing was done. In May, 1939, we were directed to report to the American Consulate General in Naples, for the required physical. While there, we saw the transatlantic liner *Conte Biancamano* depart the port of Naples headed for New York, as she had done so many times before. Mom said, "Next month we will be on board!" Alas, there would be no next month. On its way back from New York, the *Biancamano* was re-routed to Genoa to be re-fitted as a troop transport. A short time later, the United States severed diplomatic relations with Italy and all transatlantic service was halted. We were trapped!

Nonno Filippo

The restless, semi-hard-drinking vagabond and political hot head. I only have one scene in my head about him. It was the 24th of June, 1936. I was 4 and a half. My Uncle Nick took me to the feast of St. John the Baptist and there he bought me a mechanical train. I went upstairs to show "Nonno" my little train. He was taking a nap on Uncle's bed. I woke him up, wound up the train, which chugged off toward our large window doors, and there it stopped. I remember seeing his smile of approval, after which he went back to sleep. He and Uncle Nick left for America a week later, and I never saw him again.

Nonna Concetta

Nonna Concetta is the real tragic hero of this narrative, a true martyr on earth, but hopefully an angel in heaven. Although, at times, when things didn't go her way, she could rattle off a stream of vitriolic imprecations that would make a sailor blush.

THE ITALIAN MIGRATION TO AMERICA

Prior to the last quarter of the nineteenth century, Italians who migrated to America were the skilled ones like artists, masons, barbers, and tailors. Around 1875, however, the gates were opened wide and anybody who wanted to come to America could do so simply by having a passport and the fare for the ocean trip, although everybody had to have an American contact who would act as sponsor and a letter from an employer who would guarantee a job for them. As a result, a flood of Italians migrated to various parts of the United States. Since Italy is surrounded by water, one can imagine that fishermen abounded. They went to areas such as New England, the Gulf Coast, and San Francisco, creating a boom in the commercial fishing industry. Joe DiMaggio's father was among these. The majority, however, being farmers for the most part, had few skills, so they accepted whatever job they could get. Pick-and-shovel work was the most common activity for the Italian men. Their women stayed home, of course, and many of them took in "boarders," that is, friends and relatives who would stay with the family. The lady of the house would cook for them, do their laundry, and even write letters home for the ones who could not read and write.

Most Italian immigrants were so disenchanted with their beautiful but poor native country ("You can't eat beauty!" they used to quip), that they sold all they possessed, placed the few essentials they possessed in an old suitcase, some times kept closed with a string, and came to America usually on borrowed money. They set up shop somewhere and never set foot on Italian soil ever again. Ironically, it would fall upon their sons the honor of returning to Italy when, after the attack on Pearl Harbor, like so many young men from all over America, they, too, rushed to their draft boards enlisting in droves to help their native land. Once on Italian soil, many American servicemen traveled impervious roads in the mountains of Abruzzo, Irpinia, Calabria, and elsewhere to meet their relatives. One such was the Most Reverend Louis A. De Simone, Auxiliary Bishop of Philadelphia. He is the bishop who graciously consented to introduce this book for me (in spite having the same last name we are not related, although he introduces me as his cousin). During WWII, soldier De Simone was a communication specialist with the U.S. 5th Army in Italy. One of three sons of a couple who immigrated to America from Montella, east of Naples, in the Campania region of Italy, he traveled to the little city in February 1944, to meet his grandmother, Autilia Volpe. He traveled to the hometown twice more before the end of the war. It was not until he returned to the United States that he decided to enter the seminary and become a priest.

Another kind of Italian immigrant was the type who was happy neither in Italy nor in America. He didn't like America when he arrived and did everything he could to save up for the return trip and go home. But, alas, when he got there, he usually learned that he had made a mistake. Once you cross the ocean, America gets in your blood, so inevitably, he repeated the procedure. I've met some families who have gone back and forth several times. This invariably hurt the children, especially if they were born in America.

At this point, since we're on the subject, I would like to narrate a short episode, parenthetically, that will serve to illustrate the problem. As an educator for over thirty-five years, I am well known. When some people greet me with the prosaic: "Are you behaving?" I always answer: "Of course! I have no choice. After teaching for thirty-four years, everybody knows me. If I deviate from the straight and narrow, I would get caught the very first time!" But, even I was shocked one year when I was spending a month in my hometown visiting my daughter in Fossacesia. I was in a piazza in Lanciano waiting for a bus to begin boarding to take me to Chieti, my other stomping ground when I was at the G. B. Vico Academy. It was a large piazza, but there was not a soul on it at 9:30 in the morning; just the locked bus and I. In the far distance, however, three young men sat at a table outside a caffè. Within five minutes, one of them got up and started to walk toward me. Immediately, I smelled trouble. This guy is going to rob me, taking advantage of the lack of people around, I thought to myself. Immediately, I began to excogitate some sort of plan to protect myself. I was a soccer player in my youth: I kick things. Now I began to plan the specific target. Besides the obvious place, where else is he vulnerable? I decided on the shins. A well placed extra point kick to the shin would drop him like an overripe pear. So, I waited. The young man, however, figuring that I might have precisely the thoughts in my head that I indeed had, said, way before he got to me, "Are you Mr. De Simone from Bishop Kenrick High School?" Well! I knew it! I'm not even safe in my own home town! No wonder I have no choice but to behave. He was the elder son of a family such as I have just described. His family lived in Ortona. They had gone to Canada, first, then to Norristown, and then back to Ortona whence they had come. I had not taught him since he did not go to regular high school in America, although he had gone to the eighth grade in Montreal. But, I did teach his younger brother, and since his parents did not speak English very well, it fell upon him the burden of coming to the school for parent-teacher meetings to inquire about his brother's progress (or lack thereof!). But, now, both brothers, at 23 and 18 years of age respectively, found themselves in a country that they regarded as their own only peripherally, they had no job, and they completely lacked any kind of prospect for the future. So, we talked for a while until the bus began to load up. I advised him to go back to America, and take his brother with him as soon as possible. Sever your mother's apron strings and start to live your own lives. It's time. They did, too. I saw them in America again a few years later and they had set up a firm that imported Italian marble and tile. They're both millionaires now. Even their parents returned to America, their tails between their legs, as the saying goes. It takes some people an entire lifetime to grow up.

Then there was the type of immigrant who simply came to America to earn some money over a period of a few years, then return to Italy, buy a piece of land and maybe even a modest house. This type of immigrant could better be called a periodical migrant worker: five years in America, one back in Italy, with a few variations here and there. The one thing most of them failed to realize was that once they crossed the Atlantic, America got into their blood, and things would no longer be the same for them. In extreme cases, some of them would forget to go home, leaving their wives as virtual widows to work the land or whatever it was they invested their hard-earned money into. There is a well known anecdote in which one such migrant after many years during which his two sons had grown up to adulthood, finally decided it was time to go home. He reached the hometown on a Sunday morning. The sons hired a car and went to the train station to pick him up. As they pulled into the town's piazza they met their mother who was on her way to Sunday mass. They stopped the car and said to her that they had their father in the car, expecting her to want to greet her husband. Instead she said coldly: "Good, take him home. I have to go to mass now!" And she proceeded toward the church. If there was a flicker of love for her husband still left in her, it was buried somewhere in the remote recesses of her heart. Absence, they say, makes the heart grow fonder it's true, but up to a point. It's like a bottle of good wine. It grows better with age, but only until it peaks. After that, it dives right into the garbage pail.

Unfortunately, these were the type of immigrants both my grandfathers were. Nonno Donato was cured of this unsettled lifestyle when, in 1926, after he bought his nice piece of land and built a small villa on it, he decided to stay put and enjoy it. He never returned to America again, although his love for America remained strong and even grew. Nonno Filippo, on the other hand, was forced to return to America in 1936, as previously described, due to political pressures. His only mistake was in not bringing the rest of his family along. I still find it difficult to try to figure out what went through his mind at the time, because the decisions he finally made were senseless, and irrational.

MY INCREDIBLE MOTHER

My mother, Maria Sorgini De Simone, was born on April 7, 1907, in Fossacesia, like the rest of us. She was of school age during the teen years of the twentieth century. Her elementary grades coincided precisely with the duration of the First World War, in which the fledgling nation of Italy participated on the side of the Allies. Italy, in fact, declared war on the Central Powers on May 24, 1915, two years before the beginning of the American phase of the war.

My august mother. Maria Sorgini-De Simone

Five foot two, maybe, or maybe not, and all energy. She challenged, constantly challenged, whether it was the school board, municipal authority, or even the Nazis. She only completed the fourth grade because that's all there was in the local elementary school. Her school years coincided with the duration of World War I, and with her father in the military, her education ended with whatever was available in town. Unable to continue her studies, she took advantage of other things that came her way: she learned to knit and do fine needle work; she took advantage of a school for designing, cutting and sewing women's clothes; and, learned how to cook like a master chef. And what a writer! If I have any talent at all in that respect, it came from her.

After finishing the four years of elementary education available in Fossacesia, my mother was offered a scholarship to go to Lanciano to continue her education. She wanted to be a teacher. She would have made a superb teacher, too, though a severe one. In order to accept the scholarship, however, she would have had to commute daily to Lanciano on a horse-driven coach. It might have been disastrous for a ten-year-old girl to travel alone on a public coach, so Nonna Concetta opted to keep her at home. Mamma was disappointed, but she understood the situation and accepted her fate. She learned to write beautifully, with a flair in her handwriting and an unusual inclination for original, interesting expressions. Nonna, too, had learned to read well, even though she never saw the inside of a school. She could not really write very well, but she could sign her own documents when necessary, and she learned to read with blinding speed and unerring comprehension. Every day she would send me to the newsstand in the piazza to purchase two newspapers: either *Il Giornale d'Italia* or *Il Messaggero,* politically neutral dailies, and one of the leftist newspapers, *Avanti,* the socialist paper, or *L'Unità,* the communist daily. To those who inquired as to the reasons she bought the "red" papers, she replied that she read them "just to keep my fingers on their pulse." She wanted to "keep track of their thinking," as she described it. Invariably, she read every page from top to bottom and side to side. She even read the name of the newspaper aloud, and its date of issue, to make sure I had not made a mistake and bought the previous day's issue.

My mother was a very ambitious woman, a true precursor of the feminist movement of the latter part of the 20th century. Since she didn't have the opportunity to further her education beyond the fourth grade, she made sure that I had better luck with mine. She never missed a chance to show me off. She got me involved in everything: I was a member of the children's corps of Catholic Action, a *Balilla* (Mussolini's boy scouts), and she enrolled me in the *Schola Cantorum* (children's choir) at 5 years of age. I've sung in church choirs ever since.

5... mi ha detto vai a casa che qua dai fa
Aldo (in campagna) non fai bene oggi
queste sarchiamo e tu vai a cucire
non so che cosa per Anna Maria
nzellina per non ringraziarmi
che l'ha fatto comandare da tuo
padre allora io eseguisco l'ordine
vado a casa a cucire una vestina
allo bambino. Poi ha piovuto dopo
8 giorni si ritorna a sarchiare
le fave per l'ultimo giorno io vado
appresso tua madre mi ha incon
trata per la compagna mi ha fatto
ritornare dietro dicendomi non
ci andare è casa tua, non lo ai
mai fatto, non lo sai fare sempre
cara la sua gentilezza falsa. Cer
to è che la sera sono rientrati a
casa come 3 briganti, prima tuo
padre e poi la figlia e la madre
muti senza parlare. Dopo si è fal
ciato l'erba alla vigna, con la fal
cetto questo caro marito non ci son
provata ad andare perché della

Sample page of my mother's handwriting
Even to an American who doesn't understand Italian, it's obvious
that her penmanship was neat, even and easy to read. Not bad for a
fourth-grade education. As a native born and a professor of Italian,
I can attest to the fact that her narrative is similar to mine. The leaf,
as they say, does not fall far from the tree that produced it.

Il beniamino

In the Old Testament, Benjamin was the youngest and most beloved of Jacob's sons. By adaptation, in modern times the *"beniamini"* represent the youngest "angels." I got to be one because, being her first-born, mamma went out of her way to show me off. She made the white suit I'm wearing from a pattern she bought from the San Carlo of Rome, a catalog house from which she bought all her big item supplies both for the house and for her sewing business.

Il Balilla (Mussolini's Boy Scouts)

In history class we studied about a boy in Genoa during the revolutionary movements of mid nineteenth century named "*Balilla*," who was asked by the Austrian soldiers to help them dislodge the wheels of a cannon that had gotten stuck in the mud. The young Genoese "hero" refused to help them, knowing that they were getting set to bombard his city. Instead he picked up a rock and hit the soldier in the head. No doubt the story was embellished and exaggerated, but Mussolini decided to call his boy scouts *Balilla's*. If I look somewhat disheveled, it's because mamma's cousin Nino who came to school to take my picture, was at least two hours late, so I did what every five year old in his right mind would do, I ran around with my friends during that whole time. So instead of a neat little *Balilla* in uniform, I look more like the only survivor of a major cataclysmic event.

My first Holy Communion, June 9, 1940
On June 9th, 1940, the feast of Corpus Domini, I received my first Holy Communion. Mamma ordered a tailor-made suit based on the uniform of a Navy officer. Mamma took me to a tailor in the next town so no one would know about it. Unfortunately, she forgot to warn me not to tell anyone about it. Well, I blabbed the whole thing in great detail. A friend of mine's aunt immediately went to the same tailor and had him make one for him exactly like it. Mamma was so mad she refused to pay the tailor for the longest time. Five-year-old Filippo is in the picture with me.

By the time I was born, the elementary school in town had added a year, bringing its curriculum to the national minimum requirements for that time, the 5th grade. She started me in kindergarten in the fall of 1935. I was three and a half. Since I was born in January while my friends in the neighborhood were all born in the summer and fall of 1931, I would not have been able to go to the same classes as my closest friends. So, mamma excogitated a plan: the law said that children were to be admitted to school at the age of six, with a number of complicated guidelines as to their date of birth. It was the latter complication that excluded me from entering school at the same time as my friends. The law, however, didn't say anything about a child having to enter school in the first grade. So, she kept me in kindergarten for two years instead of one, asking the good Passionist Sisters to instruct me in all facets of the first-grade curriculum. They used a Montessori system of instructions, and I adapted to it like a hand in a glove. As a result, in the fall of 1938 I entered public school—in the second grade. The superintendent of schools was caught totally by surprise. He gave my mother a great argument about the lack of established precedents for what she wanted to do and that I would have been out of place and other such calamities. But, at her demand that he find a paragraph, line, sub-line, or addendum that provided an answer to the question of what grade a child should be in upon entering school, he was at a total loss for an answer. They gave me an interview which was nothing short of a thorough oral examination. I read, I did arithmetic, I told them where Sicily was on a board map; I even told them where the *Massiccio della Marmolada* was, in the Alps. I knew that because hanging on the walls in the hallway of the kindergarten section there was a series of photographs depicting various alpine scenes, including the Marmolada. I had been fascinated by the name itself (perhaps because it suggested the word marmalade). Other mountain scenes that adorned that hallway were the *Sierra Nevada,* and *Valparaiso* in Spain. I can still see them in my mind today. The school authorities were stunned, baffled, and ultimately angry with my mother but after consulting provincial school authorities, they were told that I was *"idoneo,"* that is, qualified to enter the second grade. Their only concern was that I'd be six years old, which I was, so mamma proved to be right once again. With some reluctance they admitted me to the second grade in Miss Catalano's class. Miss Catalano was an old, dried-up spinster who didn't really know much, but she was a benevolent soul. I used to call her *la Befana,* the Italian female equivalent of Santa Claus. She became ill shortly after I entered school and died before the end of the academic year.

I didn't know of all the machinations my mother was contriving on my behalf, so that when I went to school the first time, I was shocked to see all my friends from my neighborhood in the same class with me: Lino, Rino, Micuccio, Nuccia, Liliana, Tittina, Irma, and Ottavia. They were all there. I was happy. We used to walk to school together, with one of the parents taking turns escorting us to and from school each day. By the time I entered the third grade, however, we had already moved in with Nonna Concetta, and I had a new set of friends.

The kindergarten class of 1937
This is an interesting photo in so far as it depicts life in Fossacesia prior to the war. I still recognize a good half of all the children in the picture. I am in the third row, fourth from right, the only one with a brown shirt collar. My best friend Lino is to my right, while at the end of the row at my left are Angiolino, Peppino, a.k.a. Cooperativa, who became a singer of note. At the end of the row is Nuccia Toscano. The last kid in the top row, right, is another of my childhood buddies, Rino Sichetti, who grew up to be the strongest man I've ever known and the gentlest. Directly in front of me, in the second row are my friends Marisa, Bucciante, and Ninì.

THE GREAT RED SKY PHENOMENON OF 1938

One event I remember with great lucidity took place before we moved from the De Simone household to Nonna Concetta's house. It was the unusual atmospheric phenomenon that occurred on the night between the 24th and the 25th of January, 1938. The event had been predicted by Our Lady of Fatima in 1917, when she appeared to the three Portuguese children, Lucia, Jacinta, and Francisco, asking them to convey the message that the world should pray for the conversion of Russia. Said she: "This war will end soon, but unless mankind changes its sinful ways, a new and much worse war will plague humanity!" She added that an unusual phenomenon seen throughout the world would take place announcing its beginning. The phenomenon did take place, consisting of a red glow that covered the sky extending to the entire globe. It began in our area at about eight P.M. on

the night of the 24th and by 9:00 P.M. the entire sky had turned rusty red
with an east-to-west gradual movement. My mother was petrified by it all
and would not go outside to look at it. She prohibited me to stick my head
out the door, too, as if that glow would blind me or something. However,
we had large windows downstairs and upstairs and I kept on climbing and
descending those twelve steps in our hallway to see it better. Soon I got tired
of it and fell asleep. The world's press labeled the event, "an aurora borealis
of unusual splendor, but perfectly natural." Natural? It had never occurred
before, nor has it occurred again since.

TEMPEST INSIDE; STORM OUTSIDE

One night in October of that year, there was a particularly virulent verbal
attack against my mother at home. It was over a trivial matter which one of my
aunts kept prolonging over Nonno Donato's advice to stop it. Unfortunately,
he didn't have the firmness to be able to stop it. At one point, mamma had
had enough, so, being a stormy night, she bundled me and Filippo up, then
she packed a large tote bag with a few days' change of clothing for the three
of us and we left the house for good, heading for the middle of town and to
Nonna Concetta's house. The trip was no more than half a mile, but it was a
memorable one because a wind and dust storm had been raging all evening.
As we approached Mastro Peppe's shoe store, about halfway between the two
houses, the wind and the dust clouds generated by the storm became so strong
that we had to stop and hold onto a tree in front of the store to keep from
being blown away. While clutching the three-year-old Filippo in her arms,
mamma held onto the tree for dear life, while I held onto her. We remained
there a good ten minutes before we could resume our trip in safety and
proceed toward our destination. When we reached Nonna Concetta's place,
mamma let go with a long crying spell. In the process of trying to calm her
down, nonna suggested that the next day she would send one of our trusted
relatives to fetch the rest of our belongings and we could remain in her house
permanently. So, that's how I ended up living in what is known as *Cardelle's
Lane* (*Cardelle* being the nickname given to my wife's family in town, being
the most distinguished personage who lived on that street), the long alley-like
side street off the Via di Lanciano that was to become my stomping grounds
for the next five years until the war came to our town, and destroyed Nonna
Concetta's beautiful home.

I was somewhat disconcerted by the entire event that evening, but I
preferred serenity to bickering, and so I quickly adjusted, settling down to a

new life. The school was much closer, and I was able to get to it by myself. I made new friends without losing the old ones, and the atmosphere of my maternal household was more conducive to intellectual pursuits. If nothing else, in this house there was always a newspaper to read. After Nonna Concetta was finished with it, that is!

The first event that took place downtown after we moved in with Nonna Concetta was the return of Agapito. Who was Agapito? Well, for one thing, he was the mason who built Nonno Filippo's new house, or at least he had something to do with it. But, he was one of the thousands of Italian young men who had fought the Spanish Civil War on Francisco Franco's side. Giorgio Perlasca was one, too. Giorgio became disillusioned with the fascist regime in which he had believed. He got a job with an Italian meat importing firm in Hungary, and saved 5000 Jews in Budapest in 1944. But, that's another story. Agapito, supposedly, had died in battle. Two years before another young man from our town reported that Agapito had died in his arms and had brought some personal items back to his family. With that, his family had a memorial mass celebrated for him as was the custom, went through a period of mourning and all the usual prescribed rituals reserved for the dead. But, somehow, two years later, he reappeared in town unexpectedly. The town was full of people that night, waiting the return of the local hero (sort of). I can still see the throng of people milling about at the top of our street, waiting for an automobile to arrive from Lanciano. I remember, too, that that night was the first time I ever saw, let me rephrase that, I took notice of Anna Maria Fantini. I wasn't quite seven years old, and I wasn't impressed. Ironically, after WWII was over, our Spanish hero became a communist.

THE NEW TEACHER ARRIVES

In the fall of 1939, as we reported to school to begin the third grade, we were told to report to Signor Tozzi's classroom on the second floor of Fossacesia's elementary school building. All the kids in the upper grades who had had Tozzi before as their teacher had given us sufficient warning on how tough he was. "He grabs you by the short hair in the back of your head and lifts you from your seat," was the foreboding admonition. After a few days, I concluded that Mr. Tozzi was indeed a serious teacher, but a fair one. You do your work properly and he didn't bother you. Unfortunately, he didn't last very long as our teacher. He had been an artillery officer during the Great War, so by the end of the second week of school he was recalled to active duty. He left almost immediately. School authorities merged the two third-grade classes, pending the arrival of a new teacher. The combined classes totaled about fifty children under the tutelage of an inexperienced teacher, a young man by the name of De Sanctis. Signor De Sanctis tried to handle all those screaming kids for about a month after that, but he failed to make an impression on me.

Finally, the new teacher arrived—a stunning young lady in a fascist uniform. Signorina Dora Cacciavillani obviously had been smitten by the regime, but so were many others. She was young, energetic, and future-oriented. They had to split the two classes again, of course. Signor De Sanctis was probably hoping they would do so alphabetically, but she had other ideas. She stood at the teacher's desk, looked at each one of us and began to point to the kids she wanted: "I'll take him, her, the little girl in blue, that boy with the red sweater, etc." In other words, she chose the best of the crop just by looking at us. Signor De Sanctis, a year or two older than she, was so intimidated by the tone of command in her voice that he didn't utter a word. He just let her have her way. I've thanked God ever since, however, because she chose me, and she turned out to be one of the best teachers I've ever had. She taught me at a crucial time in my intellectual development. She was so innovative that she even taught us the Morse code, giving each student a wooden contraption—a poor imitation of the touch switch of a real telegraph. The practice sessions always consisted of the students transmitting messages to each other within the classroom. Besides being a useful tool, it was fun, too.

For the next year La Cacciavillani, as she soon started to be called, encouraged us to be alert to the political events that shaped our lives, and so I began to follow them by listening to the 1:00 P. M. news. We didn't even have a radio, but my mother would send me every day to the home of some friends of ours who did, and when I got home I had to repeat what I had heard.

The night of June 10th, 1940, each town in Italy was ordered to install loudspeakers in central locations so that the people who did not possess a radio might be able to hear a special address by the Duce himself. I remember that broadcast. In boastful, bombastic tones, typical of dictatorial rhetoric, Mussolini announced that Italy had declared war on France and England. "Great!" Mamma exclaimed. "Can the United States be far behind?" Mamma and nonna wept that night. They knew that it was going to be downhill all the way after that. They just fell quite a bit short in their assessment of exactly how far down hill we were going to go.

A year and a half would pass before the Japanese attacked Pearl Harbor, but when that happened mamma's prediction came true. Now, Italy was at war against the United States, as well. Even I, young as I was, could tell the Duce's decision was insane. Italy had marked her doom. He had been told that the nation and its people were not ready for war materially, psychologically, or spiritually, but he was a stubborn and spiteful man, so there was no reasoning with him. That was the beginning of a very tragic period for my family, and for the entire country.

THE REFUGEES

Early in 1942, strangers began to be seen around town as never before. A family had moved in with a neighborhood family across the street from us. There were people around with strange names and even stranger movements. Most people moved at night in the security of darkness. Because of the imposed "blackout," every household was in darkness, even those who had electricity, which on our street represented no more than three or four houses. We were given instructions to cover all window panes with a dark cloth. The lamps themselves had to be covered with a dark blue or black cloth. Curfew was imposed, too. After 10:00 P.M. everyone had to clear the downtown area and return home unless one had a special permit issued by the municipal authority. Everyone tried to comply.

I had followed the war in its every aspect from the beginning. Controlled by the government, the media reported only what they wanted us to know (although, if truth be served, the Italian Fascist regime was not very strict in that respect, as is being revealed by the flow of documents continually being released from the State archives, after the mandated fifty year period of secrecy). Of course, they never mentioned the way the Germans had invaded Poland and Eastern Europe. They reported it, but in glowing terms as if the Nazis had been invited and welcomed into Poland with open arms by the Polish people. Once I saw a news clip at the movies showing smiling Polish girls welcoming the German soldiers with armfuls of flowers, even as their tanks rolled into Warsaw. It would be several years before I would even hear words like Auschwitz, Treblinka, Birkenau, Dachau and others. As for the problem the unfortunate Jewish people were having in Eastern Europe at the time, the people of Abruzzo had not a clue.

A number of years ago, Susan Zuccotti published a book called *The Italians and the Holocaust,* in which she refutes the notion that the Italians did not enforce the so-called Racial Laws. Her argument makes sense at the level of reason and logic, but not at the people level. The people rose above their petty interests and helped anyone in trouble, most of the time at the peril of their very lives. This was particularly true of the central and southern regions of Italy. The Catholic Church was continually harboring Jews, with the full cooperation of the civil authorities, in Assisi, at Campagna near Salerno, in every convent or monastery in the south of Italy, in Rome itself, and elsewhere. Even though the Italian parliament had passed the racial laws in 1938, their enforcement was left to the discretion of the local official in charge of any given situation. So, while Susan Zuccotti is generally accurate in her assessment of Italian culpability regarding the Jewish situation, she failed to recognize that those laws were ignored in many places, especially in provincial areas. In Abruzzo, we saved thousands of refugees, regardless of who they were. The comment made by a Jewish survivor of those days is relevant, "At least," said she, "the Italians didn't kill us."

One thing that was not enforced in most of Italy was the request by Mussolini that every Jew on Italian soil wear the yellow star that identified them as Jews. Pope Pius XII said that if Mussolini were to impose that ignominy on the Jews, be they Italian, foreign or *apolide* (without a declared nationality), he would wear a yellow star himself and order every priest in Italy to do the same.

Sometime around the early phases of the war, an Italian underground began to operate, clandestine and invisible like all the others. The Italian underground protected all refugees who sought shelter on Italian soil. In the summer of 1943, however, il Duce lost control of the situation into which he had gotten himself in, and on July 25, 1943, after receiving a vote of "No Confidence" by the parliament, he was arrested by the Polizia di Stato and sent atop the Gran Sasso d'Italia, the highest mountain in the Apennine range, and held in a palazzo probably belonging to the State. I guess they figured, who could possibly get to him that high up. Well, they didn't figure on the Germans landing a small airplane in those open plateaus. I read many an article over the years as to Mussolini's state of mind at that time, and I came to the conclusion that he was relieved that it was all over. We will never know, of course, but I truly believe that it was so. It is my sincere belief, supported by many writers and journalists, that he wanted to surrender to the British or the Americans, and he had a large case full of documents that he had planned to surrender to the Allied governments. Unfortunately, he didn't make it. The next day, a small plane landed on an air strip atop that mountain and "rescued" him. Benito must have thought: *"Eccoci di nuovo!"* (Here we go again). That episode left thousands of questions unanswered, unfortunately. They set him up in the north in the lake region in a puppet republic, and the *Repubblica di Salò* was born.

Telegramma decifrato del Ministero dell'Interno in
data 28/8/1938 XVI

Prefetti Regno

N.32547 Risulta che in varie località esistono colonie
agricole che ospitano gratuitamente ebrei stranieri at
scopo dichiarato farli impratichire agricoltura Alt
Pregasi accettare et riferire massima sollecitudine in
quale località esistano tali colonie facendone
quindi segnalazione a questo Ministero con indicazione
numero preciso persone che le compongono Alt d'ordine
Ministro Interni Bindi

Looking for Jews in Italy, in '38

This document was sent to me by my friend in Fossacesia, Alfredo
Tozzi. It is a decoded telegram sent to the Prefects of all the Italian
provinces by the Minister of Internal Affairs, named Bindi. It is
interesting to note the date of August 28, 1938, followed by the
Roman numeral XVI. I checked on the Internet and the official
date in which the infamous racial laws were promulgated was
November 17, 1938, XVII. The Roman number designates the
16th and 17th year of the Fascist Era. The reason the November
date has increased by one is that the so-called Fascist Era began
with the march on Rome which occurred on October 28, 1922.

So, on October 28, 1938 it was a new year of sorts. I think the meaning of the telegram is that Bindi was trying to locate the Jews present in Italy in anticipation of the need to round them up if Mussolini would so decide after the new laws would take effect. They did, in fact, round up thousands of them and placed them in "concentration camps," similar to the Lanciano camp of Villa Sorge. The translation follows:

> Decoded telegram issued by the Italian Ministry of Internal Affairs, dated August 28, 1938. (To all) Prefects of the realm of the Kingdom [of Italy]

> N. 32547 It has been brought to our attention that in many areas (of Italy) there are agricultural colonies that are giving free hospitality to foreign Jews for the declared purpose of giving them agricultural experience—stop—Please, check this out and refer to us with the utmost urgency as to where such colonies are, then report to this ministry, indicating the exact numbers of which they consist.

> The Minister of Internal Affairs, Bindi

After Mussolini was deposed, the king asked Marshall Pietro Badoglio to take the reigns of government. Badoglio was one of two highest-ranking army officers in the Italian military, the other being Rodolfo Graziani. Badoglio did take over the government, but he did so in a shabby way. As his first official act, he should have rescinded the Duce's infamous "racial laws." As a result, the interned people, be they political internees, Jews, Gypsies, Croatians or whatever, were not released. The lack of action in that area made him and the king just as guilty of that atrocity the Jews suffered as Mussolini had been.

THE POW CAMP OF FONTE D'AMORE

In the area of Sulmona, about 100 miles due east of Rome, at the foot of the western slope of the Majella range of the Apennine Mountains, there was a POW camp set up in an area ironically called *Fonte d'Amore* (Fountain of Love). It held 3,500 British prisoners of war taken by the Germans in northern Africa during the days of the Desert Fox offensive. The camp was guarded by Italian troops, but the guards quickly made friends with the internees, and, when the armistice was signed, the Italians simply opened the gates and let them go. About half of them, however, were told by their own officers to stay put until the Allied forces arrived and freed them, thus remaining under the protection of the Geneva Convention. The other half had already hit the road. Unfortunately, it was a road to nowhere and replete with danger. Many sought refuge among the local population, thus being absorbed into the social fabric of rural and pastoral Italy, especially in the mountainous areas of Abruzzo. Many soldiers and even some high-ranking officers spent about a year tending sheep on the slopes of the Majella Mountains in the Province of L'Aquila, blending in with the shepherds. In exchange for their labors, the Abruzzesi people fed and protected them. They didn't feed them roast beef, of course. By that time, if the people had a little salt with which to flavor boiled wheat, beans, or wild herbs, the meal would have been considered a feast.

In 1999, some of the students at the Enrico Fermi Science Institute, a high school in Sulmona, encouraged by a number of their teachers, spread out into the zone interviewing many people who had experienced the war. They published a 99-page book entitled, *E si divisero il pane che non c'era* (And they Shared the Bread They Didn't Have). It is replete with documentation of heroic acts as well as barbaric ones on the part of the Germans. One poignant and sad entry is the story of a man condemned to death by the Germans, together with a friend of his, only because they had given food to six escaped British POWs. On the day set for execution, as the local priest visited him to give him some comfort and the last rites, the man greeted the padre with: "Father, today I die because of something you taught me. You taught me that it was good to feed the hungry!" Within an hour, both men were dead.

Even Carlo Azeglio Ciampi, the President of the Italian Republic at the turn of the millennium, 19 years of age in 1943 and being sought by the Germans for some alleged "crime" against the Third Reich, hid in the hamlet of Scanno, deep in the mountains of Abruzzo. After a few months he, together with other escapees including some British soldiers, crossed over the Majella Mountain on foot in a driving snow storm hoping to reach the Adriatic coast, just south of Fossacesia, to meet up with the British 8th Army which by now had occupied the left banks of the Sangro River all the way to Ortona. There were about two dozen men in that group that night in early December, 1943. Some of them were Allied soldiers who escaped capture by the Germans after parachuting into enemy territory for whatever reason. There were many others, too, coming from the most improbable of places, who sought refuge and protection among the people of Abruzzo. And we gave it to them, too, selflessly, generously, and with total self abnegation. My own mother, by consenting to take in "strangers" into our house, stuck out not only her own neck, but that of Nonna Concetta, as well as mine and my little brother Filippo's. But, then, as Dr. Palatucci put it in 1938, "There comes a time in which we are asked to confront ourselves with our own consciences." So be it!

THE JEWS AMONG US

One day in late summer, 1942, my mother was asked to attend a hush-hush meeting at the local hotel, called by our priest, Monsignor Tommaso Tozzi. I never had the opportunity to ask my mother who else attended that meeting, but I believe the *podestà* (as the mayor was called under the fascist regime) was there, too, as well as other owners of large houses. When she returned home that afternoon, she was visibly upset, and she informed us that our two empty bedrooms upstairs had been requisitioned by the "authorities," in order to house some refugees. My grandmother was upset, too, because whenever the people who ran the town, from the mayor down to the secretaries, wanted to hide behind a flimsy curtain of anonymity, they used to call themselves the "authorities." Actually, they were local men most of whom my grandmother had seen being born and raised, but when they called themselves "the authorities," she knew she had no choice but to adhere to the letter and spirit of the law. We lived in a large modern home, as previously mentioned, with two bedrooms to spare. Naturally, while we had room to take a few people in, with the three male members of our family safely tucked away in America, both my mother and grandmother were afraid to take in strangers. Nonna Concetta was furious with mamma. She asked her. "Did you say no to them?" "Of course, I did," mamma replied, "but Monsignor Tozzi said, 'Pretend it's Jesus knocking at your door asking for hospitality. Will you slam the door in His face?' And with that, I had no choice but to sign up for two rooms." She did specify, however, women and children only. No men. On that detail, the authorities kept their word. She made no reference to any other homeowners who might have signed the paper to accept any of the refugees.

Msgr. Tommaso Tozzi, DD, PhD

Everybody in town called him Don *Tumasse*. He was a tough cookie, as they say. As an examiner he must have been a nightmare. He loved music, and he enjoyed a nightly walk with a group of us altar boys to what he called Jacob's well, on a property near the edge of town. Once there, we dipped the bucket into the water, raised it, we all took a long draft, we thanked the Lord for "Sister water," in the words of St. Francis of Assisi, and then we walked back toward downtown, each of us leaving the group as we reached our respective homes. When the time came to see what we were made of, he did not hesitate to go to work on behalf of a suffering humanity.

"Jesus" arrived about a week later, under the guise of four splendid blond girls. I judged them to be between twenty and thirty years of age and obviously sisters, they looked so much alike. When I saw them, I secretly rejoiced. I suppose the discovery of the opposite sex for a boy is a sort of internal rite of passage into adolescence. I had recently noticed that whenever my neighbor's daughter, Anna Maria, appeared on her balcony, a little way down our street, I flipped, "flapped," and eventually flopped for real as, in time, she would become my wife. These blond girls proved my suspicion that there was, indeed, something interesting in the so-called opposite sex. They were a little strange, however. They were taller than our girls in town, and they seemed somewhat coarse. Looking back, their coarseness might be explained by the rigors of their having to run for their lives, probably for several years. They took my room and my bed. Filippo and I had to move into the other room with mamma and nonna, sleeping on makeshift cots.

There was no doubt that the young ladies who came to live with us were not Italian. For one thing, I never heard them speak; obviously, they did not speak our language. They were simply transiting through Italy, chased from their homes by the German oppressors. Also, they were blond, but they did not look anything like the blonds we had in town, the color of whose hair was soft gold and curly. These girls wore their hair straight down and stringy, and it was yellow rather than gold, like the hair of rag dolls. I rarely saw or heard them. They moved upstairs into our house and never came downstairs. After sundown, they would sit on one of the full-width balconies we had in front and back of our house. Their balcony looked to the west and had a spectacular view of the Majella mountains. They liked that. They would have had access to the other balcony, as well, which faced the sea, but its view was obstructed by the rooftops of other homes. The sea was not visible, but on really hot evenings, they often sat on the rear balcony to catch a breath of sea air. On certain evenings the sea breeze was so strong and refreshing they had to put a light sweater on their shoulders (which my mother provided for them—they didn't have much luggage when they arrived). Mother provided for their other needs as well, even going to the municipal offices to collect their stipend when she went to get ours. Were they Jews? I don't know for certain. In those days, it was dangerous to know too much, and under no circumstances would mother have placed the burden of knowledge on my head or on my brother's head. German patrols rarely came into our street, but in 1943 that possibility was always in a thinking person's mind. Route 16, the north-south national highway on the Adriatic coast, in those days passed through every town and hamlet it encountered. It bisected our town right through the middle, and it was only two blocks away from our house. It was not unusual to see small convoys of German troops rumble through our normally quiet town. Whenever a convoy passed through town, they invariably stopped at our public fountain to refill their water supply. Since the fountain was less than a half mile from our house, it was not rare to see a few German soldiers strolling around our neighborhood, just out of curiosity, of course. It would have been dangerous if they saw any sign that we were harboring *"merce proibita"* (prohibited merchandise), as they often called people on the run. The convoys invariably stopped for an hour or so in the middle of town while they took advantage of our fountain with its constantly flowing water. Whenever a few soldiers ventured onto our little street, they were peaceful, discreet, and even polite. Besides, they were just passing by our town, and their principal motive was not to capture Jews or Allied personnel on the run. Still, one never knew.

In late September, 1942, there was a notice affixed on the outside wall of Fossacesia's town hall. It was typed in Italian and began with the usual greeting: "Cittadini" (Citizens). It reminded us that the German soldiers were making untold sacrifices to "protect our *freedom.*" Yes, that's exactly what it said! We were expected to give them full cooperation and even to provide food for them. The gem of the day was that every citizen was expected to report to the "lawful" authorities any suspicious person coming to or transiting through our town. These orders invariably concluded with a peremptory, *"It's the law!"* It was signed Field Marshall A. Kesselring. I read the notices myself and the name Kesselring frustrated me because I thought the "r" should have come before the "l" and not after. But, then, I was thinking in Italian, and the name was German.

Most of the strangers transiting through our town in those days were Jews, as attested by documents still found today in town halls all over the Abruzzo Region. They came to us from the sea and the Yugoslavian coastline, as well as from Rome, Assisi, and cities in the north. They were trying to escape persecution by the Germans. If caught, their final destination would have certainly been the concentration camps in Dachau, Auschwitz, and even Trieste, where there was a "crematory," built in 1943 at the *Risiera di San Sabba*. The *Risiera* was an abandoned rice-processing mill built in 1913. Being very old and inefficient for the function for which it was intended, the *Risiera* was abandoned. In the early forties, it was turned into a crematory, built by the engineer who built the crematories at Auschwitz, at the request of his buddy, Colonel Adolph Eichmann. The victims of *San Sabba* were mostly Italian partisans. Only about fifty Jews met their deaths there. But, there is much to be learned from it. Today it is a museum.

Over the years, I often thought about that hush-hush meeting called by Monsignor Tozzi in the summer of 1942. It bothered me that I saw no activity around town that suggested the presence of other refugees in Fossacesia. Only recently I found plenty of documentation that as of August 23, 1943, there were at least 214 refugees living in town, and more coming in all the time, under extremely trying conditions. There were Jews practically in every town of our region of Abruzzo. I am also convinced that there was a lot of underground activity in our area in those days and that Monsignor Tozzi was, if not the leader, at least an important cog in the machinery that had sprung up overnight in central Italy to meet the needs of the thousands of people who needed our help. It churned silently and unseen, but with great efficacy. I came to the conclusion that our house was not the only house requisitioned by the priest, the municipal authority, the underground, or all of them together, to give shelter to the refugees. There were quite a few houses even bigger than ours in town and just as empty. I was fascinated for years about the possibility of other people hidden away in our town by the time the war actually arrived. There were several names of people in town mentioned by mamma and nonna from time to time. I assumed that those were members of the underground whose job it was to protect the various *"Jesuses,"* those who lived in our house as well as others who found refuge in houses scattered all over town. Recently, a young relative of Monsignor Tozzi's wrote to me from Fossacesia. He had read a printout of the Italian version of this book and was excited and happy that I spoke so well of his great uncle. I answered him, thus beginning an epistolary relationship that endures to this day. Seeing that he was very much interested in what occurred in our town in those days, I gave him some guidelines on how to conduct further research, and he came right through for me. He found a letter from the *podestà* at the time, Costantino Mayer, addressed to the Prefect of the Province of Chieti dated August 23, 1943, three weeks before Italy signed the armistice with the Allies. Here is the English translation of its text.

> In this municipality there is only one ancient public fountain which pours out less than a pint of water per second. In the meantime 63 displaced families, a total of 214 individuals, have flocked to our town. We have placed them in decent living quarters, but without running water and many without bathrooms. We have placed six families, totaling twenty-six individuals, in the local school. It will be difficult to find houses for them. There are no more places available. We are in urgent need of at least sixty beds complete with mattresses, sheets, blankets. We are also in need of cooking utensils for 30 families, as well as undergarments for sixty people. The refugees came to us from Bari (4), Rome (78), Naples (17), Civitavecchia (2), Milan (16), Ancona (5), Foggia (51) and Tripoli (41). As I write, another family has just arrived from Naples, and two from Foggia. Their conditions are bad. I am in the process of opening an office for refugee affairs and a place for the distribution of rationed goods reserved just for them.
>
> Il podestà,
> Costantino Mayer
> August 23, 1943

The zones of origin are significant, especially Foggia. The name Foggia did not refer to the city of Foggia because that would not have made any sense. More likely it referred to the province which bears the same name. That means that the refugees probably got there through one or more of the fishing port towns of *Peschici, Vieste, Manfredonia, Margherita di Savoia,* and any number of other small ports along the Adriatic coastline where fishing boats or small-tonnage merchant ships could have docked to discharge refugees coming from the eastern shores of the Adriatic. Many, no doubt, were part of the six thousand Jews saved by police commissioner Giovanni Palatucci in Fiume. Some were probably trying to reach the holding camps of Campagna whose protector was Bishop Giuseppe Maria Palatucci, Giovanni's uncle. Campagna is in the province of Salerno, clear across the Irpinian Mountains, about forty miles south of Montella. Any number of unforeseen events could have occurred to prevent those people from reaching their destination. So, with the help of the Italian underground, they were spread along the coastal towns, reaching all the way to the Sangro River Valley, 50 miles north of Foggia. It is not difficult to conclude that the Italian underground had things well under control as early as 1940.

THE JEWS IN ABRUZZO, 1940-44

My friend Antonino di Giorgio, of happy memory, wrote about the three hundred Jews, all males, who were housed in an abandoned movie house in Casoli, a small town atop a peak at the foot of the Majella Mountain, no more than twenty miles from our coastal town of Fossacesia. His book, *Un'estate in bicicletta* (A Summer on Bicycles), however, is largely "fiction based on fact," hence unreliable as a source of accurate facts. Armando Liberato, however, in his *La linea Gustav* (The Gustav Line), speaks about the Jews in Castelfrentano, which is territorially adjacent to Casoli. Sometime during the summer of '43, thirty-five Jewish refugees from the Trieste area sought refuge in Castelfrentano. Among them there was a woman of undeclared nationality *(Apolide)*, who happened to like Italian wine. One day in late September, she was indulging in a wine-drinking bout with some of the local young people, when a German motorcycle approached carrying a German officer in its sidecar. The two young Germans went into the bar and each had a beer. As they emerged, however, they were affronted by the Jewish woman who, emboldened by the wine she had drunk, took that most inopportune moment to address the Hitler problem. Speaking to the officer in German (or in her own Slavic language—those present couldn't tell), she told him that he and his men were stupid to place their very lives in jeopardy just to please a mad man, referring to Hitler. It was not a wise thing to do. The motorcycle left heading toward Fossacesia and Route 16. Everyone gave a sigh of relief when the Germans departed, thinking that the danger had been averted. The next day, however, a small German truck came into the same area carrying a number of well armed German soldiers asking for her. They found her. They loaded her on the back of the truck and took her away and she was never seen again. Not only that, but the following day, a larger truck arrived, and the rest of the group was arrested. To this day, the people of Castelfrentano use this story to teach their growing children the prudence of keeping their mouths shut under all circumstances.

Recently, I looked on the Internet for information about the presence of Jews in Abruzzo during the war. I was amazed at the wealth of information available. First and foremost, there is the very thorough work by Costantino Di Sante, *Gli Ebrei in Abruzzo, 1940-44* (The Jews in Abruzzo, 1940-1944). The first ironic statement Signor Di Sante makes is that the Marche and Abruzzo regions were chosen by Italian political and military leaders before the war started as the most logical location in which to build *"Campi di concentramento e di confino"* (concentration and confining camps), because of their "scarce war interests." That judgment turned out to be a cruel joke, but that was the very reason why there were over seventy camps in the province of Chieti alone. Di Sante's book gives numbers, ethnic identities, and even names. Since the extermination camps in Auschwitz, Treblinka, Dachau and the like are referred to as *"concentration camps,"* I will refer to the Italian camps as "holding camps," because there was a vast difference between the two. I will list a few name, merely samples from a long list.

HOLDING CAMP OF CASOLI (MEN ONLY)

Arensberg, Willi German Jew
Berolz-Heimer, Kaus German Jew
Brasch, Kaus German Jew
Bettinger, Salomon Mannes Stateless Jew
Zylbergerg, Jukiel, Stateless Jew

HOLDING CAMP OF ISTONIO MARINA (NOW VASTO MARINA).

Bonfantini, Corrado (MD) Italian Jew
Cesare, Salvatore (Chemist) Italian Jew
Damen, Onorato (Humanities professor) Italian Jew

HOLDING CAMP OF CHIETI

Fried, Ignatz, (Opera singer) Slovak
Saarsfield, Salazar (Businessman) English
Singer, Egan (Engineer) Czechoslovakian
Remj, Simon (Mechanic) French

HOLDING CAMP OF LANCIANO (WOMEN ONLY)

Roth, Raisel 30 (Homemaker) Stateless Jew
Hubschamann, Federika, 34 (MD) Polish Jew
Centawer Ruth 22 (Student) German Jew
Korn, Klara, 45, Polish Jew, (homemaker).
　　Has two children with her
Steinfeld, Hela, 42, (Clerk) German Jew.

Di Sante fails to list Maria Eisenstein in the Lanciano group. Maria (née Maria Moldauer), was the author of *L'internata n°6,* (The Internee Number 6), which she wrote while under confinement in Lanciano. At the time she wrote that book, I was ten years old and a sixth grade student in the Liceo Ginnasio Vittorio Emanuele II, in that same city. Those camps were meant only for the confinement of people considered to be politically dangerous to the party or to the military. The war ministry didn't expect the large number of people that came into Italy at the onset of the war. With so many political agendas to resolve, they simply put the excessive number of refugees in the camps originally meant for internment of Italian politically dangerous suspects. After the promulgation of the Racial Laws, the Jews, be they Italian or foreigners, were considered mildly dangerous. So they put them into those camps, providing them with the bare necessities of life. The Church helped in one form or another. But, the region of Abruzzo was supposed to be a safe place. The war was not expected to go there. The people there are traditionally known as "Forte e Gentile," (Strong and Gentle). The assessment was correct, because the region was heavily mountainous, had very poor roads, and was completely devoid of any structure of military interest. Moreover, its people had a very mild political consciousness. As previously stated, the Abruzzese people were basically agricultural or pastoral, and they had no desire to go and kill people who had done them no wrong. As it turned out, the war roared right into our innocuous little towns and into our very neighborhoods.

A LETTER SIGNED BENITO MUSSOLINI

Each camp had a director; usually the mayor was given that added responsibility. In order to alleviate the plight of the suffering, the Italian Fascist government passed a bill that would grant a stipend to families whose major source of income was from a country against whom Italy was at war. I know about that because with my father unable to send us money from America, we were eligible to receive the stipend too. My mother read about the provision passed by the parliament and she used to go to our Town Hall on a weekly basis to inquire about it. Unfortunately, the authorities never knew anything about it. One day, after her fifth or sixth inquiry, one of the men suggested that perhaps, she had "misunderstood" the article. A woman scorned hath no greater fury than my mother spurned by anyone who dared impugn her intelligence. She became so furious that her screams could be heard at the lower-end church (as the church of Saint Donato was called by the population due to its being built at the bottom of a depression in the terrain). She went straight home and wrote a letter directly to Mussolini, never really believing that she would get an answer. She decided to mail it out of town for fear that the postal officials would intercept it. I went with her to Lanciano to mail it.

Two weeks later, an express letter arrived from Rome. It was signed *Il Capo del Governo, Benito Mussolini* (The Head of Government, Benito Mussolini). It reassured my mother that what she had read was correct and that the appropriate office would look into the matter immediately. She was encouraged to return to the town hall for more positive information. Mamma was stunned. Still, she feared a trick, so she took the letter to Aurelio Santeusanio, a young friend of the family, and a former tutor of mine. He looked at it and said: "The Duce is the only one who writes an M that way." He referred to a certain flair in the Duce's signature that was standard, because it was a machine-generated signature, and so it was always the same.

The letter caused a mild tremor in town. The "authorities" at town hall felt betrayed. That she should not have gone over their heads was their cry. But, they too had received a letter from Rome, one of reprimand for dereliction of duty, so they had no choice but to act upon the government directives. The money, not only for us, but for all eligible recipients in town, arrived shortly thereafter. Later, I found proof that the money was not intended just for us "Americans," but for all "transients" forced into Italy by the extraordinary circumstances of the moment, including the Jews. We received the money in February 1943, retroactive to July 1, 1942. It was a very nice sum, so mamma decided to splurge. We had been invited to Nonno De Simone's household, the home where I was born, for the engagement of one of my aunts. So she took me and Filippo to Lanciano, to do some shopping for the occasion. Lanciano is a fairly large city that briefly borders Fossacesia to the west. Fossacesia students who wished to continue their studies beyond the fifth grade had to travel there by bus. The people from the surrounding towns still go there to do some serious shopping. In summer, the situation is reversed as the Lancianesi come to Fossacesia to take advantage of our beaches. With a tidy sum in her purse, she bought a beautiful hot pink cashmere sweater for herself and a blue-gray Borsalino hat for each of us. She had already prepared a suit for both of us, so the hat completed the outfit. We looked like two miniature senators.

The money was really not much, as it was intended only to make sure that the people, especially the children, would not have to go to bed hungry. Mamma wrote about it to papà a couple of years later in the famous thirty-six page letter to him on November 13, 1944. She even told him how much we received. She got six lire *per diem* and each of us boys received three lire. Nonna Concetta also applied, but she was refused the subsidy because she owned property. It made sense to me, but she immediately smelled a political rat—not for nothing had Nonno Filippo returned to the United States, in 1936. He had been a Socialist, while the authorities were Fascists. Hence in Nonna Concetta's logic, it automatically translated into "no money for me."

In 1995, when I read Antonino Di Giorgio's, *A Summer on Bicycles*, I finally had proof that it wasn't all a dream. The reference is to the summer of 1943, which is the period about which I am writing. He, too, speaks of a small stipend given by the government to the more than three hundred Jews who were being sheltered in an old movie house in his town. I knew then that I didn't just dream about the money. It was later confirmed by Armando Liberato in his book *La Linea Gustav* as well. Both of these gentlemen established beyond a doubt that the money was intended for anyone transiting through Italy in those chaotic days, no matter who they were. It was intended to make sure that those people had at least something to eat while on Italian soil. Although I have no proof of this, I would venture to say that our four blond sisters who lived upstairs in our house between September of 1942 and February, 1943, also received the money, the transaction probably being handled by my mother when she went to collect her own stipend.

The final proof of the stipend being given to all transients, including Jews, is given by Maria Moldauer Eisenstein. She reports that she received six and a half lire per day, just about the amount that my mother received.

FIUME'S LAST POLICE COMMISSIONER

Dante Alighieri in his *Divine Comedy* sets the natural limits of the Italian nation to the north, between Arles, in Provence, to the west; through the Alpine arc in the north, and to Pola in the Quarnaro Gulf to the east *(Inferno IX,* 112-114). That was early in the 14th century. Unfortunately for Italy, the political forces that tried to pressure her into submission never recognized what could well be profoundly logical. If we look at the topography of the northern crest of Italy, it's easy to see the practicality of Dante's idea about the natural borders of the nation. The people of Fiume, a port city deep into the Quarnaro Gulf, consider themselves Italian. Yet, the city was Italian only from the end of World War I, until the end of World War II. Now, there exists in the region a situation similar to that existing in Miami which has a large population of Cuban people in exile until Cuba becomes "*libre,*" that is free from the Castro regime. The Italian Miami is Trieste, but, unlike the Cubans, the Fiuman community of Trieste has no hope: Fiume is gone forever. It is now Rijeka, and it is part of Croatia. As the only port that opened directly into the Mediterranean from the eastern countries of Europe, Fiume became the logical escape route for thousands of Jews after the Nazi concentration camps became operative. But they needed some help.

Dr. Giovanni Palatucci, a lawyer turned cop was stationed in Fiume between 1938 and 1944. As the last police commissioner of Italian Fiume, he saved well over 6,000 Jews during those four years. On September 13, 1944, however, he was himself arrested by the Gestapo and sent to Dachau where he was killed on February 10, 1945. After five months of torture and deprivations, he was felled by a volley of automatic fire. As the functionary in charge of the Foreign Office in a border port city, Dr. Palatucci was the first to receive a copy of the so-called Racial Laws passed by the Fascist government in October, 1938. When he read them, he consulted his boss, Dr. Feliciano Ricciarelli, and concluded: "We have reached the bottom of our shame. It is now time to confront our consciences." So Palatucci stated his purpose at the very beginning unconditionally and without hesitation. Dr. Ricciarelli must have agreed with him, because he too ended up in Dachau. The only difference between the two was that while Palatucci was executed for his "crimes," Ricciarelli somehow survived the rigors of the camp.

In 1978, the Most Reverend Ferdinando Palatucci, Bishop of Nicastro in Calabria, cousin of our hero, came on a pastoral and personal visit to

Norristown. Since I was teaching Italian at the time in the now defunct Bishop Kenrick High School, in Norristown, it was natural for him to visit our school and offer mass for our students. It was he who first told me about his illustrious cousin and their equally illustrious uncle, the Most Reverend Giuseppe Maria Palatucci, Bishop of Campagna, in the province of Salerno (about twenty-five miles due south of their native town of Montella).

Dr. Giovanni Palatucci, hero at Fiume and Martyr at Dachau.
This is the official medallion issued by the State of Israel, in 1952, on the occasion of the naming of a grove at the Yad Vashem Memorial Forest after our hero who had managed to save over 6000 Jews when he served as Police commissioner at Fiume Italiana (now called Rijeka, and is no longer part of Italy, but part of Croatia). The Nazis killed him on Feb 10, 1945. The State of Israel honored him almost sixty years ago, whereas the Catholic Church is just now studying the case, with the intent of naming him a Saint and a Martyr.

In March of 1939, the sea-going ferry Aghia Zoni steamed north-west on the Adriatic Sea, with 800 Jewish passengers aboard who had paid to be taken to Palestine. In reality, the passengers had been betrayed by someone. Actual destination, Fiume and one of those infamous death trains.

ITALY

Venice

Turin

Abbazia
Fiume

Genoa

Jugoslavia

Aghia Zoni

Fossccesia

Adriatic Sea

Rome

Sangro
River

Gaeta

Montella
Campagna

Sicily

Mediterranean Sea

Gela

Map of Italy

This plain map shows in the upper right corner the city of Fiume and the smaller town of Abbazia where the drama of the Aghia Zoni took place in March of 1939. After being alerted by an Italian Army officer about the ship's passengers being in possible danger, Commissioner Palatucci halted the ship along the Quarnaro Channel leading to the port of Fiume, and, with the help of Fiuman Jew, Rodolfo Grani, unloaded the 800 refugees at Abbazia, placing them in the care of the bishop of Abbazia, Msgr. Isidor Sain, who hid them and eventually sent them to Campagna where the Commissioner's uncle in Campagna. After the war, all eight hundred were safe and sound and living in Israel, Grani included.

The first question that has obsessed me from the very beginning was: "How many of the refugees who lived in my house and other houses in every coastal town of Abruzzo were part of the 6,000 Jews saved by Dr. Giovanni Palatucci?" The question is more than legitimate, considering that Fossacesia is on the Adriatic Sea, halfway up the Italian boot. Fiume and the Quarnaro Gulf are across the narrow body of water from Fossacesia, although much farther north. One of Dr. Palatucci's biographers says: "He hid them (Jews) in a thousand ways." Well, what did Palatucci have that facilitated his work? The Adriatic Sea, of course! And he used the sea as much as he could. Every fishing boat, every small-tonnage merchant vessel, every pleasure boat that left the port of Fiume heading for the Italian coast was a potential instrument for transporting his protégés to safety. The regions that front the Yugoslavian coastline, from Ancona to Bari, is still a hotbed of information that must be uncovered before it is too late. Every municipality in the regions of Marche, Abruzzo, Puglia and Campania should be researched in order to write the closing chapter to the saga of blood and tears that is the legacy of World War II. There is much to be learned there about what the Italians did for the Jews at that time. And we must keep in mind that the Palatucci's of Montella were a family steeped in the Franciscan community, since three of Giovanni's uncles, his father's brothers, were Franciscans in high positions in the order. Giuseppe Maria Palatucci was the Bishop of Campagna, a small town just south of their native Montella, but in the province of Salerno. Campagna had not one, but two camps of Jewish internees. The bishop did all he could to maintain the detainees in good spirit, even so far as securing a large sum of money from the Vatican to help maintain their camps in decent condition. Giovanni used to correspond with the bishop, his uncle, through his aides, who traveled into Italy from Fiume for various reasons.

In the biography in Italian issued by the Polizia di Stato, the author states that the very nature of the Commissioner's clandestine activities barred his leaving behind any written documents descriptive of his doings which might "incriminate" him vis-à-vis the Gestapo. Many years later, on November 4, 2004, I interviewed Albertino Remolino at his home in Campagna. Remolino is the last of Palatucci's collaborators. He confirmed to me that the Commissioner would use any and all policemen who might be on their way to Italy for any reason, personal or police business, asking them to escort refugees to a thousand destinations in Italy, singly or in groups. He would provide them with some money and false documents so that the identities of his protégés, as Jews, Gypsies or whatever, would be concealed. It is possible that Nino was one such policeman. Being the top man in the *Questura* (Police

Headquarters), albeit as a temporary regent, Palatucci was able to destroy all records that identified people transiting through Fiume as Ebrei (Jews). The following narrative, then, is based on conjecture, simply because there is no paper trail and, as an adult, I was not able to verify much. As an eleven year old boy, I was supposed to keep my mouth shut, but my ears and brain were open and alert to all whispers, innuendos or rumors that might have been poorly concealed by my mother or grandfather. So, this is what I'm sure really happened.

In 1939, Bathsheva (Eva) S. found herself all alone in Trieste. She had been studying at the University of Trieste and living with a family in that city, when the war began. She was denied an exit visa, and somehow managed to escape the Fascist raiders who rounded up all Jews for the purpose of sending them to an internment camp. She had traveled to Fiume hoping to be able to find transportation to Budapest, but there she met many people who told her that the trip was impossible under current conditions. So she took up temporary residence with old friends. Once there, she spoke to people who confirmed to her that both her parents and an older sister had been captured by the Gestapo and sent to Auschwitz, so now she was alone in the world. She was advised to seek out Dr. Palatucci's help. He responded by hiring her on the spot to help him destroy all documents that identified thousands of Fiuman residents as Jews. There, she met Nino Del Re and the two fell in love. They had a brief romance and then decided to get married. In late summer, 1943, as the war intensified, Nino decided to try to take her home to mamma in Benevento. But she got pregnant almost immediately, and by the time they reached the fishing pier at San Vito in mid-November, 1943, she was due to give birth any day. After an all-night trip by boat from Fiume, she was a wreck. With Nino's help and that of another couple that traveled with them, they managed to make it up the hill to Pete's house, but she could go no further. They decided to knock there and trust in divine providence for whatever help they could find.

POSSIBLE LINK TO COMMISSIONER PALATUCCI

Palatucci's involvement in saving all those Jews began in March, 1939, when a Greek passenger ship, the Aghia Zoni, was steaming up the Adriatic headed for the port of Fiume. It was carrying 800 Jews taken in consignment by the Italian Army in Greece (I have no idea how or why). There is no documentation beyond the fact that one night in March, 1939, eight hundred Jews were aboard the Aghia Zoni and were told they would be taken to Israel.

Instead, they had been betrayed. They were headed for Fiume into the hands of the Gestapo to be taken to Auschwitz or some other extermination camp. The passengers were completely unaware of their intended destination. An Italian officer, however, got wind of something strange going on, so he contacted Police Commissioner Palatucci, who immediately sprang into action. He alerted Rodolfo Grani who secured the help of the Most Reverend Isidoro Sain, Bishop of Fiume-Abbazia. Somehow, the three of them managed in one night to get all those people off that ship before it reached Fiume and to hide them somewhere in Abbazia. When the *Aghia Zoni* docked at the port of Fiume, there were no passengers on board. The Gestapo arrived the next day and found that there was no one to load onto one of its infamous cattle trains. At that time, however, the Gestapo had no control, legal or otherwise, on Italian soil, so there was nothing they could do about it.

In 1952, Rodolfo Grani, then residing in Israel, wrote a scathing article which he published in the Israeli magazine *Hoboker,* probably in Hebrew. The Rev. Don Franco Celetta of Montella, Palatucci's hometown, sent me a copy of the article in Italian translation which I then translated into English. I have, therefore, irrefutable proof that the 800 passengers of the *Aghia Zoni* in March of 1939 were saved and in 1952 were safely living in Israel. Mr. Grani inveighs against all his Jewish co-religionists who were critical of the Vatican as a do-nothing entity in trying to save the Jews during the war. Here is the complete text of Grani's letter.

THE VATICAN'S EFFORTS IN SAVING JEWS DURING WWII

From the Israeli periodical *Hoboker* (Morning), August 10, 1952. (Translated into English from the Italian translation of the original in Hebrew)

It is with great surprise and consternation, unfortunately, that I realize that almost weekly efforts are made by some editors to attack the Vatican with unjust and ridiculous accusations. I have often protested decisively, albeit just verbally, against these defamation campaigns and unfounded allegations. The stereotypical answer is almost always the same: the internationalization of Jerusalem!

We have finally discovered that IT WAS NOT the Vatican that was behind these internationalization maneuvers, but, rather, the United States and Great Britain. And this cannot automatically point to the Vatican, because most American and British Christians are not Catholic.

With that we must deduce that it is improbable that the Vatican is behind these Christian groups to push the buttons.

Considering then, more specifically, the finding of a suitable solution to the final settlement of the Holy Land, I must assume that the Vatican would be satisfied with such a solution.

Aside from this, a presumption on my part, I fail to understand with what authority does the weekly *Hapoel Hazair* take upon itself the right, as an official organ of the Mapai Party, to launch the calumnious accusation that the responsibility for the extermination of over six million Jews, which was Hitler's personal pet project, should really be laid upon the shoulders of the Vatican.

I do not find it fair in the least, or even correct, that the great majority of our media should have taken heed of the journalistic duel which took place between *Hapoel Hazair* and *L'Osservatore Romano,* without questioning its authenticity, even in the face of solid citation of Jewish sources proffered by the Vatican newspaper.

I had the good fortune of living in Italy for nearly a half century, and I know well both the people and the clergy of my former country. I can decisively affirm that never, within the entire forty-seven years of my residence there, have I ever perceived, even minimally, a sense of anti-Semitism in them.

Few are those who know that the much-maligned Pope Alexander VI, the Borgia Pope, (1492-1503), who was indeed responsible for the death of many, at the moment that Ferdinand and Isabel of Spain chased the Jews out of Spain, ordered that they be accepted into the Papal States, and that they be treated with respect.

But we need not go all the way back to the XVth century. All that we, the people of small and fledgling Israel, need to know is the real situation that occurred between the Vatican, the Pope, and the few who managed to slip through the Nazi noose and to save themselves from the tragedy that Hitler enacted in those days.

It is important that we know the deep sense of human solidarity and the generosity of the Great Head of the Catholic Church, Pius XII [demonstrated toward our people]. *I can affirm with absolute certainty that there are here [in Israel] eight hundred people who in the month of March, 1939, shortly after the election of Pius XII to the chair of Peter, lucked out and escaped the Nazi police. They were saved, in fact, by the Bishop of Fiume and*

Abbazia, Msgr. Isidor Sain, who hid them in Abbazia until he could arrange transportation for them to go to Palestine.

The sad fate of these poor people had been marked: to be handed over to the Gestapo. To prevent that tragedy was the intervention of Police Commissioner Dr. Giovanni Palatucci, who informed me of the imminent danger that these, our co-religionists, faced. After spending an entire night trying in vain to get them off the ship, at dawn I went to see Bishop Sain, who comforted me and promised me the full backing of the newly-elected Pope Pius XII.

The above-mentioned Political Commissioner, Dr. Palatucci, was the nephew of Msgr. Giuseppe Maria Palatucci, Bishop of Campagna, SA. He did his utmost to save the lives of eight hundred Jews, the passengers of the Greek ferry boat, the *Aghia Zoni,* by utilizing the help of his illustrious uncle. This is an episode that must never be forgotten.

One year later, WWII exploded. Immediately Mussolini, surely responding to pressure from Hitler, decreed that Italy, too, should force the Jews to wear the ignominious yellow star that had its origins in medieval times.

The Holy Father (Pius XII) declared that he would be the first to wear the mark that identified him, too, as a Jew and would order the entire clergy in Italy to do the same.

The fact is that in a radio address, Mussolini attacked the pope on the subject, but never managed to impose the use of the yellow identification mark on the Italian Jews. In Italy, unlike all the other European nations, the wearing of the yellow star never got off the ground.

Cardinal Bergoncini, the Vatican's Secretary of State, visited every concentration camp in Italy. The high prelate had close rapport with all the internees, without paying any attention to the differences of religious creed, helping, freeing or saving many Jews.

In the same way, we found a noble protector in the figure of Most Reverend Msgr. Giuseppe Maria Palatucci, Bishop of Champagne, Province of Salerno. It was there that we Fiuman Jews were interned en mass.

Bishop Palatucci rendered his person unforgettable to the thousands of our people, helping us, consoling us most generously, without shying away from being photographed repeatedly with us, being ostracized by most unusual circumstances. This Bishop did more than all the great leaders that history concerns itself with, rising above them all.

On September 29, 1943, the Nazis decided to evacuate the city of Rome. On that occasion, they captured 200 Jewish hostages, demanding 50 kg. of gold as ransom. All the Jewish people donated gold most generously in order to save their brothers. Many Catholics donated their gold, as well. There were some military officers, and even a general, who went personally to the collection place in order to make their contribution of precious objects.

The situation was terribly difficult! Time was of the essence. Some Jews, who did not possess gold objects, gave money instead so that gold could be bought on the black market.

As soon as the Vatican got wind of it, they informed us that they were willing to provide gold in sufficient quantity to make up the difference.

It is also important to note that at that time a young Jewish man had managed to infiltrate the Nazi officer corps and had managed to pass on important information that helped the community whenever necessary. It was he who suggested that the Israelite Community fill a sack with 59 kg. of lead and give it to the Germans instead of the gold, but his suggestion was rejected.

Despite the fact that their demand was met, the Germans, as usual, failed to keep their promise: the two hundred hostages were barbarously executed in Rome's *Fosse Ardeatine.* All of this happened on October 16, 1943. From that point on, the Germans stopped deporting Jews. Instead, the order was to execute them on the spot.

Even on this occasion, the Holy Father did his best to save as many people as possible. ***He mobilized the entire clerical force of the Vatican***—and even a number of non-clerical people simply dressed as priests in order to save as many Jews as possible. Let's not forget that this humanitarian effort cost the lives of many who generously lent their hand.

The figure of Padre Benedetto remains unforgettable. Also, during the nine months of Nazi occupation, Padre Francesco Morosini did his utmost to the point that he was himself arrested and shot. During the occupation of Belgium, the Cardinal of Bruxelles kept a Jewish young man he had personally saved from the Nazis and made him his secretary.

Of course, the man who, more than any other went through a lot of trouble on behalf of the Jews, was Dr. Giovanni Palatucci, whom I personally knew. Before arriving at the city of Fiume, this young functionary had no clue as to the meaning of the word "Jew." As soon as he arrived in our city, he was given the responsibility of running the Foreign Office as State Police Political Commissioner. Using the information I would furnish him, he became one of the most active elements in the salvation of Jews. He was the nephew of the above-mentioned Bishop of Campagna.

In order to succeed in his intent, Palatucci had to engage in a game of double standards: officially, he appeared to be in line with the fascist directives on anti-Semitism, but secretly he did all he could to save as many Jews he could.

He issued permits of temporary stay and other appropriate documents that might have given a little breather to those poor people who were at their wit's end. It was precisely due to his interest that we, Fiuman Jews, managed to be interned at Campagna. Eventually, the young commissioner was promoted to the rank of Regent Commissioner, but his continued presence in Fiume was not appreciated by the Gestapo, who arrested him on September 13, 1944, sending him to the extermination camp of Dachau, where, after five months of torture and deprivation, he died a premature death on February 10, 1945.

The city of Ramat Gan honored this Christian martyr with a permanent memorial by naming a street and a park after him on the main Haifa-Tel Aviv road. Its genial mayor, Lady Krinizi, has set aside a lot behind the Palatucci Park where another memorial will be erected in honor of the Hungarian Jew, Dov Gruner, who was hanged by the British a year, or so, ago. Thus, two adjacent areas will forever help to keep alive the memory of two martyrs, both of whom gave their lives on behalf of us Jews, the first an Italian Christian, the other a Hungarian Jew.

Mayor Krinizi, taking advantage of the presence in Ramat Gan of Msgr. Antonio Vergani, the representative of the Latin patriarch of Nazareth, proudly showed him the realization of the project. In response, Msgr. Vergani reiterated the idea of wanting to donate an abandoned monastery for the realization of related social works.

After all that's been said, again I ask for what reason certain elements of the press continues to spread calumnious information intended to sow discord in the rapport between the Hebrew world and the Vatican? May I invite these journalists to abstain from any further diffusion of vicious rumors that damage the interests of our nation.

Rodolfo Grani

THE ARRIVAL OF NINNI

One day at the end of February, 1943, mamma went to the town hall to draw her monthly subsidy, as well as that of our guests. When she returned home, she saw that the blond girls were getting into a car parked in front of our house. She had just time to give them their money and say good bye. I was in school so I didn't see them depart. When I came home, I remember seeing Mamma upstairs cleaning up the rooms where they had lived during all that time. A few days later, somebody at the town hall told her to prepare for another family which would be coming the following week.

The new group consisted of a grandmother in her sixties, her daughter of about forty, and a nine-year-old boy named Ninni, evenly placed in age, between my brother and me. We were ecstatic, thinking that we would have a playmate. Alas, the boy acted more like a girl than a boy: he played with dolls, did crochet, and sewed dresses for his doll. I tolerated him, but my brother used to harass him unmercifully, though without malice. Ninni never joined in our games, regardless of their nature. Filippo and I were all boy. We played soccer (in a sort of way—our ball was made of old socks stuffed with rags) and *"a sticchie,"* a kind of bocce game involving a half brick stood up on its end upon which buttons were placed and a flat round stone that could be shuffled toward it to knock it down. And we ran, always ran, constantly ran, often accompanying our runs with sounds that mimicked the engines of racing automobiles, including the shifting of gears. Ninni could have never kept up with us. On the other hand, my brother and I could never play with dolls, either. So, there went the dream of having another boy with whom to play.

These people were Italian, however, although I could not tell, by their accent, from which region of Italy they came. Were they Jews? I think so. The film *Assisi Underground* would support that theory. The pastor of San Damiano in Assisi, Padre Rufino, whose name and picture are featured prominently in the Holocaust Museum in Washington as well as in the Yad Vashem Museum in Jerusalem, hid thousands of Jews in the cloisters, in the churches, even in the hermitages. They even pitched tents in the woods in order to house the ever-swelling number of refugees. He used to procure transportation to the town of *Pescocostanzo* in our mountains, not far from the mountain where the Sangro begins its run toward the Adriatic Sea. From there they would help them get across the Sangro and consign them to the British authorities on the other side of the river. However, the Sangro at the point near *Pescocostanzo* where the passage to freedom took place was but a small creek. In the film, it looks more like the Mississippi.

During the period between late 1942 and 1943, there was a constant flow of refugees, Jewish and not, moving south, coming mostly from Assisi. Occasionally, they would run into difficulties ranging from bad weather to the presence of German patrols. When that happened, they would spread themselves along the northern bank of the river with the help of the underground forces. Our town is the last hamlet before the Sangro flows into the Adriatic Sea, and Casoli is about 12 miles inland at the top of a small mountain, still on the northern side of the Sangro.

The film, *Assisi Underground,* also featured Gino Bartali, one of the great bicycle racers of my youth and, after 1973, a personal friend of mine (he came to Fossacesia on the occasion of the tragic death of Sandrino Fantini, Fossacesia's own bicycle champion—he liked the town, so he bought a condominium there for his summer retreat). In 1943, Gino had won the world title in road racing, and in preparation for his next races, he would ride his bike from Florence to Assisi. The truckloads of German soldiers he passed along the road used to applaud him because they knew who he was. What they didn't know was that on each trip from Florence to Assisi, Gino carried dozens of false documents hidden in the tubes of his bicycle. The documents were prepared by a printer in Florence. When they reached their destination in Assisi, Padre Rufino would distribute them to the Jews. That sort of activity was very much in vogue all over the world during World War II. Even Cardinal Roncalli, the future Pope John XXIII, who was serving in Turkey at the time, distributed thousands of them. On August 1st, 1989, my wife and I attended a dinner dance in Fossacesia, and Gino and his wife sat at our table. I asked him about the scene in the movie. He confirmed its authenticity, but said he was upset with the film's producers because they failed to mention many other young racers who did the same thing. Some were caught by the Germans and shot on the spot. The movie totally ignored their sacrifices. We in Abruzzo didn't bother with documents, genuine or false. We simply gave them hospitality until the Allies arrived.

NINNI, VUOI L'UOVO? (JOHNNY, DO YOU WANT AN EGG?)

Some of the people who still live in our old neighborhood in Fossacesia, remember that Ninni used to sew, play with dolls, and do crocheting. I am certain that if he is still alive he is involved with fashion designing. It would be nice to see him again, some day. My wife remembers that every day his grandmother used to call out to him: *"Ninni, vuoi l'uovo?"* She was concerned because he was so thin, so she wanted to give him a more substantial diet. Ninni, of course, never wanted an egg. My mother used to save pieces of cloth for him that she would trim from the material she used to make dresses for her clients. According to Susan Zuccotti, by 1945 there were 45,000 Italian Jews and 7,500 foreign Jews in Italy. Through my research, I have come to believe that Ninni's family was Jewish and that they were probably from Rome. They might have been warned earlier in the year of the impending *"retata"* (dragnet), as everyone used to refer to those horrible roundups the Germans used to stage without warning. They had an opportunity to run as early as late February, 1943, and they took it.

It must be understood that there were two types of Jews among us. The first group was made up of people detained by the government as far back as 1938, after the promulgation of the cruel Italian racial laws. Their "crime" was that of being Jewish. Another group, however, came to us through the efforts of the underground, aided by the local clergy and municipal authorities. These were the ones who had managed to slip through the strands of the Nazi net. Following are thoughts expressed by some of the Jewish detainees in Casoli:

> "There are seventy-five of us here between life and death, in a state of pitiful vegetation . . . we are detained without being charged, without a trial and without defense . . . or verdict."
>
> *Maria Moldauer-Eisenstein*

> "I'm in good health . . . if we could await here in Casoli until the end of the war it would be a good thing . . . nobody knows what's going to happen to us."
>
> *A German Jew writing to his brother in South America*

> "No one is starving, tortured, killed or mistreated here . . . but we have had our freedom taken from us . . . The uncertainty and the

uselessness of our situation, the boredom of our mere existence, the total lack of hope for tomorrow lurk in the very folds of our souls."

A Stateless Jew being held in the Tortoreto camp

These attestations are ample proof that many Italians, being of little anti-Semitic consciousness, accepted both types of Jewish refugees and soon befriended them. There was a young man in Casoli who used to play soccer in the Casoli team. He came to play at Fossacesia twice in the summer of '43. We used to call him Zinni. I don't know why, but I think that his last name might have been something like Zinnman or Zinnerman, and so the Italian fans reduced it to Zinni. And we, the kids, didn't like him either, because he scored twice against our team in each of the two games played, one at home, one away. We didn't hate him because he was a Jew. We didn't know what he was. We didn't like him because he was a good player and he hurt our team badly both times. Still, we enjoyed watching him play.

How the internees were treated was up to the director of the camps. In many cases, there was an exchange of sexual favors in order to obtain a little more food, an extra hour of freedom, a slightly higher ranking in the hierarchy of human misery. Myriads of personal dramas took place in those days which will never be known, most of them being intensely personal.

The fact that the Italian people were not profoundly anti-Semitic did not escape the notice of the Duce, himself, although Susan Zuccotti is virulent in her accusations against the Italians of the Repubblica di Salò, and with good cause. After the September 8th armistice, the internees of Lanciano and Casoli were transferred further north into the Marche Region. Here, Mussolini was only the puppet of the Nazis, who ruled with their usual ferocity. As a result, some of the Italian die-hard fascists became as ferocious as the Nazis themselves, and were responsible for arresting eleven or twelve of the Jews interned in Lanciano, sending them to Auschwitz. But, without even considering the Salò violence and deportations, the very idea of detaining thousands of people after 1938 simply because they were Jewish is imputable to the Italian State without mitigating factors of sorts. The historian Spartaco-Capogreco puts it this way:

> "Given that in the fascist detention camps for the Jews, Man's dignity was observed (more or less), it is also true that the very existence of those camps represented the trampling underfoot of the very dignity some people still think was upheld."

And then there is the story of Samuel Grauer and his wife Rosa Jordan Grauer, Jewish escapees from Poland, as reported in Gianni Orecchioni's book, *I sassi e le ombre*. Samuel and his pregnant wife Rosa arrived in Trieste from Danzig in November of 1939, running from the Nazis, who had just invaded Poland. They thought they were safe in Italy. Their first child, Marco, was born on February 6, 1940, in Trieste. Unfortunately, on June 10th, Italy, that every one expected to remain neutral, entered the conflict on the side of Germany. Immediately Samuel Grauer was detained because he was a Jew. He was sent to Casoli. Soon Samuel made the request of the government that his wife and young son be allowed to join him at Casoli. His request was granted and the reunited family was reassigned to the camp at nearby Orsogna, still within the Fossacesia-Lanciano area. They were declared "free internees," a cruel oxymoron if there ever was one! Such a status, however, permitted Samuel to work as a carpenter. On February 4, 1942, another boy was born in the hospital at Lanciano, six miles away from my own birth place. They named him Tito.

On September 8th came the armistice, and with it wave after wave of Nazi troops rolled into Italian territory. The Grauers were arrested in Lanciano and transferred to the prison of L'Aquila (the capital of Abruzzo), then to Milano, and finally loaded onto one of those infamous cattle cars. The train identified with the number 6 left the Milano station on January 30, 1944, arriving in Auschwitz on February 6, Marco's fourth birthday. Tito had "celebrated" his second birthday two days before locked in that terrible death car. Professor Orecchioni reports, "We know the two boys were killed the same day they arrived at the death camp, but the fate of their parents remains unknown." At this point, the professor attempts to place in perspective the cruelty which the Nazis and the fascists dealt upon the Jews on Italian territory, not even respecting the rights to life of the Grauer children, innocent by definition, Italian by birthright, human beings by the will of God, yet betrayed by Italians. True, it was the few Italians who stuck to Mussolini's ideals to the bitter end, but one rotten apple in a basket makes for a rotten basket of apples. It is not within my prerogative to assign culpability. That's God's job, the creator of us all. Let us leave it to His infinite wisdom to exact justice or dispense mercy and forgiveness as He wills. All we can do at this juncture is leave to future generations the task of writing the final chapter about the Italian fascists and their conduct during those horrible days. It will provide, no doubt, for some very interesting reading. And, may God have mercy on all—who must bear on their consciences the guilt of having contributed to the evils of a most vile page in the history of mankind.

Bishop Palatucci amid his Jewish protégées

Bishop Giuseppe Maria Palatucci, Police Commissioner G. Palatucci's uncle, photographed amidst Campagna's Jewish detainees, mostly professionals. This is obviously not a picture of hostility. To the left of the bishop, in the white uniform, is the director of the two camps in Campagna. Above the bishop there are three Carabinieri, wearing black military caps with the silver flame. The rest are all Jewish detainees, including the bearded man in the foreground, bottom right. He looks like a rabbi if I ever saw one!

NINNI'S FAMILY DISAPPEARS AND THEN REAPPEARS, SAFE AND SOUND

Ninni's family was with us throughout the summer of 1943, until the air raid of October 12. At that point, they disappeared and we never saw them again. We knew they made it though, because one day in the summer of 1945 they sent a truck to get their belongings. Mamma had a difficult time with them, too. The fact was that we had lost our house completely. Before the British demolished it, they allowed mamma and nonna to enter it and try to salvage whatever they could. But, they had nowhere to put our furniture, our clothing and other things we ourselves owned. Our refugee family had come to us with two trunks filled with fine linen and other expensive things. Mamma had to ask friends and relatives to keep the contents of the trunks in their homes until the family came to retrieve them. I was away at school when the truck arrived, but nonna told me they complained that mamma "had given their stuff away." She had given it to other people to hold, not as a gift. Our house had been razed to the ground, after all. Of course, even as an incentive, she told the people who took the trunk, in consignment they could keep the articles after a few years if the proprietors failed to return. So, Ninni's family got everything back and we, their benefactors, lost all of ours. Life is not fair at times! They made a big fuss over the loss of their radio, too. We had no clue as to the whereabouts of their radio. We certainly didn't have it, because we were living in a one-room hovel with one wire that went from the electric pole outside directly to the one bulb that mamma had hung from the open ceiling. Nonna paid a minimal, fixed, semi-annual fee for the service of powering one forty watt bulb just to have some light in the shack we called home for nearly three years. There were no electric outlets into which we could plug a radio and make it function. As for their trunks, the family that kept them for us never even opened them, and so mamma was able to return them intact. They did not appreciate the fact that my mother became obligated to the various families who held them for us.

Being a ten, eleven-year-old boy, I wasn't privy to any money transaction that might have occurred between mamma and our guests, but I don't believe anyone was ever compensated for his efforts on behalf of the refugees. No one had any money, and the little stipend the government passed on to us, as Americans, and to the transients, was sufficient only to keep body and soul together. But, then, no compensation was ever expected. Our people were at the other end of the Holocaust, catching those poor people who had been fortunate enough to slip through the Nazi net. My most pressing personal obsession after the war has been a nagging "what if" question in my mind. What if I had been the adult in question, in place of my mother or grandmother, would I have risen to the occasion? I'd like to say yes, and hope that I would be correct, since I have a personality akin to both of theirs. It seems to me that when we anticipate similar dire situations we are terrified by the very thought of the unknown. And, why not? The most critical psychological element in such occurrences is the fear of the unknown. When a dire situation arrives for real, however, and one finds himself in the middle of it, he simply deals with it, often surprising himself at his own resiliency in handling any and all adversities.

THE SUMMER OF '43

In the fall of 1942, I entered middle school in Lanciano. The students from Fossacesia and surrounding communities who wanted to pursue their education beyond the fifth grade had to take public transportation daily to get to Lanciano. The ride took almost an hour, since the bus stopped at other surrounding towns to pick up their students.

The year was marked by the death of one of my favorite aunts in the hospital in Lanciano, and this set the stage for a turbulent year. Then there was my celebrated tonsils operation that Professoressa De Benne forced on me. She thought the reason I was so distracted all the time was because I needed a tonsils operation. She even recommended a doctor who would do it. My mother, who revered all teachers, bought the idea lock, stock and proverbial barrel. The operation took place on March 22, 1943. It was a brutal intervention *in vivo*, without anesthesia. I don't remember the pain, but there were buckets of blood flying around everywhere, especially since my dangling legs were kicking at a hundred repetitions a minute. The one picture I have in my mind of the aftermath was that of my Aunt Rose (the one who would be temporarily kidnapped by the Nazis six months later), holding four ice cream cones she had gone to buy at a caffè nearby. Normally I would have devoured all four at the same time, but with my mouth still oozing blood, I had lost my appetite, even for ice cream. For the next three weeks I was confined to my home, and mamma kept me home even after I had returned to school on days that were too windy or rainy. So, I lost about a month's time. Why that operation could not wait until school was closed for the summer, I'll never know. It is my firm conviction that that lady and that doctor had something going for themselves: she provided the patients for him, and he did the work—a butcher's work, at that! And then, De Benne had the nerve to fail me for having lost too much school time.

One incident I'll never forget took place in late April. One day, after I had recovered sufficiently from surgery, as I came out of school, I crossed the "Corso Trento e Trieste" in Lanciano, and I headed for the stairs that lead to the upper level, on a street called Corso Bandiera, not far from the school. Even today, Corso Bandiera is a commercial strip that runs parallel to the main central artery of the city. Bandiera store prices were decidedly lower than those along the main strip. It is on a high plateau, accessible from the Trento e Trieste via a wide staircase with over fifty steps. I don't even remember what I was doing up there. Probably mamma had asked me to buy some sewing supplies such as thread, needles, and the like. Suddenly, sirens began to wail. "Oh, oh! What do I do now?" I thought to myself. That time I was really scared, not so much because of the air raid alarm, but because I was alone. So, the first thing I did was get behind a building as per my mother's instructions in case of an air raid, and I awaited the arrival of the bombers. I didn't panic, however, as I awaited patiently for things to develop. After about ten minutes, seeing that all was calm, I decided to make a run for it, and headed for the bus stop in the *piazza*. My bus would not depart for another hour or so, but there was a possibility for me to get home on another bus. I lucked out. Just loading was a limousine (a very modest one, that is—it was just an oversized 1934 FIAT), but it did carry seven passengers comfortably. They used it almost like a taxi, to transport special categories of passengers, such as the very old or the handicapped. I asked the driver, Giovanni Toscano, if he had room for me, and he told me to stick around: there were two ladies who had gone to the hospital to visit relatives there. If they didn't come back on time, I could take the place of one of them. Besides myself, also waiting (and no doubt praying that the ladies would not return), was none other than Monsignor Tozzi. His mere presence there made me feel more comfortable. Since the ladies were nowhere in sight, we were both invited aboard. The car left almost immediately, and, unlike the bus, which made many stops and took a wider route, the limo was an express, reaching Fossacesia by the shortest route possible. Within fifteen minutes I was home. I told my mother what had happened and she immediately thought of not sending me to school for the balance of the year, but I wouldn't hear of it. I had already lost too much time with that stupid tonsillectomy in March, and I was trying to salvage the lost time. Three weeks later, however, schools did close, a full month before usual, and I wouldn't be surprised if those wailing sirens that day were not the catalyst that precipitated that hasty decision. By now, of course, we had been given ample notice that things were going to be rather "interesting" for the next few months.

Since Professoressa De Benne didn't promote me in June, I had to prepare to take remedial examinations in September. The task of preparing me for the make-up examinations fell upon Flora Fizzani. She held classes in her home, and there were about a dozen of us studying with her throughout the summer of '43. Miss Fizzani had been my mother's *cummare*, that is they had exchanged a solemn friendship bond. In Italian the word is Comare (*la cummare*, in dialect, with some slight regional variations), while the male counterpart is Compare (not Goombah!). These reciprocal titles were the result of an adult standing for a child in baptism, or first communion, and confirmation. Later, as adults, they were also used for maid-of-honor and best man at weddings. I don't know why my mother was *cummare* with Flora, but it militated against me, because mamma asked Commare Flora to send her a note every day reporting on my progress, or lack thereof. The note was rarely positive, and I had to be the bearer of the note, too. Looking back, it is amazing that I learned so much, given that, according to many of my teachers, I was little more than a "bench warmer." But, that's what they did in those days. I suppose the system worked.

Unfortunately, that year September exams were not given; the war came, instead, and schools never reopened until two and a half years later. Consequently, I did not attend the seventh and the eighth grades in a regular school. A number of our mothers (with my father being in America, and the fathers of many other kids in town in the military, the mothers had to do everything) arranged for some of us to take private lessons with Miss Fizzani. She taught us a variety of subjects, from Italian to Latin, from math to a science of sorts. She had had polio as a little girl and, as a result, her right arm was completely paralyzed. She was the only person at the time I had ever seen write with her left hand. While her right arm was useless to her, she could deliver quite a wallop with her left, as I found out one day. I was doing a translation from Italian to Latin, and I was looking for the Italian indefinite article "un" ("a, an" in English). I had a large dictionary so I began to leaf through it but I couldn't find it. I tried several times: nothing! Finally, I slammed the book shut, and I placed it on the table with a loud bang, announcing at the same time: "It's not there!" That's when she let go with an open-handed left hook that caught me right over the right ear and for a few minutes I couldn't hear with it. That's when I remembered a fundamental rule: Latin has no articles; that's why it wasn't in the dictionary. Well, that was standard procedure in those days. They did hit us once in a while, but it didn't hurt, really it didn't.

As a matter of fact, my two favorite teachers ever, Cacciavillani and Fizzani, hit me only once each (well deserved both times!), but I hold no grudges against them. On the other hand, after the war had passed, two of my teachers humiliated me in public for no reason at all. Those I have never forgiven. In fact, I even pray for them because they, more than any other, are in need of God's mercy!

At recess time, throughout that summer, Flora Fizzani would take the class to her back yard and make us water her garden. In the process, she would give us a few lessons in botany. It was an enjoyable way to learn, even as we were all aware of the difficulty of the historical moment. We knew that as of July 10, 1943, the Allies had already invaded Sicily and it was a matter of time before they would arrive in our area. Occasionally, one of the students would swear he heard explosions in the distance. Of course, he heard nothing of the kind. Before July 10th, the Allies were still in North Africa, and after that in Sicily, therefore the war was still hundreds of miles away from us, so we heard nothing. And yet, the imminent danger of the approaching war was all too real to us, so the teacher would make us practice safety measures in case of an air raid: get under the table for a few minutes, until the all clear was given. Sometimes, I think that some of the boys spent the time under that table holding hands with the girls!

When August arrived, Miss Fizzani ceased instruction for the entire month, since August in Italy is vacation time, even if there is a war going on. The biggest feast day of the year, that of Saint Donato, the saint protector of the town, is celebrated on August 7th. It was her intention to restart school in September, unless the regular schools reopened first. We were to keep in touch. When September arrived, however, she checked with the Carabinieri and was told to await notification from them; the situation was somewhat precarious. Schools would not reopen and she felt she would be better off not to take the responsibility of all those kids in her home in such dire moments. So she didn't. Unbeknown to her and to us, there was a dark, dark cloud approaching. For the next three months, we would be engaged in a period of sheer primeval and instinctual attempt to survive. Most of us would survive; sadly, Miss Fizzani would not. As soon as the month of August rolled around, she closed the summer session and told us to enjoy our vacation despite the uncertain circumstances. She, like many others in town, expected the Allied Armies to roll onto town without much trouble. I believe she had anticipated that by September, or October at the latest, things would be back to normal and everyone would be back to school. Oh, how wrong she was!

My three wonderful teachers

These are the photos of my three great teachers, who are responsible for putting into my head such a strong linguistic base. They did so in Italian, of course, but that base served me well, as I was able to build several foreign languages upon it: classical Greek, Latin, French, Spanish and even English.

Dora Cacciavillani, the dynamic one

She taught me in grades 3, 4 and part of 5. At that point she began to train me for the so-called Admissions Exams. She had the reputation for getting physical with the students. All teachers did that in those days. She hit me once only, and I deserved it. She died on March 16, 2007, age 92.

Maria Fantini, the meek, the modest, the humble

She was somewhat of a maintenance teacher who made sure that what I learned in school stayed learned. She was the daughter of Monsignor Tozzi's sister. She was really a beautiful girl to whom life has been less than fair. She deserved more, much more! Maria is in her eighties.

Finally, and by no means least, is Flora Fizzani, the profound one.
She was profound because she was possessed with a very strong
moral backbone which she was able to pass on to us, her pupils, in
a thousand ways. Her teaching was the type that kept on teaching
for a lifetime. She had had polio when she was a little girl and it
completely paralyzed her right arm, but she packed a wallop in
her left.

After teaching a group of us during the summer of 1943, she,
like the rest of us, was forced to leave the town. After nearly two
months of running from one refuge to another, one day in early
December, in Ortona, she and her 7-year-old nephew, Enzo, were hit
by shrapnel from a cannon shell's explosion just outside the entrance
to the cave where they were staying. Enzo died instantly, but Flora
lingered on until December 14 and then died. I pray for her, but
mostly to her, because she was a saint even when she was alive.

THE ARMISTICE

Late in the evening of September 8th, 1943, about 8:30 P.M., Signor
Attilio Del Raso, our mailman, came to our neighborhood to deliver a special
package to one of our neighbors, and announced that Italy had just signed
an armistice with the Allied Governments. The war was over! So he said, and
so we thought. Signor Del Raso enjoyed a good glass of wine even during
his routes, so being in the neighborhood, he stopped at our house, knowing
that he would find a glass of good wine there. He and nonna discussed the
situation with great optimism in their voices. Even the church bells began to
peal at an unusual hour. The war must be over.

Unfortunately, our optimism was premature. Not only was the war not
over, but it was about to pounce on us with all its fury. Within a little over
a month, on October 12th, our town would be the target of an unexpected

and unannounced air raid, later described in this narrative. It was to be the first of many during the next three months.

At the end of summer, however, in the year of Our Lord, 1943, none of this loomed even remotely in our minds. Yes, an ominous atmosphere lay over the town like an invisible pall; yes, the food that had been scarce for the past two years seemed even more scarce now; and yes, the rumbling of motorcycles, trucks, automobiles, half-tracks, and even tanks could be heard from time to time, almost daily, as they hurtled down the hill headed south toward the Sangro River. Yet, there was a lull in the town that didn't prepare us for the approaching disaster. In the words of Armando Liberato in his book, *La linea Gustav*: "Our populace knew that the Allied armies were coming, and they expected a bit of a noisy confrontation, perhaps, together with an occasional explosion, but no one, absolutely no one, expected that the front line with all its destructive force would descend upon our peaceful towns, with its devastating fire storm coming from land, air and sea. We awaited the development of events with calm trepidation, hoping for the best and trusting in the mercy of God." Again, in Liberato's words, "Many of our towns were half destroyed, our schools reduced to rubble, and quite a few people killed," not only by the bombs, but by pure German rage, as well.

AN OPPORTUNITY NOT TAKEN

According to a magazine article I read many years ago, sometime in August, 1943, in a pre-arranged move, an American transport plane landed at Ciampino Airport in Rome. On board was a team of Allied diplomats. They were taken to a secret location where they met with Marshall Badoglio or other government representatives. The Allied plan was simply to land troops in Italy like the largest group of tourists that sunny country had ever seen. On another occasion I read something about the 82nd Airborne Division possibly conducting a massive drop of troops on Rome. Whatever! It was a good plan, but in order to do that, they asked Marshall Badoglio to put two Italian Army divisions at the Brenner Pass, the only Alpine pass between Italy and Austria, to block any massive invasion by the Germans. Could they do that? The answer was yes, Italy did have two divisions on national soil, but Marshall Badoglio was afraid that two divisions would have been overwhelmed by the Germans. He agreed at first, but then failed to go through with it. I believe this was the reason General Eisenhower reneged on his own promise to hold off the announcement of the armistice until September 11th. Instead, he announced the signing of the armistice between Italy and the Allies on

September 8th. This caught everybody by surprise and caused panic at all levels. That very day, the King and Queen, Prince Umberto, the heir to the throne, Marshall Badoglio, General Staff, fled from Rome and headed for the East coast. They traveled to the small hamlet of Crecchio in Abruzzo, about ten miles northwest of Fossacesia. The population of Crecchio is less than 4,000 people, but it has on its territory an ancient yet functional castle that dates back to the 12th century. It was originally a fortress, but in 1789 it was changed to an elegant residential building. It was eventually purchased by the De Riseis family as their principal residence. Prince Umberto, the future May King, Umberto II, had stopped there on his honeymoon trip in 1926. Again in 1928 and 1932 he slept there while on official visits to various towns in the area. In 1943, the De Riseis family still lived in the castle, and Lady Gaetana De Riseis was the primary figure in the family. According to some articles about the history of Crecchio downloaded from the Internet, Lady Gaetana was the last person to try unsuccessfully to persuade Prince Umberto to return to Rome and take over the reins of government. It would have been a heroic act which might well have altered the course of history in a positive way. His mother, *la Regina Elena*, they say, talked him out of it, fearing that he might be killed by the Germans. And so he relented. Of course, I never heard of a hero being talked out of performing his great deeds by his mother!

The next day, the royal family, Marshall Badoglio and the entire *Stato Maggiore* (Joint Chiefs of Staff) moved the seat of government to Brindisi, in the deep south. They sailed from the nearby port of Ortona aboard the yacht *Gabriele D'Annunzio*. A new era for Italy was about to begin, but not before a disastrous war practically razed it to the ground.

After the war was over, Umberto became king of Italy, but his reign lasted a mere forty days. He is still mockingly referred to as *"the king of May,"* because that's how long he lasted as monarch—the last ten days of April, and the entire month of May, 1946. On June 2nd, the Italian people, in a national plebiscite, opted to drop the monarchy in favor of a republican form of government. As a fourteen-year-old student in the city of Chieti, I played a tiny part in that historical event. My school in that city was one of the polling places for the referendum. The resident students were asked to help during the election. The people chose the latter, and the new Italian Republic was born. It is still going strong.

What should have happened back in September of 1943 was that King Victor Emanuel III should have abdicated in favor of his son Umberto, and the latter should have heeded the advice of Lady Gaetana de Riseis and returned to Rome, taking the reigns of government into his hands. Then he would have governed as a leader, instead of returning to Italy from exile after the war, expecting the Italian people to welcome him with open arms. Even if he had been killed by the Germans, he would have died a hero, instead of dying in exile, a dishonored man. Had he made the right decision back in August of 1943, and taken over the reigns of the government at that point, he would have saved thousands of lives on both sides, spared us untold destruction, and avoided many tears and much grieving on the part of the civilian population, especially the children.

But then, the Allies blundered, too, on an even grander scale. Having decided to invade Italy, they did so on July 10, 1943, but they opened a beachhead at Gela, one of the southernmost towns in the Island of Sicily. Not even Hannibal did that, for heaven's sake! He took his elephants to Spain, then through Gaul and over the Alps, before descending into Italy and toward the city of Rome. From Gela, the Allied forces had to occupy the island of Sicily first, and then conquer the entire peninsula inch by inch, foot by foot. No wonder they became tired and it took them almost a year to get to Rome. They should have asked my mother to plan the invasion of Italy. She used to conjecture as to the possible routes the Americans could take to save Italy from Nazi oppression. She thought they would send an expedition force up the Adriatic Sea that would land somewhere between the Po and Adige rivers, south of Venice, and another up the Tyrrhenian Sea to land between Genova and La Spezia. Had they done that, the Italian campaign would have been over in less than a month, sparing thousands of lives on both sides and avoiding the massive destruction the war caused, including that of my own beautiful house, that reduced my family to live in a shed. I'm not going to get into speculations as to what should or should not have happened with regard to the invasion of Italy. But I know this, I believe that it's going to go into history as one of the greatest military blunders in the history of warfare.

There is an anecdote I would like to share with my readers, parenthetically, that illustrates the dilemma in which the Italian soldiers found themselves. On the one side, with King Victor Emmanuel III being the legitimate ruler, the army was a duly constituted instrument of the State, and the soldiers were bound by law to fight. Many of the young men had family in America, however. Some of them had already been to America and had returned for one reason or another and were trapped there by the war. If they were still Italian citizens and of draft age, they were drafted by law and found themselves having to fight against their own countrymen. Naturally, the entire armed forces just didn't have a large enough national agenda to go out and fight anybody. Now, it happened that the day before the American Army was to board the ships in North Africa to proceed to the shores of Gela, the commanders asked any soldier of Sicilian descent who spoke the Sicilian dialect or the Italian language to be among the first to touch the island's soil to greet the inhabitants in their own language, thus reassuring them that they had come with peaceful intentions, hoping to convince the Italians to surrender. The morning of the invasion, on the first ship to hit the beach, there was a young man named Harry Bilella (he spelled his name Billela) from Norristown, Pa. He spoke the Sicilian dialect very well, so he was the first to jump off the landing vessel. Years later, I met Mr. Bilella. He told me that the first thing he looked for was the tomato gardens that produced tomatoes the size of cantaloupes his father used to brag about. What he found instead was an Italian machine gun nest staring at them from a nearby hill. If they had fired, Harry and his friend would have been dead. Instead, within a few minutes, they saw an Italian soldier coming down the hill carrying a white flag. When he got within voice range, he shouted: "Are you guys Americans?" "Yea, who wants to know?" "I'm from Patterson, New Jersey," came the reply. And with that, the white flag went flying one way, the rifles were put down, and there was a grand reunion of Americans. The Italians also revealed that they wouldn't have fired at them, no matter what, but an even more disturbing reality was that they couldn't fire even if they wanted to—the Germans were supposed to supply them with ammunitions and they didn't. So, they surrendered. The Italian from Patterson was quickly taken "prisoner" aboard ship, together with the rest of the Italian machine gun crew, and he was promised a ride home with the POWs, but when they got to America he would be sent home to New Jersey. He thought that was the luckiest day of his life.

"LU SFULLAMENTE" (THE EVACUATION PERIOD)

Thus began the very significant period of our lives known in town as "*Lu sfullamente*," that is, the evacuation of the town first prompted by the air raid of October 12, then made official two weeks later by order of the German Command. Here is the order, in translation, issued on October 25, 1943, and posted on the doors of the city halls of all the municipalities on the list—twenty three of them.

Citizens

The Command of the German Troops is forced to take under consideration the possibility of a general evacuation of all the population of the following communes and localities with the possibility that at a later date other towns further north may be asked to evacuate their populations, as well.

[Here followed a list of 23 towns that included Fossacesia, but also small cities like Lanciano, Ortona a Mare, and Guardiagrele, fairly large urban centers. The total population to be evacuated surpassed two hundred thousand people—where do you put that many people?]

The grave necessities of the hour require that all citizens obey with the strictest discipline the dispositions of the authorities in order to confront and overcome with calm and spiritual strength the inevitable discomfort that war brings on. You must have unshakable faith in the destinies of our Fatherland and for its benefit follow with prudent discipline and willing spirit of cooperation the directives that for your own good the Command of the German Troops has studied, so that this temporary evacuation from your homes and your lands will take place in an orderly and solicitous fashion. You will soon return to them in freedom and peace, as it is the hope of all the Italian people. Your mayors will give you all the necessary instructions and will personally supervise the evacuation operations. The Provincial Prefect will control very closely the provisions set aside for this purpose for your comfort and assistance.

The Prefect of Chieti
October 25, 1943

While most of the people in town heeded the order to evacuate, only a few families actually moved north. Most of the people went into the countryside and, when pushed by German patrols, they simply moved in circles. None, however, conducted that maneuver with more guile than my mother, as she outsmarted the Germans at every turn. Our home was almost at the very center of the town, and although we moved eleven times in forty-five days, we stayed within a radius of no more than two miles from our house.

HERE COME THE AMERICANS!

On Sunday, July 11, 1943, a most unusual event took place: Nonno Donato came to our house and asked my mother if it was all right for me to spend the day with him in our country home at Caporale. Surprisingly, mamma said yes. So, while nonno proceeded into town to do some errands,

I went to mass and then waited for him to return. He did so around noon, and together we walked back to Caporale. On the way, we stopped at nonno's house in town, the house in which I was born. In the few minutes we were there, nonno showed me a large case he kept in a shed in the back of the house. He told me that it was full of books, mostly Italian classics, that my father had brought home from America in 1934. There was even a gramophone, and at least two complete operas on disc. I wanted to look inside, but he said he hadn't opened that case since 1935 and he had lost the key years ago. He would have had to have a new one made, or break the lock. Neither of the above actually happened. Instead, in November a cannon shell would hit the shed and break the case apart like an eggshell. I would not get my hands on the contents until December 1st, the day of our liberation.

That Sunday in July, we proceeded down the hill to Caporale, arriving just in time for dinner. After dinner, Nonno suggested that we take a walk to our relatives, the Marrone family, better known in town as Casimine, a nickname derived by the name of their son, Casimiro Marrone, whose name was reduced to Casimine. He was my favorite cousin. As we were walking the half-mile distance between the two farmsteads, we walked along Route 16. On the way, we ran into Signor Ernesto Fantini, Anna Maria's father, my neighbor in town and future father-in-law. He gave us the news that American forces had invaded Sicily the day before, July 10th. Being an American himself, Signor Fantini and my Nonno Donato had a great time, as they danced and pranced in the middle of the road with great unrepressed jubilation. They even attempted to sing the Star Spangled Banner, managing only a bit of *la-la-la* because neither one knew the words to the anthem (most Americans don't, either!), sung off key and out of tune, but with a great profusion of patriotic spirit. Fortunately, there wasn't a soul on that road who could have witnessed that spontaneous burst of loyalty to America. Few Italians had cars and those who did, couldn't get gas. The Germans had not yet arrived, so the road was completely deserted. After the "dance," they stopped to talk and concluded that with the Americans already on Italian soil, the war would soon be over. They thought that the Americans would arrive in town within a week. Boy, were they ever wrong! Between then and October 20th, when he came to fetch us to "reunite the family," a couple of major events had happened that were not foreseen in July: Italy signed the armistice with the Allies on September 8th, and our town suffered an air raid on October 12th. Thus, the optimism of summer was replaced by the anxious trepidation of autumn. What's going to happen to us? We had not prepared for this.

Donato De Simone, the Elder: American

This mustachioed, pipe smoking, highly respected gentleman was my grandfather, the first Donato De Simone, for whom I was named. Even though he opted to retire in Italy, he loved America with genuine reverence and devotion. Nonno Donato took a big chance when he hid a downed British pilot for five days in an area that pullulated with Nazi soldiers. On November 3, 1943, he delivered the pilot to the beach area where a local fisherman took him by row boat to the southern banks of the Sangro River where the British 8th Army was. From there he was able to rejoin his outfit. Unfortunately, he would be killed in combat about a year later in France. Nonno Donato was proud to have helped in the war effort. It was his way of "giving back," as the modern expression has it. He loved America, after all!

F. Ernesto Fantini, Anna Maria's father: Another American
Mr. Fantini served in the U.S. Army in 1919-20 in some fort in
Kentucky. With him served another gentleman whose first name
began with an F. They were both named Francis, but were better
known by their middle names, Ernesto and Scott, as in F. Scott
Fitzgerald, the famous writer.

PFC. Ernesto Fantini, with the U.S. Army in Kentucky, 1919.

OCTOBER 12, 1943

Tuesday, October 12, 1943, began in Fossacesia with the same hum-drum monotony that had characterized the previous day, the day before that, and all the days of that unbelievable year—a year that was to change our lives forever.

It has been established already that schools in our region of Abruzzo were ordered closed on May 20, instead of June 17, as originally scheduled. The end of the war loomed on the horizon, after all, so it would not be long until things would return to normal. Unfortunately, within a few months things were to become much, much worse.

That morning, a group of boys were gathered in a circle in front of my house. Elide Fantini, who lived down the street from us, joined us at one point while her sister, Anna Maria, was on her balcony, brushing her luscious, waist-long hair, trying her best to ignore me as I tried to impress her with my "prowess as a soccer player," a few minutes earlier. She had turned twelve in July, while I would have to wait until mid-January, 1944, for my own twelfth birthday.

The circle of neighborhood youths that had gathered in front of my house ranged in age from 8 to 14. The prolonged vacation had resulted in our having reached the point of maximum boredom, so we were discussing the possibility that schools might soon reopen. The older boys told horror stories of this or that teacher's atrocities toward the students who misbehaved. Those who thought they knew more felt obliged to exaggerate the descriptions, so the younger students would react with stunned effect and dismay to their stories of woe and sorrow. I, too, threw my own two cents into the confabulation, being the only one who had experienced middle school in the city of Lanciano, so I told of the difficulty of the sixth grade. "Whatever you do, don't go into Professor De Benne's room." I warned them. "She's crazy!"

Suddenly, we heard what sounded like the engine noise of airplanes approaching from the south, but we couldn't see them yet. A few seconds later, however, I saw a group of six fighter planes emerging from beyond a tall building at the end of our block. They were dark in color and menacing in appearance, probably Spitfires, although I was not yet an expert at identifying the shape of military airplanes. These were the very first British airplanes we had ever seen. A year or so before, the local contingent of the Carabinieri had persuaded our pastor, Monsignor Tozzi, to rent the entire rectory to them. The rectory was adjacent to the belfry of the church and separated from it by a large terrace. Monsignor agreed because he owned his own home where he lived, just a block away from the church. Moreover, it was important that the population of the town be warned in case of approaching danger. This arrangement gave the Carabinieri access to the bell tower from the terrace. They retracted the long rope that went from the bell internally to one of the corners of the sacristy, and dropped it onto the terrace on the outside of the steeple. They could easily ring the smallest of the three bells in the belfry whenever they got word that an air raid on the town was imminent. Whenever there was the possibility of an attack, one of the men would simply walk across the terrace and ring the bell to sound the alarm. At the first toll of that little bell, practically the entire population of our town would abandon their homes in an orderly fashion and quietly leave town by the quickest routes, finishing the night under some olive trees on the outskirts of town. This was almost a nightly ritual throughout the summer of 1943. Within twenty minutes, the entire town of 5,000 people was virtually deserted. Summer passed, however, without a single air raid actually occurring—not until that fateful Tuesday morning of October 12, shortly past 10:30 A.M. Ironically, when the real air raid did come, no bell ever rang to give us a warning.

That morning, while in the circle of my friends, I happened to be facing south, so I was in a perfect position to see the airplanes as they appeared suddenly to my left, at ten o'clock high. Somebody said; "Hey, look, they're dropping leaflets . . ." Before we could react, we heard the first explosion. Instant panic ensued. My brother and I, being right in front of our own house, dashed toward it and literally ran into our front door and into our kitchen. The front door being wide open was a normal procedure in good weather, so we got inside in two jumps. The others quickly ran to their own homes as fast as they could.

Mamma and nonna were in the kitchen. At the first explosion, they ran to us and gathered us in. We all took our places under the door frame between the kitchen and the dining room, as we had previously rehearsed several times since the beginning of the war. Mamma finally got a chance to put into operation one of the first things she had read in the newspapers on what to do in case of an air attack. Frightened to the core, we huddled in that door frame between the kitchen and dining room, shaking like leaves. Actually, mamma had made one very important tactical mistake: she forgot to close the front door. But, it proved to be providential, too, as it permitted me to see the planes again as, having dropped their bombs, they made a 180° turn and headed south whence they had come. It was then that I realized that it was not one, but two groups of six air-planes each that executed the raid on Fossacesia: twelve fighter bombers carrying at least one bomb each. The attack had lasted less than two minutes. The planes entered Fossacesia's air space from the south, judging from the path of destruction they left behind. They started to bank left as soon as they approached the school building. The bombs fell in a straight line from south-east to the north-west, about a quarter mile contained between the school and the church. The pilots dropped their bombs, making sure to stay on the very edge of town, perhaps thinking that, in so doing, they were being nice to us by killing just a few of us. But the Mario Bianco elementary school, which also housed the preschool and kindergarten classes, was their first target. The planes approached the school from the front, but the very first bomb they dropped missed the building entirely, falling in the middle of the street behind the school. As for the school itself, it would be charitable to believe that those noble aviators knew that the school was not in session. At the beginning of October, however, the Allies were still in the deep south of Italy, and the rest of the country was trying to function as normally as possible. Yes, our school was closed, but some schools in towns south of Fossacesia were open and functioning. So it is difficult to repress the nagging thought that our school had been targeted for the purpose of inflicting damage that would result in the greatest psychological impact upon the population, that is to kill a few of their children. Psychological warfare was Churchill's favorite war tactic!

The last bombs hit the corner of the Basilica of San Donato, inflicting slight damage to it, and another hit the Contini family residence, diagonally across from the church. The Contini apartment was part of the Mayer complex, the largest building in town, where two rooms were seriously damaged. A few bombs fell harmlessly in the ravine immediately behind the church. Between the school and the church there were a few homes, and beyond was an open area, the backyards of the homes on the main street of the town. I believe that the majority of those twelve bombs fell into that open area, so they did not hurt anyone, but at both ends of that open field there were a number of casualties. Near the school, a passing woman and her two small children were killed, and near the church, half of the Paolucci family was wiped out, as their home suffered a direct hit. Four of the nine members of the family plus the fiancé of one of the girls, unfortunately, were in the home at the time.

The very first victims were twenty-seven-year-old Anna La Caprara, whose husband was in the military service, and her two children, Donatino and Eufemia. That morning, she had taken her three-year-old son, Donatino, to the doctor because he had run a fever all night. Not having anyone at home to watch her five-year-old daughter, she had taken her along, too. Anna lived in the countryside on the other side of town, so being in town with both her children, she decided to stop to see her own mother, who lived near the school. They were walking from the doctor's office toward the grandmother's house, unaware that the entire route lay within the airplane's line of fire. They were walking alongside the school's playground area, not more that a hundred yards from the grandmother's home, when the first bomb exploded in the middle of the street right in front of them. Anna was carrying little Donatino in her arms, and Eufemia was walking beside her when the first bomb exploded. All three were killed instantly. They were the very first civilian victims of the insane war in our town; there would be many more casualties before it was over.

Hearing the explosion, Anna's mother rushed out of her house in total panic, trying to figure out what was going on, and seeking shelter for herself. She was hardly prepared for the shock that awaited her as she looked down the street and saw the victims on the ground, mortally wounded. According to stories that circulated in town after the tragedy, she had recognized the little girl's blue-and-white dress that she had recently sewed for her birthday. Simultaneously, some people had rushed to render whatever aid they could and were already tending to Anna when the mother reached the scene. She saw Donatino lying face down on the gravel road. She picked him up and carried him home in her folded-up apron. He had a gash in his forehead and a completely exposed shoulder joint. Weeping and wailing inconsolably, the grandmother took him to her home, not knowing what else to do with him. In the end, the grandmother's home was turned into a sort of morgue as they carried all three victims there to await official investigation. All were dead. The "officials" didn't show up until the next day. Meanwhile the neighbors tried to render whatever comfort they could give, but given the restrictions of the time, there was precious little they could do. But at least they stayed with the family all through the night, even as the three bodies, horribly mangled, lay in state in the middle of the room.

For the Basilica of San Donato, the town's main place of worship, that was the first of many attacks. The church was located about a quarter mile northwest of the school. The church at that time on a Tuesday morning was empty, so no one was hurt. After the front arrived, it would suffer many more daily attacks.

One of the bombs hit the Paolucci residence dead center, reducing it to rubble, killing all five members of the family who were home that morning. Alberto Nicolucci, author of a historical account of those days, interviewed Mario Paolucci, one of the surviving brothers of the victims, who was 13 years old at the time. In his book, *Storia e società a Fossacesia,* (War and Society in Fossacesia), Nicolucci reports the entire conversation he had with Mario, 73 years old now, about the events of that fatal morning. Here is the translation of that interview:

> There were ten of us living in the house. Only five survived the attack, by the grace of God. Mamma had gone to the Town Hall to receive our monthly allotment of food stamps. Dad had gone out early trying to see if he would be hired by the day to earn some money with which to feed his family. My sister Olga, 21 years old, had gone next door to spend a little time with Nicoletta Valente, her best friend. My brother Tonino, ten years old, was outside playing with some of his friends, and I was also outside, a few yards from the house, attracted by a couple of German military vehicles that had stopped to fill their water containers at the town fountain almost directly across the street from our house. Suddenly there was a roar overhead, followed immediately by a deafening explosion, and the entire three-story house crashed onto itself right in front of me. A gigantic cloud of black dust filled the air, so that I was not able to realize immediately the enormity of the disaster that had suddenly wiped out half of my family. I ran toward the house and almost ran into my sister Olga, who had dashed out of Nicoletta's house in the grip of sheer terror. She pointed to a bundle on the ground and asked, "Who is it?" Instinctively I called out: "Massimiliano!" He answered with a groan. His face was lined with blood, he had a gash in his head, and a brick embedded in his chest. Nicoletta and I tried to lift his head, but then a number of men surrounded us. They took over the awful task and rushed him to the clinic of Dr. Saraceni about a block away. He was dead on arrival. Massimiliano was the only member of my destroyed family that I saw, because the others were buried under tons of bricks and cement. It took until the late-night hours to recover their bodies. An emergency crew quickly organized by the authorities found them all, but they didn't allow me to look at them. It would have been too ghastly for a young boy of my age to see such a macabre scene.

The raid was swift and deadly. How many bombs those little planes dropped we will never know, but they were small fighter planes. Assuming that each plane carried one bomb, we can judge that they dropped a minimum of twelve bombs—on a sleepy little town that posed no threat to anyone. In retrospect, one can see that only two bombs did all the damage, killing eight civilians and destroying one house, while a third damaged the church. The Contini household, on the northern end of the Mayer palace, across the street from the church, also received extensive damage, but it's not clear if it was damaged by the same bomb that damaged the church, or if it was the result of a fourth projectile. Fortunately, no one was home at the time. Signor Contini, a municipal employee, was at work, while his wife, a school teacher, was temporarily idled by the fact that school was not in session and she had taken her two children to Lanciano by bus to shop for shoes. Therefore no one was hurt. The rest of the bombs fell and exploded harmlessly in open areas. It was a miracle that the planes stayed on the edge of town, because had they decided to drop all of their bombs on the center of town, there would have been a slaughter of unspeakable proportions. Still, the raid made no sense at all. There was nothing in town that could have even remotely been considered a military objective.

The Nicolucci book reports that during the summer of 1943, there was indeed a contingent of the Italian Air Force under the command of a colonel, which had taken temporary refuge under the trees that lined some of our streets. They had a military contingent consisting of seven trucks, several motorcycles with sidecars, and a field machine shop. They had set up the shop under a tent in the lower part of our piazza (square), across the street from the eastern wing of the Mayer palace. The trucks had been parked in *Viale dei Tigli* (Linden Boulevard), not far from the piazza, because of the large trees that flanked the beautiful boulevard. They made an ideal camouflage for hiding the motor vehicles from air attacks. There was one incident that I personally witnessed which lends credence to the story. In April of that year, while going to school in Lanciano by bus one morning, as we headed north on a long stretch of highway, we noticed to our left literally hundreds of Italian airplanes flying parallel to us and heading in the same direction. I remember that one of my friends made a wise remark that the bus was going faster than the airplanes. Everybody laughed, but it was a tragic commentary on the insane decision by Mussolini to go to war with that kind of outdated equipment. They were biplanes of the type that flew in World War I. They were probably being flown north in order not to prevent their falling to the Allies. But that was also odd—these planes were totally worthless. The Americans had at their disposition thousands of B-17s, B-24s, B-25s and other sophisticated modern bombers, and they had no need to confiscate Italian junk.

Nicolucci further reports an incident that took place on the 10th of September, 1943, two days after Italy signed the armistice, pulling out of an insane war that the Duce thought he could win. According to an eyewitness, after the 8th of September, the Germans sought to confiscate all arms and other equipment held by the Italian armed forces. On the 10th, a lieutenant and three German soldiers arrived in town and, after locating the colonel in command of the Italian Air Force contingent, ordered him to surrender all his equipment and placed him and his crew under arrest. The Italian colonel, however, refused to surrender his equipment or to recognize the Germans' authority to arrest him. Many of the airmen, as well as a large crowd of civilians that had gathered there, began to press inward toward the German soldiers and the colonel. The outnumbered Germans became fearful for their safety, and decided to abandon their plans, leaving the area empty handed but warning that they would be back. At that point the Italian colonel ordered his men to break camp immediately and they set off westward toward the Majella Range of the Apennine Mountains, which were no more than thirty miles away. Within a little more than two hours, they had loaded everything and were gone, taking with them everything except two trucks which could not be started. When the Germans returned several hours later, they found no one there. By this time, with several hours advantage over the Germans, the Italians were well hidden in the valleys of the Majella Mountains. The Germans couldn't start the two trucks, either, and they were never seen again. The story is true—but could it be possible that the twelve British planes had been after the two ancient and disabled trucks? Definitely not! I reiterate, then, that the attack that morning made no sense at all, other than to inflict psychological damage on the harmless and peaceful population of our little town. Nor could the civilians themselves be considered armed in any way. Within its municipal boundaries, Fossacesia contained no more than half a dozen privately owned shotguns and one Colt 45—our family's. It belonged to my grandfather Filippo, who had returned to America and by then was already dead and buried, anyway. The hunters in town were even scarcer than the game they used to seek, always unsuccessfully. So there was no possible justification for that air raid. The killing of those eight innocent civilians was utterly senseless.

PANDEMONIUM FOLLOWS

The moment the bombs exploded pandemonium set in. The acrid smell of gun powder had settled all over town within seconds. There were mothers running around in panic trying to locate their children, crying out their names. Screams from the downtown area could be heard all the way to our neighborhood, several blocks away. People frantically tried to dig out the victims buried under the rubble. All this had given our people their first taste of war. Not the war they had read about in newspapers up until then, but the real war, the war with shootings and bombs—a war which within a few weeks was to tinge even the placid waters of the Sangro River crimson red.

Ten minutes after the planes had left we heard the tolling of church bells urgently calling for help. But there was no one to help, although the two doctors in town stayed on the job, heroically rendering whatever assistance they could under the circumstances—and that wasn't much. Neither they nor the only pharmacy in town had any medical supplies. The military, considering that they needed them more urgently, had taken all. The casualty count was also unusual. During the previous three years I had listened to the one o'clock news on a friend's radio every day since the war began. It wasn't rare to hear reports of bombings in Torino, Milano, Napoli, and other Italian cities. They often gave reports of the estimated number of civilian casualties. Under normal circumstances, the number of wounded was always four or five times higher than the number of people killed. Not in this raid! Our casualty count was eight killed and none wounded. Among the rescuers were four Franciscan monks who, having heard of the raid on Fossacesia, had pedaled seven miles on bicycles all the way from Lanciano to lend a hand.

Among the dead was a soldier from Sicily, Salvatore Correnti, Olga's fiancé, who had been stationed near Torino. When Italy signed the armistice on September 8, Mr. Correnti, like thousands of his comrades, received vague and sometimes conflicting orders. With Mussolini gone, members of the Italian armed forces, by then spread all over Europe, were abandoned to their own fate. Many were taken prisoners—by the Germans, the Russians, the British, and anyone else who thought they had power over them.

Salvatore Correnti, known as Turiddu, from Paternò, province of Catania, in Sicily, had been stationed in Pinerolo, near Torino, as part of an elite army division. When the armistice was announced, he decided to run to his girlfriend's house in Torino to discuss the situation with her and her family. He had met Olga Paolucci at a dance, and the two had fallen in love. So, while awaiting further instructions from his military superiors, he decided to stay with her family, even as he kept in touch with whatever was left of his military headquarters in Torino. He didn't want to be declared AWOL. Officially he was still part of the army and was reluctant to move too far away from his command post. He had planned to marry the girl as soon as the war was over, anyway, so he agreed to move in with her family.

Then things got complicated. Mussolini, had created a make-shift Republic in the north which he called *La Repubblica di Salò* (The Republic of Salò). Salò is a small town in northern Italy on the western shore of Lake Garda. It quickly became known as the "Little Republic." All military units "caught" in uniform in that part of the country were expected to bear arms in its defense, side by side with the Germans. Most Italian soldiers refused to fight alongside the Germans and were taken prisoners by the Nazis who sent them to Germany. Those lucked out, because shortly after that the order came from the Fuehrer himself that any member of the Italian armed forces who refused to fight along side German troops were to be shot on sight. The rest tried to get away, often heading south by means of whatever transportation they could find, but mostly on foot. Turiddu Correnti had sworn allegiance to the Royal Army, not to the army of any "Little Republic," so when the Paolucci family decided to move back to Abruzzo and Fossacesia, where they had family and where they felt safer, he decided to tag along.

When they arrived in Fossacesia in late September, Abruzzo was technically under the jurisdiction of the Little Republic, which meant under Nazi rule. But, it was so far south that it was simply impossible for the regime to enforce its directives, so he felt safe. Unfortunately, he did not make it. The single bomb that smashed through the roof of the three-story building where they lived killed him and half of the Paolucci family, exploding with a tremendous roar and lifting up a cloud of dust. Ironically, all five were killed right in the little town of Fossacesia where they thought they were going to be safe.

The people of Fossacesia reacted to that first raid as expected—with total panic. Most of the families left their homes immediately. The majority of the people, thinking, perhaps not wrongly, that the open spaces provided greater safety, headed for the countryside where they had relatives or friends. Staying away from town seemed the prudent thing to do, just in case the planes returned to drop a few more bombs. The general uncertainty of the situation was momentarily dwarfed by the absolute certainty of the air attack we had just experienced. To get out of town was the urgent goal of most people. Some people, being afflicted with serious infirmities, couldn't run. Some could not be moved at all. Others had no one to help them. On our street lived two elderly women who were bedridden. They both died in their beds when the heavy bombers arrived and our very street was turned into a living hell.

As soon as the planes left the area that morning, my mother ran upstairs, grabbed some clothes for all of us, took some food from the pantry, and placed everything in a wicker basket. In the manner that was common in those days, she rolled up a kitchen towel, made it into a donut, placed it upon her head, and put the basket on top of it. Women routinely carried such baskets, often quite heavy, by balancing them on their heads. They could walk for miles without even holding the baskets with their hands. While mamma carried the basket on her head, nonna took a smaller basket with an arched handle and put the food in it. We boys carried our own clothes inside pillow cases. Before we started out, I had the brilliant idea of grabbing my school anthology so that I would have something to read, and we headed toward the western end of town. We had two aunts who lived in that direction—Aunt Anne, whose house came first, and then Aunt Florence, who lived on the same road but a half mile farther west, near the edge of Fossacesia's territorial extension to the southwest. It was quite a walk, but we were used to it, having done it innumerable times before, albeit during happier times.

After an hour's walk through fields and dirt roads, we arrived at Aunt Anne's home. My mother was very close to both Aunt Anne and Aunt Florence, even though I was not sure how we were related to either one of them. We had to stop at Aunt Anne's, because it would have been considered a bad thing to pass in front of her house on our way to the other aunt's without stopping there first.

Aunt Anne was in her sixties, although she looked ancient to us kids. She looked like an Amazon. She was a big woman and a very energetic one. When Mamma suggested that we could go to Aunt Florence's house, a much bigger house, she wouldn't hear of it. Within a few minutes, she had brought out a number of quilts and other bedding that could, in a pinch, double as floor mattresses. She also had a large supply of food and treats of which we knew we would partake as the evening wore on.

Within an hour, details about the air raid began to filter into the countryside. By late afternoon we had learned the identity of those who had been killed and what damage the town had received.

That night, Aunt Anne prepared a frugal but abundant supper for us all. We numbered over twenty people as other relatives had followed us, as well. There was bean soup for everyone along with some cheese and freshly baked bread, delicious in the best tradition of Italian domestic bread making.

After supper, we sat around the fireplace, all huddled together as if to seek protection in our closeness. There were several mothers with their children who showed particular solicitude toward them, now that we had had tangible proof that the war was indeed coming. At one point, as we sat there well into the night, we heard the rumble of a lone night prowler passing overhead, mysterious, foreboding, threatening. Within an hour, it passed overhead twice. The second time, it actually dropped a bomb, but we heard its explosion in the distance, well after it had passed over us. We heard the explosion and trembled. The engine noise then faded away into the night, after which things quieted down and we all went to sleep.

The next morning, mamma got up early and, hearing some voices outside near the road, ventured out and spoke with the people who had stopped to exchange information. They confirmed the identity of those killed in the bombing of Fossacesia the day before, but reported that things were now pretty quiet in town. People had begun to trickle back to their homes. Hearing this news, mamma and nonna discussed the wisdom of returning home, and they decided to try. If things should change, we could always hit the road again by the same route we had used the day before. After having had some breakfast of sweet bread and goat milk, we prepared to depart. I did not drink any of the goat milk. Before leaving, mamma made sure Aunt Anne knew that in case it became necessary for us to abandon our homes again, we would continue on to Aunt Florence, especially since some of Aunt Anne's own children were expected home from Rome within days. Aunt Anne agreed, and we departed for home.

Wednesday, October 13, was a bright enough day, although the sky was covered with a thin layer of high clouds. It was very much like the day before, which meant that airplanes could indeed be flying in that kind of weather, and they might return to bomb us again. Things were pretty calm, however, so mamma decided to take a chance and go home. The air raid had caught them by surprise and they had not completed all the work there was still left to do in preparation for whatever calamity was approaching. We left Aunt Anne's place at ten in the morning, reaching home by eleven. All was calm. There was an eerie feeling in the air, now that our little hamlet had been violated and could be violated again. Still, no one said a word about it. Few people passed by, and those who did went on their way rapidly and guardedly. Since none of our friends were around, Filippo and I stayed inside, afraid to drift too far from our mother and grandmother. We lent a hand as they began the work of bricklayers, trying to create a secret hiding place for some of the family treasures: money, jewelry, mamma's two fur stoles that papà had brought her from America, and most of her fine linens, which she herself had designed and made by hand. They placed everything under the stairwell that led upstairs. The stairs were made of reinforced cement, each step covered with a slab of granite. Underneath, there was an ample open space usually reserved as a storage room. After they filled the whole cubicle with everything they could think of, they walled it up with cement blocks and a few bricks. Then they plastered it over. Once the plaster had dried, it looked like a normal wall. I was surprised at the good job they did, not being professional masons. After the plaster had dried a bit, they pushed a rather heavy closet against it to camouflage it, and prayed that the Germans would be fooled into believing that the stairs rested on a solid block of dirt or cement. After the war was over, we found the wall still intact and we were at least able to save some of the family's most treasured heirlooms.

That night, at about eight P.M., we heard screams coming from the area of the piazza. It was the heartrending wailing of the surviving relatives of the victims. They were having funerals at that unusual hour because the authorities had not released the bodies until 6:00 P.M., and, due to the rapid decomposition of the remains, they had to dispose of them immediately. We were much moved by the event.

We went to bed rather early but completely dressed, just in case. Though somewhat scared, we passed a peaceful night. The next day, the atmosphere around town was a bit more tranquil. One or two of my friends had returned, and we were able to play outside for an hour or so. I was kicking a rag ball around when suddenly a thought came to my head for which I needed to consult mamma and nonna, so I went inside. "Ma, have you seen Ninni, his mother and grandmother?" I said. "No," she replied with surprise, "I haven't." In the panic that had followed the air raid, we had completely forgotten about them. She called upstairs, but got no answer. She climbed the stairs and noticed that the door that led to their two rooms was ajar. She approached, called out again, and, receiving no answer, she cautiously went inside. There was no one there. Nothing had been disturbed in the two rooms they occupied. Even their radio was still there. They could not have been captured by the Germans, because there were none in town at the moment of the air raid nor were there any now. Not yet, anyway! Had they been there, the radio would have been the first item looted. We hoped for the best and waited for events to unravel. Over the years, I came to the conclusion that when the bombing raid on our town took place, members of the Italian underground came and whisked them away. Who the so called "underground" was, of course, no one knew. Thinking back, though, I remember an odd fellow in town named Nunzio who had made several visits to our house during the previous year. It was very possible that he was the local contact and a member of the underground. His visits were unusual. It was not that mamma and nonna, in the absence of the male members of the family, had any kind of social life, especially involving Nunzio, a man with the reputation as a busybody. So it must be assumed that Nunzio had begun to make quick stops to our house for a different reason. I now think that he was the one who kept a protective surveillance upon the refugees who were hiding in our town.

The night of October 14th we again went to bed with our clothes on. The peaceful atmosphere that lay over the blacked-out town gave no indication of another danger that was about to pounce upon our town: a German Panzer division was approaching from the north. Completely unaware of this peril, we went to bed and quickly fell asleep. The night was quiet and peaceful. The church bells did not ring during the entire night, so everyone felt a sense of security.

At 5:00 A.M. on the morning of October 15th, however, we were awakened by the sound of truck and tank engines coming from the center of town, two blocks away, together with the typical clanging of a moving battalion of soldiers. Those who saw it reported that the caravan must have consisted of more than a hundred vehicles: tanks, half-tracks, trucks filled with troops, Mercedes-Benz sedans carrying high ranking officers, motorcycles with sidecars, and anti-aircraft guns mounted on small flatbeds pulled by smaller trucks. They said that when the caravan came to a stop, its head reached the southern end of our town, while the tail end hadn't even entered the north end of the town, almost a mile away. It was the first time that such a large contingent of German troops had reached our town. They were on their way to intercept General Montgomery's 8th Army, which had already reached, uncontested, Brindisi and Bari, at the "heel" of the Italian peninsula.

By the time we realized what was happening, the column of military vehicles had stopped. We began to hear loud banging coming from the entire length of our main street, Via Roma and Via Sangro, all part of the National Route 16. The soldiers were waking up everybody; the German command had ordered the evacuation of twenty-three towns of the province of Chieti, including ours. The official announcement would not be made for another ten days, but this contingent began to implement it ahead of time. Mamma immediately got us up. Being already dressed, we tumbled out of bed, grabbed the bundles she had prepared for me and Filippo the night before, and in less than ten minutes we were outside and headed toward the end of our street. In order to get out of town without being spotted, we did not take the main road a half block to our left, opting instead to follow a dirt path alongside a creek at the bottom of a ravine that ran near our neighborhood. In order to reach the ravine, we had to turn left at the end of our street. Just then, we heard furious banging at the end of via Commercio, the street that formed a T with our little alley and led to the center of town. There too, German soldiers were waking people up and informing them that within 48 hours they would be implementing the order they had received from Hitler himself to evacuate the town. At the exact moment we turned left to head toward the ravine, mom said: "Don't look back, and walk, don't run, as rapidly as you can." We obeyed even as, in the distance, we could hear heavy boots hitting the pavement on the run. When we reached the edge of the ravine, we jumped into it, sliding down more than walking. It was fun! There was a little hut made of cement blocks halfway down the cliff. It was the tool shed belonging to one of our neighbors. We followed mamma's lead and hid behind it. There was also a bush right next to the little hut. Mamma hid behind that bush so that she could observe without being seen. From this vantage point she saw two German soldiers walking back and forth at the top of the hill, perhaps looking for us. Suddenly mamma said: "Get down, get down!" Although she spoke in a whisper, there was an unmistakable sense of urgency in her voice. She had seen one of them raise an automatic rifle toward us as if intending to fire. We fell flat on our stomachs, although the hut certainly would have stopped the bullets. We lay there, our hearts in our throats with fear, expecting the worst. The German did not fire, and within a minute or so, they both left. We remained motionless for well over fifteen minutes, because mamma was afraid that those two soldiers might be hiding, waiting for us to show ourselves so they could fire. The town clock rang twice, five thirty and five forty-five, while we lay there. The sun had not risen yet, but the "dawn's early light" was bright enough to allow us to see everything. I suppose that the Germans did not want to venture too far away from their vehicles, and so they didn't come after us.

Five minutes after the second ringing of the town clock, we cautiously got up and started on our way again. We had come pretty close to being captured or even killed. We moved out of town as fast as we could. Following the creek bed until we came upon a dirt road, we turned left on it and within five minutes we reached the provincial road that led to the Sangro River Valley. There we relaxed a bit and headed toward the rural homes of our relatives. Walking quickly but without urgency, we passed in front of Aunt Anne's place. Since mamma had already told her that we would be going to our other aunt's place, we didn't bother to stop. It was still quite early and there was no one outside. We figured they were still asleep, so we kept on going toward Aunt Florence's place. We got there just as the town clock faintly announced that it was seven thirty.

Throughout that day, other relatives of ours began to arrive. They told us how they were awakened by the Germans and told to get out of town, but they were only given until noon to do so. They had barely enough time to pack some clothes and other necessities in wicker baskets and abandon their homes. They left at noon and reached Aunt Florence's house at various times throughout the afternoon. By evening there were about thirty people there.

FRIDAY, OCTOBER 15, 1943:
DAY OF FEAR AND ANXIETY

In the afternoon rumors began circulating that it was all right to return home, that the majority of the German troops were only passing by on their way to the front lines. They had occupied only three strategically placed homes in town, using them as command posts or lookout points.

Encouraged by these reports, mamma and nonna decided to join other relatives who were determined to return to town and try to rescue more of what they considered their valuable possessions. Before leaving, they asked some adults who stayed behind to keep an eye on me and Filippo. I had pleaded to be allowed to go along, but mamma was immovable, saying that it was too dangerous. Was it not dangerous for them to go? I wanted us to stay together; if it were dangerous, it would be so for all of us. But my mother was not easily persuaded. Besides, someone had to stay behind to watch my little brother, and so Filippo and I reluctantly stayed behind. Filippo was too young to realize our plight, but I was old enough to become deeply worried. I got into all kinds of trouble that day—not on purpose, but more because I was distracted and filled with anxiety. I was so worried about my family's safety that my mind was not on whatever it was that I was doing at any time throughout the day. At one point, Filippo and I were playing with an old rubber ball with a hole in it, when I kicked it inside a chicken enclosure. As I went in to retrieve it, I was attacked by a jealous rooster. I had left the little gate open so that I could quickly grab the ball and scoot out of there. Unfortunately, with the gate open, another rooster and several chickens escaped, much to the consternation of old Aunt Florence, who then had to catch them and put them back in the coop. Later, I kicked the ball into one of her flower beds, and it landed on top of her luscious chrysanthemums that she was preparing for her visit to the cemetery on November 1st. Her husband, old Uncle Bernard, had died the year before. Fortunately, the damage to the flowers was minimal. At lunch time, I even knocked over a glass of wine. I lucked out there too, because in Italy traditionally, when wine is spilled, people always shout, *"Allegrìa!"* (Cheers!) While the word translates into the traditional British exclamation for drinking a toast, the Italian word in the case of accidental spilling of wine simply means that happy times are here again. So nobody got mad at me. Still I was in a state of apprehension, and I felt as if I had a heavy object resting on my stomach. I kept looking down toward the road that bordered the property of our aunt, where I could have seen any returning travelers. There was no one to be seen.

Finally, later in the afternoon, I spotted Cousin Lilia and her brother Mario, who had accompanied the entire homebound group early in the morning, coming up the driveway. When I first saw them they were quite a distance away and the fact that they were not accompanied by the others gave me another jolt of trepidation. They had left together in the morning, so why were they now coming back alone? It would have taken them a good ten minutes to arrive, but I could not wait, so I ran out to meet them. No, they had not seen my mother, nor grandmother, and yes, the Germans were in town. It appeared that the German command had established its headquarters in the Alberto Mayer villa, the most sumptuous structure in town. That was really a villa, situated at the southern edge of town, on a hill that commanded a breathtaking view of the entire Sangro River Valley from the sea to the mountains. It contained about a dozen rooms on two floors and a tower, a sort of rooftop play room where the Mayers would hold parties on warm summer evenings. The Germans figured that if they were going to make a military stand on the Sangro River Valley, this would be the perfect spot from which to orchestrate and conduct it. They had already established the northeastern head of the Gustav Line, their winter line, right at our river. From the party terrace on the roof they had a visibility of at least twelve miles all around and total control of six miles of river banks on both sides, including its two bridges. The villa had been built in the early part of the century, and it almost seemed that Don Alberto Mayer did it in anticipation of the arrival of his "paesani," with whom he shared ancient ancestors. The original Mayer family had come to Fossacesia from Germany more than four centuries before. Unfortunately, those modern Germans didn't appreciate the common ancestry. When they started to round up men for forced labor, some of the Mayer men were taken along with the others, without regard that their name was decidedly German. And they weren't exactly young men, either. The youngest, Don Giulio, was in his mid sixties. He was obese and suffered from severe chronic asthma. The Germans didn't care—they put him to work digging ditches with the rest of the "low caste men," an activity he had never experienced before in his life. Lilia had no more information than that, but she did add that there were rumors that the Germans had rounded up a number of civilians and taken them away in trucks. In the group was

Aunt Rose, Grandmother's sister. She warned me not to say anything because it wasn't certain about the fate of our relatives and she did not wish to alarm the rest of the family unnecessarily.

Shortly afterward, however, another group arrived, and they made the announcement that Aunt Rose had indeed been taken away on a truck toward Rocca San Giovanni. This report placed our entire household in a state of frantic turmoil. It was devastating news for us all. Everyone was affected by it, especially me. I immediately added two and two and came up with five. I quickly assumed that mamma and nonna were part of the group that was captured by the Germans. Panic set in. I made an instant decision—I was going to rescue them. How? I never asked myself that question. I simply started to run like crazy toward the main road. Where was I, an eleven-year-old silly kid going? It didn't matter. All I knew was that I had to do something, and so I ran through the recently plowed field, on a diagonal, in order to gain time. I had already learned that the shortest line between two points was a straight line, so, instead of taking the long driveway, I headed east through the fields toward the corner of the property, a good quarter mile away.

I had barely started my trek toward heroism, when I realized that cousin Maria was on my tail in hot pursuit. Did this sway me from my resolve to do something? Not on your ancestors' vaults! When I realized I was being chased, I renewed my efforts, increased my speed, and lengthened my stride, running downhill like a gazelle. I had almost reached the road when all the strength seemed to abandon every fiber of my being. At that moment cousin Maria overtook me and grabbed my right arm. As she did so, I simply dropped to my knees, hyperventilating as I fell onto the dirt on my face. Maria, who by now was also exhausted, collapsed on top of me. She kept admonishing me that whatever I had intended to do was insane, but I was in no mood to listen to a lecture. She dragged me back to the house, and I simply followed along, sobbing with what little breath I had left. When we reached Aunt Florence's threshing plaza, I headed toward a pile of hay, dropped on it, and quickly fell into a profound sleep. I was exhausted as I had never been before, nor would ever be again.

Meanwhile, the story of Aunt Rose's capture, though true, was somewhat exaggerated. The Germans who had arrived in town, being confronted by a bunch of yelping women yelling at them in a language they did not understand, simply decided that if they were to accomplish what they had been ordered to accomplish that day, it was necessary to remove those hyperactive tongues from their midst. To Aunt Rose's misfortune, she lived on Via Sangro, or Route 16, and the column of military vehicles had stopped right in front of her house. Some soldiers wanted to store a number of machine guns and ammunition in her dining room. She was horrified at the thought and began to scream at them that this was her house, not theirs, and who knows what else. Aunt Rose hurled at them a litany of epithets not only in Italian, but in our particular dialect. She, like Nonna Concetta, her sister, had the reputation of possessing a rich and varied vocabulary of colorful and descriptive invectives. The Germans didn't understand any of it, of course, but they did get the spirit of the message. They reacted by picking her up bodily and placing her in the back of a small military truck, together with a half dozen or so other neighborhood women. The truck and passengers took off heading north. Meanwhile, her daughter, cousin Lydia, who had walked to a neighbor's house across the street while the encounter was going on, witnessed the entire episode from across the way. She was so horrified that she started to join her mother on the truck but was held back by neighbors. Young and beautiful as she was, it was not a good idea to put herself in jeopardy. As soon as the truck left the area, not knowing what was in store for Aunt Rose, Lydia, in total panic, together with a couple of cousins, returned to Aunt Florence's house. She arrived shortly after I had had my little drama with Cousin Maria. Sobbing non-stop, she threw the family mood into an even greater frenzy of panic.

Fortunately, the German soldier who drove the truck that carted the women out of town, after reaching open country, stopped the truck and allowed the ladies to descend. Then he got back on the truck and left the area, figuring he had taken them far enough away that they could no longer interfere with whatever work they had planned to do. So the women found themselves in the middle of the highway, half way between Fossacesia and Rocca. They knew exactly where they were, but now they faced a long walk back to town. According to eyewitnesses, when some of the women got back to town and attempted to reenter their homes, they found them occupied by new "owners." When they tried to enter through their front doors they were greeted by the menacing nozzles of automatic weapons.

Aunt Rose opted not to return to her home. She hoped that her daughter had joined the others in the original group and had gone back to Colle Castagno (Chestnut Hill), three miles to the west. She knew she had a lot of walking to do, so she wasted no time. Instead of heading toward the town, she skirted its northern perimeter, walking through fields, along the creek bed, and in a little while she was on her way to Aunt Florence's house. She started out at about 3:15 P.M. and arrived there at 4:45 P. M. By that time, I was still asleep on the hay, having been there since early afternoon, and my mother and grandmother had returned at 4:30 P.M. Aunt Rose's daughter, Lydia, was all but ready for the nut house from fear that her mother had been kidnapped by the Nazis.

Aunt Rose arrived at a quarter to five like a countess going to a gala reception, atop a horse-driven surrey. A local young man had given her a ride for the last mile or so. Everybody rejoiced, and a sort of calm was quickly restored once everybody realized that, after all the drama of the day, everybody was safe and accounted for. Complete calm was out of the question; life had been disrupted and the future was bleak indeed. Everybody's nerves had been frayed to the limit that day, but at least everyone was home and in good condition.

When I woke up, they were having a celebratory glass of wine. It took me a few minutes to figure out where I was. I suppose the intense emotional stress of the day had taken its toll. Maria told my mother what had happened. I thought I would be in trouble, so I stayed at a safe distance, but I was surprised to see that mamma was all solicitude toward me. She led me to a tub of water, washed my face, and suggested that I take a short walk to try to clear my head. I followed her suggestion and I even tried to sing along the way, but somehow I couldn't do it. A deep-seated sense of anguish had set in, which robbed my mind of the necessary serenity to make any kind of music.

When I went back into the house, mamma brought me up to date on the events of the day. Apparently, the German army had taken over Fossacesia, leaving a platoon of soldiers there. They had been exploring the town to see which homes they could take over for their needs. The first thing they did was to set up their command post in the Villa of Don Alberto Mayer, as already related. Its upper playroom must have been the envy of every scholar of military strategy who ever planned a battle. Its only drawback was the fact that it sat at the top of the hill at the very edge of the northern rim of the Sangro River Valley. Totally exposed, it was a sitting duck for anyone with a weapon powerful enough to be able to reach it. Of course, this meant that we were not going to go home again until the British came to liberate us. It was not prudent for two women and two children to be at the mercy of a platoon of Germans. So, mamma and nonna decided to settle in and wait. Out of sheer boredom, we went to sleep rather early.

AN UNEXPECTED VISIT

The next day, shortly after noon, I saw a man turn onto our driveway and start up the hill. He looked like a dot in the distance. He walked with the slight stoop typical of my Nonno Donato. Within a couple of minutes we all could see that it was, indeed, my grandfather. I was happy. I always liked Nonno Donato, whose name I carry. There had been significant friction at home between my "educated" mother and my aunts who were somewhat coarse, if not actually illiterate. When we lived in the same household, they never got along with each other. Aunt Zelina couldn't read or write, and neither could my paternal grandmother, Minguccia (short for Maria Domenica). The friction was inevitable. That's why on that stormy evening in October, 1938, our mother had gathered up me and Filippo, and we moved to our maternal grandmother's house.

When Nonno Donato finally arrived at the house, mamma came out and greeted him somewhat awkwardly. After a bit of clumsy conversation, they began to talk, and things got better as they went on. What Nonno had come to say was that, because of the seriousness of the moment, he felt an obligation to my father, who was in America, to safeguard his family. He was wondering whether it would be possible to regroup the family into one nucleus. Would we consider going with him to rejoin the rest of the family? Well, mamma thought that it might not be a bad idea, but under the circumstances, she wanted to think about it. Would he give us until the next day? "Of course!" He agreed to come back the next day either to take us back with him, or go back alone and hope for the best. With that, Nonno Donato left the area.

Naturally, there were many factors to consider. We had our maternal grandmother with us. She, like my mother, was a rare specimen herself. Nonna Concetta would have had a difficult time living with the members of the other household, even though neither group was in their own home at the time. Of course, there was no way that my mother would have abandoned her own mother in these direst of circumstances, but would she come with us? That was very much in doubt. For the rest of the evening, mamma and nonna had some very heated discussions. They even consulted the other relatives. They decided to sleep on it and make a decision in the morning.

The rest of the afternoon was boring, to say the least. I tried to read, but was not able to concentrate. Filippo and I, together with some of our cousins, began to gather the gigantic acorns that had fallen off the oak trees on Aunt Florence's property. We gathered several basketfuls and then tried to figure out what to do with them. We explored the hedges of the property and I spotted some hawthorn shrubs that had sprouted some equally enormous thorns. So we began to snap the thorns off the bramble bushes. First we were able to push the thorns into the acorns four at a time to simulate animal legs, and we made a whole bunch of "pigs." But then, noticing that each thorn had a rather large base at the point where it had been attached to the tree, I started to push them into the acorns two at a time at the top of the oval nut, so that we made a number of "soldiers." The base of the acorn, called *cupules* in botany, resembles the helmets worn by ancient soldiers in battle, and that gave us the idea of having a battle between the Romans and the Goths. Why the Goths? No reason. It's just that that name was the first one to come into my head as possible opponents to the Romans. So we began, and in a short period of time, we had made hundreds of them. Even the girls in the group helped us, at least until we began to align them in battle mode, at which point they lost interest. This activity kept us out of the adults' hair for a couple of hours.

While we were immersed in this activity we heard the drone of airplane engines. We reacted in unison—we ran for cover. From the safety of the house, looking south through the windows, we saw two small planes slowly and loudly making their way north. When they reached the river, they began to release a trail of white smoke behind them, right over Fossacesia's flatlands. We had never seen anything like this before. What could it mean? We were suddenly very scared. As the planes flew northward toward us, they were parallel, but at a considerable distance from each other. When they reached an area almost overhead, they stopped emitting the white trail. Then they turned. One made a complete circle, and when it reached the end of the white line to our right which the other plane had traced, it let go with the white smoke again, stopping the release upon reaching the end of the white line which it had made earlier. The other plane did the same, except that it only made a half circle before it reached the other end of the white trail. It, too, restarted the white vapor emission and continued until both planes reached the end of the opposite white line. In other words, they traced a perfect square in the sky; we judged it to be about one square mile in size. We were fearful but puzzled. What could this mean? Now, everybody knows that in any group of people thrown together by fate or accident, such as ours was, there is always one person who knows everything, has seen everything and knows the answer to the most complex questions. Cousin Maria, the one who had chased me through the fields the day before, having a boyfriend in the Italian Navy, considered herself an authority on all things military. She took it upon herself to instruct us poor, uninformed cretins (her opinion), that the planes traced that area to mark the spot for bombers that would surely follow and would drop their bombs when they reached the inside of that square. My mother, however, had a way of completely unplugging her with one word, after which Maria always stammered a bit and then walked away. Mamma simply asked: "Why?" The question was totally logical. From Aunt Fiora's house, which sat atop a pretty substantial hill, we could see south all the way to the river and beyond, and from east to west, the vista was open from the Adriatic Sea to the Majella Mountains, a radius of at least five miles. There was nothing there but farmland. Unless the Allies were planning to plow the fields using expensive bombs, Maria's theory was completely senseless. We watched as the white square in the sky, pushed by the wind, began to migrate toward the sea, changing its shape slowly. The once-perfect symmetry began to collapse. In a few minutes it completely lost its shape and within an hour it disappeared altogether. No bombers ever came. We never did figure out the reason for that exercise in futility engaged in by those two airplanes that afternoon. The entire episode was, nevertheless, very mysterious and a bit unnerving. We felt as if we were being visited by alien ships.

After the planes had left, we boys tried to resume our game of fantasy and take up again the battle between the Romans and the Visigoths (or was it the Goths?). But the magic was gone, and we quickly tired of it all. Aunt Florence had seen us sticking big thorns into the acorns and she made us gather them up and throw them in the fire which she had just started as she prepared to cook supper. She explained that some animal might try to eat an acorn and get the thorns stuck in its mouth. We did as we were told, cleaning up the entire area, and learning a valuable lesson in the process.

When supper was ready, everyone sat around the tables, arranged in the shape of an L. It took several tables to accommodate the entire gang, stretching from the large utility room in which the family did farm work in the summer all the way into the granary, where the ubiquitous kids' table was placed. Besides two kilograms of pasta (that's 4.5 lb.), Aunt Florence killed and cooked four rabbits and two chickens in order to feed everyone. So we ate well that evening. There was an air of joviality in the house. They even laughed at Aunt Rose's adventure on the German military truck. Aunt Rose herself told the entire episode at least three times, adding color and increasing its dramatic impact with each retelling. At about nine P.M. everyone went to sleep. We slept mostly on the floor, although some people found some strange bedding upon which to rest. I myself slept on top of several sacks of wheat. My makeshift mattress seemed soft when I first lay on it, but soon it felt hard as rock, and very uncomfortable.

Before retiring, mamma and nonna discussed at length the pros and cons of going with the De Simone branch of the family. At times, the argument was rather heated. I was not privy to their discussions, but even from far away

I could tell by their intense gesticulation that they didn't agree on everything. By morning, however, there must have been some compromises, because a decision had been made: We would go with Nonno Donato when he arrived. Still, Nonna Concetta was not particularly happy at the prospect of going to live with the "other" family. Looking back, even after all these years, it turned out to be a mistake, because for the next eight months, life became sheer torture for her. But, we couldn't foretell that at the time. Having decided to go, we hoped for the best.

In the morning, we gathered all our belongings, which really did not amount to much. We informed the others of our decision, wished them good luck and waited for Nonno Donato to arrive. The rest of the extended family decided to stay there but to try to locate an alternative to the house, just in case, so they went on a cave exploration. That area is replete with caves. I was scared to live in caves because they usually were the home of bats, foxes or other wild life. They found a large cave and opted to spend the war there, with the help of God. They remained in that cave until the end of the war, even though the bulk of the British 8th Army chose that particular area as its path to reach the top of the Fossacesia-Mozzagrogna ridge. They cleaned up the cave and placed bed covers on its walls in order to protect them from the intense humidity that those sandy walls produced.

When Nonno Donato returned in the morning, he announced that we would not be returning to our own Caporale home, but to the house of some friends about one mile due south of Aunt Florence's house. The day before, he had forgotten to tell us that little detail. Because we had to travel precisely into the area over which those two little planes had traced that perfect square with white vapor the previous day, I remember being somewhat apprehensive. What if those planes came back to finish the job, whatever it was? That was the thought going through my head as we began our journey down the hill. I didn't say anything, not wanting to alarm my eight-year-old brother. We walked expeditiously, but without urgency. Along the way nonno brought me up to date on what he knew about the "Americans" that were coming. We reminisced a little about that Sunday afternoon in July when I had spent the day with him at our country home and Mr. Fantini gave us the news that the Americans had landed in Sicily. "Things didn't turn out the way we thought, did they?" I asked rhetorically. "No, they didn't!" he replied. Still, Nonno Donato assured us that everything was going to be all right. The American Army would reach us in no time, so speculations for the immediate future were on the positive side. One had to maintain a hopeful attitude, especially toward us children. No use putting fear in our hearts. We must take each day as it comes; such was Nonno Donato's philosophy, and we departed. With both sides of my family reunited physically, if not spiritually, the family was now composed of the following members.

A ONE-NIGHT STAY

We soon arrived at the home of the Stante family. I had the impression that it was wheat thrashing time, judging by the number of people gathered in that home. The other side of my family was there, consisting of my grandfather and grandmother, Maria Domenica, and three aunts with their respective children, my cousins. What I remember most about that day was when it came time to go to bed, the owner spread out a couple of thick quilts on the tiled floor of his spacious dining room. It served as a kind of community bed. The floor was hard and cold and the room was noisy because my cousins, being so very young, decided to cry all at the same time. Their mother chose a spot right next to me to lie down. I had no problem with that arrangement, but within a few minutes she began to snore like a snorting bull. So, between the children's crying and her snoring, they kept me awake all night long.

Around midnight, we heard the sound of airplane engines again. Faint at first, but getting steadily louder until the noise reached its maximum level as the single plane passed right over us, it then began to regress to a faint level, finally fading altogether into the night. It was the *ricognitore*, the scout, as it had been labeled by my cousin Maria the day before. She was the one whose boyfriend was in the Navy; therefore, it followed that her assessment of any situation of military nature had to be accepted as gospel truth. Although, in this case, she was probably right, since the word *ricognitore* does mean "scout." But then, I had a difficult time imagining what they could possibly be scouting, flying as they were in total darkness.

While the plane flew over us, the tension in that room was very high indeed, especially among the children. One of my little cousins began to weep, slowly and plaintively at first, but getting progressively more terrified as the plane got closer and closer to us. As it flew directly over us, the noise got so intense that it seemed to be just a few hundred feet over the roof. As the drone of those engines got louder and louder, the silence in the room became commensurately more profound. Even the children barely breathed. My little cousin kept on weeping but ever so quietly. Even after the plane's engine noise had faded away into the night, the child's mother couldn't stop her sobbing which continued for a few more minutes until she fell asleep. She was absolutely terrified.

The next day, before anyone had a chance to wake up completely, there was a tremendous explosion not too far from the Stante household. Its roar reverberated throughout the valley. There was the usual common concern, although it wasn't as laden with panic as was the raid of October 12th. My mother went to the door, but without venturing outside. She saw nothing. Then she went to the side window, again without seeing any sign of smoke or other tell-tale clues associated with an explosion. It wasn't until much later that a passerby told Nonno Donato that the Germans were blowing up homes in the valley to prevent the Allied troops from finding ready shelter. Debris caused by the explosion could also be used to block the streets, thus delaying the movements of Allied personnel and machinery.

As the morning progressed, nonno, mamma and some of my aunts held a conference among themselves. By noon, they called everybody together and announced that we were moving to cousin Casimiro Marrone's house, whom everybody affectionately called Casimine (years later, Casimine moved to Montreal and the Canadians re-baptized him Cazmine—Caz for short). As I was growing up in the mid 1930s, Nonno Donato and I often spent summer weekends in our summer cottage. I used to love to get up very early and see the sun rise over the Adriatic Sea. It was a spectacular event. Our cottage was less than a half mile from the Marrone farmstead, so I used to visit Casimine almost every day. He was my favorite cousin, and I enjoyed going to his house to play. Once or twice, as I recall, I even slept over. So, now, we were going to go and actually live in his house for a while. I couldn't wait.

Country roads then were still made of packed dirt. It had not rained yet so the roads were dusty rather than muddy. There was not a soul in sight. This was the time of the year that the farmers should have been getting ready to harvest olives, and to plow the fields and sow wheat for the following year's harvest. Not that year: the fields were desolate. The normal sight of oxen pulling plows was nowhere to be seen. It was a sad thing to see all those empty fields in the fall.

We started out early in the afternoon. Fortunately, this trip was downhill all the way. That helped the elderly in the group and Aunt Filomena, my father's sister, who was "very pregnant" and due to give birth within a week. Since the family had just reunited, my mother was surprised at this. Since the situation was somewhat awkward among the two groups, mamma used the imminent birthing event to thaw the icy disposition of some of the family members. It worked! Before we reached the elder Aunt Filomena's house, mamma had asserted herself once again as the leader of the pack. Casimine's mother, was one of the most benevolent and generous creatures on earth. In the past, when we lived at our paternal homestead, whenever my mother had a skirmish with one of the family members, which was quite often, she would run to Aunt Filomena's place for comfort and advice.

About half way through our journey that day, we had to pass close to one of the very sharp curves of which Rte. 16 was particularly rich. It was almost a cul-de-sac, where we could not see who was coming, especially from the north, that is in the direction of the town itself. Mamma stopped the group. There was a brief consultation about whether we should proceed by the main road which, while not exactly covered with asphalt, was at least topped with a compound of small pebbles held together by synthetic lime. In summer, whenever an automobile passed, it invariably lifted a cloud of dust behind itself; in the winter, when it rained, that lime became a thick white mud that not only covered one's shoes, but it soiled a man's pant legs up to his knees. In late October, since it had not rained yet, that road was decent, and Nonno Donato wanted to go that way. I knew why. He wanted to check his wine cellar to make sure his wine barrels weren't touched. Once we rounded the curve going south, the road traveled due east for about a half mile up to the gates of our country cottage, before sharply turning south again. The situation had not yet turned so drastic that one should have had second thoughts about stopping at the house. From there the branch of Rte. 16 that passed just south of our house in town as it came out of the center of Fossacesia was clearly visible, a half a mile up the hill. It would take any truck five to seven minutes before it reached the sharp curve at Campidoglio, so that we would have had time to scamper to safety if necessary.

Suddenly, the noise of a motor-driven machine of some sort startled us. I had never heard that kind of noise before. We couldn't see anything, but nonno said it was a chain saw. Apparently, just around the corner to our left, the Germans had started to cut down trees. With that, the decision was quickly made to reach Casimine's house through the fields, and forget stopping at our house. We did not want to be seen by the Germans. Within ten minutes, we reached the Marrone household via the woods.

The elder Aunt Filomena, greeted us with great enthusiasm, which turned to even greater jubilation when she realized that my mother and all of us had rejoined the rest of the family. She was a peace-loving soul. She invited everybody into the house, and announced that she was going to kill some chickens and make a stew. I had not had chicken since the previous Christmas, almost a year before and now we had it twice in two days. Since the war began, we had managed to subsist on one meal a day. The fare was at poverty level. The main meal consisted of a homemade pasta dish or a leafy vegetable. There was no meat, fish or poultry to be had. Aunt Filomena explained however, that, according to scuttlebutt, the Germans were going to all the farmhouses in the entire zone confiscating farm animals, large or small, so we might as well eat them ourselves before the Germans arrived. No one objected.

Aunt Filomena said that many people had opted to flee Fossacesia and travel south across the Sangro's main bridge to the town of Torino di Sangro. When the British 8th Army finally arrived, the area on the south side of the river would be liberated first. Some, fearing that the bridge was under surveillance by the Germans, actually waded across. The river could still be waded up to the first rain. Many people did just that, taking advantage of the lack of rain. If we had to move ourselves, she reasoned, we will have to abandon these poor animals with no one to feed them or to give them water. So we might as well kill them and eat them. The logic of the argument escaped me, actually, but having a chicken dinner, especially the way Aunt Filomena prepared it, resolved any possible fallacies with her reasoning that the poor animals were better off dead and eaten rather than being left alone to starve to death. All the women, except the younger Aunt Filomena, who after that long trek on foot looked as though she was ready to give birth at any time, went into the house. In minutes, they divided the chores among themselves, and within two hours we had a feast on the lawn. Casimine, who had been out in the fields, returned, washed up, and joined us with two bottles of Montepulciano wine. That evening we ate a marvelous dinner, the first of five such meals. While we ate, all the guests caught up on the latest news, accepting every detail as gospel truth without verification.

When dinner was over, two men came from the house across the valley, and informed my mother that they planned to dig a deep trench right on the farm's staging area. It would be an air raid shelter for us to sleep in when hostilities began. Nobody had any idea what those hostilities would be like, so the planning was not exactly according to the tenets of military logistics. They reasoned that if we were below ground level, we would have a greater chance of survival. Only a direct hit would put us in danger. As it turned out, these were prophetic words, indeed. Mamma thought that it was a good idea, although they didn't consider its location to be of any importance, so they never even discussed it. The men had already planned to dig the trench at a cross between the two properties so that each household had its own entrance, and each entrance would have an emergency escape. They planned to begin work the following day.

THE LULL BEFORE THE STORM

The next day, the men from both families began to work. My mother supervised the *"cantiere,"* or work site, and in no time the men were working in perfect harmony. By 11:00 A.M. they had dug a trench twenty feet long, six wide and six deep. As the town bell rang twelve, Aunt Filomena rang her own bell and announced that dinner was ready. The men stopped, went to the well to wash up, and were coming back to the front of the house where the women had set the table outside, when the last of the boys came running and announced: *"Tedeschi,"* the Italian word for Germans (it rhymes with "pesky."). Immediately the men disappeared. Nonno remained, confident that the soldiers would consider him too old for ditch digging. He had to stay with the rest of the family, especially due to Aunt Filomena's condition.

A motorcycle with a sidecar came up the long driveway that led to the house from the main road. It came to the front of the house and stopped just where the table had been set for dinner. There were plates on that table for twenty-five people, and it looked as if a wedding feast was about to take place. The Germans knew that it was intended to accommodate several more people than the women and children visible. An officer got out of the sidecar and approached the table. He looked around and then asked where the rest of the guests were. Mamma approached and, speaking mostly in gestures, said that they were in the fields working and they would be coming home later. We were just preparing ahead of time. The officer spoke Italian fairly well, and said to my mother that they needed something, but he couldn't describe it. It took a few minutes for the message to be understood. It turned out that they needed a tool to fix one of their vehicles. Well, we had no such tool, but Aunt Filomena opened a small tool shed they had not far from the house and motioned to the officer to take whatever tool he thought might do. There were some tools there, such as hammers, saws, pliers, and the like. None were made for auto mechanical use though. The officer and the driver thanked everyone and turned to go when Aunt Filomena, perhaps grateful that they had not come with hostile intentions, offered them a glass of wine and some fried zucchini. The two soldiers looked at each other with a silent, "Shall we?" They were after all on duty. But the officer said, *"Ja, danke!"* and they drank a glass of red wine each and savored the zucchini. They motioned that everything was good, saluted and left, giving yet another proof that not all Germans were the bad Nazis everybody imagined. Almost an hour later, we heard engines starting up in the distance as they left the area. Filippo and I and a couple of other kids ran to the highway through the rows of grapevines to check and see if they were really gone; within a few minutes we gave the all clear. The men emerged from their hiding places and we had a scrumptious meal of sausages and cheese, salad and fruit. Casimine's Montepulciano wine turned lunch into a royal banquet.

With the danger gone, the men working on our shelter realized that they had better figure out a way to hide the excavations so as not to attract the attention of the German soldiers who might pay us a visit in the days to come. They devised a plan to move an entire, though small, haystack and settle it right over the initial hole. It was nothing short of ingenious! The execution proved a bit messy, but the results were better than planned. Somehow, it looked natural and the entrance to the trench was all but invisible.

Once they figured out how to do it, they moved the haystack aside and continued to work until such a time that another motorcycle or other vehicle might approach. By four o'clock the excavation was finished. The resulting dugout would have been the envy of World War I soldiers, but without the mud. It was narrow, damp and uncomfortable, but it was adequate.

They moved the haystack back on top of the mote, only to discover that it only covered a third of it. My mother provided the answer: "Place some tree branches across the top of the trench and spread the hay on top of it," said she. Done! Within a half hour, the haystack seemed that it had become tired of standing up, and had decided to lie down for a nap. And the men went to the well to wash up.

Around four o'clock, Aunt Filomena prepared dinner for everyone. Rabbit! Her theory was still a valid one: we might as well eat all the small animals because if we don't the Germans will. I still remember the announcement posted in front of the town hall in Fossacesia that urged the population to help feed the "heroic German Army soldiers who sacrificed their lives for our benefit." They could be comical, those Germans, when they wanted to be! Of course, no one in his right mind gave them food as a result of that notice. Although, if a couple of soldiers had come in saying that they were hungry, nobody would have denied them a place at their table as an act of Christian charity, but feeding their army was out of the question.

The rabbit was prepared in two ways: Oven roasted and stewed. Aunt Filomena cooked two rabbits in the brick oven that every farmstead had built just outside the kitchen, while mamma prepared two more as a stew simmered in tomato sauce. It was a Lucullian feast worthy of a Roman emperor and the compliments to both chefs by all partakers were a thing of sheer eloquence.

The day passed uneventfully while the men worked, except for the continuous noise of that pesky chain saw with which the Germans were knocking down tree after tree. Half way through the meal, however, everything stopped. "Thank God," said my mother, "it has given me a migraine!" Besides the continuous rattle of the chainsaw, two explosions had been heard in the afternoon, similar to the one we had heard early the day before, but accompanied by unusual reverberations. The sound of the explosion traveled in equal force concentrically, but its echo came back only from the west and north where there were some hills and lots of buildings off of which the sound could bounce. The south and east were bound by the Sangro River and the Adriatic Sea, hence open spaces all the way. As a result, each explosion was followed by several waves of echo returning to us from the west, an incredible tsunami of sound. I had never experienced anything like that before, or since. Those explosions occurred at two or three hour interval for the next four or five days that we remained in the area. It seems such a silly idea to destroy houses just so when the British arrived, and arrive they would, they wouldn't have a place to stay. Had the Germans never heard of tents? But, then, they never consulted the populace about anything they did; they did as they pleased, finding justification for their arrogance in that it was the will of Der Fuhrer.

BETWEEN TWO FIRES

"Into the valley of death rode the six-hundred . . ." Thus Alfred Lord Tennyson described the famous *Charge of the Light Brigade* in the Crimean war, immortalized in his poem. That charge was a disaster because the Light Brigade rode into the valley unaware that the surrounding heights concealed a bevy of loaded cannons ready to fire upon the unsuspecting horsemen. The Light Brigade was decimated by the Russian cannons that dotted the surrounding hills in Balaclava. The poem was one of the several in my anthology translated in Italian as, *"La carica della Brigata Leggera."* I knew mamma had read it, so perhaps this was what she had in mind as she repeatedly looked at the ridge of Torino di Sangro to our south and the Fossacesia ridge to the north. When the British 8th Army arrived and they would begin the battle of the Sangro River, we would be caught in the middle. From the second day after we arrived at Aunt Filomena's house, I saw my mother looking somewhat apprehensive. I sensed that she had something on her mind. She said nothing for two days. Finally, on the third day she summoned my grandfather outside. Though I was not able to hear their conversation, I could see that it had soon turned into an altercation. She kept gesticulating and pointing to the south, then to the north, while he seemed to be going around in circles, obviously annoyed at her discourse. Later I found out what they were saying. Mamma was pointing out that we were in the middle of the Sangro River Valley, an area that was obviously destined to become the staging area of one of the biggest battles of WWII in the Italian theater.

The Zamenga Bridge, that carried Route 16 and the railroad bridge over the Sangro were still intact, but the moment the Germans recalled all their forces now staged south of the Sangro to retreat to the northern side of the Sangro, it would be a sure bet that both the bridges would be blown up. Then, the British would be forced to build some sort of floating bridge to carry their army and its equipment over the river. And where would the Germans be during all of this? On the Fossacesia ridge, of course, shooting at them with everything they had in an attempt to prevent them from doing just that. We would, then, be caught right in the middle of it all. My mother didn't think that Aunt Filomena's house was the safest place to be in when that happened. She suggested that we move south, cross over the bridge, perhaps during the night, and seek hospitality at the home of some of our friends who lived in Torino. The Zamenga Bridge was no more than two miles from the Marrone farmstead and we could have made the move in a couple of hours. It was a good idea. Many people from Fossacesia did just that, some by wading across the river. The people who went south did not see much of the war, they just heard it, although my best friend, Lino, whose family did go south of the river, told me that they witnessed some fierce hand-to-hand combat in the town of Casalbordino, about ten miles south of the Sangro. I have no reason to doubt him, but they did not get the pounding we received in November from wave after wave of B-24 Liberator bombers!

Unfortunately, Nonno Donato wouldn't hear of moving south, north or anywhere else. He didn't want to jeopardize the safety of the entire family by moving to unfamiliar territory. What if the bridge was being guarded by German sentries? What if it was already mined and ready to go up in smoke at any time? And who could possibly tell what we would find on the other side? The possibility of wading across the river was immediately eliminated as a possible choice because mamma was petrified of water. The waters of the Sangro in winter were notoriously treacherous. And, of course, we had the young Aunt Filomena with us who might give birth right in the middle of the river. Nonno Donato had a point there. So, for that day, the discussion was tabled. Meanwhile, judging by the disgruntled look on Nonno's face and the mutterings of my mother to Nonna Concetta, I believe that they were both sorry for having agreed to reunite the family. It seemed that nothing had changed. How could it? My mother's brain worked like a fine Swiss watch, while the rest of the family remained in a state of deep fog. She could see things the others couldn't, and this always caused a clash of personalities and ideas. This altercation was a sure sign of a tempestuous future in the making.

Meanwhile, just before lunch, we heard the sudden noise of two airplanes roaring angrily at each other. They were engaged in a real dogfight. We boys were impressed. We had never seen a dogfight before, except in the movies. The planes began to chase each other in an area that appeared to be right over the river and the Zamenga Bridge. Mamma spoiled all the fun, naturally, by ordering us inside the house. "Watch them from inside the house. Not near the window, either!" she ordered. We had no choice but to obey. Fortunately, Aunt Filomena's house faced south so we had a fairly good view of it all. Looking through a large window, it was like watching the images on a movie screen. The two planes chased each other marking time with the rat-ta-ta-ta of their machine guns. At one point, one of the planes seemed to emerge from the ground in full alar display immediately followed by the other. They formed an arch from right to left as they appeared to emerge out of the ground and after describing a perfect arch in the sky dove into the ground once again. Since the topography of the terrain was not exactly flat, despite the area being called the flatlands, they neither emerged from the ground nor crashed into it: it only appeared that way. Their engines roared angrily at each other as they tried to down one another, both failing to do so. After a few minutes, they got tired of the chase, and the air combat was over; one plane headed south the other north. We, the young ones, talked about the great event of the day for a long time. We speculated that it was the British plane that ran out of ammunition, because if it had been the other way around, the British Spitfire would have pursued the German fighter plane all the way to its home base. German planes rarely dared to fly south past the Sangro Valley. At that point in the war, the RAF had complete control of the air, because the Luftwaffe, the German Air Force, had more than its hands full in other war theaters.

A MOST UNUSUAL "SHELTER"

After dinner, the men working on the shelter went into the woods to cut tree branches with which to cover the trench. They worked until dusk, piling up quite a collection of poles about six inches in diameter and at least twelve feet long. They quit as it got dark, and they made plans to finish the project the next day. They had considered the various ways of covering the shelter, but they began to argue with each other and so they failed to agree on how this should be achieved. What if it rains? What if both entrances get blocked?

We must be able to come out through the roof! So, they decided to sleep on the question. By the next morning a solution would surely be found.

And a solution was indeed found. Early the next day Carmine came to the work area with a roll of material called *"incerata."* It was paraffin-covered cloth from America that was completely impermeable. He only had two, however, while the service of three of them, minimum, was necessary for the purpose. Finally, Nonno Donato remembered that he had one at the house. So, he decided to walk the short distance to our house to fetch it. I accompanied him.

We approached the house with some trepidation. The Germans were known to break into homes, taking possession of everything they wanted. When we arrived, nonno opened the door and we walked in and made sure that no one had ransacked it. It was intact. We walked around the outside, inspected the wine cellar and ascertained that the wine casks were all still sealed, especially his "cooked wine," a sherry-like brew that was always the wine-maker's pride and joy. Nothing had been touched. No one had made any attempt to enter the dwelling. So we celebrated the event by taking a draft from the cooked wine vat. He took a long draft, I took a short one. Nonno Donato then decided to walk around the perimeter of the property. The house was L-shaped. As we reached the back of it, that is the inside part of the elbow of the L, he noticed that someone had actually cut an opening along the hedges that separated our property from the road that passed behind the house. It wasn't a small opening, either: it was at least six feet wide. In order to make that opening, they even had to saw off several bushes whose bases were fairly large. Nonno actually ran there, that's how concerned he was. He examined the hole they had made and he noticed that, whoever did it, had beaten a path to the corner of the house and stopped there. It was obvious that several men had done something there, but what? Nothing else seemed touched. Puzzled, Nonno Donato was at a loss to explain it, but he was troubled and felt violated to the deepest core of his being, typical of any one whose home is invaded by strangers.

We stayed a few minutes and then started back to the Marrone household. Through the fields we went, proceeding cautiously as we made ready to cross the highway. As we approached the southernmost limits of our property, however, an entire column of military vehicles started to pass. We had to wait a good twenty minutes, hiding among the vines, before we could safely cross the street. Finally, there was a break between vehicles, so we dashed across the roadway and we immersed ourselves among the vines of the Casimine vineyard. Between our own vineyards and those of the Marrone's, I must have eaten three pounds of grapes. They were very sweet because they should have been harvested at least three weeks before, but under the circumstances, it couldn't be done.

In a few minutes we entered the house where everyone was having a siesta as they awaited our return with the *incerata*. Nonno immediately told the rest of the family of the breach in our hedge on the Via Marina side, in the back of the house. They discussed among themselves, but no one could come up with a reasonable theory as to why the Germans had done that. There was no doubt in anyone's mind that it was done by the Germans. Finally, my mother suggested that it was done so that they could have vehicular access to the nearby well. But that theory raised as many questions as it answered. Finally, everyone went back to his or her task. The air shelter "engineers" stretched the new piece of *incerata* nonno had brought, put a decent roof to the shelter, consisting of a number of small tree trunks laid across the opening, and topped it with a number of tree branches complete with leaves to camouflage the engineering marvel. When they were finished, the engineering student deemed it a masterpiece. And maybe it was, but there were a number of fatal flaws in its concept. For one thing, it stood out like that famous sore thumb. The camouflage failed in its intent. Instead, it immediately called everyone's attention to its presence and its intended purpose. Furthermore, it was visible from all the heights that surrounded it. But it was judged to be adequate. Having finished the outside, the women started to decorate it inside. No, they did not hang any picture on its two six-foot-tall dirt walls, but they did hang old sheets, bedspreads, spread cloths, and anything else they could find to distance us from the humid, naked earth. We slept in it that night.

The next morning, I woke up at dawn frozen to the bone. I had pains all over my body because of the unnatural position in which I had to sleep all night. My legs were still "asleep," as they say. Obviously circulation to them had all but stopped during the night. I crawled over the other bodies and made my way out of that burrow. I believe that mamma had had a lapse in judgment at first, because we actually slept in that thing for the rest of our stay there. It was the most uncomfortable sleeping arrangement I had experienced since the air raid of October 12. It was so uncomfortable that I, usually a late riser, would awaken at five or five-thirty in the morning and walk outside to stretch my aching limbs. Once there, however, I would be enchanted by the most spectacular celestial show I had ever seen. It was the morning star, the planet Venus, putting on a show in the terse Italian fall sky. It looked like a large diamond hanging there, ready to be plucked by an eager young bride. I can still see it in my mind, today: brilliant against indigo blue. I knew then the reason the Blessed Mother is often referred to as the *Morning Star*.

Everyone got up with the birds, as they say. Who could sleep under those conditions? We had a meager breakfast of bread and olives and a herbal tea that tasted horrible. There certainly was no coffee or regular tea. Those commodities had not been available in stores since the war began four years before. The sun was barely up in the east when mamma and nonno began to argue again about moving. It wasn't a virulent altercation, but mamma's argument was a firm and sensible one. If going south across the river was impossible, she would go north to the area northeast of Fossacesia, called Piano Favaro. It was only a stone's throw from the town. She had some friends there. Surely they would grant us hospitality.

Nonno Donato kept insisting that Aunt Filomena's pregnancy and imminent delivery had to be considered first in any decision we made. Where could we go that could provide the care she needed in that most delicate situation? At least we had a home available here.

Finally, mamma made a decision: at 9:00 A.M. the next day she would gather us children, Nonna Concetta, and her friends, and move north. She told nonno exactly where we would be in case he had second thoughts and wanted to rejoin us.

The sun had been up for a while when Casimine and his two sisters announced that they were going to a plot of land they owned near the river to do a little work that needed immediate attention. Yes, they knew it was dangerous, but the work had to be done and they would reach the plot of land via back roads. Today, they reasoned everything is still relatively calm; tomorrow, who knows? They left at eight o'clock taking the proper tools with them. If they got caught by the Germans, they would simply say that they were on their way to report for duty. Wasn't that what the provincial prefect had said: "Report voluntarily and bring your own tools?" Hopefully they could finish the job shortly after noon without getting caught or shot at by passing aircraft.

After they left, the morning dragged on for us. I thought I'd read some, but I just didn't feel like it. Filippo and I, together with the son and daughter of my mother's friend, Nicole, tried to amuse ourselves by playing hide and seek in the yet-to-be-harvested vineyard that separated the house from the highway. The grapes were still luxuriant hanging from the vines, so occasionally we helped ourselves to a bunch of the white or red variety of the fruit. Aunt Filomena, seeing us playing in the vineyard, decided that we might make ourselves useful, so she came out with two special scissors and two baskets.

She suggested that we harvest as much of the grapes as we could. "Well!" I thought, "This is different!" We went to work and in about two hours we had harvested enough grapes so that Aunt Filomena was able to squeeze the juice and add it to the liquid that she had fermenting in the cellar, thus replenishing all the juice that had evaporated in the process. When we were finished harvesting the grapes, Aunt Filomena went into her cupboard and pulled out a kitchen towel whose four corners had been tied crisscross at the center. She untied the knots very carefully to reveal about a dozen beautiful *bocconotti* she had saved since Easter. They are by far the most savory of all the cookies in the world. I had not seen any of these for several years. We each got one. It was a super and very much appreciated reward.

By early afternoon, Casimine and his two sisters, Maria and Ermerina, returned from their jobs at the river area. They reported no activities whatsoever on the part of the Germans. In retrospect, one can draw conclusions from this: It was the 19th of October, 1943. It was too early for the bulk of the German divisions to come pouring down the eastern side of the peninsula to confront the British 8th Army. The convoys that we saw occasionally were small and with large intervals of time between. This bit of news was enough to retrigger the argument between mamma and nonno. She asked Maria and Ermerina if they had seen a sentry on the river. They said that they weren't that close to the bridge, but it didn't appear that it was being guarded. "See," said mamma, "there is nobody there. We could make it." But Nonno Donato was as stubborn as the proverbial mule, so she didn't take the discussion any further, but simply reminded him that the following day, October 20th, we would be moving to the northern side of town. Again, she took the opportunity to explain to him exactly which house we would be in. If, in the days to come, they decided that the rest of the family wanted to join us, we would be waiting for them. Her last sentence was punctuated like an exclamation mark by one of those mine explosions with which the Germans were systematically destroying the homes in the Sangro Valley.

Shortly afterward, Casimine called me aside and showed me a most unusual collection of military booty he had found at the farm. I immediately surmised that they were the spent machine-gun shells that had fallen from those airplanes when they engaged in the dogfight the day before. I believe they were 20mm machine-gun shells. It appeared that the bases of those shells were just about that size. He had brought home about a dozen of them. Together with the shells, he also brought home the rings that kept them together, rendering them capable of being fed into the weapon. The shells were brass, and the rings looked more like an iron alloy, painted a dark green color. Those rings were built in an ingenious manner. They started out as a piece of metal, possibly square, having approximately eight inch sides. On opposite sides of it, two cuts were made that left three tongues on both sides. Then, the center tongue of one side was bent in a machined circle toward the middle, where the two on the other side were bend toward the center of the reverse side. This formed a three-ring gadget capable of housing two bullets and at the same time permitting the rings to be linked to each other until the bullet was fired and the shell ejected. Once the shell was ejected, each tri-ring linkage also fell off, since they depended on the shell to keep them linked. By re-inserting the now empty shells into the two rings, and one on the other side (it would never work that way, actually), we were able to come up with a strange looking "weapon" of our own. It was a toy with which we began to play a war game. The "toys" looked more like small cannons and they were very, very heavy. After fifteen minutes, we stopped, our arms being extremely fatigued as we attempted to keep that gadget up as in a hand gun attack. Over the years, I couldn't help but think that we boys must have war built into our very genes. Here we are caught in the middle of a real war situation, with the possibility of losing our very lives at any moment, and all we could think of playing was war.

At 6:00 P.M. Aunt Filomena called us in for supper. She had pulled the necks of four ducks and had prepared them in the best tradition of the pluri-millenarian Abruzzese cuisine. We had another Lucullian feast, *"bene innaffiato con vino a volontà."* The phrase means that the dinner was "well sprinkled with wine at will." but it is a misapplied hyperbolic statement. Italians do love their wines, but they respect it, too. They enjoy it at will, but usually without abusing it. That night was no different. We kids were given our usual allotment of a half glass of wine, diluted with water. Nothing else was available, except water, of course. Even today, children are often allowed to drink at the table and there is no age limit for purchasing wine or liquor. However, although alcoholism was not a problem with youth in the past, in recent years, some forms of abuse have been on the rise, so something has changed for the worse.

We remained at Aunt Filomena's for five days. Her house was situated away from the road, but there was a tall oak tree in front it, and Casimine, who was an expert climber, used to scamper up that tree reaching its very summit in a matter of seconds. From there, he had full command of the entire straight section of Route 16 that went from the corner of our property at the foothills of Fossacesia, to past the Casimine area, about a half mile, and eventually to the Zamenga Bridge, two miles south of the Casimine household.

He "squirreled" his way up that tree every time the roar of military engines halted, indicating that the caravan had stopped probably for water or to pick some late season fruits. There was an apple orchard on the Marrone side, while our own vineyards were across the street. The Germans helped themselves from both sides of the highway. We didn't mind that.

Once, a small group of German soldiers, fully armed, made their way through the vineyards to the Marrone house. I thought that they were just exploring the area. I happened to be behind the house when I saw them approaching stealthily. I watched them as they headed for the farmhouse from its main driveway, which was quite long, thus giving me time to alert the others. As usual, the men who were there scrambled in every direction, trying to find a hiding place. The three German soldiers and an officer, upon reaching the house, looked around, inspected the surrounding fields, probably to see if there were any fruit plants, and then talked among themselves for a minute or so. There was a big vineyard that extended as far as the eye could see, and some late-blooming pears that were still loaded with fruit. Aunt Filomena came out and went out to meet them, mainly to give time to the men to find a hiding place. Communicating with hand gestures, she made the Germans understand that if they wanted the fruit, they could take as much as they wanted. They got the message because they immediately went into the vineyards and began to eat the grapes. They nodded that it was good. My mother came out with a pair of scissors, and began to snip large bunches of grapes off the vines. The Germans thanked her, and were hesitant to leave. Mamma figured out that, since all conversations were achieved through hand gestures and head nods, they were wondering about the basket, which was of good quality. She nodded back to take it with them, or to simply throw it back into the vineyard. We did find it later under an olive tree in the middle of the vineyard at a distance of twenty-five feet from the highway. It was carefully placed there.

The day after our group had left the place, the Germans made another visit to the Marrone house. A year later, Cousin Casimine told us that they were looking for a pig, or some other animal to slaughter. They found nothing, since we had already consumed every last creature that God intended for our sustenance, except one cow that cousin Casimine had taken to the middle of a grove of pine trees at the bottom of a ravine. No one had even suspected that there might have been as little as a wild rabbit in that grove. But the cow, named Mughetta (lily-of-the-valley), decided to moo at the worst possible time. It didn't take long for those "gentlemen" to go there, untie the cow and take off with it without even saying thank you. According to Casimine, who told me the rest of the story in Montreal in 1977, one of the Germans turned to the civilians, rattled his rifle in their directions, and vomited out of his mouth a barrage of undecipherable German words filled with obvious venom, seasoned, no doubt, with obscenities and hateful threats. They were convinced that, as members of the Aryan race, they were the legitimate heirs to the Earth and all its treasures, bar none. "We said goodbye to Mughetta," continued Caz, "with heavy hearts, and ignored the German hatred," he added.

After that incident, the enlarged family split. Nonno Donato and the rest of our family finally decided that mamma was right, and came north to rejoin us. Aunt Filomena and the rest of their family headed for Villa Alfonsina, south of the Sangro River, where the eldest sister, Lucia, lived. Ironically, as you will see later, they passed over the bridge undisturbed.

WE COME UNDER ATTACK

October 20th was a beautiful fall day. It was the third night that we had slept in the makeshift shelter, so we all had "broken bones." For that reason, we all got up in darkness to admire Venus, even though each morning it was lower and lower on the horizon. Aunt Filomena was already up: she had to bake bread. My mother joined her in the kitchen to help her and to announce to her that we had decided to leave the area and trust our luck to another zone, north of Fossacesia. Aunt Filomena was saddened about that development, but wished us luck and said she hoped we would all survive the events of the coming days. The uncertainty of the moment was unfathomable.

By eight o'clock the moving party was all set to hit the road. Mamma and nonna had prepared a bundle, mostly clothing, for everyone to carry. We said goodbye to everyone and we started up the slight incline of the driveway that led to a dirt road leading to the highway, which it took us ten minutes to reach. As we approached the main road, mamma halted the party. She wanted to make sure that no Germans were coming down from the curve that also marked the entrance to our property. She cautiously walked up to the edge, listened for engine noises, looked up and then waved us to proceed.

Once we were on the highway, we hugged the right and, after walking the length of a football field, we arrived at the southern end of our property. We entered it at its very corner where Nonno had removed a bush or two from its hedge so that whenever we wanted to go visit Aunt Filomena we could walk on our own property and not use the highway. The original reason for not walking along the highway was that whenever a vehicle passed, it would invariably kick up a cloud of white dust. The more recent reason was that, more often than not, the vehicles in question were German military vehicles. It was best not to be seen by their passengers: one never knew what they had in mind. So, we practiced the same counsel in reverse: we entered the breach in the hedge. That's the southern breach, because now we also had one in the back of the house made by unknown visitors, for unknown reasons. We walked through the rows of vines that still had the grapes upon them. Before we left the vineyard and entered the olive grove adjacent to it, mamma suggested that we pick several bunches of grapes to sustain us for a while. We were headed toward the unknown. Yes, we knew where we were going, but no one knew what we would find when we got there. Who knows when we might eat again, mamma had said. So, we all got busy, first to find some kind of container in which to put the grapes, then to fill them with a few bunches of the purple fruit. We looked around. There was a small thatched hut nearby that Nonno Donato had erected a few years before for the purpose of protecting himself from the rain in case of a sudden shower, while he was out in the field working. We went there and luckily we found a wicker bag containing a number of old leather work gloves that nonno had brought home from America back in 1926. We dumped its contents inside another container and we grabbed a pair of farming shears and began to cut the bunches of grapes. They were purple grapes intended to be consumed at the dinner table as opposed to the smaller juice grapes reserved for making wine. We filled the basket.

We were getting ready to get on our way again when we heard engine noises. Oh-oh! Mamma ordered everyone to stop. We looked around and we saw that a German military convoy was transiting on the highway heading south, but they were still in Fossacesia. They would take about ten minutes before they reached us. So, mamma ordered everyone to sit on the ground, and stay there until the convoy passed us. We were very quiet making sure that we were well hidden by the thick foliage of the vines. We waited. The soldiers stopped just as they reached our vineyard. They came into it and picked some grapes. We remained quiet until they left, and then we, too, continued on our journey, heading for the northern limits of our property. When we reached the house mamma decided not to try to go inside, fearing the presence there of Germans, even though there were no signs in the front porch that there had been intruders. One never knew! Behind the house, I showed her where the gap in the hedge was. She examined it and noted that whoever did it came there with a truck since there were tire tracks clearly visible on the dirt road.

We continued on our way by turning right from the now famous breach in the hedge and proceeded east. It was another beaten-down dirt road. It led straight to the top of the ridge that overlooks the *Golfo di Venere*, flowing into the main provincial road that leads to Fossacesia from the beach area. We followed it, but only until we reached another road that crossed it coming from Fossacesia and descending toward the river. We turned left on it, and climbed the hill toward Fossacesia, intending to by-pass the town, and proceeded at an angle through the fields toward the cemetery.

At the point that the road turned north and became Via Sangro, the town's main street, there was, and there still is, a large cross made of reinforced cement, placed there for religious purposes many years before. Every passer-by used to stop to say a prayer until the whole world became cynical and the practice was all but abandoned. We believed in those things then! We had planned to do precisely that when we reached that cross, and take a rest in the process. We were looking forward to sitting down for a while when, as we came around a bend in the road, we were shocked to see that we had run right into a German military encampment. They had taken over a house that sat a little bit away from the road; that's why we didn't see them until it was too late to back off. Mamma said under her breath for us to keep on walking as if nothing was wrong.

We were almost at the gate that led to that house when suddenly we heard the roar of a low-flying aircraft passing right over our heads. Talk about double jeopardy, this was bad timing at its absolute worst. That airplane flew so low that it scared the daylights out of all of us. The first plane was quickly followed by two more. It was an air attack, and we were right in the heart of its principal target, that German outpost. We hoped those pilots didn't hit the bull's eye while we were there.

Our moment of panic was cut short by the arrival of a giant of a German soldier who motioned to us to follow him. He took us to a small room that was attached to the two story house. It had probably been the family food storage room, but now it was open: it had no roof, just four walls with a window on one side. The German soldier helped the women remove the bundles they were carrying on their heads and told us to take cover in a corner. We did as we were told, while he grabbed his rifle, rushed outside, and joined his comrades in trying to shoot down those planes. I saw it all and it appeared to me to be a study in futility. Those planes, three twin-fuselaged P-38 Lightnings, were simply too fast to be hit with rifle fire.

The ground-to-air battle lasted no more than five minutes. The roar of the three airplanes was the dominant factor that characterized the entire episode. The engine noise when the planes flew over that encampment was unbearable, as they flew so low I thought we could have touched their wings. In addition to the roar of the engines, there was the rat-ta-ta-ta of the machine guns. Not a very reassuring situation. The planes circled a couple more times, but without firing their 20mm guns. Within a few minutes I saw them fly into the Sangro Valley, one after the other, flying south toward their bases, probably in the flatlands of the Apulia region. Before they left, two of the planes dropped their single bombs, but without doing any damage.

When the battle was over, the giant soldier came back to us, helped the women place their baskets upon their heads, gave each of us a couple of dark gray crackers and sent us on our way. This was the second time that I had seen concrete evidence that not all Germans were bad, though many were. This one was a nice guy who probably had children of his own in Germany.

We continued our journey through the fields in the back of the row of houses on the east side of Via Sant'Egidio. As we passed by the end of that street, we looked down toward the downtown area. It was totally deserted. Way down near the other end there were a couple of trucks parked, but not a living soul, military or civilian. It was strange not to see that street pullulating with children, being the most densely populated street in town.

When we began the stretch toward the cemetery and out of town, we were facing the Mario Bianco Elementary School, the school which I had attended for six years and Filippo for only two. We couldn't possibly know it then, but that was the last time I would see that beautiful building standing. But now, the Germans were going in and out of it. Obviously, they were using it as a troop shelter. We decided to avoid it, so we made an oblique right and headed straight for the cemetery.

In a few minutes, we reached the crossroads where there was a confluence of five streets, including the cemetery lane. Crossing this was a bit tricky because we could only see two of them down their entire length to see if there were any military traffic on them. Mamma thought for a while and then asked me to cross the road and get myself to the cemetery corner. From there I could see down the other two streets, all the way to the church of San Giovanni in Venere and, the other way, I could see nearly downtown Fossacesia. At the end of both streets there was indeed military activity, but I suggested that they were pretty far away, so it was all right for everyone to cross. And in a few seconds we were on our way to our final destination. We stopped briefly at the cemetery gates and said a prayer, especially for the newly buried victims of the air raid a week before.

When we reached the northwest corner of the cemetery wall we turned right onto a dirt road that ran along the northern wall of the cemetery. From there we could see a white house across the ravine standing all alone: that was our destination. In order to reach it we had to walk down to the creek level at the bottom of the ravine and then climb up the opposite slopes. It was the same ravine that ran behind the church of San Donato a half mile away. The road that ran alongside the cemetery was fairly large at the top, but it began to narrow as it descended toward the rumbling creek. It hugged the steep terrain with a series of sharp curves so that it proceeded downward gradually in a serpentine manner until it reached the creek level. In the summer, people often waded across the creek, but in winter they availed themselves of several large rocks placed in the water and it was easy to skip across it. Once on the other side, the narrow path continued up the hill in the same manner until it reached the top of the ridge, where it widened again.

We reached the white house at exactly 12:45 P.M. I knew that because from there, in a straight line, we were less than a half mile away from the Church of the Rosary, in the center of Fossacesia which housed the town clock. That clock had a two-bell system for loudly announcing the time of day to the four corners of the town and beyond, every fifteen minutes. The larger of the two bells rang the hours, while the smaller announced the quarter-hours at a higher pitch. So, just as we were entering the front yard of the white house, the larger bell of the town clock rang twelve times, and the smaller tolled three times. We had made it, but it had been the most stressful walking trip I had ever undertaken in my young life. The thought crossed my mind that my hope was that things would get better soon. Regretfully, they were to get worse, a lot worse.

As we entered the property of a lady named Memena, short for Filomena, mamma and nonna were greeted with great profusion by the proprietor. We were invited in, she offered some refreshments, but we were disappointed to learn that we could not stay there. Memena was the aunt of our next-door neighbor in the lane, Rosina De Cellis, whose son, Domenico, was our playmate. Normally, the owners of those farm houses greeted anyone who asked for hospitality without too much fuss, but for some reason Memena did not. We decided to go to her sister's home, Rosina's mother and Domenico's grandmother, who lived a little ways beyond her house. It was only a quarter-mile away, and we got there in no time. When we reached our destination, we saw Domenico inside the yard playing with a dog. We waved to him, and he ran to greet us. He accompanied us in and called out his mother and grandmother, Giacinta. Here we were accepted, but we slept in the house only one night. The other two nights we had to go down the ravine where there were several sand caves.

The reason for the strange arrangement was that on the third day after we had left the farmstead, the rest of Giacinta's family was supposed to arrive from the south. It was a common event in those days for entire families to come back to town from Milano, Torino, Genoa and other industrial cities in the north in their attempt to escape the frequent air raids by American bombers. Some cities used to get bombed every night. This family came from Naples, a favorite night target of American B-24 bombers.

A SPORTS CAR ON A DIRT ROAD

The second day we were in that house, Filippo and I were in the yard with Domenico, just standing around talking and fantasizing what life would be like when the British arrived. Somehow, we already knew by then that the Americans were *not* coming to our area, having split the task of conquering the Italian peninsula into two fronts, the British taking the east coast, the Americans staying in the west coast of the Italian peninsula. I suggested that when the British arrived everything was going to be chocolate-covered, and we would have plenty of beautiful footballs to play with (I meant soccer, of course). Both Dominic and Filippo thought that my suggestions were pretty stupid. I was annoyed at their annoyance. True, I was talking without really knowing, but we were bored out of our wits by that time, and anything anyone said was part of an attempt to pass the time.

Suddenly, we heard engine noise, but it didn't sound as if it came from a military vehicle. This noise was different. We looked toward the northern end of the street and we were shocked to see a little sports car hurtling down the dirt road. It was a convertible, no less, a tiny car, light blue in color. The top was down and there were three people on board: two men and a very blond woman. Her hair was yellow, pretty much like the color of the hair of the girls who had been living upstairs in our house. The two men occupied the front seat while the woman sat in the rear seat, keeping company with what appeared to us to be a mountain of boxes or suitcases. She appeared to be holding them in place. We looked at each other in utter amazement as if to say, where do those fools think they're going? It must be remembered that this was the same dirt road that we had used to come here from the Fossacesia cemetery. That same dirt road narrows down to the size that barely permitted two pedestrians to pass each other comfortably as it descends toward the creek, doing so with a half-dozen extremely sharp curves on both slopes. Granted the car was tiny, a sports car that after the war became known as a Spider, with room front and back for only four people, but it was an automobile nonetheless. We were able to observe its tire marks clearly visible on a dirt road that up to now had only seen agricultural carts driven by animal power. The marks of automobile tires stood out like the nose on a fibbing Pinocchio. How in the world was that little wheelbarrow of an automobile going to manage to get across a creek that, at that time of the year, carried better than a foot of water? Our reasoning was not wrong. We were certain that we would see it come back. "Let's go after it and see how far they'll get before they decide to turn around!" suggested Domenico. He didn't have to repeat it. In a single motion, all three of us took off and began to chase that little car. We had to run a quarter of a mile before reaching the edge of the ridge where the road turned right to begin its descent toward the creek bed. When we got there, we were amazed that the car was no longer in sight. High vegetation and terrain variation blocked our vision, but we could not hear its engine purr, either. It seemed that it had vanished. We listened attentively, but there was no hint of engine noise of any kind. Domenico wanted to go farther down the hill, but I didn't want to. I had not said anything to my mother that we were going there and I didn't dare go any farther. So, we just stood there for a minute or two when, to our utter disbelief, we heard engine noise coming from far away. We looked down the valley toward the creek and there was that pesky little car on the opposite slopes, trying to negotiate those narrow curves with some difficulty, but moving decidedly uphill toward the cemetery on the Fossacesia side. They had made it, after all! How in the world did they do it? We were amazed. We stayed there until we saw it transit along the cemetery wall, and then it turned south and out of sight. It's amazing what a tiny little skirmish like World War II forces man to do! Under normal circumstances, the owner of a small car like that would have never dared to cross a creek where the water level was higher than the car's undercarriage; but, in war times, when danger lurks around every corner, everyone had to dare the unimaginable.

We quickly ran back to the house and, to my amazement, mamma, hadn't even missed us. We told her about the tiny car and how they had made it down and up the creek slopes of the ravine behind the cemetery. She conjectured that they were trying to avoid the main highway either to avoid the Germans or the frequent air attacks by British fighter planes or both. Two or three times, those planes would swoop down and strafe anything on wheels moving up or down the roadways of our area. Later on we learned that, after the armistice, many Allied soldiers who had been freed by their POW camps in northern Italy traveled south in an effort to rejoin their armies, British or American. They did so on foot mostly, covering about ten or fifteen miles a day, according to their ability to hold up under a sustained march all day long. Sometimes they were given a ride, but in those days the vehicles they encountered were animal-driven carts. Many stopped at farmhouses and asked permission to sleep in their barns or hay lofts. Most of the farmers were gracious permitting them to do so, but not all.

NONNO DONATO COMES TO HIS SENSES

Shortly after noon on October 23rd, I saw a group of people coming down the road. I immediately recognized my grandfather leading the troop. Everybody was there, and wobbling right in the middle was my very pregnant Aunt Filomena, surrounded by the rest of the women, like a queen bee surrounded by the rest of the swarm for protection. "Well," mamma said, "I see it hasn't happened yet!"

After the initial exchange of greetings, Signora Giacinta, the owner of the house, explained to Nonno Donato that she had already too many people in the house and she couldn't accommodate everybody, but she would make an exception for his pregnant daughter and one more person to stay with her. It was decided that my paternal grandmother, Minguccia, would stay with her daughter, just in case. Everybody else had to sleep in the caves in the valley below the house.

SIGNOR CHICKEN

That day, after the rest of the family had finally come to their collective senses and concluded that mamma was correct in her judgment and decided to rejoin us, Nonno Donato followed mamma's instructions and amazingly they found us, precisely where she had said we would be. However, he quickly realized that he'd better be looking for a different house for his grandson or granddaughter to be born in. A cave or stable might have been all right for Jesus, but He arrived under very different circumstances. These were war times. Besides, nonno had several friends in the area whom he had helped when they were in America. Surely one of them would take us in. So, that very afternoon he set out to see his old "American" friend, Frank Moretti, better known as Mister Chicken, who lived a mile or so from Giacinta's house. When in Norristown, in the early 20's Mister Chicken, as he was called there, had lived in the very same boarding house as Nonno Donato and my teen-ager father, on Franklin Street, in the east-end of Norristown. He resolved to go visit him early the next morning. Hopefully, he would give us hospitality. I went with him.

On the way, I asked what Mister Chicken meant. Up to that time, I had never heard even one word of the English language. He told me he and the man we were going to see had worked together for a while in Norristown. He was a curious character, he added, who couldn't even read or write, but was quite a resourceful person. At one point, around 1923, there was a scarcity of jobs in Norristown, foreshadowing, perhaps, the Great Depression of the 1930's. Mr. Moretti was laid off from his job at the Norristown Water Company. After canvassing the sidewalks trying to find a job for several months unsuccessfully, he had an ingenious idea: seeing so many people coming out of the stores on Main Street or the Montgomery County Court House for lunch around noon, and walking two or three blocks to go to a luncheonette, he thought, why not bring lunch to them? So, he went home, designed and built a cart using two bicycle wheels on one end and a wooden leg on the other. He placed a charcoal grill on it, and began to grill chicken legs and wings which he got for practically nothing from the "live chicken stores in town." He bought some wax paper cut in squares and placing himself at the corner of Main and Swede Streets in Norristown, he sold grilled chickens from 11:00 A.M. to 2:00 P.M. For fifteen cents, you could get two drumsticks or two wings or a combination of both. For two bits, you could have three pieces of chicken and a soft drink. It was an instant success, anticipating the Colonel and his Kentucky Fried Chicken by two generations. He made twenty-five to thirty dollars a day, an unheard of amount in those days. By 1926, he had made so much money that when my grandfather and papà returned to Italy that year, he went along taking all his money with him. With that, plus the money he had already sent to his wife over the previous years, he was able to purchase the home and property that we were about to visit. And that's how he became known as Mr. Chicken in Norristown and vicinity.

Nonno Donato made me laugh when he added an interesting anecdote about Mr. Chicken, alias Frank Moretti. The first Saturday of each month, a group of Italian immigrant men from Norristown, Bridgeport and Conshohocken, Pa. would travel together by train to South Philadelphia to visit the Frank Di Berardino Bank to deposit money or to send money to their wives in Italy. It was a monthly ritual that everyone looked forward to. It was a holiday for those hard-working but not necessarily refined gentlemen. Some of them were totally illiterate, and so they needed help. My young father would go along precisely to help them fill in the necessary papers. They would take the train around 8:00 A.M. at the Reading station in Norristown and get off at the Market Street terminal. From there, they would take the trolley car on 12th Street and go to the area of the Italian Market. At Christian Street, they would walk to the corner of 8th and Christian, transact their business at the Frank Di Berardino offices, and then shop at the Italian market along 9th Street. Before boarding the trolley that brought them back to the Reading RR Station for their return trip to Norristown, they would stop at a sandwich window at Christian Street near 9th, and they would have a pork sandwich and a beer. Frank Moretti would join them every month. My father, being a teenager at the time, had been designated by his father as Signor Moretti's shadow and secretary. He said that papà even taught Signor Moretti how to sign his name. It looked horrible, nonno added, but it was legal, so he could at least sign for himself. Still, he had to be told where to sign. The only problem Nonno Donato had with Frank was that he always wore a pair of boots, winter and summer, whose soles were lined with large-headed nails. When he walked on those Philadelphia sidewalks in the company of ten or twelve other men who wore somewhat similar shoes, it sounded like a platoon of soldiers marching down the streets. I had seen men like that in our own town, so I immediately got the picture. Nonno warned me not to call him Mr. Chicken, however. Call him Frank, or Signor Moretti. "I'm the only one who can call him Chicken—when others do, he gets mad," he added. That was fine with me. I couldn't even pronounce it, anyway.

When we reached the Moretti farmstead, I was impressed with the house itself. It was a large two-story building featuring classical Italian lines with large windows and an impressive front door. There were no balconies, which was most un-Italian, to be sure, but it had, instead, a terrace to the eastern side with a magnificent view of the Golfo di Venere and the Adriatic Sea. The shore was no more than a quarter mile away. A man was on the threshing plaza doing some sort of chore. He had his back to the gates so he didn't see us go in. Nonno placed his index finger across his lips indicating to me that he wanted to surprise him, and when we got close, nonno shouted a peremptory order in English. I didn't understand it, of course, but he later translated it for my benefit. He said that he had told him that he was in violation of the municipal law for selling chickens on the streets without a license. Signor Moretti turned around quite startled and, realizing who it was, laughed and greeted nonno with great enthusiasm. They explained to me that Signor

Moretti didn't realize when he started selling chickens on the streets that he needed a license to do it, so about a month after he started, a policeman asked him for his license, which he didn't even understand; somebody had to explain it to him. He was fined five dollars for his "crime." With some reluctance, he went right into the courthouse and got a license, which cost five dollars. Thereafter, Frank always referred to the license as his ten-dollar permit to do an honest man's work. His biggest problem was, however, that the policeman was not only an Italian, but an Abruzzese. He considered it the ultimate betrayal!

They continued to speak to each other in English for a few minutes, laughing as they did so. He invited us into the house and he brought out a bottle of whiskey. He said it was the last of the Mohicans. He didn't know what the word Mohicans meant, but he knew that he had learned the expression from someone and knew that it meant the absolute last of anything. In his case it symbolized the last bottle of whiskey he had brought home from America. They toasted to America "and to all the chickens of the world, God bless them all!" Frank added, as nonno translated for me. That brought a chuckle to my lips. All the chickens of the world are raised for only one purpose, that of being killed, cooked and consumed, but God bless them anyhow. At least until the skillet is ready.

Then, Nonno Donato asked him for hospitality in his house for his entire family, not hiding the fact that his daughter, Aunt Filomena, would probably have a baby in his house. Chicken said, "No problem." His wife, Melania, was particularly happy to hear that she would receive a new life in her home, and the deed was done. We had a place to stay and Aunt Filomena wouldn't have to give birth in a cave.

While the men went upstairs to figure out where they were going to put everybody, Signora Moretti went into the chicken yard and tried to catch a real one to prepare for dinner. She, too, was told that if they didn't kill their livestock, the Germans would take them. The chicken must have been practicing evasive maneuvers, though, because she gave the lady quite a workout before rendering herself as an offering to man's unending need for nourishment. I became hysterical watching the operation, because the lady had become exasperated not being able to corner that poor chicken, so she would accompany each failed attempt to catch that elusive fowl with the quaint southern Italian habit of wishing that untold evils befall the object of her wrath: *"Puozza jettà lu sanghe!"* (May you shed blood!), *"Ti puozza murì!"* (I hope you die!), *Puozza cripà!"* (I hope you croak!), and other similarly descriptive maledictions. What made it so funny was that the imprecations she hurled at that poor chicken encapsulated precisely what she was fixing to do to that unfortunate creature after she caught it, anyway. Finally, she grabbed a basket and with it she cornered the doomed hen. A few minutes later she severed its neck artery, whereby the animal literally "shed its blood, croaked, and died" all at the same time, as she had previously vouched. She collected that blood, too, because coagulated chicken blood was a delicacy and treated just like another piece of liver-like substance to be added to the stew. Some people didn't like that, but I used to love it! To each his "bone", I guess!

Meanwhile, the men came downstairs and talked some more in English over a glass of wine. I could not understand what they were saying, of course, but it was obvious that they were reminiscing about America and having a hilarious time with it.

Mister Chicken had told Nonno Donato that he was delighted to give us hospitality, but not until the next day. Apparently he used the upstairs bedrooms to store grain. He had two spare bedrooms, but at the moment they were filled with fifty or sixty sacks of grain. He was trying to avoid confiscation of that wheat by the Germans. "Give me time to clear some of those sacks and make some room. Tomorrow morning you can come." Nonno agreed, they shook hands, reminisced a little more about the good old days spent in Norristown working for the water company, and we left.

We started back to our temporary residence by the main road. We walked as fast as we could, because we did not want to run into unexpected confrontations with the Germans or with a lone Spitfire. At one point, we heard what sounded like a motorcycle approaching.

Nonno immediately motioned to me that we should duck into the fields. We found an opening in the hedges alongside the road, and we took it. It led immediately into a grove of cane shoots that hid us perfectly. Within a minute or two, a motorcycle with a sidecar came rumbling down the old gravel road. As usual, it carried an officer in the side-car, while a very young soldier drove the cycle. They passed before us like a meteor, leaving behind a cloud of dust. These casual encounters between German military personnel and Italian civilians occurred quite often. Most of the time, they did not lead to confrontations, but when they did, the results on the part of the civilians were usually deadly.

As soon as the dust settled, we got back on the street and we reached the house within a few minutes. It was 1:00 P.M. I had two confirmations of it: as we were entering the gates of Giacinta's house, Fossacesia's bells tolled a single stroke, followed within seconds by the bell of the next town, Rocca San Giovanni that echoed that single chime. Dinner was ready: Steak? Chicken?

Rabbit? None of the above! What we found was chunks of lard: just pieces of fat, frying in a pan. Under normal circumstances, the young people today would not even dream of eating lard, but we made an exception that time because the possibility of a real famine loomed quite evident. We had better eat whenever we could, whatever we found, however cooked. There might not be any food available for a while. And so we sat down at a table set up outside, since the weather was still nice, and we ate. There was plenty of homemade bread to dip in that melted oil, and that's what we did. We had no choice. The alternative was starvation. Occasionally, I swallowed a chunk of lard trying not to bite into it, but it was difficult. Bread dipped in oil was actually quite tasty.

That night, once again we slept in the sand caves. It was the fourth night for those of us who had left earlier, but the first for those who followed. This time it was more fun because my cousins and other friends were there. It was like a sleep-in to celebrate a birthday. Nonno didn't enjoy the experience, however, so he resolved to move on to Signor Moretti's home as soon as possible after sunup. The creek that ran no more than a hundred feet in front of caves that served as our bedrooms was the same that flowed behind the cemetery and that we had crossed a few days before. Here, however, the terrain rose almost straight up. In order to negotiate its descent or climb, the farmers in the area had actually dug crude steps into the turf. Therefore, we had to climb over a hundred steps. It was a rough experience. An even tougher task was trying to keep clean, considering that the area was very humid under the best of circumstances, so that the "steps" were always muddy. When we reached the top, Filippo and I were not in the best condition: our shoes were muddy, our socks were muddy, and our pants were muddy. There was mud everywhere.

Mamma hollered at us, until we called to her attention that she was muddy, too. The entire episode ended up in general laughter. We were all muddy. Nonno said that once we reached Signor Moretti's place we could all wash up. He, after all, had a bath tub. No running water, though. The water had to be first extracted from the well, then heated and then carried upstairs each time. But, that night, we all got a long overdue bath. It felt great!

CAPTAIN JOE DROPS IN, UNINVITED BUT WELCOME

We left rather early that morning because Aunt Filomena did not want to give birth to a baby in a cave, either. It was Tuesday, the 26th of October, 1943. After a twenty-minute walk we reached Signor Moretti's home. When we arrived, Mrs. Chicken, Signora Melanìa that is, was impressed by the number of people in the group. I know, because I happened to be looking at her when she let go with an unmistakable *"smorfia"* upon her face. That is a grimace of disapproval much better defined by the Italian word than by its English counterpart. Let's say that she didn't like it, but said nothing.

On the way, Nonno Donato reminded me not to call our prospective host "Chicken," not even "Signor Chicken." "Call him Signor Moretti," he warned. As we entered the gates of the property, we heard the bell of Fossacesia's clock tower toll eight times followed by the little bell chiming three times. It was quarter to nine. Shortly afterward, both bells began to chime in alternating tolls, don-din, don-din, don-din, the traditional call of the town's students: it was time for school. Within seconds, the bell of Rocca's town hall did the same thing: it was time for school there, too. "It's time to go to school," I said aloud, in an ironic yet nostalgic tone. It was that awkward situation that all pupils feel at one time or another in their lives. Happy that they don't have to go to school due to an unwelcome illness, a long period of school closing because of a catastrophic event like an earthquake, or, as in our case, an inopportune war, while at the same time sad, because we needed to go to school, and we knew it. An occasional snow day was a happy event, but prolonged inactivity, rooted in the even greater reality that we might not even survive this thing, produced a depressing feeling in all of us. I couldn't help but wonder if I would ever see the inside of a school again.

We were greeted by Signor Moretti with great enthusiasm. We were invited into the dining room, where Signora Moretti had prepared a very nice breakfast. Their supplies, though dwindling, were still fairly ample to last for a long while, even for the large group that had just invaded their home. My brother and I particularly enjoyed the toasted bread with homemade fruit preserve spread.

When breakfast was over, the women went upstairs to check out the places where everyone was to sleep that night. There were four rooms, two on each side of a nice-sized corridor. On both sides of the corridor and between the rooms were two recesses designed to accommodate two closets, but which the Moretti's had not had the opportunity to purchase due to the start of the war. It was in those recesses that they set up two cots, one for me, the other for my brother. Everyone else found a niche somewhere in the house including the wine room (they didn't have a cellar). For the balance of the day, everyone got busy doing whatever amused them. We boys did what boys do, and the two girls in the group did what girls do, especially when we were completely disenfranchised. This was not our home. It was at times such as these that one became aware of the importance of one's concept of home as a base of operations. We had all been displaced. As we went to bed, we hoped that during the night the long-awaited happy event would arrive. Aunt Filomena slept in the master bedroom, which was right next to my cot, though separated by the wall. But it would take three more days for the new baby to arrive. She simply wasn't ready!

The next morning, October 27, Nonno Donato, along with the owner of the property and a number of other men, went across the street from the house to a utility barn that Signor Moretti owned. It had been their intent to play cards. Mamma allowed me to accompany Nonno Donato, not without the usual litany of do's and don'ts that she normally recited to me in similar circumstances, even during peaceful times. In war times, she increased her efforts hoping to keep me "safe," as if she had any control over the thousand-fold unpredictable vicissitudes of war.

The barn was quite large, with plenty of free space. Signor Moretti had gathered all his working machinery to one side and secured it for the winter. He even had a small tractor, an unheard of commodity in southern provincial towns at that time. It had not been operative since the war began, due to the unavailability of gasoline. There was a long table there, too. It served primarily as a work bench for Signor Moretti, but came in handy as a picnic table in summer and as a gaming table during the long winter months when farmers had plenty of idle time. The men soon set it up to play cards, while we, the children, began to harass a number of cats that had made that barn their permanent home.

At about ten o'clock, a storm began to brew over the sea. The beach area was not very far away, but we were quite high, as Mr. Moretti's house was built on a promontory two-hundred-fifty feet above sea level. Proceeding southeast toward the sea, the terrain sloped gradually and, after a quarter mile, it dropped almost perpendicularly over the shore area. At the base of the hill, it flattened out to accommodate the Adriatica highway (still a dirt road at the time) and a single-track railroad trunk, both of which connected the north with the deep south of the peninsula. The railroad was totally inoperative because that single track had been damaged by Allied bombs during the past three months. A few miles farther south, even the bridge had been heavily damaged and rendered unusable.

We all gathered by the large barn door watching the approaching storm. Within minutes, the sky became pitch black in the southeast. Suddenly, we heard airplane engines roar overhead. Two fighter planes, flying very low, were chasing each other "What luck!" I thought to myself. "A dogfight. This is better than the movies!" I could watch without mamma harassing me. But, I was wrong: Nonno Donato was just as tyrannical as mamma in trying to keep me out of harm's way. "Stay inside! Don't expose yourself! Do this, don't do that," and similar admonitions and warnings that spoiled all our fun. With the barn door wide open, however, I could see the two planes once in a while as they flew past the front of the barn spitting venom and steel at each other. The most vivid memory I still have of that day is seeing the tracer bullets as they whizzed earthward at an angle, showing up dramatically white against the black stormy sky. The machine guns of both planes angrily spat fire at each other as they looped, dipped, and zipped through the air, trying to outmaneuver each other as each pilot went for the kill. It was very exciting for us boys.

Suddenly, the engine of one of the planes began to cough and sputter, followed by a prolonged whining sound that became lower in tone as the plane moved away from us. One of the fighters was in trouble. Within seconds, the other plane left the area, and all was suddenly very quiet. The bullets appeared to have hurt no one on the ground, and there were no bombs dropped by either plane. The men returned to their playing table, and I turned to Signor Moretti's tractor, which had aroused my interest and curiosity. It was a Ford. Nonno Donato told me it was a model designed by the well-known American car maker, but it was built in Germany on license by the Ford Motor Company.

After a few minutes, we heard a very excited voice calling for my grandfather to come out to the rear of the barn adding that a parachute was floating down toward us. We all ran out, of course. I had never seen a real parachute float down from the sky before. Alas, I was denied this time, too, because the man had touched down already and was dragging his life saving device behind him as he walked toward us. Not knowing which of the two pilots had been shot down, nonno didn't know if he should say something in English, or keep his mouth shut. But, the pilot looked very British, so he took a chance and said something in English. The RAF flier answered in his own version of the King's language. The flier gave his name as Captain Joseph Campbell and, true to the Geneva Convention manual, he added his serial number. Nonno told him to relax and come inside quickly. His name was useful but we didn't care about his serial number. He was now one of us. We would keep him safe. The captain asked if there were some Germans in the area and if they had been looking for him. Nonno answered yes to the first question, and no to the second, adding, however, that only about ten minutes had passed since his plane was shot down. The Germans might very well be searching for him as they spoke. There wasn't much time. "Come inside!"

At this point, there was an immediate flurry of activity: all the men got busy and, as if acting with one mind, they quickly provided the pilot with an entire outfit of the most horrible looking rags they could find. One of the men grabbed the parachute and, after making sure that the coast was clear, headed toward an abandoned well at the end of the property. He threw the parachute into the well and made sure it sank to the lowest point by throwing rocks on top of it. Nonno Donato told him to remove his uniform quickly. As he did so, his pants, shirt, and leather jacket also ended up in the well. All the men eyed that beautiful leather jacket, but no one would be caught dead wearing it. Expressed in another way, if the Germans were looking for the flier, anyone caught wearing that jacket might soon be dead indeed. Signor Moretti went into the house and brought out a pair of pants, a shirt, and an old trench coat he had bought in America and gave them to him to put on. They didn't exactly improve his looks, but they did the job. The only problem with Joe Campbell, as he said he preferred to be called, was that he was clean shaven and had unusually blond curly hair, typical of Englishmen, unheard of in Italy. I mean, he looked very, very English. Most of the men in the barn hadn't shaved in weeks and had long, dark, unkempt beards. Next to all those Italian men, his blond hair stood out like the ears on Topolino's round head (that's Mickey Mouse). He was told that he could stay with us until the British arrived. They were expected any day now, someone said. As it turned out, their arrival was better than a month away.

As soon as the women heard about the pilot dropping in unexpectedly for dinner, they made sure there was an extra plate ready for our guest. He had received a laceration of the left wrist as he ejected from his plane, so my mother, who had brought a first aid kit with her, applied medical care to his wound. Here, I had a chance to see the difference between Italian medical practices, at the time, and what the captain was used to: after washing the wound nice and clean, mamma applied the only antiseptic available to her. It was pure alcohol. As she applied it to the wound, the young man jumped a foot and a half off his chair from a sitting position, screaming as he did so. After that, he did not want her to touch it further. He motioned to her to just wrap it up, thank you. So she did.

The captain stayed in the utility barn that night. The men set up an elaborate access to the loft so that if the Germans were to enter, it would appear that there was no access to the upper scaffolding, which itself appeared to be just an elevated platform for the storage of hay and animal forage or bedding. Behind the hay, however, they fixed a cozy bed for the English aviator to sleep on and where he could hide rather comfortably. One of the men even set up a mirror whereby he always had a view of the door without having to expose his head. If anyone came in that door, he could see him without being seen.

Of course, the only ones who could converse with the Captain were my grandfather and Signor Moretti. Neither one was an expert at high-level conversation in the English language, but Nonno Donato could manage a down-to-earth conversation. I understood none of it then, but it was obvious that Nonno Donato's English was much better than Signor Moretti's. Of the two, he was the one who maintained a sustained flow of words, whereas Signor Moretti limited himself to a few monosyllables now and then that I would best describe as grunts. After all, nonno had completed the second grade. He said that he had even attended evening classes in America, sponsored by the Italian Catholic Church in Norristown. Neither one could have discussed Shakespeare, of course, but their English was more than adequate for the needs of the moment. I was fascinated with the language, too; it was the first time I had heard it spoken. I listened attentively to their conversation, trying to capture a sound or two that seemed to be a word or a short phrase. English would someday be my everyday language once I rejoined my father in America. I quickly learned that it is not a good thing to pick up sounds of a language and bandy them around without first knowing precisely what they mean. I had heard Joe Campbell and Signor Moretti talk to each other several times that afternoon and kept hearing a recurring word that, of course, was meaningless to me. It was Signor Moretti who spoke it almost exclusively and frequently, while the Captain used it only now and then. Nonno Donato never uttered it once. Late that night, just before we went to bed, I cornered my grandfather and asked him point blank about the recurring word I kept hearing. "Signor Moretti and the Captain say it all the time. It sounds like the Italian word *facchino* (pronounced fak-kino—it means "porter."), but it can't mean that, because they say it too often. What does it mean?" "Well," said Nonno, somewhat gruffly, "don't repeat it: it's a bad word." Many years later, thinking about it, I had to laugh as I would marvel at the irony of it all: the very first word that my ears ever perceived as a sound and a complete word of the English language turned out to be a certain f-word that's more at home in taverns than at the opera house. Perhaps that's the reason why I have had a total revulsion for it ever since. Not even my DI in the U.S. Marine Corps could force me to utter it!

As I eagerly listened as the men talked, I also caught another nuance in their speech: the two Italians spoke English with a different cadence than the Captain did. The cadence that Nonno and Frank Moretti evidenced in their pronunciation of English was nothing more than the so-called Italian accent; the natural tendency every Italian has to end every word with a vowel sound. The captain, of course, spoke the King's English, with the typical British accent.

The evening proved to be rather calm and pleasant. There hadn't been any activities on the part of the Germans to look for a pilot who had parachuted from the downed plane. We concluded that the Germans did not see the chute and assumed that the pilot had gone down with his plane into the sea. So, Captain Campbell remained in the house with the family until late, conversing with Nonno Donato and Signor Moretti, who were happy they could finally use a skill no one else had. Signor Moretti even brought out a bottle of his best wine, while Signora Moretti roasted some *ceci beans* (Pronounced chay-chee—chickpeas). Between a glass of wine and a handful of *ceci* to munch on, the conversation became animated and jovial. I think the two elder "Americans" were trying to relive their youthful rampages through Norristown and Philadelphia, while Captain Campbell brought them up to date on the progress of the war.

When it came time for the Captain to get back to the barn, Signor Moretti, his fourteen year old son, Angelo, and another man accompanied him. Some of the ladies wanted him to stay in the house, but the men, some of whom had fought in World War I, explained the intricacies of military strategy. If the Germans came and found the Captain hiding in the barn, it would simply be a case of a fugitive who had broken into the barn and was caught. But if he was caught in the house, then all the members of the family would be considered accomplices in harboring a fugitive. Signor Silvestri, another American who lived nearby, agreed. In 1924, so Nonno told me, he had returned to Italy because of an intricate family problem that took several years to resolve. By the time it was cleared, the Great Depression had hit, so he remained in Italy. *Salivestre,* as everybody called him (his full name was Silvestro Silvestri) explained that the best thing for everyone to do was to forget the Captain even existed. *"You don't know noteeng!"* he admonished everyone, especially the children. *"Shhhhh!"* he added placing his extended right index finger in front of his lips when he realized he had spoken in English and none of us knew what he had said. We were used to that by then, and we got the message loud and clear, if silently. The barn was across the street from the house, as mentioned, but not directly. It was about 150 feet farther east. This was good because it would have been less likely that the Germans, if they caught the Captain, could possibly blame the residents for aiding and abetting a fugitive.

After the Captain had climbed onto his hiding place, Signor Moretti arranged an emergency exit in the rear of the barn. If the front door were to be forced open, the captain could escape through a hole in the roof from which he could jump into a pile of hay. He told the Captain he could not go out except through that hole, unless somebody came to fetch him through the front door, because he was going to padlock the barn door to give the appearance that it had not been touched. Accordingly, after bidding Captain Joe goodnight, Signor Moretti locked the two barn doors with double padlocks. The Captain was actually quite cozy and warm in that hay loft: the women had provided him with several woolen blankets, and a hot water bottle, from America—naturally!

GUN SHOTS ARE HEARD

The second day Captain Campbell was with us, October 28, was another of those hazy sun days, typical of our area in the fall. Signor Moretti decided he would try to prepare a piece of land about the size of a soccer field, for the sowing of a legume called *lupinella*. In the spring, it is plowed under for the purpose of replenishing the soil's nitrogen supply. Young couples would go into the fields to eat *rampalupine*, (that's what we called it in dialect), and hide among the stalks to "make out." The only use for it I could appreciate was that while the young shoots are still tender, it was delicious to eat. You broke the tender stalk, peeled it, and ate the inner core. It was one of the delicacies of springtime. Unfortunately, it also had the power to give one the father of all bellyaches if you ate too much of it.

Nonno Donato, Signor Moretti and young Angelo went into the field armed with hoes and started to work. I volunteered to be the lookout. There was a fig tree in the middle of the field from which dangled a few figs the birds had missed. They were mostly overripe, but still tempting. I cleaned out the tree of all its remaining fruit.

From the top of that tree, I commanded a wide area, including the beach and the two access roads to the zone, one from the southeast, the other from the west. There was no military activity. The men worked incessantly, aware perhaps that the calm of the day might be replaced by chaotic conditions perhaps as soon as the next day. We had no source of news so we depended on an occasional passer-by to tell us what was going on. Any news obtained that way was, of course, totally unreliable.

At noon, the men stopped working and headed for the well. We all washed up and proceeded toward the house for lunch. As we approached the front door, we heard two rapidly-fired gun shots coming from the area opposite the coastline. All the women came out of the house alarmed. As far as we could tell, it sounded as if it came from the west, probably around the highway, Route 16, about a half mile away. Not knowing who fired those shots, we went in and enjoyed a beautiful meal that included pasta, cheese and a frittata (omelet) with zucchini and sausage. It was destined to be one of the last great meals we would all enjoy for several months. Angelo brought a lunch basket to Captain Campbell, carefully prepared by Signora Moretti. She included a pint of white wine.

After lunch, I thought the men would go back to work immediately, but they opted for a game of cards first, so I decided to do some reading. There was much material in that book I had not read because I thought it was boring. But, I was wrong—every entry turned out to be a revelation.

Later, the men went back to the field to resume work. I didn't feel like going back up that tree, however. I told nonno that I could keep an eye on the road just as well from the terrace. He agreed, but I kept on reading, instead of doing my job. Thank God the Germans didn't come that day, because if they had, they would have pounced on us and we would have been caught unaware. I paid scarce attention to the road, absorbed as I was with my readings. Italian anthologies carried the works of international authors, especially American authors. That day I discovered Mark Twain's, *"Quello zuccone di Wilson,"* (Puddin' Head Wilson), and several poems by various American and English poets, translated into Italian.

Meanwhile, the ladies had prepared supper, and we were summoned to the Morettis' large kitchen to partake of it. Nonno Donato went to the barn to fetch the Captain. Captain Joe didn't want to come at first. He said he didn't want to impose. At this point, nonno had to give him one of his paternal lectures. "If you didn't want to impose on us, you shouldn't have dropped in on us, like you did, and uninvited at that!" said he jokingly. "But, since you did," he continued, "like it or not, you have become a temporary member of this family. My son, Albert, is in the war, I don't know where he is or if he has a plate of food to eat tonight, so you are taking his place. And I'm the head of this family. I already checked, the coast is clear, so let's go before the minestrone gets cold. Forward, march!" Of course, nonno explained this to us later, probably adding a little ad-libbing of his own. But, there he was, Captain Joseph Campbell, dressed in rags that didn't match his spiffy and shiny appearance. Earlier that day, Joe Campbell had expressed a desire to take a bath. This required the service of several people. There was no running water in those days in small towns in Abruzzo, especially in farm areas. Every home in rural areas had a well, however. So, in the afternoon, some of the ladies present prepared a bath fit for a king. They heated the water, carried it upstairs to the famous bathtub, provided towels and a tiny piece of homemade soap. It was the only soap available at the moment. So, now Captain Joe was sitting in our midst clean and spiffy, still dressed in tattered old clothes that were a bit tight on him, but looking like he had been there all his life. Nonno and Mr. Moretti positioned him at the table in such a way that he could talk with both of them, in English, during the meal. The conversation was non-stop among them while the rest of us simply listened. They had more to say to each other in English than the rest of the table did in Italian.

Later that night we learned what had happened when we heard those two shots earlier. Tommaso Natale, a 28 year old man from Fossacesia had been shot in the back by a German soldier and left in the middle of a field to die. His death affected everyone, especially the children. I did not learn the full story until recently, when my friend, Professor Alberto Nicolucci, wrote an accurate account of Tommaso's tragedy. He says that Tommaso and his cousin Lino were on their way to Tommaso's girlfriend, not far from Mr. Moretti's place. They walked through the fields to avoid any possible confrontation with German soldiers. Earlier that week, he had been captured by the Nazis and forced to work digging ditches for mines. He had been held several days, but he planned to escape at the first opportunity. That day, while working, seeing that he was not being watched, he bolted, running for the better part of a mile. When he felt relatively safe, he walked normally, but headed as fast as he could eastward toward his girl's house. Somewhere along the way, he ran into his cousin Nicolino, Lino for short. They decided to stay together. When they reached the ravine that skirts the town behind the church of St. Donato, they decided to climb the hill opposite the church, feeling it would be safer. After a while, they reached the highway. All they had to do was cross it and they would reach their destination. There was a hedge that separated the roadway from the cultivated fields of Piano Favaro, so they walked alongside of it for a minute or two until they came to a break in it. Going through it, not seeing anyone coming from either direction, they crossed the highway. It was a fatal mistake. Just then, a lone German soldier on a bicycle rounded the curve coming from Fossacesia, headed for Rocca. There were no more than fifty yards between them. They stared at each other for a split second and, seeing the lone German on a bicycle, Tommaso must have assumed that he was after him, because he panicked and ran. His cousin panicked too, and dashed off in the opposite direction. That saved his life, because the German soldier got off his bicycle and shouted to Tommaso to stop. He did not heed the order, so the German simply shot him in the back. He then turned to Lino, but by this time the young man was pretty far away, so he missed him. The deed done, the Nazi got back on his bicycle, and calmly continued his journey toward Rocca San Giovanni. He made no attempt to see if the man he had just shot was dead or alive. He simply left him there to bleed to death.

Lino waited until he was sure that the German was gone, and then went looking for his wounded cousin. He found him under a pile of corn husks that had been left there by the owner of the property when things got too dangerous to work the fields in peace. He had tried to hide there, but he had received a single bullet in the right buttock, and had lost much blood. In a barely audible voice, he said to his cousin that he was cold. There was nothing the cousin could do, however. They were in the middle of a field; there was nothing there with which to provide a little cover. Nevertheless, he was wearing a light jacket, which he took off and put on Tommaso's shoulders. Having been hit in the back, in the act of running, the victim had fallen face first, and had remained in that position for a half hour. The cousin ran for help but he had to go all the way to Fossacesia. Before reaching town, however, he saw a German truck approaching, so he stopped it. He showed his hands dirty with his cousin's blood, he motioned to them that there was a man wounded that needed help. The Germans understood, and putting the truck in high gear, reached the wounded Tommaso in minutes. He was still alive but barely. They picked him up and rushed him to the Rocca San Giovanni field hospital, set up in the city hall building in the main piazza. But Tommaso died in the truck. Some German hospital personnel came out, and took the body into a back room. The cousin was told to wait in the lobby but he was not told that Tommaso had expired. He sat there a half hour, then an hour. Every few minutes he would ask the attendants what was happening, where was Tommaso, how was he doing. They still did not tell him that Tommaso was dead.

Suddenly, a man erupted into the room screaming and crying, "*Fije me; fije me!*" (My son, my son!). It was Tommaso's father, who, having been told that his son had been shot went out to look for him. He had no idea where to look, so he went to the German headquarters in Fossacesia and tried to make himself understood, but without success. Finally, a German soldier figured things out, and took him in a car to the hospital in Rocca, hoping that they had some news. Neither the soldier nor Tommaso's father had any idea he was indeed there, but dead by at least two hours. He was given the news just as he was entering the doors. Pandemonium ensued. Screaming to the top of his lungs, Tommaso's father hurled a few epithets at the Germans, who were sympathetic, but immovable. "*Somebody* shot your son. Nobody knows who. We think it was an accident," said an officer!

By six P.M. the relatives had gathered in the Piazza degli Eroi, Rocca San Giovanni's center square, but the body was not released until 7:30. The funeral began immediately. The priest of Rocca San Giovanni, late as it was, set up a hurried funeral cortège and the members of the immediate family followed to Rocca's cemetery, which was not too far away. To my knowledge, Tommaso's remains are still there. Local bureaucracy was such that it was a lot easier to bury him there and forget about it. To bring the body back to Fossacesia, even later in peaceful time, would have required fighting a barrage of bureaucratic red tape imposed by local ordinances and provincial decrees.

Before the sad cortège left the field hospital, Signor Natale demanded to know the name of the man who shot his son, but the commanding officer refused to reveal it, answering philosophically, in French, "*C'est la guerre!*" (That's war!) But the circumstances under which Tommaso died were nothing short of criminal. Tommaso was one of many Italians who lost their lives in their own backyard, as they tried to run from danger. Later, in America, I met some of his relatives who had migrated to Philadelphia in the 1920s. One of his cousins was Judge Sebastian Natale of the Court of Appeals in Harrisburg, Pa. I never met the distinguished jurist, because he lived in Harrisburg, so I never had the opportunity to tell him the story of his cousin's tragic death. The judge died in 2002.

We all felt very sad for Tommaso's death, of course, but we didn't have time to mourn too much because all of a sudden people started to run around frantically. "What's going on?" I asked Nonna Concetta. Before she could answer, the local midwife appeared at the door. I knew who she was, though I had no clue as to her exact function in a situation like this. I was old enough to know that babies did not come from cabbage patches, nor were they brought by the stork (I had never seen a stork fly around in my area, anyway, let alone one that carried a bundle hanging from its enormous beak containing a baby!), but I had no clue as to the details that characterized such events. We used to call the midwife, *la mammina* or *la mamminella* (literally, the little mother, or the very little mother). The older boys used to tell rowdy jokes about her. She was staying with a family not far from Signor Moretti's place, and it didn't take long for her to arrive to her job. The women, meanwhile, had made ready whatever was needed for the event. I knew that boiling water was one of the items needed to bring a child to the world, but I could not imagine for what purpose. The time had come for my aunt to deliver. My brother and I took advantage of the fact that our mother had become completely involved with Aunt Filomena's "birthing" event, so we had stayed up with the adults.

Mamma had prepared a number of items and had laid them neatly on a bed in an adjacent room, so that they would be handy at the moment they were needed. Things like pieces of cotton cloth, various containers of previously boiled water, a fine porcelain vessel together with a linen towel and a crucifix. What is that for? I inquired. I was egregiously ignored. Later I learned the reason and I was amazed at the things my mother thought of. The latter items were intended for a baptism. We were, after all, in dangerous conditions. Death lurked just behind the corner and could make an appearance at any moment; therefore the possibility was very real that the baby, conceived in love, might well be taken from us in hate by the warring parties. So mamma had planned to give her the "Baptism of Intention" immediately after birth.

I heard her first cry at 3:30 A.M. when she had received the slap on her tiny behind. I didn't even know at that age that we are all welcomed into this world in such a rough and disrespectful manner. I heard my mother shout, *"E' na citele!"* in Abruzzese dialect. Her glee was answered by a shout of joy from everyone present. So, it was a girl. That girl, my cousin Pina, is now a grandmother and lives in Toronto, Canada.

Almost immediately, I heard my mother's voice utter in clear, loud tones: *"Ego te baptizzo, Giuseppina, in nomine Patris, et Filio, et Spiritui Sancto. Amen."* It was the formula for the baptism of a child with which I, having been an altar boy, was very familiar. And I thought to myself, "What's she doing, baptizing her? She's not a priest!" but I dismissed the thought. I figured that she must have simply uttered the words much like a prayer, perhaps in thanksgiving to God for the healthy delivery. Many years would pass before I learned in theology classes at West Catholic High School, in Philadelphia that, under dire circumstances, anyone can baptize a baby, as long as it was done with water, and the proper words are pronounced.

A CASUAL ENCOUNTER

The only problem was that she was not sure if it was valid for all times. She thought that it was a temporary thing until things got back to normal and the baby could be taken to church and re-baptized by a priest.

The next day, *la mamminella* returned early in the morning to check on the mother and the baby. She reported that all had gone well and told the family that there was an emergency medical center staffed by German medical personnel who might have some blankets available. As a public official, she could issue a pass for up to three people to be received and taken care of. My mother and Aunt Rosaria, accompanied by Signora Moretti volunteered to go. They left at about eleven o'clock. Naturally, I was concerned. Whenever mamma ventured out under such perilous conditions of war, I always went into a deep feeling of anguish, which stayed with me until I saw her come home, wherever home happened to be at that particular moment.

Just as they arrived at the place where we had stopped three days before, and where we had seen the little blue sports car, the three women saw a group of people descending the narrow roadway on the other side of the creek. They noticed that they were pulling a two-wheeled wagon (well, actually, at this point the wagon was pulling them, since it was headed downward in a rather steep descent and several younger men were trying to apply the brakes on the vehicle in order to prevent it from rolling down and crashing over the hillside). There was a person lying on the wagon's bed, but the women were unable to tell if they were carrying a sick person or a dead body. The people were obviously civilians from town, so the women rushed to meet them. They met just as both groups reached the bottom of the valley at the creek bed. It was the Tozzi family led by Monsignor Tommaso. They were carrying his mother, Signora Maria Lopez-Tozzi who was dying. Signora Maria Lopez-Tozzi had been ill for some time and the war emergency did not make it any easier for her family to alleviate her suffering. They had been forced out of town like everybody else, and were now transporting her to a nearby home of a friend. After an effusion of greetings between mamma and the Tozzi's, she asked Monsignor if he could baptize a newborn baby. He said, "Of course, but not in church. Fossacesia is filled with Germans. No need to tempt fate and try to go there. Let's baptize her right here. Go home, get the baby, and I'll meet you here at noon, an hour from now." The here in question was by the side of a creek. "Remember," continued Monsignor Tozzi, "Jesus Himself was baptized in the River Jordan."

So the three women made their way back to the Moretti household. When they got there, they caused a bevy of activity. Everyone started to run here, there and everywhere: Give the baby a quick bath and put on a white baptismal dress (borrowed). Signora Moretti started to prepare a little party for afterward. Within an hour, they took the baby on her first journey. I got to accompany the party.

Monsignor Tozzi arrived almost two hours after we had reached the rendezvous point with the baby. He said that it took longer than anticipated to settle his mother in the household that was willing to give hospitality to a dying person. The old lady required special attention at the moment, so they had to set up a bed for her in a back room of the first floor as she could not be carried upstairs. That took some time. But as soon as his mother was settled in her temporary sickbed, Monsignor rushed back to the creek with the necessary paraphernalia for an infant baptism. He asked the necessary questions as to the parent's choice of a name, date and hour of birth and other relevant information. He approached the creek bed, and placing his left foot on the shore, rested his right foot on the first large rock in the water for balance. Then, reaching between his legs, he grabbed the back hem of his cassock (priests, in those days, were required to wear the *soutane* at all times, that is the cassock that represented their habit), pulled it toward the front and upward, and inserted it into the buttoned-down part of the garment which held it in place. He looked funny, but that gave him a degree of freedom of movement. Then, he summoned mamma and Aunt Rosaria to approach with the baby; he asked who was to be *"la cummare,"* the one who would stand for this baby in baptism—the godmother). He was told it was to be Aunt Rosaria, and the baby's name was to be Giuseppina. He had brought with him a water glass. He pronounced the prescribed prayers and rituals, he then bent over, scooped a little of the frigid water with the glass, and poured it over Pina's head, who let out a lusty yell as the cold water hit her warm, young head. She didn't like it one bit and let everybody know it. My mother quickly dried her tiny forehead, while Aunt Rosaria rocked her gently and spoke softly to her, trying to calm her down. Pina gave an indication even then that she was going to be a baby of good disposition; she quickly calmed down. As he was pouring the water on the baby's head, Monsignor said: "Too bad we don't have a camera. This would have made a very interesting historical photo." Unfortunately, no one had a camera, and even if someone did, there wouldn't have been any film available anyway. Film hadn't been available in stores for several years. So the event of my cousin's fluvial baptism remained a highly unusual event, but unrecorded except in our minds and hearts, and in these pages.

Giuseppina Sorgini (Pina), age 21, in Montreal

Quite a beauty for a baby born during the war and baptized in a creek!
We had no camera to photograph Pina with when she was baptized in a
creek like Christ, but I can provide a photo of her as a very pretty young
lady in Montreal. She is now a grandmother and lives in Toronto.

Franco Montefiore, Pina's husband

Franco is another gentleman of rare demeanor and character I had
the privilege of knowing in my lifetime. And handsome to boot!
Could Pina have chosen better? This photo was taken in Genoa, in
1957, while he was serving in the Italian Army as a communications
expert. He was 22. Both Pina and Franco now spend most of their
time babysitting for their grandchildren and loving it.

After a few minutes, Monsignor Tozzi proceeded to administer the salt of wisdom. Pina didn't like that either, but she limited the outer expression of her displeasure by making a series of grimaces and funny faces that left no doubt as to what she thought of salt administered outside of culinary requirements. Monsignor Tozzi then invited us all to pray for the baby that the Lord keep her and us all safe from the ravages of war, and that she would grow up in wisdom and faith. We prayed for the Monsignor's mother that God grant unto her a happy death.

Soon the baptism was over. The women covered the baby's head so that she might avoid a major cold, and after thanking the monsignor for his kindness, we said goodbye and began to climb the hill on our way "home." Pina had already fallen asleep again, giving us notice that she was not going to be a problem in those trying times.

CAN WE CELEBRATE MASS?

My mother said goodbye to Monsignor, said some words of comfort to him concerning his dying mother, and we started up the hill to bring the baby home. We were almost halfway up the path when we heard a voice calling out to mamma: "Mari, Mari!" Mamma turned. It was Miranda, the monsignor's other niece (and my teacher, Maria Fantini's sister), who motioned to her to come back down because Monsignor wanted to talk to her. Mamma told us to wait there while she hurried back down. While waiting for her, Aunt Rosaria, with the baby in her arms, sat upon an ancient Roman road marker whose Latin inscription, even while reflecting its millenarian existence, was clearly legible. The stone was white and she didn't know that it would soil her dress, but it did. When we returned home, we noticed the conspicuous white blotch on the back of her dress, and had quite a laugh over it. Under the circumstances a good laugh was a welcome diversion.

When they came back, mamma informed us that the monsignor asked her if she could set up a place for him to celebrate mass on All Saints Day, two days hence. "Of course," mamma had said. "Where could we have it?" Aunt Rosaria asked. Mamma answered, "In Signor Moretti's utility barn. We could easily accommodate fifty or more people there." That announcement filled us with excitement at the prospect of hearing mass for a change. It had been only three weeks since I had attended mass, but it felt more like three years. I always felt comfortable at mass under normal circumstances, but now, with the dangers of war ever present, the combination of faith, custom and fear, mostly fear, made the prospect of attending mass that much more appealing.

During our absence, which lasted about three hours, the Moretti's had set up a table with some quickly arranged goodies and some cooked wine. We had a little party. We even invited Captain Campbell. He particularly enjoyed the wine, of which he drank a sufficient amount to get drunk, but was able to function quite well in spite of it. Nonno Donato made a comment or two about the English liking their sherry.

After the party, the Captain decided to go back to his room at the "Royal Hotel," as he referred to the barn. He told everyone, in jest, that he had received the king's suite while His Majesty was relegated to a mere single room. He asked me and a couple of other kids in the group to accompany him. Nonno had decided to go to another nearby farm to see if he could purchase some food. Looking for food was a constant preoccupation for nonno as well as for mamma. Later, as a family man, I constantly marveled about the preoccupation they must have had. How would I have managed had I been in their shoes? There were quite a few of us who needed to be fed, and the Moretti's, while well stocked with basic necessities, could not be expected to feed a small army. So, nonno thought of going to the homes in the area where he knew there lived other "Americans" who might be willing to advance a sack of flour, some olive oil, perhaps some cheese or sausages to him. He left shortly after dinner and was gone the rest of the afternoon.

Meanwhile, back at the barn, Captain Joseph taught us boys a few games English kids play, and we tried to play some of them, but we quickly tired. Somehow, they "didn't fit us." While the other kids scattered to various places in or around the barn, I stayed with him and asked him to tell me what was the English equivalent for the Italian verb, *"dire."* I remember insisting that I wanted the infinitive. I don't think he knew what an infinitive was, but he tried to answer me, although he didn't understand me any more than I did him. He said something which I was not able to decipher. Since my grandfather was not there to tell me whether or not the Captain had understood me, I was not able to verify that the word he gave me was the correct one. When Nonno Donato did return, though, he said the Captain had indeed understood and had given me the correct word. It was "to say." The word "say," then, was the very first word I ever learned in the English language. Most people remember their first kiss, their first drink, or their first time behind the wheel of an automobile; I remember my first word I ever learned in the English language. It was October 31, 1943, and I owed it to the patience of Captain Joseph Campbell. All I wanted to do was learn how to say, "How do you say this or that?" in English.

Once I was assured that the word "say" was the correct one, I became a pest. "Captain, how do you say this thing in English?" "Captain, how do you say that?" And I would point to an object, then another, then another and another. I drove him nuts. But he stayed with me and I learned quite a few English words that day. With each word he taught, he asked me to repeat it so that my pronunciation would be correct. That was good, because I was not quite 12 years old, the perfect time to learn a language. With a native speaker coaching me early enough, I was able to acquire a fairly good pronunciation of the English language. English will forever be a foreign language to me, but at least my pronunciation of it is decent. At the same time the Captain gave me the English equivalent of the name of an object, he would ask me to give him the Italian word for it so that he could learn some Italian. This proved to be a problem, though, because I figured out then that the English language had but one word for the definite article. It was "the," invariable and applicable to all nouns under most circumstances. Italian, alas, has eight little words applicable to different words with a rather elaborate and complex system. It was too sophisticated for an English-speaking person to learn in that setting. But I tried to explain it to him, and he made a valiant attempt to understand.

While I was busy with the Captain, mamma joined us in the barn and began preparing for the mass that was to be celebrated the following day. The table the men used to play cards was selected as the altar. It was too low, in my mother's judgment, so she sent a bunch of us kids to locate some cement blocks. Signora Moretti said there were some behind the house. She located a wheelbarrow and we both went behind her house to get them. Angelo, her son, came with us and headed directly toward the stack indicated by his mom. He grabbed the very first block to place it in the wheelbarrow, when I had a moment of panic: he had exposed a nest of scorpions. While I panicked, horrified, he calmly brushed them off with his hands and proceeded to load eight blocks on the wheelbarrow. When we got back to the barn, I quickly told my mother about the scorpions and told her to be careful—there might be others. Sure enough, inside the hole of another block, there were three more of the repugnant creatures. One of the men killed them all. Angelo placed one block under each table leg as mamma stood in front of it to see if it was high enough. It wasn't. We needed two rows, so Angelo was right in bringing eight. Then mamma asked Signora Moretti for her best bedspread. She returned in ten minutes with a beautiful example of embroidery, the artisanship of our women at the time. Mamma draped it over the "altar," adjusting it to cover the front, thus hiding the cement blocks. Then she covered it all with a white sheet as prescribed by canon law for the sacrifice of the mass, and the altar was ready, complete with an enormous antique candelabra. But there were no candles in it.

After she finished with the altar, mamma's attention turned to other paraphernalia necessary for the celebration of mass. She had a rough time finding a pair of candles. She asked around, but nobody had any. Finally, one of the men opted to go to a chapel by the seashore which had opened only a few years before. He had worked in the project when the little church of Stella Maris was being built. His specialty was to decorate the inside walls, which was done entirely with sea shells. He knew his way around the chapel, so he borrowed Angelo's bicycle and went there, hoping to get inside the tiny chapel. When mamma began giving instructions on something, the teacher she never got to be always rose to the surface, and she could drive one to the nut house with her attention to the minutest details. She told him that if he ran into a German patrol, tell them your grandmother is dying, and we needed the candles for the last rites of the church.

Once inside the little chapel, he looked around, but found only three small candles of three different sizes, plus a larger Easter candle. He took the three little ones, figuring that they were better than none. He also thought of grabbing the crucifix, which my mother had not even thought about. It was a good thing, too, because the young man was indeed stopped by a German patrol on the way back. He told them that his father was dying and needed a priest and he was bringing home the necessary candles and crucifix for the last rites of the Church. They let him go. Without a doubt, that crucifix was a very powerful aid in persuading those "gentlemen," to let the kid go. It was dark when he finally made it home. Mamma opted not to go back to the barn, as there were no lights in it.

Before returning to the house, mamma had the men move the farm machinery around and had made a decent room in which she placed a number of chairs for the elderly people who were expected to attend the service. Later that evening, the ladies retired to the kitchen to bake a number of hosts to be consecrated and distributed as Holy Communion. I had never seen that done before, so I had to watch.

While putting the finishing touches to the altar, I had suggested that the floor be swept thoroughly, and before I had finished giving voice to my suggestion, I quickly regretted it as I saw someone come toward me with a large broom. I learned that day never to suggest anything that might be misinterpreted as an act of voluntarism. I wanted to add that, I didn't want to do it myself, being a kid, but the more I tried to formulate some kind of disclaimer, the more stupid it sounded. Besides, the woman who handed me the broom did so with one swift maneuver. She placed it firmly in my hands, and with the same movement she turned and walked away. I can still see the back of her powerful shoulders move away from me. I never saw her again in my life. I still don't know who she was. And, so, I had no choice but to begin the chore of sweeping and mopping the dustiest, dirtiest, most clogged piece of real estate I had ever seen. Mr. Moretti was planning to clean it up the same day we moved in with him, so while his machinery had been secured for the winter, the floor had not even been swept. What a mess! And it was up to me to clean it. Fortunately, some of the other young people volunteered to help, including my brother Filippo, who soon proved to be more of a hindrance than help. It took me over an hour to finish. Mamma praised me for the good job I had done in sweeping the floor. That was highly unusual. She never praised me for anything. The altar looked very much like an altar and except for the lack of statues, it did not look much different from our own Church of the Holy Rosary, which was rather simple in decorations. Signora Moretti did have a large picture of Our Lady of Pompei (Our Lady of the Holy Rosary), so she went to get it and mamma placed it at the center of the altar. One of the men built a wooden vertical backdrop to the altar, covered it with blue wrapping paper, and with a simple nail, our Lady of Pompei was designated as our protector for the mass and beyond. It was funny, but most of those men had only been to church on the days they received the sacraments, but now were all working in perfect synchronization for that mass. I knew, also, they would all be there!

By early afternoon, the place looked like a chapel. Meanwhile, the young man returned with the candles, so that was taken care of. "What about a little bell? Who has a bell?" I asked. Signor Moretti quickly sprang into action and returned a few minutes later with a large gadget made up of a series of leather straps riveted together in such a way that it would fit around the head and neck of a large animal—the famous cow-bells! Upon each piece of strap was attached two or more round bells. Signor Moretti shook it vigorously as he handed it to me. It made quite a racket, not unlike the sounds of Jingle Bells, which was unknown to me then, but which became the first sounds of Christmas in America that I became aware of after I arrived in the United States.

A woman came forth bearing an *oliera*, that is a salad set consisting of a pair of cruets, one clearly labeled, *olio*, the other, *aceto* (oil and vinegar). It was a wedding gift from *Cummara Teresina*, she said, whoever that was. It had never been put to use. They were perfect as the wine and water cruets normally used in church. And with that; we were all set. We were not sure if vestments were absolutely necessary, or a stole would have sufficed, given that this was a "*messa da campo*," as all the military people in the area called it, in other words, a field mass. Either way, Don Tommaso must have had a set with him. The last touch was provided by a woman who came into the hut carrying a small oriental rug, brand new. Her husband, who had served in the air force in Cirenaica, North Africa, had promised the colonel to whom he was an aide to bring it home for him. That colonel, unfortunately, was shot down over Egypt shortly afterward, and now she did not know what to do with it, since the colonel was from Sonzogno, near Milano. She theorized that, by using this carpet in the mass, we could dedicate this mass to him and he would receive spiritual benefit from it as well. Some of the men unrolled it and placed it at the foot of the altar. It was breathtakingly beautiful. Now we were really ready to go. Mamma had even thought of preparing a list of hymns. She was thinking of asking others for their input, but she quickly abandoned the idea. There would be the inevitable squabbles. Who wanted this, who wanted that—who needs it? So, when the time came, she simply intoned a hymn of HER choice, and everybody followed, calmly and peacefully. After the mass was over, everybody praised her for her musical choices.

Of course, there was no way of knowing if Monsignor Tozzi would show up. We knew his mother was dying, but he was still the pastor of his scattered flock, and anything could have happened given the circumstances. Other people might need his assistance more urgently. Everyone hoped for the best: mamma prayed for it, instead.

The evening was calm and cool, but not cold. We went to bed rather early, in imitation of the new baby who seemed to do nothing but sleep. The air must have been blowing toward the northeast because the clock bells could be heard loud and clear. It was nine fifteen, and all was well.

The much awaited battle of the Sangro River had not yet taken place, and no one knew when it would happen. As it turned out, a month would pass before it occurred, but we didn't know that. We didn't even know what an English footsoldier looked like, in case we happened to see one. Somebody said they were dressed all in white because they saw some of them with their binoculars, but I think they saw a regiment of Hindu soldiers who were members of the British 8th Army as well. Actually there were a few fearless young men from Fossacesia who moved from one side to the other without impunity. They had discovered that the British would pay cash for some homemade cold cuts and wheels of cheese, so some of the most daring young men began to make nightly trips across the Sangro River to an area nearest the beaches at Torino di Sangro, carrying double sided knapsacks loaded with goodies. Returning in the pre-dawn hours of the morning, the knapsack was loaded with foodstuffs or other goods on the way down, and with money on the way back.

ALL SAINTS DAY

We all got up early that day. Mamma, aunts, both grandmothers, and everyone else connected with my family got busy getting Pina ready for her first mass. She was given a bath, fed properly, and dressed up for the occasion with a dress that mamma and Aunt Rosaria had brought from the house two days before. It had been decided that since Aunt Filomena lived near San Giovanni, hence about a mile away from center of town, it would have been fairly secure to reach the house through the fields. They did so the afternoon of the 31st. They were only gone about three hours. They brought back diapers, undergarments for the baby and a couple of little blankets. They had hesitated before taking the baptismal dress, as Aunt Rosaria had questioned the need for such a dress under conditions of war. Mamma agreed with her that the situation hardly called for a nice dress, but one never knows, she added. It was not heavy, she had concluded, and so they added it to the wardrobe, making sure they brought plenty of items of more immediate necessity, such as diapers.

When we moved to the barn, they placed Pina in a cradle that had served as a bed for Angelo and her sister many years before, and she promptly went to sleep, as the rest of us waited patiently for Don Tommaso to arrive. The most nervous of the faithful was my mother, who checked everything several times. The best wine had been procured for the sacrifice. Since Signora Moretti did not possess a cutter with which to cut round hosts, the sheets of hosts the women had baked the day before were broken into small pieces and placed in a soup bowl. Mamma was not happy about that, but it was the best anyone could do in such dire limitations. And, so we waited for Monsignor's arrival.

Unfortunately, the priest never arrived. We learned later that his mother had again become violently ill during the night, and it had been necessary to transport her to the office of a doctor in Rocca San Giovanni. There was no way he could have possibly returned in time, especially since he would have had to walk; there was no subway. Everyone was disappointed, especially my mother, who was looking forward to hearing mass after nearly a month without doing so.

Just then, a woman approached and said that there was a military chaplain of the Alpine troops who had found temporary shelter in a house about a quarter mile down the road, near the shore. Following the September 8th armistice, his regiment had disbanded, and he was trying to make his way back to his Molise parish town. He was waiting for "a dark and stormy night," so that a boatman could take him, by rowboat, to the other side of the mouth of the Sangro River. The British had already reached the Sangro, so on its right bank was freedom. Angelo volunteered to go and fetch him. He said he could reach there in five minutes with his bicycle. He left immediately. About twenty minutes later, we saw Angelo's bicycle return, but Angelo was not on it. Instead, it was being ridden by a man of about forty years of age and nearly bald who looked like he could have played defensive tackle for the Philadelphia Eagles. It was the chaplain, the Reverend, and formerly Colonel Don Carlo Ambrosini. Angelo had given him his bike so that he could arrive as fast as possible, and Angelo came home on foot (Angelo was not particularly versed in religious activities anyway). Actually Angelo had arrived ahead of the priest, but he did not come to the barn. Instead, he went directly to his house to look for some writing material and some writing paper the chaplain had said he needed. The Moretti's being farmers, did not possess much in the way of writing utensils, but he remembered that years before his father had brought home from America many note pads and some advertising pencils. Angelo and the priest arrived at the barn at the same time. Angelo had a pad of writing paper with him. It had a fancy heading that I had never seen before. I looked at it, however, and immediately recognized it for what it was. It read Norristown Water Co. I knew that in America they had such things. Nonno told me that at Christmas time many firms gave away small complimentary objects as a way to advertise their products and say thank you to their customers for the previous year's business. Angelo handed it to the priest who was most grateful. It was over a week that he had been looking for some writing material.

Meanwhile, the priest introduced himself to my mother. He said his name was Don Carlo, originally from Piedmont, but now serving a community of Molisani in the Campobasso region. Participating at mass that morning were about forty people, including a group of men who had mysteriously materialized out of thin air, it seemed, because they were hiding in the woods to avoid being captured by the Germans, who were always looking for manpower to dig holes in the ground in which to bury land mines. Having heard that there was going to be a mass of All Saints Day celebrated in that barn, they all came out of their hiding places like nocturnal creatures of prey emerging from their lairs at dusk. That, too, was odd, because under normal circumstances, those guys would send their women to mass on any given Sunday, while they waited patiently at the nearest caffè, either engaging in a game of cards themselves, or watching as others played. I suppose that the adage about there not being any atheists in a foxhole applies to any and all war settings.

Even Captain Campbell came down from his perch atop the barn and was set to participate at mass even though he was not even Catholic. He had found a place right in the middle of a group of children and was having a great time making them say little ditties in English. His blond hair and his relatively clean-shaven face stood out while the rest of the men had long, dark, unkempt beards and hair. I was the altar boy. Don Carlo donned his vestments quickly, and facing the altar, he began: *"In nomine Patris, et Filio, et Spiritui Sancto. Introibo ad altare Dei."* I answered: *"Ad Deum qui laetificat juventutem meam."* Mass was under way.

At gospel time, I walked to the altar (there were no altar steps to climb) to pick up the missal in order to place it on the other side of the altar (the gospel side, as we used to call it). It was not the usually heavy, red *Messale Romano* that I was used to handling, but a very thin, equally red missal, titled *Messale Romano da campo* (Field Roman Missal). I picked it up easily, I turned around, and immediately froze in my tracks. To my horror, I spotted three German soldiers standing in the back of the congregation, near the front door of the barn. They had leaned their rifles against the wall, had removed their helmets, and very formally had placed them on their left forearm in the crook of their arms. After a while, I noticed they had placed them on a bale of hay nearby; I guess they got heavy. They seemed to be following the mass. I was horrified, not because of their presence there; after all, I had seen German soldiers before, armed and menacing sometimes, peaceful as lambs at other times. These guys looked more like the meek of Biblical fame, come to inherit the earth, albeit somewhat ahead of schedule. But, I was concerned for Joe Campbell's safety. Surely they will spot him. He had come down from his "lofty" place and was now sitting on the left side of the barn, playing with some children, totally unaware of the danger he was in. In the midst of all the Italian men whose unkempt black hair and beards revealed the severity of their conditions, Captain Joe's clean-shaven face and blond hair stood out like the nose on Cyrano's face. They had, no doubt, been looking for him for the past five days, ever since he had jumped from his disabled airplane, or at least so I thought. As I approached the altar on its gospel side, I leaned toward Don Carlo, and whispered to him about the German soldiers standing in the back. He asked me what they were doing. I told him that they seemed to be following the mass. So, he told me to keep my eyes on them and, if they did anything unusual to ring the bell—hard!

But, they didn't do anything strange. When the time came, two of them even received Holy Communion. It had become obvious to me by then that two of the soldiers were Catholic; the third probably was not, but he stood courteously behind them, politely observing without participating. When mass was over, they saluted very formally, and walked out of the barn. It was not possible that they did not spot Captain Campbell, nor that they might have thought he was one of our men. More likely, they heeded the strong suggestion by Don Carlo who, in a brief but strong and impassionate homily, urged everyone, "to heed the counsel of your conscience before doing anything that may bring pain and suffering to a fellow human being." He had spoken in Italian, but I believe they got the message.

Before mass began, my mother had told Don Carlo that there was a British pilot with us and that we should pray for his safety at mass. After mass, Nonno Donato introduced the captain to the priest. Much to everyone's delight, we learned that the chaplain spoke English fairly well. At least they could communicate with each other, even if in brief, curt phrases, accompanied by lots of gestures. Communication, even in gestures, could have been essential to survival.

With that revelation, the priest suggested to Captain Campbell that he go back with him to the home where he was staying, not far from the Moretti place, instead of staying where the Germans could capture him. Judging by the behavior of those German soldiers who had shared the Eucharistic Presence with us, I was certain that they would not betray us, and come back for the Captain, but one never knew. Prudence, as they say, is often the better part of valor. Don Carlo also suggested that, when the time arrived, they'd both go on the boat to the British side, and the pilot could rejoin his outfit. But they had to wait for a stormy night. On clear, moonlit nights the Germans ran gunboats up and down the shore line outfitted with powerful spotlights. There were two spotlights on shore, as well, that constantly swept the beach waters. It would be suicidal to attempt to put a rowboat on the water under such circumstances. On rainy nights, the sea swelled up and the gunboats did not run, nor were the spotlights on the shore activated. Still, it was a gamble; but in those days, those who didn't gamble often did not survive. After the group of worshippers broke up, Mr. Moretti invited everyone of us to his dining room. Mrs. Moretti had prepared a scrumptious lunch made of fried chicken, rapini (an Italian favorite green, bitter as aloe and vera combined, but to a real Italian, the bitterer the better-*er!*), and cheese. We all enjoyed it, including the chaplain and Joe Campbell. Then captain Campbell thanked Mr. and Mrs. Moretti for their hospitality, my grandfather and my mother for their courage and "heroism," as he put, he praised Mr. Moretti for his prowess as a wine maker, and said good bye to every one. He even kissed the baby. Don Carlo approached the baby, blessed her with holy water, and prayed over her that the rest of her life be rooted in peace, not in war. Then Captain Joe came to me, shook my hand, and encouraged me to stay with my study of the English language, but with a strange suggestion. Said he, "Don't try too hard in pronouncing the words because you tend to distort them. Be more natural. Don't make faces when you pronounce a word. Don't overdo it." It would take me years to understand exactly what he meant by that. Then they both left after having a bunch of us kids scout all around to see if there were any Germans in the area. When we gave the all clear, they started down the road to the other house. They would have about a fifteen minute walk.

The Snoopean "dark and stormy night" arrived two days later, on November 3rd. In the afternoon, Nonno Donato and Signor Moretti sent Angelo in a driving rain to the Chaplain to tell them they would accompany the pair to the beach area at about 5:00 P.M. Signor Moretti took his dog along, as well. They had intended to make him walk ahead of the group. They said that animals could sense the presence of mines in the soil and walk around them. In case he did step on a mine, the pooch would be killed first. Fortunately, they didn't bother to tell the dog what his job was! "He didn't ask us," said Nonno Donato in his usual dry wit, "so we didn't tell him!"

When the men returned home that night, they were soaked to the bones, as was the dog. They reported a quiet mission without any encounters with the dreaded German coastal guards. Apparently the chaplain and the Captain made it all the way to the British side, because I heard no more about them. An old proverb has it that "bad news travels fast." If they had been captured, the news would have spread like wildfire. Many years later, I spoke with several townspeople who now live in Canada. They, too, were on that boat for various reasons, and they remembered the British officer and a priest traveling to reach the British sector.

In the years that followed, I heard of a priest from Piedmont named Don Carlo who was serving in a town of the Molise Region called Guglionesi, where I had some friends. By the time I managed to visit that town, however, their Don Carlo had died, so I was never able to confirm his identity as that of the chaplain who said mass for us on All Saints Day, 1943. As for Joe Campbell, in 1946, Nonno Donato received a Christmas card from England, from a certain Reginald Campbell, Joe's father, who thanked him for saving his son from being captured by the Germans. He informed him that the Captain did manage to rejoin his outfit in 1943, but was killed later in France, during the Normandy invasion. I have always cherished his memory.

THE GERMANS DO RETURN

The German soldiers did not return to our manor after the mass, so mamma realized that they were not looking for a downed pilot at all. Still, we were certain that the three German soldiers who participated in the mass were noble and humane, as they ignored the blond young man who sat on the floor among the young people and who looked very British, indeed. However, they did return the next day for other reasons.

It was about four in the afternoon. The rain had stopped, but it had brought about a dramatic change in the weather. The storm clouds that had invaded the region had brought with them much cooler air. Mamma took sweaters out of the bundle of clothes she had quickly gathered when we left our home on October 12. She gave me a red sweater to put on, and a blue one to my brother. They were homemade, and they itched. I didn't want to put it on, but it was pretty cool, and my mother gave me an ultimatum—wear it or else! So, reluctantly I put it on, scratching and complaining, complaining and scratching. After a few hours, though, I had gotten used to it and it didn't itch any more. It even felt good.

The other detail I remember about that day was that mamma gave us our good shoes to wear. Prior to that day, we were still wearing a pair of summer sandals that looked like they had been unearthed in an archaeological excavation. She also gave us each a pair of homemade black cotton socks that reached above our knees. They were not exactly in line with the latest fashion, to be sure, but under those circumstances, they felt good against the first chill of fall. With that came that sense of melancholic coziness that accompanies the first chill in the air, harbinger of the approaching winter cold. The women had lit the fire in the fireplace in anticipation of preparing food for supper. It felt good to sit around the gigantic fireplace, typical of farm households. A few chickens were still scratching around the yard, and there was plenty of broccoli and cabbage left. Soon, we would eat.

Suddenly, we heard the hoofs of several horses approaching the manor. It sounded like an entire cavalry regiment was coming down the street that led to the sea, about 100 yards north of the house. Cautiously, from behind some bushes, I looked to see what was going on. I was surprised when I realized there were only three black horses, being ridden by three die-hard Fascist militiamen wearing their typical black shirts that seemed to match the color of the horses. Five German soldiers walked alongside of them. To my surprise, when they reached the path that passed in front of our house, they turned onto it. Oh, oh! I thought. This was unusual. Obviously these guys wanted something. When they reached the entrance to Signor Moretti's homestead, the large gate was wide open, but they didn't come inside; they stopped in front of it for a few minutes while they talked among themselves. Then, three of the Germans came inside. One was an officer who motioned to Angelo to approach. As he did, the officer said something to him upon which the boy turned and, on the run, went behind the house to call his father.

Meanwhile, an insignificant incident took place that is still vividly etched in my memory: one of the soldiers saw me, and he walked over. I immediately recognized him as one of the three who had been at mass the day before. As he approached me, Nonna Minguccia instinctively called me to her side, so as to protect me, just in case. When he reached us, he said something in German, which I didn't understand. He then tried to say it in Italian, and I clearly understood *"la messa."* That's when I got the message: he was complimenting me for serving mass. I smiled, nodded, and offered a barely audible *grazie* (thank you). My grandmother was working on a basket of red peppers. She was making a garland of them in order to hang them to dry in the sunlight. The peppers were actually sweet, but the German didn't know that. She gestured to him if he wanted some. He laughed, and contorted his face as he declined her offer.

At the same instant the soldier was contorting his face at the thought of eating hot peppers, there was a scream, a blood curdling shriek that froze everybody in his tracks: it was young Angelo who screamed, lurching forward as he did so. From under the porch where he had been standing to watch what was happening, he ran to his father placing himself between him and the raised muzzle of an automatic rifle. No one heard what that officer had said to Signor Moretti, nor what his answer had been that triggered the German's rage, but we came within a whisker from witnessing a real tragedy. The soldier who was with me and my grandmother quickly ran to his commanding officer, placed his hand gently on the weapon, lowered it and talked to him as he led him outside the gate. This was one more proof that there were many good German soldiers, and there were some great ones, as well! This one was among the great ones. At the same time, Signora Moretti dashed out of the house in a panic, and approached her husband and the German officer trying to find out what the problem was. Angelo, meanwhile, was inconsolable. He had collapsed on the dirt floor of the yard and was sobbing and contorting his body on the ground. I thought he was having an epileptic seizure. Some of the women tended to him and tried to calm him down. In a few minutes, order was restored, and our Catholic friend returned inside the yard. He explained in halting Italian that they were looking for a couple of chickens and some "cooked wine," in order to celebrate their colonel's anniversary. I remember that there was a little confusion as to what they had requested: cooked or cooking wine? They assumed it was the cooked variety, the sherry-like aperitif wine typical of our area. Nor had anyone understood if it was a wedding anniversary, a birthday, or some other occasion they wanted to celebrate. All we understood was that, for them, it was a big event, whatever it was. Mamma also commented that they, too, were capable of an act of sentimentality when they wanted to be sentimental.

At this point, everyone had found that ribbon of humanity which, linking us together, one by one, joins us to our God, the Creator of us all. Signora Moretti had risen above the human instinct displayed by her husband to protect his own, and was able to defuse a potentially tragic situation. Even the arrogance of the officer had cooled down, helped by his subordinates' calmer personalities. She went to a soldier who seemed to speak Italian fairly well, and began to speak with him. The soldiers had regrouped outside the gate. When she understood what it was that they wanted, I heard her exclaim in dialect: *"E pi tante poche!"* (All that for so little?). So she told the one soldier who spoke Italian to return the following day at four in the afternoon. She asked how many needed to be fed, and some other details, and she would have the dinner cooked and ready for the party. And the little platoon left as peacefully as they had arrived. The incident that had brought everyone to the brink of disaster had lasted no more than five minutes, and it was destined to remain parenthetical and forgotten (but, not really—some things just cannot be forgotten.).

As soon as the Germans left, the women got together and planned to cook a classical Italian dinner, Abruzzese style, to feed twelve people. Each of the women volunteered her specialty. Of course, they were limited by the availability of the ingredients. But, they managed. Unbeknown to me then, Signora Moretti had asked them for some salt because we had run out. They said yes, and one of the horsemen spurred his horse and he took off like Roy Rogers on Trigger. He returned alone, ten minutes after his comrades had departed, and brought back a fairly large bag of raw, unrefined salt. It was then that my grandmother Minguccia asked Signora Moretti if she could have some of it. Signora Moretti gave her quite a bit. Nonna placed it in a handkerchief, knotted in a special way, and for the duration of the *"sfullamente,"* she kept it on her person and would not have shared it with anyone, not even the pope had she met him walking around the chasms of the Abruzzese topography, highly unlikely as that may have been.

The next day, things in the Moretti household actually got comical, because once the women started to prepare the food for the famous party, they got so much into it one would have thought it was they who were celebrating the famous anniversary. They killed four large chickens (I never did figure out where she had them hidden!), they roasted them with potatoes and peas, then they prepared some *broccoletti di rape* (rapini, or *rabbi's*, in American parlance), and salads of various kinds, and other things. There was no bread, so my Aunt Rosaria volunteered to remedy that situation by baking some. She was the expert in that field. They even prepared two winter melons, much to Signor Moretti's chagrin. "But, they're my seed melons," he lamented. He even pulled from under a staircase a dusty jug containing one gallon of a special cooked wine that was, in the man's opinion, "at least ten years old." He parted with it with considerable sorrow. "Oh, well," he finally said, "It could have been worse." Indeed, he could have been dead instead! No doubt he could still see the muzzle of the automatic rifle pointed at his face, so he let go of the wine. Later, he was heard saying that he wished he had had a chance to taste it, at least. "Ten years old! Imagine!" said he, plaintively.

Punctually at four the next day, two German soldiers returned with a truck. Everything was ready. They loaded the food and the wine on the truck, they thanked everyone profusely, left a gift for the lady of the house (I never learned what it was, but whatever it was, it was subtracted from one of the local merchants' inventory, no doubt), and left. We never heard any more about the colonel, his anniversary, and the wine, which the owner never got to taste. Even in a hostile environment, that sense of human solidarity emerges under the right circumstances. The war, like a nameless hurricane, passed over us in a few weeks, and when the people saw each other again they rejoiced that God had spared them. When things became normal again, we often visited with the Morettis and others who had given us hospitality. My mother made several dresses for her: all "Sorgini originals." Years later, the ladies who prepared the anniversary dinner still spoke of nothing else, while Signor Moretti was still bemoaning his ten-year-old sherry wine. "I never got to taste it, even!" was his constant lament.

I often think about the psychological significance of that story. I came to the conclusion that the moment those soldiers mentioned the word "anniversary," they restored the human element to their faces, something the war had removed from their visages. The ladies responded in kind, and the special dinner was their way of saying to them, "See? We knew you guys were human, after all. Now act as such!" Unfortunately, war has a way of bringing out the worst in man, and it's almost impossible to avoid its contagious allure.

Later that evening my mother, discussing the situation at the table, mentioned the three German soldiers who had attended mass two days before. It must have been hell for those young men who were Christian—Catholic, Lutheran, or whatever else—having to execute orders that were contrary to the dictates of their consciences.

A few years ago, my brother Filippo, who now resides in Virginia, was visiting with me. While having dinner one evening, the conversation went to those days, as it often does, and so I asked him if he remembered anything about that particular incident. I was shocked, and pleased, when I heard him answer: "Yes, I remember horses!" "Yes!!!!"

NOVEMBER 4ᵀᴴ, A DAY OF TRUCE, PERHAPS?

Except for that incident, November 3rd was a rather quiet day. I no longer had Captain Campbell to pester with questions about the English language, so I turned my attention to Signor Moretti's silkworms, which he raised by the hundreds. They only ate mulberry leaves, and most of the leaves on the three mulberries on his property were gone, but I helped him gather the few that were left. An occasional British fighter plane flew overhead without bothering us.

Early on the morning of November 4th, the Germans came again, this time bearing evacuation orders. These were not the same who celebrated the famous anniversary, but soldiers of a different outfit. Their job was to evacuate the area systematically and swiftly, one rural area at a time. We had to be out of there by noon. The order to evacuate the zone had come all the way from Germany, "directly from the Fuehrer," so a young soldier told us. I considered that bit of information was intended to impress us. The soldier who had given us that little morsel of joy must have been disappointed that none of us moved a facial muscle in glee. They said that the battle of the Sangro River was imminent, and they were preparing the battle grounds for the approaching conflict. He said that it loomed as an especially bloody one. Whoever remained in this area would be *kaput!*, he added.

By nine o'clock, we were ready to depart. Nonno said that if we could reach the house of Pietro Di Nenno, another of his American friends, we would probably find accommodations there. We thanked the Morettis for their hospitality, and within a few minutes, we were on our way. Nonno Donato and I led the parade of refugees. Mamma followed carrying the baby, with Aunt Rosaria trailing behind her, ready and eager to take the baby the moment she gave the least sign of tiring. Aunt Filomena came next, happy to allow others to carry the newborn. The two grandmothers, several other aunts, cousins and friends brought up the end of the line. Filippo and a couple of other boys snaked in and out of the group, completely oblivious of any possible problem. They were discussing military strategy, no less! They always referred to bombs, especially those dropped from airplanes, as *"piselli"* (peas). That was standard jargon among boys in those days. In our active imaginations, we fought all the battles of the world, from swashbuckling sword fights, to naval battles, to air-to-air combat. We won them all. Except that now we were about to experience the real thing!

We walked up to the gravel road that led to the sea, but we turned left and headed west instead of turning east toward the shore area, as specified by the Germans. *"Mare,"* they kept saying, or *"stazione."* In other words, they wanted us to go toward the sea, where the train station was. We all made believe we didn't understand. After telling us where to go, however, they failed to leave armed guards to make sure we followed orders, so we didn't.

Turning onto the gravel road, we walked westward for about a half mile until we came to a narrow path on our right that led north. We took it and proceeded a short way to just before the path formed a T with another east-west gravel road. Signor Di Nenno lived right there on the corner property to our right. Nonno said that he owned all the land from his house to the sea, a piece of property of considerable size, characterized by hills and valleys. His home was a single story house of unusual architecture. Nonno hastily entered the gate at the front lawn. The door was wide open, as it was often the case with houses in rural areas, but there was no one inside. Nonno began to call out, in English: "Hey, Pete! Pete! Peeete!"

Unfortunately, we were not the only ones to arrive at this destination. Almost at the same time, the Germans arrived there, too. They parked a military truck on the street between Pete's house and a cluster of homes on the other side of the gravel road that belonged to a family nicknamed *Yerimunni.* Four soldiers began to go from house to house, throwing everybody out as they did. When we saw that, my mother asked us to follow her past Signor Di Nenno's garden and around the building so we could talk about the new turn of events without being seen.

Meanwhile, Pete and his wife answered the call from a distance behind the house, and he said something to Nonno, who again answered him in

English. I figured that he must have told to him to hurry up, because both Pete and his wife immediately picked up the pace. They reached the house in a couple of minutes, and asked everybody to come inside. By now, we were absolutely scared, especially since we could hear those four Germans barking orders in their guttural language. So we crouched to the floor, aware that it was a matter of time before they would come to us. There was nowhere to hide. Our group consisted of more than twenty people. My Aunt Filomena went to a bedroom to nurse the baby, but mamma told her to do it right there in the kitchen, instead, thus using the baby as a sort of shield. Surely, after seeing an infant, those Huns would not bother us.

Alas, we were wrong. After clearing the houses across the street, they began to amass people on the lawns and on the street, counting them and giving orders as they went. Then they came to us. Pete's little house was the first of three on the south side of the street. As we waited for events to develop, we could mark their progress by the sound of the heavy boots hitting the flagstones of the pathway from the gates to the door, typical of German soldiers as they trampled their way to the front door. Pete had designed and built that pathway. Nonno had told me when we walked on it the first time that the decorative garden paths had been Pete's specialty in America. He was a real artist, and that's how he made his money. I'm sure that when the first German soldier saw the intricate design on that brick walk, he wasn't impressed. It is difficult to have sentimental feelings in your heart when you are intent upon doing harm to other people. Art and malice do not mix very well.

Upon hearing the squeak of Pete's gate as it was opened, I felt a jolt in my heart like the dead battery of an automobile getting a jump-start. We could tell that two of them were proceeding toward the front door, thump-thumping their way up the walk in rhythm with the pounding of my heart. The door being wide open, they walked inside unceremoniously, without saying a word. They looked like our mountain, the Majella range of the Apennines, which was clearly visible from Pete's windows, resplendent in the glorious autumnal morning in Abruzzo. They barked some orders in German, which nobody understood, as they motioned for everybody to go outside. Some of the people scurried out immediately. At this point a funny thing happened: Pete said something to my grandfather in English. Nonno Donato answered with a peremptory: *"Statte zitte!"* (shut up!). The one thing we didn't want them to know was that we were Americans. Fortunately, the Germans failed to pick up on the linguistic difference between English and Italian. The shorter of the two soldiers told Pete, in gestures more than words, to go outside, and get a pick and a shovel. There was no doubt as to the meaning of what he said, since his gestures were more than eloquent. Pete was to get tools for digging, and go with them.

Then one of them made a mistake: he turned to my sixty-seven-year-old grandfather and grabbed him by his arm, roughly yelling something at him. Suddenly, out of the clear, a shrill cry lacerated the air: it was my mother, who had screamed as she fainted. She dropped heavily onto the hard floor, although at five-foot-two she didn't have much of a drop. She didn't hit her head, however. In other words she fell being aware as to where to place her head. Naturally, I ran to her, as did others in the room, and I noticed that she was in some sort of convulsive state. Now I was really scared. Signora Di Nenno was coming out of the dining room with some vinegar to try to "revive" her. Pete, meanwhile, unnoticed by the two Germans, had gone out the back door, taking advantage of the distraction of the moment, and disappeared. I never saw him again—ever. He simply vanished into thin air. Mamma's dramatic moment had its desired effect on the two Germans, too. Intimidated by the turn of events, they left the house in a hurry, forgetting Pete, forgetting Nonno Donato and forgetting everybody else. The entire episode didn't last more than five minutes. I often think about it. Clearly etched in my mind is my mother's round face dominated by two of the biggest anthracite eyes I have ever seen. At a distance of well over a half a century I still see a subtle, almost imperceptible line of amusement on the sides of her mouth, something faintly reminiscent of Mona Lisa's smile. Could it be that she had put on the Oscar-winning performance of her life? Later, she swore that at that moment all her strength left her. She used to say, in Abruzzese dialect: *"Mi s'è stucche la nirvature,* (my nerves snapped). But, I wonder! The moment the two Germans left, she seemed to recover her strength fast and miraculously. I wouldn't have put it past her to put on a dramatic act, despite her assertions to the contrary. And she was rather convincing, too.

After that, another surprise awaited us. Within a few minutes, another German came into the house. He was a man of a much gentler sort, even polite as he invited, rather than ordered, everybody to go outside. So we filed out one at a time. To my surprise, there was another German out there rounding up the people, but the two "mountains" were gone. We were told to relax and wait. By this time it was around eleven o'clock in the morning and the Germans decided to "serve lunch." They gave everybody a packet containing two large crackers. It was the second time I had tasted those crackers. The first time was when we were going from the Sangro Valley to the Piano Favaro and got caught in front of a German camp at the southern entrance into Fossacesia, just as three Allied planes attacked it. The crackers, described as black by the townsfolk, were of a dark gray color, and were probably made of whole wheat and barley and some other grain. They didn't taste bad, actually. It was just that Italians were not used to seeing anything edible that was quite that color. But we ate them and mamma even urged us to accept a second "helping," if we could. By then, we were beginning to feel the pangs of hunger, which would intensify before long. Food had become quite scarce.

And so we waited, and waited and waited. For the next two hours we milled about in the area as the Germans kept chasing people out of their homes. The two Germans in charge of our group were rather docile and they began to chat with us in labored, but understandable Italian. The first thing they did was to reassure us that on this day there would not be any air raids by the Allied or the German Air Forces. As it turned out, they were correct. Not one plane was seen flying in any direction throughout the day. German planes were rare, anyway, but Spitfires and American P-38s were all over the place at any given moment. The weather was absolutely beautiful, the sky sparkled and visibility was unlimited, so meteorological conditions were not the reason for this lack of air activity. However, being the fourth day of November, Armistice Day in Italy and in the countries allied in the Great War, it was possible that a truce had been negotiated between the warring parties. Germany was the losing nation in that war, which means they may not have celebrated the signing of the armistice, as a nation, but perhaps they agreed to a temporary cease fire for that day, just to catch their breaths.

The other thing the Germans made quite clear to us was that we were to head for points north. To me, that meant that we would be pushed toward the towns of San Vito, Ortona, or Tollo, no more than ten, fifteen miles north of Fossacesia. But I think what they had in mind was Bologna, Pavia, Milano or Torino, far north on the Italian peninsula. That's what we were waiting for: trucks to take us there. Entire families from towns northwest of the Gustav Line were moved indeed to the far north with trucks, trains, and other means. Some of them didn't get back to their towns before 1948 or even 1950. Divine Providence must have been watching over us, however, for the trucks never arrived.

Soon we became restless. Milling around between the gravel street and the threshing plazas of the two manors in the area, the younger members of the group were becoming a little hard to handle. By one o' clock, there were a couple hundred people assembled there, representing inhabitants of the area and refugees to whom they had given hospitality. The two soldiers were armed with the usual automatic rifle. They would have had no problem maintaining order if they wanted to use those weapons, or at least threaten us with them. But, those two were much more docile than the average German. Soon the crowd, being a crowd, began to act like a crowd, and the two were obviously beginning to lose control of the situation. So around 1:30 P.M., they gave orders to start walking west on the gravel road toward the asphalted road, the national Route 16. By following the itinerary ordered, if the trucks were to come, we would certainly meet them along the way. The order to move defused a potential riot. The head of each family began regrouping their families and counting heads. We were the first ones to depart, because, being already in "traveling mode" since morning, we simply kept going, having no idea where we were headed. The only one that needed tending was seven-day-old Pina. She had to be changed and washed and fed on a regular basis. We were ordered to make single files along both borders of the road, in order to permit the movement of military vehicles in the center of the road. Nothing passed, however. The so-called road was barely six feet wide.

After we had walked a few hundred yards, I looked back and noticed that the two Germans were walking along with the group. They walked in the middle of the road, one toward the front, slightly behind us, the other at the very end of the two lines of people, automatic rifle at the ready. We reached the highway in about ten minutes. Just as we did so, we saw another group approach the highway coming from the opposite side, walking along the spur of what was the continuation of the gravel road we were on. We were coming from the sea side, they came from the mountain side. Our armed escort gave orders to turn right toward the town of Rocca while the two Germans who escorted the other group told them to turn left. Each group was told to consolidate the two columns into one and form two new single files and to proceed toward Rocca San Giovanni on both sides of the highway. With this, the number of people swelled to an estimated three hundred. My mother made some comments as to where in the world were they taking us, but no one could venture an answer. The steeple of the only church of Rocca San Giovanni loomed in front of us plain and tall, though it was separated from us by a deep and fairly wide ravine. This was familiar to us. We didn't panic. Not yet. Nobody had eaten anything except for the crackers the Germans had given us, but nobody complained, not even the children.

Soon we reached the edge of the mini-canyon that separated us from Rocca. The bell tower of the church of Saint Matthew appeared so close that that we could see its bell housing very well. Perched in it like a vulture awaiting the death of its prey, was a German sentry, a pair of powerful binoculars firmly planted upon his face and trained south, looking at Fossacesia and at the Sangro River, several kilometers to the south. From that height, he had a clear view of the entire Sangro Valley. He was probably monitoring the movements of the first units of the British 8th Army, as they finally arrived at the natural barrier of the Sangro River. All bridges had been blown up, so they would have to pause and study the best way they could devise in order to cross the river with all those tanks and heavy cannons.

As we came up to the spot where we had to turn, we stopped for a few minutes. My family was at the head of the parade and mamma might even have been contemplating some sort of evasive move. Other people, catching up to us, stopped as well. Within a few minutes, however, we heard heavy boots double timing it toward us. The German soldier from the rear of the column must have sensed something, so he ran to his comrade and both came up to us urging us to keep moving, their rifles raised threateningly. They told us to turn left and follow the road as it descended toward the creek. We had no choice but to continue on our way, walking downhill toward the little bridge that carried Route 16 over the creek. We crossed over it and began to climb up toward the first houses of the town of Rocca San Giovanni.

Beginning at Fossacesia, north to the city of Ortona, a span of about 14-15 miles, there was a series of deep ravines, the result of water run-offs coming down from the Apennine Mountains that rise to a height of over 9,000 feet, scarcely thirty miles away. In the arc of several million years, each rivulet found its way to the Adriatic Sea, eroding the terrain little by little and creating the ravines. Between Fossacesia and Rocca, perhaps less than a mile from each other, there were two such small canyons. Early in the twentieth century, with the advent of the automobile, it became necessary to build a road that would permit cars to cover the entire peninsula. Those ravines presented quite a challenge to the civil engineers of the time, who decided to carve the road on the side of the cliffs with a gradual incline until it reached the water level of the creek. There they built a small, narrow bridge that would carry the road over the creek, and then they dug out the road on the opposite ridge, the same way. Under normal circumstances, pedestrians who went to or from Rocca San Giovanni would take a shortcut at this point, instead of going all the way to the bridge. The Germans, not being familiar with the area, blocked us from taking the shortcut, and so we had to walk the entire length of the road to the creek bed. After crossing over the bridge, we began to climb up again toward the little town of Rocca. Upon reaching the piazza, we sort of sneaked by the church, scarcely daring to breathe, lest we awoke the sleeping vulture. The irony of it all did not escape me, either: the purpose of a bell tower was to call the faithful to prayer, not to be used as a commodity for waging war.

We entered Rocca's south entrance. The church blocks the road at that point, so we turned left and entered the piazza. Almost immediately, however, the road turned left again toward its western exit. Mamma thought that the Nazis were taking us to Rocca San Giovanni, but that was not the case. We had walked for well over an hour, and we were tired, but more importantly, we were beginning to worry. Where were we going? The two German soldiers were still with us and they gave no sign that might have indicated that we were close to our destination. Actually, there was no destination. We were just moving like a bunch of sheep without a plan as to where we were going and why.

As we entered the piazza, I was shocked to see it pullulating with German troops. Hanging from the balcony of Rocca's Town Hall was a giant red flag with a white circle in the middle upon which was the well known swastika, like a giant black widow spider. It intimidated all it surveyed. This was the German Army's official headquarters. It was the central command from which the German high officers ran their war operations. Next to it was another flag, much less intimidating, which showed a red cross over a white field: the symbol of the International Red Cross. This was the hospital where Tommaso Natale had died. There was a bar next to Town Hall, and, in typical Italian fashion, a few German soldiers sat at outside tables. The weather had warmed up since the day before, so they were sitting at the sidewalk tables, as is the custom at Italian bars, drinking. There were quite a few soldiers sitting at those tables drinking something that didn't appear to be espresso coffee, which would have been the drink of choice for Italians at that hour. It was probably beer. I had heard of beer, but I had never seen any one drinking it up to that point in my life, so I didn't know if you drank in a cup, or a glass, or what. I wondered if Tommaso Natale's killer was among them.

Rocca San Giovanni is a small town of barely 3,000 souls. It sits between two deep ravines so that it has no north end, but does have a west and an east end, both of which extend for about a quarter mile on either side of the piazza. At its western end, on the road to Lanciano, was the town's cemetery, with tall cypress trees typical of Italian burial grounds, that gives its interior a lugubrious, scary atmosphere. We passed in front of it just as it was beginning to get dark. Nonno asked the German escort where they were taking us. There was no answer; just a gesture to keep walking. Darkness was decidedly getting more pronounced, and the people were becoming more restless with each passing minute. The children especially, being cold, hungry, and tired, became more difficult to pacify, except for Pina, who kept on sleeping.

A few hundred yards beyond the cemetery's western wall, the road splits, forming a Y. Its left arm proceeded due west and headed for the city of Lanciano, six miles away. The other headed northwest toward the town of San Vito. The ravine that passes north of Rocca is not very deep at this point, though it becomes quite deep by the time it reaches the town itself. Positioned at the crux of the Y was one of our "friendly" Germans blocking the way toward Lanciano, making sure we took the right branch of the road. As mamma passed by him, she gestured impatiently, asking without words, "Where are we going?" He smiled and gestured back, "Just keep walking!" Meanwhile, the darkness was closing in on us rather fast.

In addition to the incipient darkness, nobody had eaten anything since noon, when the two good Germans had given us two crackers. It was at that moment I was convinced that my brother Filippo would go a lot further in this life than I: he had gone for a second helping and had received another packet. I wished I had done the same. I was hungry! But he gave me one of his, and that calmed the growling of my stomach for a while.

We walked a little more. I was glad that after we passed the cemetery the road was downhill! That section of road was rather short, though, because the little bridge that took it across the creek came upon us almost immediately. We crossed the bridge, and with a distinct eagerness to get this trip over with, we assaulted the hill, perhaps trying to get to the top before it got dark altogether. Everyone hoped it was the last segment of our peregrination that had begun almost two hours earlier.

A BARK IN THE NIGHT

We had just begun climbing the hill when something unexpected and absolutely miraculous happened: a dog barked. Of course I didn't recognize the bark, but something inspired me to try to locate the animal. To our left, the terrain rose up about fifteen feet from road level. I looked up and down until I located a narrow path that led to the top. I climbed it and, to my amazement, I saw a very familiar white dog. Could it be Bricco? I whistled. His ears perked up and he quickly turned and ran toward me. At first, I was scared, thinking that it might be some strange dog that would attack me, so I made ready to jump quickly down the path toward the road where all the people were, figuring there would be safety in numbers. But, I soon recognized my great friend. We had a grand, festive and slobbery reunion. Well, he did the slobbering! He could not have seen us from the middle of the field where he was, and we could not see him, yet he had barked at the most appropriate time to alert us to his presence there. As a result, we were able to find lodging before it got completely dark. Somebody up there put that dog in our path in order to lead us to safety. It was a miracle. There was no other possible explanation for it.

Signor Ernesto Fantini was my neighbor. He was the most respectable man I had ever met, and an American citizen. He migrated to America in the early years of the twentieth century. Like many Italian young people of his era, he had a third-grade education, but the third grade was sufficient for his time to be able to function very well in society. Born in 1891, he was in school until the turn of the century. He had learned the basic skills of reading, writing, and arithmetic. He could do arithmetic calculations in his head with amazing speed and accuracy. The very first day out of school, most students aged nine or ten, went out to look for a "*mastro*" (master craftsman) who would teach him his particular skill as a tailor, cobbler, barber or similar. Signor Fantini chose to be a blacksmith. I don't know why he chose such a hard line of work with which to earn a living, given his gentle disposition and his refined demeanor. Physically, he did not appear to be particularly strong, either. He looked more like those men who preferred going to the theater or the opera, instead of fishing or hunting (like me!). But, in those days and in the little town where he and I saw the first light of day, opportunities were extremely limited, and so, after a few years of training, he worked for a local smith. In 1911, he had a chance to migrate to America, and so he did. He headed for Philadelphia, where there were a number of our paesani, and he secured a job with the Pennsylvania Railroad as a blacksmith. He worked in a forge during an era in which, if a locomotive needed a part, it had to be specially made, often right on the spot, so that's what he did. He made iron spare parts for the rolling stock, from scratch.

In 1919, he was drafted into the U.S. Army, serving two years in a fort in Kentucky. One of his buddies was a man named Francis S. Fitzgerald. "Everybody called him Scott," he told me in 1956, when I returned to Fossacesia and married his daughter. He showed me some personal photographs of the two together. "I wonder whatever happened to him," he asked plaintively. So I filled him in on the vicissitudes of one F. Scott Fitzgerald, the writer. I told him Mr. Fitzgerald had become famous as a writer and social elite, but that he had died, in 1945. That made him sad.

Although Ernesto Fantini appeared to be a man who was fittest for the indoor life, he did develop a love for the outdoors. But, it wasn't just his recreational and sporting spirit that prompted him to do so. It wasn't rare that his work required that he sleep in railroad cars for weeks at a time. In 1980, shortly before he died at the age of ninety in Toronto, Canada, he told a wide-eyed number of his grandchildren that his work often required him to board a train and be transported to the middle of a forest, in Illinois or Missouri, to work on a disabled locomotive. Being many hours away from civilization, there was nothing to eat and nothing to buy. McDonald's was a half century away. On occasion, it became necessary for him and his coworkers to go into the wilderness and literally shoot their supper—wild turkey, pheasant and quail were abundant in the wild. If they were near a stream, they fished for their supper. His choice of fare was pheasant. That's how he developed a love for hunting. While in the army, he had qualified as a sharpshooter, so he bought himself a double-barreled shotgun, and he maintained his shooting skills by hunting. Long after his need to hunt for his meals had ended, he turned that love into a hobby, becoming quite a sportsman.

In 1924, family pressures required his presence back in Italy. His first wife, whom he had left back in Fossacesia with a small child, (Lisa was born in 1921), had caught the *Spagnola,* or the Spanish fever. I don't know for sure, but I don't think he ever saw her alive again. She died in November, 1924. Being totally uncertain about his future, he brought all his money with him, thus avoiding the upcoming great economic crash, and the depression that followed. By the time these things came to pass, he had purchased a home and quite a bit of fertile land in the choicest areas of Fossacesia. In 1927 he married Rosaria Santeusanio, the daughter of his first *mastro* and a beauty in her time. They had two more daughters, Elide who now lives in Toronto, and Anna Maria, my wife of fifty plus years.

The depression never touched him, but his good heart did. Many people would beg him to lend them money, and he couldn't say no. Consequently, he lost a lot of his savings, mainly due to the inability of those who owed him, to pay him back. After the war passed in our town, our money was devalued to practically nothing, and those who had borrowed his money when it was worth its face value would return that face value at a time that it was not worth the paper it was printed on. Eventually, he sold his lands, but even there he lost out. Post war laws favored those who worked the land rather than those who owned it.

In addition to his money, Signor Fantini also brought back to Italy with him his love for hunting and his shotgun. As I was growing up in the neighborhood, it was a daily occurrence during hunting season to see Mr. Fantini pass in front of my house early in the morning on his way to the town's flatlands, where he would spend the entire day and come home late in the afternoon, maybe with a small bird or two. Once in a while there would be a jackrabbit in his game bag. Italy, he quickly learned, was not Illinois or Missouri: wildlife had long been depleted.

As soon as he settled his affairs, having decided that he would not be returning to America any time soon, he decided to get himself a hunting dog. His first dog was given to him by a friend who could no longer care for his old hound named Fido (Fee-doe in the Italian pronunciation). But, Fido was old indeed and so, after a couple of years, he died. After Fido, someone gave Mr. Fantini a puppy which he named Bricco. It was pure white. Bricco was tall, playful and intelligent to an extraordinary degree. That was one of the reasons we, the boys who lived on the block, named him the official neighborhood pet. I had an added reason for seeking him out: his young mistress, Anna Maria, approximately my age, was gorgeous. I sought out the dog every chance I got just to get a glimpse of her.

Mr. & Mrs. Ernesto Fantini, Anna Maria's parents
Rosaria Santeusanio Fantini was a real beauty in her time, but she was an extremely reserved and private person. She was a woman of great charity, as well. Ernesto Fantini spent a lot of time in America. He was a gentleman of sterling quality, highly respected both in Italy and in America. This photo, which I took in 1956, clearly shows, to the left, just above my mother-in-law's right shoulder, the lot where my house used to be before the Liberators liberated us out of it. Directly behind my father-in-law is the one-room hovel in which my family was forced to live for three years before we finally made it to America.

Bricco, the white hunting dog.

Bricco was little more than a puppy. He was very affectionate and exceptionally intelligent. His bark out of nowhere at dusk on November 4, 1943, alerted me to the presence in the area of the Fantini family. Five days later Bricco was dead, the victim of a German rogue who thought it would be fun to shoot the poor animal as it walked alongside its young mistress. Bricco was never photographed, because in those days only a few people in town had a camera and those who did could not find or afford to buy film. The above sketch was drawn by my friend, Salvatore Pizza, of Montella, AV, Italy, who drew it according to my description. In grateful appreciation, I salute Mr. Pizza.

COINCIDENCE OR MIRACLE?

That early evening, then, after meeting up with Bricco, being high up, despite the ever increasing darkness, I could see the very end of the two columns of refugees. I did not see either one of those German soldiers who had been our "escorts." So, I ran to Nonno Donato, and said: "The Fantini's are here. Let's stop. The Germans are gone." Mamma quickly joined the group, and, together with several other men, after making sure the German guards were indeed gone, gathered together all the members of our family, and we sneaked out of the column of walkers. We climbed the little path and, running as fast as we could, we headed for a house that appeared in the distance, directly in front of us and barely visible due to the ever increasing darkness.

It was a very nice two-story stone structure, modern in appearance, quite large and sturdy. We knocked on its massive front door with a sense of urgency. A lady greeted us. She knew why we were there, because there had been others ahead of us who sought her hospitality. She let us in without question. She said that we could stay the night, but that we had to sleep upstairs on the floor. She provided us with some blankets and some rough cotton sacks, so that we would not have to sleep on the bare tile.

Mamma told her that we hadn't had any food all day, so this kind woman gave us some bread and cheese, some wine for the men, and water for the rest of us. We could finally relax. As darkness descended over the area, two oil lamps were lit. We settled in for the night. All was quiet except for the women chatting about the baby: how cute she was, how big she was for being just one week old, and other such small talk. That night we slept on the second floor—thirty-seven of us, including a dozen children suffering from an untold number of infirmities, from intestinal worms, to a rash between their fingers, to boils all over their bodies. They cried all night and all at the same time, it seemed. Unlike the other children, our little Pina slept all night, "like a baby."

I slept well that night, too, despite the hard, cold floor. No bombs exploded, and no night prowler flew by. Once, we heard the engine noise of a military truck passing on the highway nearby causing every dog in the neighborhood to start barking furiously in unison. I wondered if one of them was Bricco.

BRICCO COMES TO WAKE US UP

My mother got up early the next morning and went out trying to locate the Fantini's. As soon as she opened the door to go out, Bricco rushed in uninvited. He was looking for me and Filippo. Once again we had an emotional reunion, highlighted by an effusion of petting, hugs and lickings. Mamma could not ask the dog where its family was, of course, but it wasn't necessary. As we walked out, we simply followed him. It didn't take long for us to reach a group of single-story rural dwellings belonging to a man named *Cesare* (Caesar). Anna Maria and her family were staying in one of those houses. I was overjoyed to see my "sweetheart" again. Even under rigorous war conditions, she was gorgeous!

It seemed that all the neighborhood ladies were there. Their husbands were either in hiding somewhere or serving in the military and the wives had no idea if they were dead or alive. They had started out in the home of Anna Maria's aunt, just out of town, but one day they were chased out of there by the Germans. The men had found refuge in a wooded ridge just out of town. They were safe there, because the area was inaccessible to anyone who did not know the points of entry. It was an excellent hiding place, provided the Germans didn't follow somebody into the area. The local contingent of Passionist Sisters, five or six of them, who staffed the local kindergarten and "finishing school," were also there. The men, some of whom had been taught by the sisters as children, provided food and protection for them. With the group, there was an elderly gentleman named Don Romeo (Don is a title of respect, not a first name—it reflects one's position and it means Sir), an import to our town, originally from Bari, where he and his wife, it was rumored, "had season seats to the opera." This impressed some of the people in town. He was a government employee assigned to our town in the 1920's. When he retired, he decided to remain with us, even though there was no opera house in Fossacesia. For several years after the war, neighborhood ladies had quite a hilarious time as they told and retold a funny episode that happened during those early days of our evacuation period. To avoid being taken by the Germans, Don Romeo decided to join Mr. Fantini and others who took refuge in a cave within those woods, while his wife, Donna (Lady) Lucia, and her sister, Lady Brigida, had remained in the company of the neighborhood ladies. The cave wasn't exactly an opera house environment, but it was safe, under the present conditions. One morning in late October, Don Romeo and three other men sneaked out of the cave, and came to the house. They, like the men almost anywhere in the zone, were looking for some dried tobacco with which to make cigarettes. Don Romeo did not smoke, but went along just to see his beloved wife. The timing couldn't have been worse, however, as they were caught at the house by a German patrol. Those ladies did not figure that they would be chased even from the houses in the rural areas just outside of town, so they were caught totally by surprise. At the first alarm that a German patrol was approaching, the men ran into the stable. There were six cows in residence there, so the men ran there and hid among the cows. The Germans ordered the ladies to evacuate the area and head for the town of San Vito to the north. The Germans had not noticed the presence of the men in the stable with the cows, but they stuck around to supervise the departure of the women. Just before departing, however, Donna Lucia in a demure, genteel manner, approached the stable door and, in a plaintive voice announced: *"Romeo, io me ne vado."* (Romeo, I'm leaving now). Upon hearing this, the Germans decided to take a closer look. They went inside the stable and not only captured the four men, but they took one of the cows as well. Some days later, Don Romeo was seen in the vicinity of the Sangro River, close to the railroad bridge, busily digging holes in the ground for the placement of underground mines. A few days later, however, the Germans released him, as he appeared too old and feeble to do manual work. He then painfully made his way back to the caves with the rest of the men (and the nuns), walking through fields and woodland, a distance of about three miles. The women, meanwhile, had made their way to Caesars' place, but nobody knew that, so he was filled with great grief. He rejoined the men in the cave and awaited the arrival of the British. Donna Lucia and Don Romeo, both having survived their respective ordeals, were happily reunited on Dec. 4th, 1943, after the British liberated the area.

A NEIGHBORHOOD REUNION

After an effusion of emotions in seeing each other again, the ladies caught up on the latest news about the war, and there was much, including the death of a certain young man from a nearby town who had rebelled against the Germans and was shot unmercifully. My mother knew his mother, having sewn several dresses for her. Mamma filled the ladies in on the death of Tommaso Natale, as well.

The most compelling news, at the moment, was that the Germans were evacuating some of the areas across the main road. We knew that, but we were hoping to be left alone for a few days, at least. As usual, there was a woman who reassured everyone that that particular zone was safe. She gave a number of "reasons" she had from "reliable sources." My mother knew better, but said nothing. Instead, she gave some instruction to all the mothers present on how to combat the many infections children were subjected to during those days. We lacked the most basic hygienic facilities, but she gave them some recipes of herbs that would be good to combat various illnesses and parasitic infections. There were many children there, equally afflicted with all kinds of contagious diseases: they had staphylococcus infections, gastrointestinal maladies, infestations of various parasites, including lice, and, of course, colds all over the place. My brother and I lucked out, since we did not catch any of those things, despite our proximity to these people. Anna Maria said that the children who shared the room where she had to sleep suffered all night long, and they cried and cried. Being a girl, her maternal instinct made her sad. I told her that we had our share of sick children in the house where we were staying who did the same thing. As a boy, I was angered by it all. My anger was not aimed at the children, but at the grownups who caused all this havoc. I was constantly aware of the fact that the children are always the real victims of stupid adult behavior.

In addition to the children having problems, there were a number of elderly women with a variety of geriatric problems ranging from "pains all over," as one lady put it, to advanced senility that required constant vigilance to make sure they didn't hurt themselves and others. There was one old lady who always needed to go home because she "forgot to feed the chickens." At any time of the day and night (she had trouble sleeping, too), she would get up and walk out the door, to go and "feed the chickens." This meant that members of her family had to guard her at all times, day and night, lest she walk out into a mine field and get killed. The daughters had placed some pots and pans next to her, so that she would make noise if she tried to get up. Unfortunately, the old lady kept knocking them down all night long simply by moving around.

A POOL OF BLOOD

We stayed in that area a total of three full days. On the day after we had arrived, I joined Anna Maria, her sister Elide, and several other young people from that rural neighborhood and went to look for some fruit that might still be on the trees or on the vines. Being very young, we were always hungry. We did find lots of grapes that had not been picked when it was vintage time, although much of it was rotting on the vine. We gathered some, sat down on some boulders that marked the boundaries between two properties, and enjoyed a sort of picnic. Being overripe, the grapes were practically pure sugar, but it was the only thing available to eat. As we ate the grapes, we talked for a while and enjoyed the exuberant spirit of our young years. I think the gathering of the grapes was only an excuse to be together for awhile.

Soon we started out for "home" through the fields. That's when we noticed, in the middle of an apple orchard, a large red spot. It was a pool of blood. Someone had been killed in that spot, probably during the night. We didn't think it was a civilian, but it was a toss up between a German soldier and a member of an Allied night scouting party, which were frequently noticed on moonlit nights, furtively going about their mysterious war business. Or could it be the blood of an animal, perhaps? The farm boys assured us that it was human blood, because animal blood was a much darker red. Naturally, we were all quite disturbed at the sight. When we got home, no one said a word about it. Anna Maria and I have been married now over fifty years, and we never talk about the war. Once in a while, though, she'll say: "Remember that pool of blood?"

Anna Maria Fantini, age eleven
This picture was taken in the spring of 1943. Her father had taken her by train to Francavilla to visit the De Medio family, the family friends of the Fantini's, who had had such a terrible tragedy at the hands of the German soldiers at the end of 1943. Looking at this picture, can anyone blame me for spotting her even at such a young age?

The rest of the day was rather peaceful. Nonno Donato, as usual, tried to figure out whom he knew in that area who might have been able to sell us some food, regardless of what it was. The lady of the house had assured us that they had in the house enough food to share with everybody, at least for a couple of weeks, then, *"Dio provvede!"* (God will provide!). It was the standard punch line in those days. She prepared food for an army every day, although it was of the standard, boring variety: home-made pasta with little condiment, left over greens, or some legumes.

WE MOVE AGAIN

The day after the pool of blood episode, my mother decided to pay a visit to her cousin, Donatina, who lived nearby. She took a couple of her women friends with her and me. We departed around ten o'clock. She judged it to be a twenty-minute walk from "Caesars' place" through the fields.

When we reached cousin Donatina's house (her name was the feminine version of my own first name), we found a number of men there busily engaged in an unusual activity: they were trying to make cigarettes. Since our area was an established tobacco growing zone, dried tobacco leaves were plentiful. They had been sun dried, but had not been processed with the removal of certain chemicals that would lessen the raw effect they had on the smokers. But those men were not going to be denied. When we arrived, they were engaged in the delicate operation of slicing the tobacco leaves ever so thinly, after having first fashioned them into a giant sausage-like object; literally, an enormous cigar. They had baked it slowly for a couple of hours, allowed it to cool for several more hours, and now they were in the process of slicing it. They finally chopped it up and were trying to fashion some crude looking cigarettes. The only paper available was some old heavy wrapping paper with which grocery stores in those days wrapped the merchandise they sold. It was not intended for cigarettes, but it was the best, the only paper available, so it had to do. Naturally, mamma took that opportunity to give me an impromptu lecture on the evils of smoking. Smoking and card playing were the two worst demons of society, according to her view of things.

As we were making our way to cousin Donatina's house that morning, we had spotted three German anti-aircraft guns aptly camouflaged under olive trees. They were positioned exactly due south in relation to Caesars' locality. Each gun was attended by a small contingent of German soldiers. They were too busy to even notice us as we were passing by. I knew mamma's brain was racing at breakneck speed at that point. The presence of those little cannons did not presage warm days and gentle breezes for us. We had come upon them quite unexpectedly, and my mother did not think it wise to run or behave in a panicky manner. We kept on walking rapidly, but calmly. "If they want us, let them make the first move," Mamma had said. Fortunately, they didn't want us, so we continued on our way undisturbed. I could tell mom was troubled, however. "This is not safe for us," she said finally. "When the British start to shoot in an effort to take out those three little cannons, we will be exactly downrange and in the line of fire," she said. By the time we started for home, she had already begun to make plans to hit the road.

We remained at cousin Donatina's for about an hour. She gave us food and drink as well as some warmer articles of clothing for me and Filippo that had belonged to her son, Bernie, when he was our age. He was now in the military. We said good-bye with the apprehension common in those days.

Hopefully we would see each other again soon. In order to avoid those cannon positions, we took a different route home.

As soon as we arrived, mamma shared her concerns with Nonno Donato and said it was necessary for us to move away from the Caesars' area. She announced to all that the next day we would be moving on. She told him that we were directly in the line of fire.

The announcement went over like the proverbial lead balloon. Having a baby with us that was now nine days old, I could understand the family's reluctance to move again, but under the circumstances, it was decidedly unwise to remain there. After much bickering and controversy, my mother gave her usual ultimatum: she would take Nonna Concetta, and us boys, and some of her friends and would leave the area the next day, November 8th, at noon. The rest of the family would have until then to decide if they wanted to go with us or stay. If they chose to remain and we all survived, we would see each other at war's end.

Having made her decision, she ran to the Fantini's and invited all who would listen to come along. This triggered a lot of controversy as well, but it was quickly decided that they would stay put because they had no way of alerting their men, including Mr. Fantini and Don Romeo, that they were leaving the area, headed for an unknown destination. Bad mistake! The German evacuation continued, and they were next in line to be persuaded to abandon their refuge, although they didn't know that then. The Germans' plans for the evacuation of the entire area was not very clear, however. One of the ladies criticized my mother's pessimistic approach to the war conditions. Nobody wanted to leave *anyway,* but to abandon an area you thought secure for an unknown place and circumstances, was sheer madness. Mamma agreed with her, but we were leaving nonetheless. After wishing everybody good luck, she returned to "our house."

A BOLD MOVE

At 10.00 A.M., November 9th, Nonno Donato still had not made a decision whether to come with us or stay. As previously stated, he had a difficult time to make a quick decision; he had to think about it, and sometimes that's all he ever did—thought about it without making an actual decision. He was very critical of mamma's tempestuous decision to move, "just because you saw three little guns," he had said, not without a snicker or two.

Suddenly, at about eleven o'clock, there was an immediate turn of events that precipitated a new and instant decision: we move. What was it that suddenly helped Nonno Donato decide to move? A cannon shell arrived unexpectedly and exploded right in front of the house, not fifty feet away from its front door. No one was hurt, although there was an immediate rush of physiological activity in everybody's lower intestines. After the October 12th air raid on our town, no more bombs had exploded in the entire zone until now. That explosion increased everybody's anxiety level and made it easy to make quick decisions. So, it was decided that my mother had been right all along and we should get the hell out of there—fast!

My mother had made her plans with or without the rest of the family. Now that the others had decided to join us, she said: *"Mo' vinete appress'a me e statteteve zitte."* (Abruzzese dialect meaning, "Now, everyone follow me and shut-up!"). We left within the hour. It took that long to prepare the baby. While waiting, Nonno Donato made a smart remark under his breath lamenting the fact that fate always made things happen so that they favored "her." I wasn't supposed to hear it, but he didn't know I was there. This time, he followed quietly and meekly, without further comment. When my mother was right she was right, and she was right most of the time.

This time mamma exhibited a great deal of intuitive skills as a "military tactician." First, she decided not to return to the main road by the same path we had used to get to the house four days earlier, when I heard Bricco's bark. Instead, she took another route a quarter mile farther north. She had not said anything to anyone as to her overall plans for the trek, but it soon became apparent to me that she had no intentions of following the route usually suggested by the Germans: she did not want to go to San Vito, and definitely not to the north of Italy, "where it was safe!" as the Germans had often put it. Over the years, I often thought about those orders to go north. Is it possible that the Germans were sincere in wanting us to go north so we would not get hurt? I doubt it, but then one never knows.

After walking about five hundred yards, she spotted a path to her right. She took it and headed east toward the sea. Route 16 was a short distance away. We headed for it. She knew that at that point the main road ran straight away for about a half mile, thus giving her a chance to spot any military vehicles that might be traveling on it, in either direction. That's why she went farther north, instead of following the original path. If we followed that original path, it would have led us to the stretch of road that was replete with hairpin bends and we could have been caught by surprise by the Germans.

Just as we approached the highway, however, we encountered two stumbling incidents: first, we heard a strange sound that resembled the sizzling of frying eggs coming from above the clouds. The sky that day was heavily overcast, so we could see nothing. We froze in our tracks. Mom gave orders to squat low, the ground being too muddy to lie flat. It definitely was not the sound of airplane motors. It was some sort of a projectile but it had to be self-propelled because, judging by its sound, it was traveling above the clouds heading north with a steady, unswerving path. We had not heard the boom of a cannon that might have fired it. It simply passed overhead and kept on going. Whatever it was, it passed above us with a steady sound, altered only by the way we perceived it as it approached and after it departed from us. It was quickly gone. Though puzzled by the experience, we were not overly concerned by the nature of the object, so long as it didn't hurt us. We got up and proceeded a little ways only to be confronted after a few hundred feet by our next barrier: there was a flat, black wire stretched out across our path. It had been laid north and south as far as one could see in both directions. Mamma stopped as she reached it and waited for nonno to come abreast to us. They discussed it. It was obviously a communication cable, a telephone line, perhaps, but nobody was a hundred percent sure. I remembered that just about two or three weeks before, a poster had been pasted on the wall of the Town Hall which specifically targeted communications lines. Normally, those posters were titled "AVVISO," which suggests "an advice." Under the circumstances, however, the word carried much more weight, more like a warning, and they were usually signed by the Italian provincial officers. This one dispensed with any of type of normal pleasantries, and went straight to the business at hand. It began with the following statement: "For the purpose of maintaining order and tranquility, I ORDER . . ." A list of don'ts followed, beginning with the voluntary consignment of all hunting firearms, target weapons, handguns, stilettos and other knives, and all explosives, even fireworks, to the Germanic military units. It was followed by a list of the dire consequences that would be incurred by anyone who wounded or killed a German soldier or officer. It reaffirmed the absolute interdiction of giving shelter or hospitality to members of the armed forces of any nation enemy of the Third Reich, or aiding and abetting any unauthorized civilian refugees (this was directed against Jews and Gypsies specifically without naming them). The printing and distribution of pamphlets derogatory to the interests of the German cause was strictly prohibited. The possession of radio transmitting or receiving equipment was forbidden, as well. That's why, when Ninni's family came to us in March of 1943, they whisked their beautiful Telefunken radio inside and upstairs in a flash and kept it well hidden. Each of the orders was followed by the penalty incurred by all transgressors and it concluded with the underscoring of the fact that these injunctions would be applied under the "German war law." It was dated 9/28/43, and signed: the Commander of the Southern Germanic Forces, A. Kesselring. Immediately next to the "Order," there was a smaller *"avviso,"* almost an afterthought, or postscript that's worth translating:

NOTICE

All existing telephone lines and cables have *been confiscated by the German Armed Forces!* Any damage inflicted upon these lines as well as communication lines built by the German troops will be considered an attack upon the German Armed Forces and punishable by death by firing squad. If the guilty party cannot be found and captured, a number of hostages will be taken from the municipality in which the damage has occurred. If the guilty party will not turn him-self in to the German Authorities within 24 hours, the hostages will face the firing squad.

The Superior Commandant of the German Armed Forces
Albert Kesselring

This was one such cable. All communications, military or civilian, were under the strict surveillance of the Germans, and anyone caught tampering with them, or, worse, actively engaged in the act of sabotaging them, would be dealt with in the severest manner possible, which usually meant facing the firing squad. My mother told everyone not to touch it and jump over it quickly! She went over it first and we quickly imitated her. Nobody seemed to die instantly from it, so we kept on going, moving as rapidly as possible. A minute or so later, we came upon the highway. We halted there while mamma stopped, looked up and down, and listened for the approach of military vehicles. Not having seen any, nor heard the whir of engines, she waved us on with a motion of her arm that not only suggested we could cross, but that we should do so quickly and silently. We did as we were told, and the entire group was on the other side of the road in seconds.

The fields were completely open and we had no protection from anything: there was not a hedge, nor a bush, not even a clump of trees. There were a few straggling olive trees, ironically the symbol of peace, but they hardly afforded us much protection. There was precious little else we could hide behind. We had to take a chance, if we wanted to survive. Even the children cooperated, especially Pina who slept placidly and tranquilly, with the angelic innocence of babes.

Everyone followed my mother as she headed east in the direction of the Adriatic Sea, walking through those wet and muddy fields with a sustained pace. We marched more than walked. There was a beaten path that we followed, but it was as muddy as the cultivated fields on both sides of it. The seashore was less than a mile away. I still hadn't figured out what my mother had in mind, or where we were going. We passed about a quarter mile north of Rocca San Giovanni. We could see the two German sentries still perched like two vultures atop the belfry of Saint Matthew's Church, their powerful binoculars still trained southward where the British were, hence away from us. That was good. Being a quarter mile away, we were well within range of their powerful machine guns, but they couldn't possibly swing it toward us, what with the tightness of the bell housing, the presence in that turret of two bells, and the fact that that weapon was really a small cannon, hence very, very heavy. Still, we proceeded with our hearts in our mouths, filled with fear and anxiety. We moved swiftly and silently. Even the children cooperated without being told. Fear has a tendency to make people behave well under the worst of circumstances.

But the Germans had their backs to us, and paid no attention to us as we sneaked past their perch. We assumed that they did not see us. If they did see us, there was precious little they could do about it, anyway. They were understaffed and too busy with more important tasks, like the preparation for one of the most grueling battles of the Italian theater, the Battle of the Sangro River, which was imminent. Besides, we had another protection: we were on the northern side of the ravine from which I had heard Bricco bark, but quite a bit farther downriver where the two ravines that hug the residential section of Rocca San Giovanni in the north and south sides converge on its eastern end and become much wider and deeper. Even if the Germans had seen us, it would have been impossible for them to capture us.

When we arrived at the general area that, in my mother's judgment, was situated directly across the valley from the Yermunni farmstead, the place from which we had been chased five days earlier, she gave orders to turn south. Suddenly, her brilliant plan dawned on me: we were sneaking back to the point of departure from which we had been chased four days before. It made a lot of sense, too, considering that the Germans had already evacuated the area, and they weren't about to do it again. Of course, if they were to return to the zone, they might have evacuated us with the nozzles of their automatic weapons, to make sure they wouldn't have to do it a third time!

We walked to the edge of the ravine, located what appeared to be a path that led to the creek, and began to descend the steep slopes toward the torrent that rumbled at the bottom of it. It had rained hard all night and the narrow lanes of beaten earth that led to the bottom of the ravine toward the creek's bed had become muddy and slippery. Carefully and laboriously, we made our way to the bottom of that mini-canyon. It took us more than twenty minutes to reach the bottom (in my estimation, of course, because no one had a watch). The crossing of the waters was no less precarious, due to the high water level and the rapidity of the current, but we made it.

Climbing back up on the southern slopes proved to be even more challenging. The mud made it extremely slippery and difficult for our worn-out shoes to get a grip on the terrain in order to negotiate our next step upward. Despite the physical effort, and the precariousness of each step, we finally made it to the top. My brother Filippo and I were proceeding together and with us were a couple of other kids. We had been playing some sort of game of advance and retreat. The one who reached the top first would be the winner, but he had to have touched certain landmarks on the way up first, or he would be disqualified. Of course, there were no prizes to be awarded. We would all have opted for a plate of *pasta-e-fagioli* as a prize if we could, but, alas, there was none to be had. Even a few crackers would have been considered a great prize, but, at that point, the food supply was all but gone.

Normally, my mother always made sure that we, her two children, were in front of her at all times, where she could keep a vigilant eye on us. This time, however, having reached the top just about thirty feet ahead of us, she went immediately to the house which was situated on the edge of the gravel road, about a football field away from the edge of the ravine. In part, she wanted to make sure it was all right for us to stay there for a few days. But, perhaps the real reason was that, having outmaneuvered the Germans in a big way, she relaxed her guard momentarily. Filippo and I reached the top ahead of the other children (although, as I recall, I made up the rules as the game progressed!), but, an unpleasant surprise greeted us just as we reached the plateau. Looking directly south across the Yermunni farm's threshing plaza, we saw in the sky and in the distance, four puffs of black smoke. They looked very much like the classic cartoonist's interpretation of four cannon projectiles spiraling toward us. That's exactly what they were: four cannon shells of the type that exploded in the air as they spiraled toward their targets. As soon as we spotted them, we dropped flat on our stomachs, right in the middle of a particularly large puddle of mud.

The four projectiles passed perhaps no more than fifty or sixty feet over our heads, and exploded harmlessly at the bottom of the ravine, close to the creek. Fortunately, when they exploded, no one was there, so there were no casualties. Had they arrived but ten minutes earlier, our entire group would have been caught at various stages of descent or ascent: the massacre would have been total. When the smoke cleared, some of the women, especially the older ones, began to thank, in a loud voice various saints, even some strange ones: St. Anthony, St. Pantaleone, St. Pancratius, and of course, the ever present Saint Rita, the saint of impossible cases. Then there were the various Madonna's, Our Lady of this and Our Lady of that. Everyone had a favorite title for the Madonna. Meanwhile, Filippo and I got up looking like we had rolled around in a pig sty.

AUNT ANGELA'S STABLE

We had no sooner gotten up from that mud puddle, when we heard our mother running toward us, screaming our names: *Natù* (truncated appellative for Donatuccio, my childhood nickname), *Filì* (truncated appellative form for Filippo). As soon as she heard the four explosions, she remembered that she had two boys roaming around the area, somewhere, so she ran *"a scenna liereghe"* (with spread wings—an Abruzzese saying indicating a person's reaction to a frantic moment). As she looked at us, her eyes got as large as two giant black olives, indigenous to that zone: she was horrified. We must have looked like the defeated remnants of a fierce Civil War battle. She nearly had a heart attack looking at our sorry state, but we reassured her that we were all right. She counted heads. All twenty-four in the group were there and accounted for, and we were all in one piece besides. It was then that she announced we had been given permission to stay in the stable that, up to a week before, had been the official residence of Rosetta, the cow. Alas, Rosetta was no more. She, too, had been inducted into the stomachs of the modern Huns, as they proceeded to make the "glorious" Third Reich "the *caput mundi* of tomorrow." (The head of the world).

The stable was attached to a house that belonged to a little old lady, a widow, who looked very much like the old lady in the Tweety Bird cartoons. She spoke with the same high pitched voice, and had quite a sense of humor. Her name was Aunt Angela. I didn't think she was as old as Noah, but pretty close. She gave us permission to stay there until the war passed, giving mamma a set of rules and regulations concerning noise, screams, smoking, and card playing. She wanted none of these as she admonished everybody to that fact. Well, those were the same rules I had lived under since I was born, anyway. We would easily adjust. The entire group of refugees followed our mother as she led us to the stable. It was attached to the house in the shape of an L.

It smelled, naturally, since it was not yet cleaned. It was fairly large. There was enough room to accommodate all of us in relative comfort. There was a bit of cleaning up to do, but there was plenty of fresh straw around that we could use for sleeping, There was a "manger" upon which baby Pina could sleep. We knew of another Baby who used a similar arrangement in which to sleep when He was born, and He survived (well, at least for a while, anyway), so our baby was well taken care of. We brought in innumerable buckets of water from the nearby well, managing to eliminate most of the smell by throwing the water on the floor, and sweeping it out. We didn't succeed in eliminating it entirely, but after a while it blended with other odors. Mamma and her friends went out and brought back armfuls of autumn flowers. They didn't particularly smell very nice, either, but their colors brightened the atmosphere. Everyone got busy dusting, sweeping, carrying things in and out, selecting hay from the haystack and carrying it into the stable with pitch forks. Twice during the operation we had to scurry inside because we heard the sound of approaching aircraft. They were mostly British Spitfires that used to patrol the Nazionale, Route 16. It was not rare to hear them scream overhead, as they flew low to attack a German truck, or a half-track vehicle.

In a couple of hours the "palace" was ready for occupancy. We would be spending the last three weeks of the Sangro River Battle in that stable. It was not the Ritz hotel, to be sure, but there was a warmth and coziness among all the occupants that gave everyone a sense of security. The common danger drew us together. In the evenings, Aunt Angela would tell us stories of her youth, which my brother and I quickly titled "a lesson in ancient history." She had a seemingly inexhaustible repertoire of tall stories coupled with an unstoppable willingness to tell them at any given place and time, often punctuated with salacious little anecdotes that amused us, but upset mamma because the old lady's choice of words was not particularly refined. Once in a while she would exclaim, in her particular dialect, *Chi l'ha fatte la vosce?* (All right, who broke wind?). This amused everyone, including my mother, who found the quip harmless enough. At least, we still could laugh. There were no guarantees we could still do so the next day, or the next hour, for that matter. The odds in favor of crying were much, much higher.

The lady who lived across the plaza, Aunt Angela's daughter-in-law, came to help by bringing us a couple of mattresses together with as many sheets and blankets she could find. She also found all sorts of baby sleepwear. Pina, not quite two weeks old, was everyone's favorite toy.

BRICCO'S TRAGIC END

About a year after the war roared through, we learned that the day following our move to Aunt Angela's stable, that is, Tuesday, November 9th, 1943, the extended Fantini family were routed from their sleep early in the morning by the Germans, and told that they had two hours in which to evacuate the area, under penalty of being shot on sight. My future mother-in-law, even though she did not know how well we had managed to escape the German traps, must have had some regrets about not accepting my mother's invitation to come with us. Suddenly, there was panic in their midst. What do we do? Where are we going? What about Papà? Well, the German's didn't want to hear any of that. They had orders to evacuate the area, period. The order that had come from Berlin made no provisions for resettling the people. "Just get rid of them," was the order.

At eleven o'clock, two Germans came back and ordered everyone to move out. No one understood a word they said, but the rage in their voices translated into sheer terror, so the families quickly gathered the few bundles of clothes and blankets they had prepared, and they began to file out of the neighborhood.

Problems arose immediately. Bricco was nowhere to be found and Anna Maria started to scream: she would not go anywhere before she found her dog. One of the Germans who escorted them out, fortunately, was kind enough not only to give her time, but actually joined in the search. Anna Maria was crying calling out to Bricco as she went. Perhaps he had sensed the imminent danger he was in, and that's why he had disappeared.

Suddenly, out of a thicket jumped a rabbit, hopping scared, running for his life, with Bricco hot on its cottontail. He dove into a pile of firewood and disappeared. Bricco stopped, perplexed, and that's when he heard his mistress calling out to him. That was enough to distract him, so, forgetting the rabbit, he came straight to her. As it turned out, it would have been better if he had stayed lost, for, unbeknown to him or anyone else, this day, November 9th, 1943, was to be the last day of his existence.

The group of refugees began to walk, slowly and reluctantly, unlike our group which, led by my mother who was always trying to stay a step ahead of the Germans, had a precise plan and at least in theory, a precise direction. This group had no specific plan as to where they were going. However, along the way, my future mother-in-law, Rosaria Santeusanio Fantini, remembering they had some friends who lived very near the seashore at San Vito, decided to try to reach them.

The group proceeded east toward the shore area. They could already hear the noise of the waves breaking against the *scogli*, the boulders placed all along the shore line in attempt to reduce shore erosion. Four or five hundred yards more and the road would begin to descend toward the sea; not far from there was the home of the family that they had been hoping would give them hospitality. The older women began to encourage the younger walkers. A little more and we'll be there. One of them even began to sing some sing-along kind of songs, but not many people, especially the young, joined in. Somehow, certain situations just don't call for singing.

As they walked, Anna Maria was proceeding on the road's edge, with Bricco walking alongside of her. There was a one-story bungalow with a front porch that was set away from the road. As they slowly approached the front of the building, they noticed two German soldiers leisurely leaning against the door frame, arrogantly acting as if they owned the building and the earth upon which it stood. They were observing the parade of refugees, hundreds of them, wearily walking past them. As soon as Anna Maria and her dog came into view, one of the Nazis said something to the other, and they both laughed. Then the one who spoke went inside the little house. Moments later, he reappeared brandishing a rifle. He calmly waited until the dog came within range right in front of him, then, raising his weapon, took aim and calmly, in cold blood, fired two shots at poor Bricco, completely unconcerned that, if he missed the dog, he could have hit his distraught mistress instead. Quickly, the adults sheltered the distressed Anna Maria and whisked her away, fearing that the soldier would turn the weapon on her, as well. Meanwhile, the animal, mortally wounded, looking at its mistress with imploring eyes and dragging its entrails, made its way toward some bushes on the side of the road, and there he died.

Almost a year would pass before we learned about the death of that poor dog. When I did, though, I was stunned. I was so angry at the senseless killing that, given the opportunity, I might have killed that idiot myself. On a positive note, though, Bricco's death magnified in my mind the extraordinary significance of his bark in the middle of nowhere that evening of November 4. He probably saved, if not our lives, at least much discomfort as we proceeded toward nowhere and into the night, hungry and cold, and with a six-day-old baby to care for.

BACK TO AUNT ANGELA'S STABLE

That day, of course, we were totally unaware of the drama that was going on about a half mile away from us. We settled in our stable and we were relatively comfortable. Mamma would recite the Rosary every night, all fifteen decades of it; we had, after all, nothing else to do, and nowhere to go. Most of the people chimed in, responding in phonetic Latin, but without understanding what they were saying. The old ladies had no clue as to what they were saying, but they had recited their prayers in that manner all their lives and were comfortable with it. Occasionally, somebody would make a snide remark about people praying only when they're scared. Actually, my mother was an exemplary woman who prayed even when she wasn't scared. She had a deep, genuine faith, and I am forever grateful to her for passing it on to me and my brother. Knowing that ignorance takes many forms, she ignored the remarks, and kept on praying for everybody, including her critics. Perhaps it was precisely the awareness of this reality that reduced the intense boredom to which we were all subjected. We were, after all, trying to live in a 15' x 20' shack, if it was that big. There were twenty-four of us, sixteen adults, seven children and one newborn. We stayed put inside that stable for three weeks. No one ever ventured outside except to answer an inevitable call of nature, and then it meant a quick run to the side of the building, in full communion with mother nature, for man is, indeed, capable of rising to heroic levels, but also squatting to lower ones, when necessary.

A number of incidents took place that kept us on constant alert. Occasionally, we would hear a mine explode in the vicinity. Sometimes, it was a stray dog that stepped on a buried anti-personnel mine, thus being put out of its misery. Many animals had been abandoned and had to fend for themselves for food and water. Other times, it was an itinerant stranger passing through the area who stepped on an anti-tank mine, and was blown into pieces. It was not rare for people passing through a rural area to come across the very disturbing sight of a dead body in various stages of decomposition. Also, British Spitfires constantly flew over the main roads strafing military vehicles, motorcycles, and anything else that moved along Route 16, often killing German military personnel. Death was present everywhere. One late afternoon, a horse-driven cart carrying a body on its flatbed passed by our area followed by five or six people, mourning and wailing. We did not talk with anyone about it, so we didn't know who the person was or if he or she had been killed or had died of natural causes. Because, despite war conditions, life went on unabated, so people were born and people died of natural causes like always.

Occasionally, we would see a few birds flying freely in the sky, moving from tree to tree, searching for food from the bounty of creation, oblivious of the war. But, the war affected them, too, because it had prevented local farmers from sowing the usual crops that fed us for the year and whose remnants in the fields fed them, as well. We were all hurting. We had to provide our own food either by cultivating it or buying it, so Nonno Donato had to make several trips to Pete Di Nenno's house or other homes nearby, searching for food. It must be remembered that we had returned to the area from which we had been chased on November 4th, a sort of manor comprised of several homes among which was Aunt Angela's home with the stable where we had taken up residence, the homes of two of her sons, and Pete Di Nenno's home across the street.

All he could find each time he went out was a half sack of wheat. Boiled and seasoned with a little bit of olive oil, it wasn't bad. Nonna Minguccia still had some salt the Germans had given her on the occasion of the famous anniversary dinner. It rendered the wheat edible. Another problem we encountered was the scarcity of dishes and utensils. Aunt Angela provided all she could and the families in the vicinity helped out, as well, but we ate with the most diversified collection of eating vessels and utensils imaginable.

Three weeks is a long period of time to pass when you have nothing to do, nothing to read, not even writing material with which to record the events of the day. I had read my anthology cover to cover twice already. Time passed slowly, aggravated by the uncertainty of our immediate future. Everyone was encouraged to remain inside the stable, and go outside only when it was absolutely necessary, and never alone. So, life trickled by one painful minute, one Hail Mary, one word of encouragement at a time.

MIND IF WE PASS BY?

One day, Nonno Donato saw three men passing through Aunt Angela's property, moving rapidly, surreptitiously. Nonno Donato, who was always near the door so as to keep an eye on what was going on outside, spotted them as they emerged from the rim of the ravine that we ourselves had crossed a week before. He waited until they were within voice range and then called out: *"Olà, Paisà."* One of the three, startled, but without panic replied: "Do you mind if we walk through your plaza?" The man had replied in Italian, so Nonno called them over to the door. One of the three introduced himself as Carmine Imperiale, an Italian army MP trying to make his way back home to Reggio Calabria, at the very toe of the Italian boot. His two companions were British officers who were trying to meet the front lines and hoped to rejoin their army comrades. Having established friendly contacts, nonno invited them in. He spoke English to the officers, who reacted with great enthusiasm hearing someone capable of speaking their own language. Carmine explained that as an Italian Army MP, he had been assigned to guard the prisoners of war in a POW camp near Sulmona. On September 8, as Italy signed its armistice with the Allies, he was quietly ordered by his Italian superiors to let the prisoners go a few at a time so as not to arouse the suspicion of the Germans, and then they themselves could go home. About half of the prisoners did abandon the camp, but the other half were advised by their own officers to stay put so as to remain under the protection of the Geneva Convention. It was just a matter of time, anyway, until the British would arrive to the area and liberate them. As it turned out, the British did not reach that area until late spring, 1944.

It took a few days to dispose of approximately twelve-hundred of the prisoners who chose freedom. As they were released, the British and American soldiers and their officers blended in with the local population. Most of them headed south, choosing mountain routes and other impervious paths that led away from the German positions, so it would be unlikely that they would encounter much German traffic. The two British officers who had established a very close friendship with Carmine, however, had panicked at the thought of trying to survive in a country where they couldn't even speak the language, so they asked Sergeant Imperiale if they could tag along with him. Actually, the Italian was reluctant to take them with him because they represented a liability. The Germans would eventually be looking for those prisoners, since they were considered escapees. As he thought it over, however, he realized that more than their being a liability to him, he represented an even greater liability to them. Since he had helped many of those prisoners during the entire summer of '43, the Germans had placed a bounty on his head. They were equally being hunted, so after thinking it over, he said, "Oh, what the heck! Let's go!" And so they began the long march home. After the war was over, the British government sent him a citation for his efforts on behalf of the members of the commonwealth being pursued by enemy forces. He is very proud of that certificate, which was accompanied by a medal and an unspecified sum of money intended "to compensate him for any expenditure encountered in the process."

HEADQUARTERS
ALLIED SCREENING COMMISSION (ITALY)
A. P. 0. S 351
C. M. F.

ESTEEMED MISTER

Carmine Imperiale

It is with great pleasure that we are sending you the enclosed Certificate of Merit granted unto you by the Allied Governments as a token of gratitude for the invaluable assistance you have rendered to the Allied Prisoners of War, to our soldiers and to all those who were attempting to avoid being recaptured by the Germans, after the Armistice with Italy, in 1943. We are enclosing also a check for a sum of money to cover any expenses you may have incurred in the rendering of said assistance.

We would appreciate it if you would affix your signature to the enclosed receipt, and mail it back to this office at — Corso Italia 25, Roma — as soon as possible.

We regret that we were unable to assign an Allied officer to come to you and make an official presentation of the certificate, together with the money, and to thank you personally. Our mission is about to end its activities, but the concluding amount of work is still vast.

We express, nevertheless, our deepest gratitude, and our most heartfelt thanks, in the name of the Allied Governments and on behalf of all the soldiers whom you have so courageously assisted, and who will forever hold in their hearts the most genuine sense of gratitude. We trust that the sentiments of reciprocal esteem and respect, born out months of troubles, filled with dangers, difficulties, hazards and risks, during which you rendered to them such invaluable services, will be renewed and strengthened with the passing of the years.

Signed, sealed and dated
Lt. Col. A. B. De Witte,
A. S. C. Commander (Italy)
March, 24, 1948

Certificate of Merit
Facsimile of a Certificate of Merit given by the Allied High Command in the name of the King of England to people who had risked their lives protecting soldiers of the British Commonwealth nations. It came with an unspecified amount of money, "to cover any expense you may have incurred."

After spending a couple of weeks in the mountains around Sulmona, they headed east, on foot. They had to go around the mountain, so they headed for the coastal city of Pescara hoping to reach the Adriatic littoral with its railroad and road traffic. It didn't dawn on Carmine that there were no trains passing because the track was in total disarray, and Route 16 only carried German military traffic. But, they had to cover well over two hundred miles before reaching the British sector, so they figured they'd better get going. They would meet up with the front lines at the Sangro River, so the day they passed in front of our stable, they had practically reached the end of their journey. But, the Battle of the Sangro had yet to be fought and that very afternoon they realized that they had better stop until the front had passed. In the meantime, however, they were hungry, so Carmine asked Nonno Donato for food. Nonno replied that we could not provide them with any, but he suggested that they stop at Pete's house, which they could see across the street in the distance, where they might be able to get some bread and cheese. Pete did indeed provide the men with food for the moment and provisions for a couple of days afterward. The two British officers particularly enjoyed the classic Italian sandwich of *prosciutto e formaggio* (ham and cheese), chased down by several glasses of Pete's Trebbiano wine. Signora Grazia gave them a couple of sandwiches to take along with them. There was no guarantee they could find food for quite a while, because when they left Pete's house they were heading right into the jaws of front line battle. But, they did not go far. They had a quick conference among themselves and decided that, with the front lines so close, they might as well wait for the British army to come to them. It would be safer. Pete suggested they stay in his barn until the danger passed.

Incredibly, four decades later, during the 1980's, when I was teaching English at Bishop Kenrick High School, I had a beautiful girl in class named Maria Rosa Imperiale, Marisa for short. She told me that her parents came from Italy and that they didn't speak English. So, I took her under my wing, figuring that under the circumstances, she was more vulnerable than most students her age. One day, her father came to the school during an open house event and we spoke about war times. I was shocked when he told me that after the armistice of September 8, 1943, he walked home from Sulmona to Reggio Calabria, stopping only for a few days when they met up with the front lines, "at the Sangro River." "Sangro River? That's my river," I said. The more we talked, the more he looked familiar to me. With the daughter in my classroom we met again and again and the more we spoke the more I realized that he was none other than the Italian MP who escorted the two British officers to safety that day in November of '43.

THE EVER PRESENT SPITFIRE

Meanwhile, the preparations for the crossing of the Sangro continued. Allied fighters "swept" the area incessantly. Every day during those three weeks, several times a day there was the inevitable drone of passing Spitfires. They attacked any and all vehicles they surprised traveling between Fossacesia and Rocca San Giovanni, on Route 16, dive bombing and strafing them with their 20mm machine guns. Whenever they attacked something, the engine noise would be faint at first, then there was a sudden change in tone. As the plane dived upon its target, the noise of its engine would get louder and louder in a tonal arc that was perceived in ascending pitch while the plane was in diving mode. During the dive, its powerful 20mm cannons rained fire and steel upon the target below with an angry ta-ta-ta-ta-ta. When it reached its lowest point, the plane would level out and then it began to climb to regain its prescribed flight level. During the climbing maneuver, the engine pitch would reach our ears in descending tones, getting lower and lower as the plane moved farther and farther away from us until it reached its cruising altitude. This nearly always coincided with the explosion of the single bomb it released at the point of lowest altitude. It sounded like an exclamation point at the end of an admonishing sentence. The sound of its engine would then level off before fading away altogether. This happened several times a day, because the Allied Air Force had become very active during the second week of November. The Allies had total control of the air and flew at will. It appeared the Luftwaffe had nothing left in our area that was capable of challenging them. The front was getting ready to move north, past the Sangro River.

A storm of B-24 Liberator Bombers on their way to a mission.
The B-24 bomber was the workhorse of the Sangro River Battle. The photo shows only seven airplanes, but a mission usually consisted of hundreds of bombers plus their escorts, namely P-38s, P-51s and British Spitfires. Despite my mother's objections, several times I, too, lay flat on my back next to my grandfather with my head on the stable's down step and looked at them as they approached

our area. They were ominous, foreboding, threatening. After pummeling Fossacesia for ten days, they began to fly into southern Germany every day for the next year and a half, since they moved their operations to the former Italian airfields of southern Italy.

GOOD MORNING, EVERYONE!

From about the tenth of November until we were liberated, we acquired a strange new way of waking up in the morning. All the roosters were gone from the hen houses, so we no longer had an alarm clock. Every morning, beginning at 5:00 A.M., a small caliber cannon would let go with a dozen rapid-fire shells aimed at the British, who were now well in control of the right bank of the Sangro. It fired from the direction that we judged to be in or around the area of the church of San Giovanni in Venere, at the extreme east of the Fossacesia plateau. The barrage of shells would be followed by about five minutes of silence. Then the answer from the British would come: boom, boom, boom. Only these shells were of much bigger caliber, judging by the sounds they made as they were fired or when they exploded. Now was the time of our greatest danger. We didn't know where those shells would fall. If our little stable were to receive a direct hit, we would all have been dead. There was nothing we could do to protect ourselves, so we just sat there, praying and hoping for the best. Of course, no one could sleep any more. And it was not yet quarter after five in the morning.

At about five thirty, the ritual would start again, only this time the German small caliber gun fired from a different position, further west: bam, bam, bam. And the British returned the greetings, boom, boom, boom. Every morning this ritual repeated itself four times or five times; each time the German gun firing from a position farther and farther west. At seven o'clock, the firing ceased. "They all went to breakfast," Nonno Donato used to quip.

The story of the "mobile sniper" was told by Armando Liberato. He says the Germans used the same tactic at Castelfrentano. We concluded then that the Germans were pathetically short of armament, munitions, manpower and sensible judgment. The Sangro River represented the beginning of the end for the Germans, but they were not yet convinced of it. They obstinately held on to their belief in the invincibility of their Fuhrer despite the hard reality that the Allied armies were just on the other side of the river. And they had tons of equipment, while the Germans were running out of armament and ammunition with which to fight, and even food to feed their men, who were reduced to pillaging whatever was left from local farms.

NOT ALL GERMANS WERE BAD—ANOTHER EXAMPLE

The day the German military forced us to evacuate the area on November 4th, Pete's wife, Grazia, did not follow their instructions. Instead, she grabbed some vittles and some blankets, and, slipping out of her back door, moved rapidly toward the far side of their property, which reached an area close to the beach. Pete had already slipped out and was watching what was going on from a distance. When he saw Grazia come running down an embankment well past their back yard, he whistled to her, joined her, and they both ran to a small hut that served as a shelter during the summer, when they worked in the fields. It was intended as a shelter in case a sudden storm came up from the sea. It was pretty well hidden from the road, so Pete and Grazia stayed there that night. The next morning, they returned home and all was quiet. They did not see another German soldier ever again after that.

On the 17th of November, a couple knocked at Pete's door. When Pete opened it, a woman, visibly pregnant, collapsed right into his arms. The young man with her lunged forward and prevented her from hitting her head on Pete's cement front steps. Pete and Grazia helped the young couple inside and guided the young woman to a sofa. Grazia heated some leftover soup and gave it to the young woman, who, after drinking it, felt a little better. Meanwhile, the young man introduced himself as Giovannino Del Re, Nino for short. His wife was Batsheva W., Eva for short. He was Italian from the Benevento area, and she, so rumors had it, was a Jewish refugee from Hungary whose parents and an older sister had been arrested by the Gestapo in Budapest while she had been studying in Trieste. Grazia asked Nino if they were hungry. They had not eaten since noon the day before, so she immediately solved that crisis by preparing some sandwiches of *prosciutto e formaggio* just as she had done for Carmine and the two English officers the day before. Nino told my mother later they had not slept more than a few hours at a time for about a week, trying to avoid German traps. That night they slept twelve hours straight.

Within a few days after their arrival, Eva gave signs that she was ready to give birth. It soon became apparent, however, that she needed medical assistance. The midwife was available nearby, so Pete went to fetch her. She came, and Pete even arranged for her to stay at their house overnight, but after examining Eva, she agreed that she had neither the knowledge nor the necessary medication to solve the problem. While not potentially fatal, her condition was serious enough that she needed the assistance of a doctor. No one knew where any of the local doctors were. Having served with a contingent of German soldiers in Africa a couple of years before, Nino spoke some German, so he decided to go to the German military command in Rocca San Giovanni and ask if they had a doctor available. They had two: Dr. Cacchione, Rocca's local physician who had been pressed into service at the field hospital, and Dr. Ingemar Walter, a medical captain. Both agreed to accompany Nino back to Pete's house, a trek of about a mile on foot through muddy fields that rainy afternoon. When they arrived, the German doctor examined the patient. Dr. Cacchione was an elderly man and basically a country doctor. He had not kept up with latest medical discoveries, especially in the field of obstetrics. Dr. Walter explained to him what the problem was and its possible solutions. He gave Eva some sedatives and did other necessary procedures within the limitations of available medical supplies, and the two doctors left.

The next day, Dr. Walter returned to the household alone. This time he arrived on a motorcycle with a sidecar, driven by a young soldier. By early afternoon he delivered a baby boy of "unusual size and demeanor." and left. At the request of the mother, the doctor pronounced the baptismal formula, as my mother had done for Pina three weeks earlier. Conveniently, Dr. Walter happened to be a Catholic. They gave the baby the name of Samuel Peter, in honor of Eva's father and Signor Pete. The parents of the child asked Pete and Grazia to stand in baptism for the baby, and so they became Compari (*goomba*, as the American uninformed version would have it; and then there is the Spanish forms of *Comadre* and *Compadre,* godmother and godfather).

The doctor returned once more a couple of days later. It was the afternoon of November 21st. He examined both mother and son and declared she had overcome her difficulties. Pete opened a bottle of *vino cotto* to celebrate the event. With my mother's help, Grazia made a cake and they had a very modest, but dignified celebration. After the doctor and his young driver left the area, Grazia sent a small piece of that cake to everyone in our stable, except little Pina who wouldn't have appreciated it anyway. While eating it, I delighted my mother by singing a student generated satirical song about Marie Antoinette being transported on a cart, on her way to the guillotine. "It's ironic," I explained. "We haven't had anything solid to eat in weeks, but now we're eating cake. Is that crazy or what?" Unfortunately, our cake was the size of a large ice cube; but it was better than nothing, and it was delicious.

The party was a modest but jovial affair, according to mamma and nonno, who attended it. While there, she had a long conversation with the doctor about the war. He spoke in general terms, but he let it be understood that within months, if not weeks, the war would be over. He didn't reveal whether the final victory belonged to the Third Reich or not. When the doctor left, he gave a piece of cake to the young corporal who popped it in his mouth and started the motorcycle in a single motion. They departed with a roar.

The pair made their way back to headquarters by taking the gravel road to Route 16, turned right onto it and began to travel the short distance toward the piazza of Rocca. And, then it happened: the motorcycle was attacked by a Spitfire that suddenly pounced upon them. From our stable, we heard the noise typical of those fighter planes when they attacked a target along the highway. Everyone was horrified, fearing the worst. My mother immediately reached for her rosary beads. Nonno Donato, looking toward Pete's house, saw that Nino had started running toward the scene. He intercepted him, suggesting instead that they wait until it got dark enough that they could venture out safely to investigate the incident. He and Pete offered to accompany him. The young man realized it was a wise suggestion and agreed to wait. Later, as dusk descended on the hills and valleys of our region, under the protection of darkness the three went out and found the banged-up motorcycle. There was some blood on it, so they assumed the worst. The family was devastated to learn of the supposed tragedy. That night, in our stable, we said a rosary for "the repose of their immortal souls." In 1992, however, I met the "baby." By then, he was a forty-eight-year-old successful wholesale wine merchant, and I got the rest of the story from him. He told me that in 1947, he received a birthday card from Bremen, Germany: "Happy Birthday, little Samuel," it read. It was signed, "Your Godfather, Ingemar." It was from Dr. Ingemar Walter! The doctor had survived the attack, after all. The blood splattered all over the motorcycle must have belonged to his young driver. Was he killed or simply wounded? We will never know.

SAMUEL, THE WINE MERCHANT

I met Samuel Del Re in 1995 when he was visiting our area and I was there on vacation. He was 52 years old and a successful wine merchant. He told me that everybody involved in the story surrounding his birth was dead. Aunt Angela died in 1954. The house was sold by her heirs to a young couple who had moved to the area following the industrialization period of the 70's and 80's of the entire Sangro River Valley. Route 16 was replaced by a modern turnpike, the A-14 (Bologna-Bari). This brought many young people to the area. The little stable that had served us as a refuge for over three weeks had been made into a bedroom by the new owners of the house. They turned the building into a modern *villino,* as the Italians love to call their suburban single homes. I met the young couple who now owned Aunt Angela's house. On the edge of the ravine, they had built a swimming pool. At the time of sale, they were told that at one time there was an almond tree in front of the house. They assumed that it had been cut down because, like the fig tree of Biblical renown, it had not produced any fruit for a time. I knew better!

LIBERATION DAY

Tuesday, Nov. 30th, 1943—There were no air bombardments that day. Nonno Donato theorized that the 8th Army had launched its offensive to cross the Sangro, and the Allied Air Force suspended operations in order to give the advancing British 8th Army a chance to move the front line forward. There had already been a case of "friendly fire" in the area around Casalbordino, just south of Fossacesia, about a month earlier, causing many casualties among their own men, so the air support was suspended for one day as a precaution.

The southern end of the Golfo di Venere.
The northern end of the Golfo di Venere reproduced on the cover of this book is the more picturesque of the two, but the southern end (above) is richer historically. Slightly above the center of the photograph is the gulf's southernmost point. It's there that the Sangro River flows into the Adriatic Sea. A whitish, barely visible

trail juts out into the sea for a quarter mile or so. It is the muddy water of the Sangro as it empties into the sea. Beyond it, there is another, smaller gulf and to the right one can clearly see the Torino di Sangro Ridge. This is where General Montgomery amassed his troops before launching the Sangro River Operations on November 29, 1943.

The German cannons and automatic small weapons to whose sounds we had become accustomed during the past three weeks, were strangely silent, as well. "All was quiet on the eastern front." Something was definitely happening! This might well be the end of the period that will be forever known in town as *"Lu sfullamente,"* or the evacuation period. It had lasted seven weeks.

General Montgomery considered the Sangro River Valley his own terminal point. In fact, he used the name of the river as part of the title of his own memoirs of war: *From El Alamein to the Sangro River.* His last visit to the front lines, before he was relieved of command and recalled to England for a new assignment, took place right in Fossacesia. There is a historical photograph that shows him inside the roofless church of Saint Donato, the church where Anna Maria and I were baptized and received our first Holy Communion. It appears that the general is inspecting the damage inflicted upon the church. Actually, he was just posing for the photo. That church, together with the elementary school, seemed to have been the target of the bombers from the very beginning of the siege of Fossacesia that began on October 12th and ended with heavy bombings the last week of November by the B-24 Liberators. Those bombers carried sixteen 500-pound bombs each with which they proceeded to liberate the daylights out of us. I believe the roof of the church collapsed simply as a result of the reverberation from explosions in its proximity.

General Bernard Montgomery (Monty)

The General was photographed inside the Church of St. Donato in Fossacesia. The church's ceiling had collapsed to the floor below. This photo was taken by a Canadian photographer on December 2nd or 3rd in Fossacesia. The young cameraman wanted to take a picture of the inside of Saint Donato, the church in which both Anna Maria and I were baptized. Just as he focused his camera, however, he became aware that it was sort of cold and incomplete; he needed the human element to add warmth to the picture. So he walked out of the church and seeing a small group of British officers and one civilian, he asked if one of them wanted to come into the church and have his picture taken. The officers in the group, naturally, deferred the honor to the highest ranking among them. That high ranking officer turned out to be none other than the commander in chief, himself, Gen. Bernard Montgomery, who seems to have no problem hamming it up for the camera. Incidentally, the lone civilian with the group was Mr. Ernesto Fantini, Anna Maria's father, who served as an interpreter for the General during his stay in Fossacesia.

With the British entrenched on the southern bank of the Sangro, and the Germans on the heights of Fossacesia, the two factions sized each other up for several weeks, but nobody moved. Meanwhile, the rains came. And it rained, and rained, and rained. The rains swelled the river to the point that it was no longer possible to wade across it, and it was even more arduous to try to build a pontoon bridge large enough so that Sherman tanks would be able to rumble across it. Finally, the British engineers decided to try to build the bridge in an area below *Mozzagrogna,* about four miles up-stream, where the river bent and narrowed. The first tanks rumbled across the Sangro late in the afternoon of November 29th, together with a division of Indian troops trailing behind.

Meanwhile, beginning on the 20th day of November, in anticipation of the final push, the B-24 Liberators began to pummel the area north of the Sangro indiscriminately. They called it "carpet bombing," because they covered an area with bombs as thoroughly as if they were laying a giant carpet over it. The bombers, B-24s, B-17s, B-25s and other types of aircraft, would arrive in the skies over and around Fossacesia by 10:30 A.M. each day and bomb the designated area unmercifully. According to the Imperial War Museum of London, a large part was played by the British twin engine Baltimores. I never saw a Baltimore in those days, however.

It isn't difficult to figure out that each air raid carried out by hundreds of bombers, produced thousands of intense personal dramas on the earth below among the enemy troops and the defenseless civilian population. In 1956, shortly before Signor Fantini became my father-in-law, he told me of the sad story of many a Polish teenager forced into the German Army and caught into the hell of those air raids. They were kids, just a few years older than I. On the 27th of November, for example, at the height of one of those bombing raids, a young soldier in a German uniform burst into the cave where he and the rest of the men from my neighborhood had found refuge. He had a name tag pinned on his uniform that ended in—ski. Mr. Fantini had met and even worked with many Polish-Americans, so he was able to identify the young man as being Polish, and not a real German. The story was confirmed about a year ago by Donato Natale, Anna Maria's cousin who lived in Florida. He died recently at age 83. He was in that cave, too. He said that at the height of the conflagration, the young man burst into the cave, frightened out of his mind, sobbing uncontrollably, his eyes revealing a very high degree of sheer terror. No one knows how he managed to find the cave the men hiding in it considered undetectable. The men made him sit down on a makeshift bench they had rigged up. They gave him a little wine in an effort to calm him down a bit. It was the only ingestible thing they had. Since no one in the cave spoke either Polish or German, they had to limit their conversation to gestures. Even so, the young soldier understood that the men were inviting him to remain with them. It was dangerous out there. The young man, calmer now but still remaining silent, shook his head from side to side indicating no. And then, without giving any indication of what he was about to do, he darted toward the cave's entrance, went outside and ran down the only path that led to the creek below. He had stayed in the cave no more than ten minutes. Everyone was shocked at his sudden move, to the point that the rest of the cave dwellers, including some of the nuns who were in an opening deeper into the cave, rushed outside to see where he had run. Mother Costantina, the Superior of the six or seven Passionist nuns in the cave, said a prayer that God protect the nice young man.

THERE ARE NO ATHEISTS IN AN AIR RAID

A curious incident occurred the last day we were bombed, November 29th, which helps to underscore the nature of the human mind. Each night, my mother would recite the rosary, as usual. It was not an unusual activity for us at home, but the present danger gave her an added impetus to pray harder. And so we all did. It was then that I memorized the short prayer that introduces each of the fifteen mysteries of the rosary. In Italian, that is! She would recite the complete fifteen decades of the rosary. Quite a few of the people present joined in. There were some who didn't, but respected her right to pray, perhaps hoping that her prayers might effect them, also.

There was a woman, however, who used to criticize my mother unmercifully. We called her "Turner." She would wax philosophically, almost suggesting that she was not afraid of those bombs. "The rosary isn't going to help us," she would say cynically. "If it's our time to die we will die, and no amount of prayer is going to change that!" She knew this would irk my mother, but that time mamma remained calm and collected. She never even answered her. Each bombing raid lasted no more than ten minutes, at the end of which Nonno Donato would announce the all clear. When she knew we had been spared once again, she would reinforce her criticism.

Beginning around the 20th of November and up to the last major raid which occurred on the 29th, we would be visited by swarms of bombers, mostly B-24's. Aunt Angela's stable, like most stables in the area at the time, was built in such a way that the animals entering it had to step down, and step up when exiting. Nonno Donato used the step as a pillow that allowed him to observe the wave after wave of bombers that arrived in our area each morning, and he would observe the exact moment they released their bombs. This gave him an idea if the bombs were going to hit us, or some other zone. The planes would release their killer loads, and then veer left and return to their bases in southern Italy. Most of the time, he would announce that we were safe. And he would be right, too, because within a few seconds we would hear the bombs explode far away.

The morning of the 29th, however, the bombs were released at just about the distance nonno judged to be the right spot for them to fall directly on top of us, so he said rather stoically: "I think we're all going to be dead in the next five minutes!" And he was almost right, too! Within a minute or so, we heard the first explosion, louder than any we had heard before. That first burst was followed by many others with an ever increasing degree of loudness. The reader may try to remember war scenes we have all seen at one time or another in movie theaters or on television, of actual clips from WWII bombing missions. From inside the plane the bombs are seen being released. The next scene they invariably showed the bombs dropping earthward. Then the scene shifts to the ground level where you see them explode in carpet coverage manner. Well, we were down below in the middle of those explosions. Their bursts became so loud that each detonation was more unbearable than the previous one. The last one exploded so close to our stable and it was so loud that the nucleus of every cell in our bodies must have rattled around its confines for about fifteen minutes before we could calm down. Throughout the duration of the air raid, mamma covered me and Filippo with her own body, while Nonna Concetta tried to protect the entire group with her body, as well. My brother, being the smallest, was at the bottom of the pile. After every detonation, mamma squeezed my arm hard. She hurt me, too. At the height of the conflagration, the noise was so unbearable that even Turner began to scream, *"Madonna di li Grazie, Madonna di li Grazie, aiutaci tu!"* In Abruzzese dialect, she was imploring Our Lady of Grace to come to our aid. Well, Our Lady of Grace must have heard her plea because we survived the most harrowing experience any of us had ever had. A number of years later Turner joined the thousands of Italians who were allowed to migrate into Canada. One day in the 1960s I happened to be in Montreal, and I saw her again. She had become a blond, frequented the local night spots, and was living a very nice life, thank you very much; Our Lady of Grace all but forgotten. The Neapolitans say it best when they remark cynically, *"Avuta la grazia, gabbato lo santo."* (Once the favor has been granted, the saint is left looking like a fool). But, then, thank God for that, too. Life goes on and it is in the nature of man to rise above his misfortunes and adversities. That was the last bombing I ever experienced with me in the middle of it. I hope it's the last.

The B-24 Liberators

The workhorse of the Italian campaign was the B-24. They bombed Fossacesia for eight days straight, pummeling it unmercifully. We, of course, were not in town, having escaped to the countryside after the October 12 raid, but many innocent civilians, especially the chronically ill who could not be moved, were killed right in their beds. There were few German soldiers in town at the time, with very little equipment, but the pervasive war philosophy of the Allies was, "Bomb the heebie-jeebies out of them!" The result was the so-called carpet bombing, with all that the term implies. It's for that reason I find little difference between Nazi atrocities wrought in hate and rage, and the Allied indiscriminate butchering of innocent people wrought in defense of freedom. This photo, compliments of the Imperial War Museum of London, may also serve to illustrate the story of the bomber I saw crash in the Sangro Valley in the spring of 1945, after dropping eight men by parachute. From the hill upon which I was standing, I saw the plane at about the same angle, size and perspective as the second bomber in this illustration, marked on its nose with the #15. (Photo: Imperial War Museum, London)

Bombs exploding somewhere in the Sangro River area
Between November 20th and the 29th, clouds of B-24's would
visit our area and bomb the daylights out of us. According to the
Imperial War Museum of London, sometimes they were different
airplanes like the twin-engine B-25 or Baltimores. They would
bomb one section at a time, hence the term, "carpet bombing."
Somewhere, in all that muck, were my family and I (Sorry, I forgot
to smile!). They missed us, thank God. Most of that bombing was
unnecessary, however. The Germans were gone, and they had little
in the way of military equipment left anyway, so all that destruction
was senseless. Fossacesia was literally cut in half by the destruction.
(Photo: Imperial War Museum, London)

DECEMBER 1, LIBERATION DAY

The afternoon of November 30th, holed up in our little stable, not being
very far out of town, we could actually hear the rumble of tanks as they
moved from west to east. Nonno was puzzled by this. He expected a south
to north movement along the Nazionale Route 16. In reality, having crossed
the river four miles upstream, the first 8th Army units climbed the ridge at
Mozzagrogna, west of Fossacesia. Since that town was very small, they entered it
from the south and crossed it in five minutes. There they found the Fossacesia
Marina-Lanciano provincial route, and so they formed a three pronged wedge:
one turned eastward and occupied Fossacesia, a second turned west and
proceeded toward the town of Castelfrentano, and the bulk of the division

headed toward the city of Lanciano, straight ahead. From that road, each town was connected to the river areas to the south by a local road. It permitted the inhabitants of the still rural towns to have access to their farmland. Fossacesia's road, being a national highway, was paved, albeit with technologies of the twenties, such as they were. But the others were covered with gravel, and it was barely adequate for the oxen-driven rural vehicles to make it to and from the flatlands of the Sangro. Sherman tanks were a different matter, however. Still, they too, made it to the top, churning up the pavement as they went.

MOTHERHOOD PREVAILS ONCE AGAIN

Meanwhile, on the evening of the 29th of November, while the bulk of the army was conducting advancing operations all across the Sangro Valley area, a small contingent of British demolition specialists set out at dusk from the vicinity of the Fossacesia train station, adjacent to the shore, and proceeding along the railroad tracks, now inoperative, reached the area of San Vito Marina unmolested and unnoticed. Their objective was to demolish a villa that rose above the sea on a hill a short distance from the shore. British intelligence had reported that German commanders had set up their headquarters there from which to direct the Sangro River operations. However, once the German high command decided rather hastily to abandon the Sangro Valley and fortify the Moro Valley instead, they moved their headquarters farther north rather quickly. The villa slated for demolition was a scant half mile south of the Moro. Unaware of the German move, the British soldiers examined the situation and decided to set up shop right on the railroad tracks, which were useless anyway, having sustained heavy damage all along the trunk from Pescara to Vasto. Their objective rose 300 feet almost perpendicularly above the railroad. There they were free to assemble the explosives necessary to do the job. Meanwhile, they sent out scouts to climb the hill and take a closer look. According to some chroniclers of the war, the two men who climbed the hill on their hands and knees, beside a map of the target area, had also been given a reconnaissance photo of the villa to be demolished. The photo showed several military vehicles parked on the gravel covered terrace. Once they reached the top, however, they discovered there were no military vehicles at all in the villa's ample front patio, as the air photos showed. While they considered what to make of this, one of the men thought he saw a faint light in one of the windows. Stealthily, the two approached the building. Inching their way toward that window, they looked inside. The window had originally been covered with a black cloth (wartime blackout), but probably in their haste to get away from there, the Germans had torn half of it off. Since they were moving, anyway, they had not bothered to fix it, and the inside scene was completely visible. To their horror, the British scouts observed a scene that was rather more reminiscent of a manger tableau at Christmas time than a war scene: a young mother was nursing a child by the light of an oil lamp. Civilians had moved into the villa like air rushes into a vacuum, a few hours after the Germans abandoned it. One of the soldiers ran to the track to alert the rest of the men who, obviously, scrapped all plans for the demolition. Motherhood once again had saved the situation. I wasn't there, of course, but I understand there were well over one hundred people inside that villa, including several British soldiers who had escaped from POW camps and had been taken in by local families until the British arrived.

WE SEE OUR FIRST BRITISH SOLDIER

Our little stable was no more than a mile south west of that villa. Part of the same contingent of British soldiers decided to do a little scouting around, and so they took to the road that led them toward Rocca San Giovanni, and they reached us at dusk. The sporadic firing of small caliber weapons, of which the Germans had made wide use, was strangely silent. Nonno Donato had a feeling that the German Army had pulled back. The British could not be far behind, he thought. As evening approached and the sun's rays began to soften, Nonno Donato cautiously walked out of our stable. I went with him, much to the consternation of my mother, who was deathly afraid that something terrible could happen to me. Nonno reassured her that I would be safe: a tranquil atmosphere reigned all around. As we reached the next house in the cluster, we met up with Nino, little Samuele's father, and Pete. Nonno Donato inquired as to the health of the baby and his mother. Nino answered that the baby was fine; as for the young mother, she was very weak and had a fever. She still needed medical attention. They spoke briefly about the German doctor who had delivered the baby ten days earlier, only to be killed by the strafing fire of a British fighter plane (at least, so we thought at the time). Nonno assured him that as soon as the British arrived, he would speak with them in their own tongue, and get medical help for her and the baby.

And then we saw him: a British officer emerged from behind a hedge, brandishing a small handgun. It looked more like a toy than a lethal weapon, its barrel was so narrow! Nonno Donato walked toward him cautiously and spoke to him in English. I didn't understand anything, but the fact that the officer appeared to have the personality of a baboon did not escape my notice. He seemed to react to Nonno Donato's enthusiastic greeting with a "so-what?" attitude, and he was annoyed that people here didn't speak English. I suppose he expected all Italians to be able to speak English . . . like all English subjects speak Italian! Within a few minutes, several soldiers joined their commanding officer. These reacted with a little more spirit to learn that there was someone who could speak to them in their own language. They told us that the Germans had pulled back to Ortona and beyond, and that the bulk of the British Army would start rolling into our area early the next morning. Meanwhile, Pete had rejoined the group and nonno explained his situation to the British officer. There were two British officers who had been freed after the Armistice who wanted to rejoin their outfit. That officer didn't seem very impressed or even interested. He told Nonno Donato to tell them to wait until the next day and report to the commanding officer of the first outfit which had room for them in their vehicles.

While I ran back to the stable to announce the war was over, the men spoke for a little while longer, and then the soldiers saluted and went back down the street toward the sea whence they had come. We had been expecting tanks, half-tracks, trucks and cannons, flags flying in the victorious breeze, flowers being thrown at the soldiers with an occasional Italian beauty offering free kisses. None of that! All we got that evening was a single officer with a pea-shooter, and three enlisted men.

That evening, for the first time in three years, we experienced a sense of freedom. It was as if an enormous burden had been lifted from our shoulders. Mamma quickly organized the recitation of the fifteen decades of the rosary in thanksgiving to God for having helped us come through that terrible period with our lives intact. As usual, some of the people joined in the prayers. This time, however, nobody teased my mother about her rosary: we had all come too close to rendering our soul unto its Maker.

A CLOSE CALL (see page 27)

THE BRITISH ARMADA ARRIVES

Early that morning, there was a knock at the stable door. It was Pete with the Italian soldier and the two British officers. They were so anxious to rejoin their comrades that they wanted to get an early start. The Italian escort, however, wanted some guarantees lest they think he was their captor. As a result, he had told the two officers to go on their own. They, on the other hand, wanted some guarantees, too, lest their fellow soldiers think they were deserters.

As a result, each felt that Nonno Donato, who understood both languages and knew the situation first hand, could be the guarantor for both parties. Nonno told both to go back home and wait until they saw more action. Up to then, we could hear the rumbling of tanks and other motorized vehicles, but had seen no one yet to whom to consign the two former prisoners and their ex-guard. By 8:30 we heard the first engine noise coming from our dirt road. It was a half-track, a tank, and two trucks full of soldiers. The soldiers got off, and they called the highest ranking officer among them, a colonel. Nonno spoke to him, explaining the situation. The colonel started to laugh: there had been others since they had occupied the mainland of Italy who rejoined the British Army, so he knew the exact procedure. He even had some pre-typed forms the two officers had to fill. No other explanation was necessary. Nonno went to call the three, and there was a grand reunion. The colonel summoned a jeep which would take them to headquarters, and their ordeal was over. The three shook hands with nonno and Pete, and they were gone.

The British military might arrived, as expected, shortly thereafter. Hundreds of vehicles, including tanks, trucks, jeeps, half-tracks, flatbeds, and other rigs hauling troops, ammunitions, supplies, food provisions, and a myriad of military equipment, the likes of which we had never seen or heard of before, began to rumble past our stable by 9:00 A.M. The trucks had a funny front end that required getting used to. That might have been the first time a contrast was noticed between the British "design" for a motor vehicle, and its Italian version. Their trucks were ugly, to be sure, but they were practical. Most of them had the dual function of hauling a load of materials of various types, or troops, and also of towing small or medium caliber cannons. The really heavy cannons were pulled by huskier vehicles, custom built for that purpose. One of the first unusual things I noticed was that each vehicle carried gasoline containers capable of holding, in my estimation, seven to eight gallons of gasoline in each container. The smaller jeeps carried one or two, while some of the larger vehicles had a whole row of gas cans in the back. The British were very friendly, too, as they waved to us from their vehicles. A couple of times, they threw chocolate bars at us, the first I had tasted in a long time. It was a Hershey bar and I didn't like it. "It's not exactly a Perugina or a Motta chocolate bar!" I complained to nonno. One soldier gave us chewing gum, a confection item completely alien to us. The first that I put in my mouth I swallowed after a few chews. The soldier who had given it to me laughed: "No, no, no!" he said, following with a barrage of words in English. Nonno Donato then explained to me that the purpose of chewing gum was simply to chew it; it's not to be swallowed. It took me a while to swallow that one.

Why? It seemed like such a useless activity to me. What can its purpose be? But no one could tell me the reason for the chewing. Just chew and shut-up, kid! seemed to be their attitude. One of the soldiers tried to speak to us with an open English-Italian dictionary in his hands. He made a serious attempt to speak Italian, except that he used every verb in the infinitive. In other words, he was trying to use Italian verbs in the manner of the English language, without conjugating them. It would be a few months before I understood the reason for that. But at least he tried. The Italians countered that bit of linguistic confusion by calling every British soldier, Charlie.

GOING HOME

By eleven o'clock we were on our way back to our homes, hopefully. We said goodbye to Aunt Angela, who smiled at us. Yeah! She could smile, after all! Up to then, although in a benevolent manner, she always pontificated to us: "You should do this!" "You shouldn't do that!" "I'm going to tell your mother!" and similar aphorisms. That morning she even cried, although she tried to hide it behind an enormous red handkerchief. "Be sure to drop by soon, you hear?" My mother assured her that she would come by often, thanked her for her gracious hospitality, and we departed. Before we actually left, she said: "Wait!" She disappeared into her bedroom. She emerged a few minutes later and handed each of the several children a handful of frosted almonds. They tasted as if they had been the last of the sweets from her wedding day, but after several years of deprivation of anything sweet, we all agreed that they were delicious. Filippo and I received five each, so we gave two each to mamma and nonna.

Finally, we got on our way. We went out onto the dirt road and turned right, intending to walk on the main highway, Route 16. The dirt road was the link to the shore line, where the British had a phalanx marching northward on another more important road. They had established a communication route on our dirt road that linked the two. Still, the Strada Statale Adriatica was of less importance than Route 16, so we only saw a few small vehicles. The real heavy traffic was on the highway, however. It was there that I saw my first Sherman tanks—hundreds of them, together with vehicles of all sizes and shapes: Jeeps, half-tracks, trucks pulling a cannon or a supply trailer, or a tough-looking muscle machine pulling a large, heavy, long distance cannon. It was a massive armada. Seeing all this, nonno remarked: "With all this equipment it took them twenty-seven days to cross a little river?"

But, I thought that was precisely the reason it took them so long to arrive, because moving all that equipment must have represented a logistical nightmare.

The logistics of moving such a massive assemblage of men, machines, cannons, and even mules, must have been mind-boggling. Occasionally one of those trucks became entrenched in the deep mud and required a tank to pull it out. The smell of diesel fuel permeated the entire area. Engine noise could be heard all over. Nonno Donato jokingly asked one of the soldiers if they had any baby carriages. He laughed and said no. The women took turns carrying Pina. Fortunately, she continued to be a good baby: she never cried.

As we started out, it was our intention to take the main road in order to avoid the muddy condition of the dirt-covered roads. Nonno, however, inquired about the traffic conditions on the highway, and he was told that it was not safe to try to share the roadway with all those vehicles. Each vehicle, except the ubiquitous Jeep, occupied three-fourths of the road surface and we would have had a hard time negotiating for the little space that was left for us to pass safely. The tanks, especially, spanned almost 90% of the roadway. As we approached the same back roads that we had taken in October, when we first arrived in the area, we stopped for a family conference. Of course, that meant mamma and nonno. The others just followed along. It was decided to turn back; it was too dangerous to walk along a highway that had no shoulder or sidewalk. We quickly back-tracked the couple of hundred yards we had already covered moving toward the main highway, and began to walk on muddy, but safer roads.

The first stop we made was at Pete's house. Grazia was able to provide us with some milk for the baby and even some diapers. She had found quite a supply of them in caring for little Samuele. The milk must have made Pina's day, because she went to sleep and didn't wake up until we reached our final destination, which, though not planned, turned out to be our summer cottage at Caporale. Since it was the first time that the majority of the stable dwellers had seen little Samuele, Grazia went into the bedroom and brought him out. His debut was a resounding success, judging by the oo's and ah's of the ladies in our midst. Even Turner was impressed. Then we said goodbye to Nino and Eva and wished them luck. They, in turn thanked both my mother and nonno profusely for their help, as they found themselves all alone and far from home. Eva confided to mamma that as soon as it was feasible to do so, she would have liked to go up north to try to find her sister and her mother. She knew her father had already died at Auschwitz, but she was hoping her mother and sister might have escaped Nazi rage. As it turned out, we had another year and a half before the war would actually be over and even more than that before she could travel by train to the north. At any rate, in 1995, I met the now adult Samuele and he told me that no more was heard of his grandmother or aunt. No doubt they ended up in one of the death camps at Auschwitz or Treblinka.

When we left Pete's house, we took the dirt road traveled by the small blue sports car we had seen six weeks earlier. I thought about those three people aboard the tiny car that day. I wondered if they had made it to their destination. We passed in front of Giacinta's house and mamma stopped to inquire about her daughter, our next door neighbor in town. She spoke to her for about three minutes and then she rejoined the group. She was crying profusely, having learned that our next door neighbor's house had crumbled to the ground. Our house, she was told, was still standing, but she could not tell if it was livable. Nonna was ahead of the group, so mamma didn't share the bad news with her. Give her a few more minutes of hope, she must have figured.

DEATH OVER THE ADRIATIC

Within a half hour, we were transiting behind Fossacesia's cemetery wall. There was a group of people standing around almost as if undecided as to what to do. Mamma, seeing one of her friends in the crowd, asked her what the problem was. She replied that the British had blocked both the road that led into town and the road that passed in front of the cemetery. We could see that up ahead there was a line of mortars at the corner of Cemetery Lane and Via Polidoro, and they appeared poised to fire their pieces. The shot that nearly killed us all that morning most probably came from them. A soldier was trying to stop the flow of people so that they could fire over the roadway. It would have been dangerous for them to fire their mortars while people walked in front of their pieces. But the people were having a difficult time understanding the orders. Suddenly, the first rounds were fired and the noise was enough to stop the people in their tracks. Some of them even retreated behind the wall at the back of the cemetery.

The town's former and future mayor and brother to the present mayor, Don Ernesto Mayer, happened to be there, too, as he was trying to make it back to his house nearby. Hearing all those cannons fire their rounds almost simultaneously, he panicked. Spotting my grandfather, and knowing that he spoke English, he came to us and asked him to inquire if it were they who were firing or if these were incoming shells. It was a silly question, actually, because even I, a boy of not quite twelve, could tell that they were outgoing shots. Nonno Donato obliged, however, and asked a sergeant about it. The sergeant replied, in some form of English dialect: "Yea, it's us, but there ain't no guarantee that the Jerries ain't gonna answer, so take cover for about ten, fifteen minutes." We did as he suggested. The cemetery's southern wall provided ample protection for us, so our entire gang went behind it and waited. Filippo and I, spotting some boulders placed there by some ancient owner of the place, ran toward them before the others, and sat on them. They weren't exactly soft, but they allowed us the necessary respite from our long walk.

We were sitting on those rocks but a few minutes when we saw the first wave of B-24 Liberator bombers arrive from the south, flying over open water in a formation of twelve planes each. This was actually the first time we had a chance to see the planes flying combat missions instead of just hearing the noise of their engines and the blasts of their exploding bombs. I remember very well the four engines and the twin tails of the Liberators, although some of the veterans of the 15th Air Force have been giving me an argument about it. "What Air Force unit were they from?" they'd ask. How in the world was I supposed to know that? I was just a boy and had never seen those airplanes flying that low before!

Filippo and I began to watch, fascinated by the spectacle. We watched one squadron fly by in the distance and disappear beyond the *Cavalluccio Point* before another squadron appeared. It was difficult for me to judge how high or how far from us they were flying. Due to the uneven terrain, we were not able to see the actual sea, a half mile away, so I wasn't even sure that they were flying over water, but when I saw them disappear behind the cape of the Cavalluccio, I knew their flight path was at least a mile off shore, heading north.

Just as the third wave of bombers flew over the mouth of the river to our south, we began to see puffs of black smoke softly explode just ahead of the planes as they proceeded northward. German anti-aircraft guns had found their range and were firing at them. It was impossible to figure out where those shells were being fired from. The thought crossed my mind that it might have been the work of the three anti-aircraft cannons we had seen on the way to cousin Donatina three weeks earlier, but they could not have been firing from that same area, because it would have been in British hands; hence they must have moved somewhere between San Vito and Ortona. But that was a long distance away. Still, they were reaching their targets without any problem. Our eyes perceived the black puff of smoke almost immediately after each shell exploded, but since sound travels at a much slower speed, we did not hear its report until a second or two later. It was all very mysterious. Filippo and I were mesmerized by it all. To young boys, this was better than the movies. We enjoyed the spectacle of live-action war.

Within a few minutes, we began to hear the bombs explode in the distance to our northwest, as the first group of planes reached their targets. It sounded like the fireworks that we used to hear in peaceful times during the processions for the feast of San Vito or Saint Thomas the Apostle in Ortona. My mother speculated that they were hitting the port of Ortona. Shortly thereafter, in confirmation of her suspicion, a very large column of black smoke appeared in the direction of Ortona and began to rise to the sky. "They must have hit an oil tanker!" Nonno said. Meanwhile, the storms of American bombers kept coming unabated, and the puffs of black flack kept on exploding in front of the planes, softly and mysteriously; and they were about to become deadly, as well.

THE FIRST HIT

Suddenly, there was a flash in the middle of the third group of bombers, and the first plane went straight down into the water, trailing a tail of black smoke. It happened very fast, and it didn't take long for the ill-fated plane to be lost to our sight. We didn't see it splash into the sea due to the undulation in the terrain, but we could imagine it. Soon we saw a second plane explode and fall into the sea, and then a third, and a fourth, and a fifth. Within the space of fifteen or twenty minutes, we saw eleven of those bombers being hit and dropping into the sea, with its full crew on board. Many years later, I studied the B-24 Liberator bomber's flight manual. In full bombing mission it carried ten men. Therefore, I saw one-hundred and ten American flyers die in the line of duty that day, in their efforts to liberate us. Today, they are all but forgotten. The U. S. Air Force has them listed as "missing in action." Except that I saw them die that December 1, 1943. Over the years I made a valiant effort to induce American government agencies to erect a small memorial in that area to commemorate the event, but they were not interested. Three and a half years later, when we finally managed to rejoin my father in America, papà showed me three bundles of local newspapers he had saved that covered the Battle of the Sangro River. He had saved the issues of November 29th and 30th as well as those of December 1st, 2nd and 3rd. Besides the *Norristown Times Herald*, he had saved two from Philadelphia, the *Philadelphia Inquirer* and the *Evening Bulletin* and, of course, his favorite newspaper, *Il Progresso Italo-Americano*, the Italian daily. Not one of them carried the story of the eleven American bombers lost over the Adriatic Sea on December 1, 1943. Over the years, I was shocked to realize how many Americans took the fact that it was not in the paper as proof positive that it never happened, including the United States Air Force. I know one thing: I didn't dream it. I saw it happen with my own eyes. Today, according to the scuba divers and boaters who frequent the Adriatic in the gulf for recreational purposes, as well as commercial fishermen, there's not one plane in sight at the bottom of that sea. I was told that many fishing boats often drag nets along the floor of the sea to harvest shellfish. If the planes were still there, the nets would become entangled on them. And they invariably look at me as if I lost my bearings. But, it is also true that given the proximity of the mouth of the Sangro River, which creates very strong currents in the *Golfo di Venere* all year 'round in well over sixty years they were probably tossed around the bottom of the sea by the currents, and they may have been transported deeper into the Adriatic channel. Could be! According to data sent to me a few years ago, the Air Force lost fourteen B-24 Liberators that day, worldwide. I saw eleven of them go down in my gulf. The other three might have been part of Air Force groups operating elsewhere in Europe or Asia. Or they could have been hit after they passed the point at which they were no longer visible to us.

Since WW II ended, a number of former B-24 personnel formed a group of volunteers that keep what was left of the Liberator fleet flying. Today there is only one B-24 Liberator still capable of flight. From February to November each year, a number of veterans fly that lone airplane together with a B-17 as they visit small airports all over the country, somewhat of a flying museum. Naturally, they attract many visitors, especially those who served in or around the airplane so long ago. I, too, try to visit the planes whenever they come to within driving distance of the Philadelphia area, in a strange, symbiotic attraction to it. It's like being repulsed at the sight of scorpions, yet being curious enough to look at them. I even purchased a B-24 cap which I wear proudly, I don't know why. Whenever I talk to those veterans, seeing my hat, the first thing they ask me is how many missions I flew in the Liberator. Invariably, I tell them that I flew no missions at all. In fact, I was on the receiving end, *"and you guys missed, ha-ha!"* When I tell them that I saw eleven planes downed that day, however, they deny it. Well, I will not place my hand on the fire to make my point. I was a kid then and as of this writing, it is over sixty years after the fact, therefore my memory of what I actually saw may have become somewhat obfuscated. They may call into doubt the kind of airplanes they were, or which Air Force they were part of, but I saw what I saw. Maybe they were not B-24's, perhaps they were part of the 12th Air Force, or there might be some other explanation for the mix-up. Still, I have those flashes of light in the middle of the flying group of bombers and the planes that were hit falling straight down into the sea, indelibly etched in my memory. Eleven of them!

The insistence of the 15th Air Force Veterans that it was impossible for me to have seen eleven B-24's shot down over my sea on December 1, 1943, is in contrast with what I read later. Stephen Ambrose says that by early 1945, only four Liberators were left out of the original 24 the 741st Squadron had assigned to them. What happened to them all? Another bit of information came from the internet. In an article from the Cape Cod Times written by

Robin Lord, the writer quotes from a book by Robert F. Dorr: "The B-24 was a cantankerous, lumbering, draughty, unforgiving son-of-a-bitch heavy on the controls, over grossed and difficult to fly in formation." Later, he adds, "Flak was a particular problem for the B-24. The shrapnel loaded mini bombs, pre-set to explode at a certain altitude, launched by German anti-aircraft guns from the ground. Since the Liberator could not go above a certain altitude and were ordered before each mission to stay at a specific height, if the flak operator was accurate that day, it was like flying through a mine field." This proved to me that I indeed saw eleven B-24's shot down that day. Perhaps the reason for their denial lies elsewhere: maybe they were not all B-24's, perhaps they did not originate from the same base in southern Italy, or maybe their reports were not exactly accurate. Who knows? But I saw what I saw, *punto e basta!* (That's the Italian phrase for, *Period!* It has a greater sense of finality than its English counterpart!)

Over the years, people often asked me if anyone had tried to rescue the flyers, and I have to laugh when I hear such talk. It is very difficult to paint a picture of the situation as it actually existed that morning, in that area. No one can possibly understand. After all, modern Americans have never been in any situations that could even remotely be compared to the realities of war. That was the "front line" of the Sangro River Battle. Everybody in the military was very busy killing while trying not to be killed, and the civilian population was running around seeking refuge, praying and hiding, trying not to get killed. I doubt that any of those fliers survived, because no one would have been in a position to be able to help them. It is very possible that a few of them might have survived the crash itself and, being very good swimmers, might have dived into the frigid water and made it to shore. It is possible, but not very likely. Swimming a couple of miles in frigid water would have required a Herculean effort even from the best of swimmers. The other thing that is hard to imagine is that life in the war zone was totally disrupted. There would have been some fishing boats available as rescue vessels, but the fishermen were away trying to save their own skins and those of their families, like everybody else.

HOME AT LAST, BUT . . .

After witnessing such cataclysmic events on that first day of December, after about twenty minutes of waiting behind the cemetery wall, we continued our journey home. We entered the town, not knowing what we would find when we got there. From a distance, everything seemed fine, but it couldn't be. People had gotten killed there, so some damage had to have taken place.

Well, we didn't have to walk much farther before we began to see the first evidence of the heavy damage inflicted on our town.

After we left the cemetery area, we took via Polidoro, which led straight to the center of town, but at the lower level of our central *piazza,* the marketplace, as it were. It was the street where, on October 12th, Anna La Caprara and her two children were killed. The hole the bomb made had been partially filled, but it was clearly visible. From that point, we also had an unobstructed view of *Fossaceca* (Old Fossacesia) in ruins, and that sort of sapped our hearts of any hope that we might find our home intact.

As we got closer to the center of town, we reached the fish market where, each morning, in more peaceful days, the farmers and the fishermen came to sell their respective products. Just as we entered the *piazza,* and the Church of the Holy Rosary came into view, as if planned, the bells of the town clock began to ring. The larger of the two bells rang twelve times and the smaller one followed with two strokes at a higher pitch: it was 12:30 P.M. This caused a lot of emotion in the entire group. Mamma had tears in her eyes. It was as if the town was happy to see us again, and its clock welcomed us home. We had been gone forty-five days.

We walked another hundred yards and arrived in front of the church in the center of town. From there, we could see the Basilica of Saint Donato down the hill to our right. It looked intact, but its roof had crashed down to its floor.

Fossacesia Martoriata (Fossacesia scourged)

Thus read the caption in the town's newspaper years later as they commemorated the 50th anniversary of the war. The steeple top visible at left is that of the Basilica of St. Donato. This is the old city, but the rest of it didn't fare much better. Our house, located to the left of this photo, about three blocks away, was completely destroyed. (Photo: Imperial War Museum, London)

My "palace" before the bombers arrived
The above photo was take during the winter months of 1930. It was the day that my maternal side of the family occupied the brand new house. The event drew the entire neighborhood. Recognizable are my mother and my Uncle Nick at the center of the balcony.

Our main street was actually the well-documented Route 16, but in town it took the name of *Piazza del Popolo,* literally, the people's gathering place. As that artery entered the town in front of the church of Saint Donato at its northern end, all the way up to the corner of the smaller Rosario church, it became part of the *piazza.* From there it became *Via Roma* and ran with that name for one block only. At that point it became a three-way intersection: *via Sangro* proceeded straight south carrying Route 16 with it. *Via Lanciano* went west to the city of Lanciano. The third arm was a secondary local street, *Via Romanelli.* As we reached *Piazza del Popolo,* we began the arduous task of trying to cross the street as one military vehicle after the other, heading north, passed in front of us at a steady thirty miles an hour without interruption.

They didn't even notice us. There had never been such traffic there before, ever! While waiting in front of the *Dopolavoro,* a former recreation center set up by the Fascist regime (that's where Filippo and I used to go before the war to get an occasional ice cream cone during the summer), as we waited by the side of the road, forever it seemed, I became fascinated by the unique manner in which the vehicles that moved on caterpillar treads actually proceeded forward, vehicles such as tanks and half-tracks. I suddenly understood the principle of the system. Each link of those steel belts would actually come to a complete halt the second it came in contact with the road surface and would rest there motionless for a second or two until the rear wheels picked it up again. Then it moved faster than the tank itself toward the front until it came in contact with the road surface again and it stopped anew. The action was repeated over and over as the tank moved forward. Being completely mesmerized by this, I didn't notice that other groups of people had joined us on the side of the road trying to get across the street. Finally, Nonno Donato spotted an MP nearby and shouted to him to stop the traffic and let us get across. With that, the MP halted the flow of military vehicles and suddenly a lot of people all along that road walked across the street in both directions.

The street to Lanciano
This is the street that leads to Lanciano in my neighborhood. This is the devastation that greeted us on December 1st. At the extreme right is a building with two door frames. It was a fabrics store. On both sides of it were our two streets, One Street and

Two Street. Our house was behind it about one hundred yards down both streets. The building destroyed at the center of the photo belongs to the Saraceni family. The last member of that family lives in Toronto. The building obviously received a direct hit. The repeated raid on our town was an absolute massacre. The jury, as they say, is still out to determine the reasons for it. (Photo: Imperial War Museum, London)

My "Palace" after the bombers left
For unknown reasons, the British engineers left the single hovel pictured above still standing. It was across the street from our house and about fifty yards north of it. It had been the habitation of a very poor woman and her young niece. My grandmother Concetta was so happy to get back to her old neighborhood that she rented it. We lived in it up to June 9, 1947, when we finally left to go to America.

We proceeded across and both mamma and Nonna Concetta nearly had a heart attack: Via Commercio, the street that we normally took to get to our house was blocked to all but local pedestrian traffic. Looking up via Commercio toward our neighborhood, we could see that it was not passable at its upper end, covered as it was with debris three feet high. As it turned out, our neighborhood was the most devastated area of town, and our family was the hardest hit.

Not being permitted to enter our street from that area, we proceeded another block to *Via Lanciano,* hoping to be able to reach our house from the upper end. So instead of walking up *Via Commercio* and then turning left onto our back or front street (I'll call them *One Street* and *Two Street,* as our house was built right between the two, without a single inch to spare on either side, and, of course without a sidewalk either), we would approach it from the other end on Via Lanciano and turn right. When we did that, though, we ran into some real destruction. There were two piles of debris on either side of the main street, and a very narrow path in the middle of the road so people could pass. It reminded me of happier times when it snowed and the people made a path right in the middle of the street. Only this was not snow, but debris of bricks, stones, and dust: mountains of debris on either side of Via Lanciano.

Just as we rounded the corner from Via Roma onto Via Lanciano, my mother spotted a book lying on top of a pile of stones. She had to climb onto the rocks to retrieve it. It was titled *Fabiola* by Cardinal Wiseman. Once she had it in her hands, she looked on the inside pages to see if there was a name written somewhere indicating ownership. There was none. So she kept it and gave it to me to carry. I couldn't wait to get home so I could read it. At that moment, though, there was no time even to glance at it because we quickly reached *One Street.* We looked down, and our home was standing there in all its glory. Mamma and nonna shouted with joy seeing that our house was intact. Their joy, unfortunately, was of a very short duration. For one thing, we couldn't reach it: there was a giant crater right in the middle of the street where the back entrance to our home was. So we walked the few steps that separated us from *Two Street,* and looked toward the front of the house. It was the same thing there: another crater in the middle of that street prevented us from entering our front door. In other words, two heavy bombs exploded, one in front of it the other in the back, without budging it, that's how well built it was. At this point we spotted a group of military personnel looking at some maps. Nonno called out to them. A young lieutenant came to us, and told us the entire block was slated for demolition in the next few days, as soon as the heavy equipment arrived from the Vasto area. He said that the houses against which our house had been abutted on both sides were completely destroyed, so our house was declared uninhabitable. "But," Nonno Donato protested, "it looks in great shape. Whatever is wrong with it can be fixed." "Well, Sir," added the lieutenant, "we didn't come here to work as masons. The military damage assessment team has declared it uninhabitable, and that's the way it stays." Of course, there was another reason they mined and finished to destroy our house: they used the material to fill in the two giant craters the bombs had made. Nonna Concetta said it would have been better if the bombs had made a direct hit, instead of seeing such a beautiful house willfully destroyed as an afterthought, thus adding heartache to all that physical destruction. And so another thorn was added to my poor grandmother's crown of thorns. She had such a horrible life that when death came to her on January 3, 1951, in America, she must have felt totally liberated.

While trying to figure out what to do, we noticed that some of the neighbors had made it back, for not all the houses had been destroyed. Mamma and nonna thought that the following day they would return and try to reason with somebody in authority. There was a quick conference that included my mother, maternal grandmother and grandfather. Mamma wanted to go into the house squatter-like. "What could they do to me? Carry me out bodily? It's my house!" she protested. But, nonno pointed out that, with hundreds of foreign soldiers running loose, that was not the worst thing they could do to her. It was a dangerous situation for two defenseless women and two children to stay there. "Come to my house and we'll talk about it with calm, to see what can be done." Mamma understood Nonno Donato's implications perfectly and agreed to move on.

Of course, we didn't know the conditions of our two paternal residences, either. They might have been destroyed, too. So, it was decided to continue our journey and check out the house in Via delle Croci, my birthplace, and hope for the best. If that house was damaged or destroyed, we could always go to Caporale, our summer cottage, if the Germans had not blown it up already.

So we began walking again. Nonno's concern about the condition of that house was not unfounded, as it was located right on the edge of town, at the top of the hill overlooking the Sangro Valley. It was wide open to all kinds of firepower. Luckily, we found it damaged but intact and there was no one there to prevent us from entering it, so we went in. As the adults inspected the upstairs and the rest of the house for damage, and the women anxiously checked the walled-up areas to see if the Germans had gotten to them, I went into a room in the back of the property where I knew there were some books. It was wide open, so I cautiously went inside (Did I mention that I was particularly repulsed by the sight of scorpions? And there were plenty of those around the area). Carefully I lifted what used to be a closet lid, and there I found a treasure—the books my father had brought home in 1934 and didn't bother taking them back with him were all there. Among them was a beautifully bound copy of Manzoni's, *I promessi sposi* (The Betrothed).

What luck! Suddenly, I had more reading material than I had ever before possessed, and they were my father's, hence mine. I hadn't even known they existed. Besides Manzoni's great historical novel, there were a number of shorter classical novels, such as Verga's *Storia di una capinera* (The story of a blackcap), several adventure stories by Emilio Salgari, of which I was an avid reader, *Le avventure di Huckleberry Finn*, that's Twain's Huck Finn in Italian, and a book on American history, but that one was in English and I couldn't read it—not yet. I took it anyway.

One book in particular attracted my attention. It was entitled *L'inglese in tre mesi senza maestro* (English in Three Months without a Teacher), by Lysle. "How is that for self confidence!" I thought to myself. Even the name of the author was strange—Lysle, after all, is not an Italian name. (Several decades later I learned that there was a series of similar books, published in Torino at the end of the 19th century that promised to teach, beside English, French, Spanish and German, all in three months and all without a teacher. Embedded within the text there were also advertisings for cigarettes, liquor, and tomato paste). I decided to check it out, so I took it. I began to study the English language with it from that point on. In keeping with the spirit of the book's title, I was able to study on my own, literally without a teacher. Not only was the book very well done, but my three favorite teachers, Dora Caccciavillani, Maria Fantini, and Flora Fizzani, had given me the necessary grammatical foundation that enabled me to navigate through it with great profit. That book with the lofty title became the basis upon which I was able to harness the mysterious meanderings of the English language.

The house itself had been damaged by a cannon shell, although it was not in danger of collapse. However, we could not stay there, either. Another quick conference ensued, and it was decided to head for our country cottage. From the balcony of the room where I was born, we could see its red roof at the bottom of the hill, a half mile away. From that distance, it looked intact, although that did not mean that it was. But, everyone hoped it was. We were all very tired and hungry by then. We soon got under way, although now I had the extra burden of carrying four or five of my father's big books. Nonno suggested I leave them at the house that he would get them the next day, but I would not be denied. Looking around, I found a bisaccia, a double sided knapsack, distributed the books equally in both pockets and I put it around my neck. Alas, I was too little and the two sacks nearly hit the ground. So Nonno came to my rescue. He took the bisaccia, which was his anyway, gave me the bundle of baby things he was carrying, and we started out for Caporale.

Because of the muddy conditions that prevailed along the dirt road we normally took to go from one house to the other, we opted to take the "Nazionale," Route 16, which was paved up to the point where it leaves the urban area. From the edge of town, as it descends to the Sangro River Valley, it was covered with crushed stone. At least it was not muddy. That decision, while taking us another half mile out of our way, may have saved our lives because, unbeknown to us then, that muddy road, at a point very close to the entrance gate to our property, had been booby-trapped with dozens of underground mines of the anti-tank variety. The Germans had buried thousands of anti-tank mines in a 650-foot-wide area that went from the shoreline to the Apennine mountains. The mines were particularly numerous in the roadways that could have been used by tanks. We would not have survived it unscathed. Luckily, within a half hour, we reached our gates. It was 3:30 P.M.

On our front lawn several vehicles were parked. A British soldier greeted us with a rifle and barked for us to halt. "Here we go again," I thought to myself. "These guys are nuts, too." But the threat didn't last long. Nonno had stopped momentarily to talk to some of our old neighbors who were making their way home from the south, so he had to run to catch up with us. As soon as he did, he spoke to the soldier in English, and calmed him down. "Who is the boss, here?" he asked. A captain came forward and said, "I am." "Well," said Nonno, "I am the other boss." Meaning, this is my house. Very diplomatic he was, my grandfather. This was dramatized a few days later when we learned that the man who lived across the street from us, another "American," upon entering the gates of his own house, finding it full of soldiers, began to shout "Out, out. This is my house. Everybody get out of here." It required a sergeant armed with a machine gun and a large foot to literally kick him out into the street. With that kind of arrogance, no wonder they did not take him to heart. They were, after all, the conquerors, and they occupied his house, just as they had occupied the rest of the country. As a result of that initial altercation, the British soldiers did not leave his house until Good Friday, 1944, when the entire division was called back to England.

In our home, nonno's diplomatic approach to a difficult situation paid off. The captain decided to clear one of the rooms, the largest, and invited us to occupy that one for the time being and he would see what he could do about leaving it altogether in a few days. Two days later, they moved out, giving us back the full use of our house. Of course, the dwelling was only a three room cottage. We were still cramped, but after living in Aunt Angela's stable for three weeks, this was much better. Besides, I had grown up in it. The distant relatives and friends that made up the original group had all gone to their respective homes, so there were only thirteen of us left, including the baby. Still, the three rooms were not sufficient, but they would have to do for the time being.

Meanwhile, as we waited for the soldiers to move their equipment from the one room, Nonno decided to check out his wine cellar, which was accessible from the outside. He approached the door cautiously, noticing that it was ajar. Even more cautiously, he descended the stairs. In less than a minute, he came back upstairs, out of breath and white as a ghost. He said something to the captain which he later translated for our benefit: "It's full of dead bodies down there," said he. The captain and the other soldiers burst out laughing: "They're not dead—they're drunk!" said the captain, "They drank all the sherry wine you had down in your cellar." My grandfather sighed in relief.

THE FATE OF OUR "SAFE" SHELTER

Later that afternoon, nonno decided to walk down to Casimiro's place. My aunts tried to discourage him mainly because of the danger of underground mines, but he thought he could see where the earth had been disturbed. He was curious to know if Casimiro's family had made it through the war safely. When he came back, he had some surprises for us. First, he said that he had passed by the bottom end of our property, where our vineyard was. The grapes were still on the vine and, although much of the crop was rotten, most of it was salvageable as wine. Soon, we would have to go in there to harvest it. But first the vineyard had to be checked out for mines. Within a week, the British sent a squad of ordnance deactivators who scoured the entire property with several mine detectors. After four hours of slowly walking up and down the field, earphones upon their heads and the round sensor plates in front of them, they determined that it was completely mine free.

Secondly, cousin Casimine and his family were all safe. However, they had to move south to Torino di Sangro. Nonno Donato reported that detail somewhat begrudgingly, because it proved once again that mamma had been right all along. The elder Aunt Filomena said that three days after the rest of my family had left their place the Germans came with evacuation orders and forced them to abandon the house, as they had done with us at Mr. Moretti's place and the Fantini's at Caesar's place. Fortunately, the young lieutenant who came to alert them that morning was a very gentle and accommodating soul. Aunt Filomena told him she had a daughter who was married in a town south of the Zamenga Bridge (true), and that she was pregnant (not true), and she was due any day (not true, either). She needed her mother's assistance. Could they go there? To everyone's amazement he said yes, and that he could give her a pass to present to the sentry at the bridge. To further amaze everyone, the lieutenant said he would come back in the afternoon and take everybody to the bridge with a truck, which he did. This underscored even further the validity of my mother's idea to go south. It often happens that we create monsters in our heads out of fear. We had an opportunity to do the same. We could have gone to the bridge and, if it was not feasible to cross it, so be it, we could have retraced our steps and proceeded toward Rocca San Giovanni. Fortunately, we had all survived the war and it was useless to keep talking about it, so nonno changed the subject. But even though no one made any further comment, what followed was nothing short of a grave silence—the famous pregnant pause, if you will! Everybody was thinking it even if nobody said it!

Finally, he let go with the biggest surprise of all, the one that had everybody in stitches (it could have easily been the opposite): that shelter the men had dug on the side of the Marrone house in October, the one that was supposed to keep us safe from cannon shells and airplane bombs, had been centered with geometric precision either by a fortuitous cannon shell, or by a super-skilled (or super-lucky) fighter pilot. We could not tell with certainty, although British experts ascertained later that it was an airplane bomb, because the trajectory of a cannon shell would have been at an angle. This was straight down into it and had dug a crater twelve feet in diameter and six feet deep. So much for safety strategy, and thank you God for another little miracle, or, perhaps, a big one!

Meanwhile, I spent the next days reading my father's books. The book that caught my fancy the most, however, was the one my mother had picked up among the debris of our destroyed town on December 1st, Cardinal Wiseman's *Fabiola*. It was a novel about the early Christians, featuring the martyrs of the early Church, such as Saint Sebastian, Saint Agnes, Saint Cecilia, Saint Pantaleon (a Roman military surgeon), and Saint Pancratius. These were the early heroes of our faith. I began to read it, and couldn't put it down. After I went through it in a few days, I read it so many times more than I can remember some passages by memory. I took it to America with me where I read it many more times (I still have it today, minus the first twenty-six pages). Meanwhile, I kept studying English with my father's book about learning English in three months without a teacher. The title's super confidence notwithstanding, however, as already noted, I believe the reason why I had such great success was that I had been given a very solid base in grammar and syntax, conceptually, by my three early teachers. When the author spent entire pages explaining what a noun or a verb or an adjective was, I could simply move ahead to "usage in the English language" because I knew these things already. Summing up our Odyssey, it was a seven week ordeal during which we dodged bombs, Nazis and hunger, but we survived it all. Thanks to my mother's shrewdness, we never moved farther north than a three mile radius of Fossacesia. Here is a schematic of our peregrination away from our home.

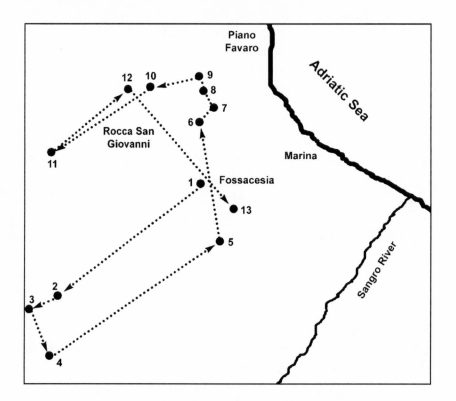

Map of Fossacesia's immediate surroundings.

Between October 12 and December 1, 1943, we were forced out of our homes by the daily threats of air raids and Nazi orders. The Germans wanted everyone to go north. But my mother kept going in circles, so that we never ventured out of town for more that a couple of miles. During the seven week Odyssey everyone calls "*Lu sfullamente,*" (the evacuation period), we changed "residence" eleven times. Twice, the residence in question was nothing but a damp cave. In two instances, we moved twice on the same day. Here are the points of "habitation" and direction of our movements during that period.

1.   Home in Fossacesia, October 12.
2.   Aunt Anne's place.
3.   Aunt Florence's place.
4.   The Stante residence.
5.   Aunt Filomena's place (Casimino).
6.   Signora Memena's place. This was the only time we were refused hospitality.
7.   Signora Giacinta's place. Actually, we slept in caves for three days.
8.   Mr. Chicken's place, the Moretti household. Pina was born here, Captain Campbell dropped in, All Saints mass.
9.   Brief stop over at Pete's place until the Germans chased us again.
10.   I Cesari (Caesar's place). Here, Bricco barked at us; we move to avoid danger; Bricco's demise.
11.   Aunt Angela's little stable. Three weeks of relative calm, but we were the target of heavy bombardments.
12.   Home, at last! Except there was no home to go to.
13.   We ended up in our little country home at Caporale

DECEMBER 10, 1943, MY PERSONAL DAY THAT WILL LIVE IN INFAMY.

Friday, December 10, 1943, was a bad day for me. It turned out to be my personal day that, in the immortal words of FDR, "will live in infamy," just as December 7, 1941, does in the heart of every American. Nothing really happened to me to make it so, but all day long I had a premonition of impending disaster, mostly imaginary as it turned out, that left an indelible mark on my psyche. Every year after that, when December 10th rolls around, I commemorate it with a silent prayer for the lady whose death at 10:30 A.M. started it all. I am probably the only one who ever prays for her! It was the tenth day of our liberation, and as noted, we had been living in our little country home since getting home from the evacuation period. Nonna Concetta was invited to stay with us, because her home was due to be demolished by the British around December 15th. That house was full of furniture and all the material possessions they had so carefully hidden from the Germans. They couldn't lose everything now that the war was over. So, for the next two weeks both mamma and nonna got up early every morning and walked up to the town trying to salvage as much of the house's contents as possible. Their most difficult job was trying to find people around town who would have enough room in their house to store some of the furniture, including our beautiful three-piece mahogany dining room set with six chairs, plus my mother's expensive sewing machine. I often think about that: it must have been a nightmare for them first to find a family with room to spare in their home and then to carry everything there. In addition to trying to find storage for our things, there were two trunks that belonged to Ninni's family which had to be stored somewhere, especially since they might come back at war's end to retrieve their belongings.

The morning of the 10th, mamma and nonna left earlier than usual, so I didn't see them leave. Around nine o'clock, Nonno Donato found an old rubber ball that had belonged to me when I was younger. With an awkward motion, he kicked it toward me, then he grabbed his harvesting tools and baskets and headed down the path to the vineyard to begin the much overdue grape harvesting. Filippo and I began to kick the ball around. At one point, I tried to kick it backwards, but I hit it with the tip of my shoe instead of my instep. The ball didn't leave my foot as intended, heading, instead, in the opposite direction and straight to the top of the roof. It bounced a couple of times on the red roof tiles, then rolled down toward us. We were ready to engage it in play once it came down, but it never made it. It failed to clear the gutter and stopped in its concavity. So, I had to walk all the way to the vineyard to call nonno and ask him to come back to the house and retrieve our ball. With infinite patience, he stopped what he was doing (actually, I think he was looking for an excuse to take a break, anyway!) and came back to the house, took a ladder, set it to the roof's edge, climbed it, grabbed the ball and threw it down to us, and started back down.

He was half way down the ladder when an explosion rocked the entire neighborhood, accompanied by the inevitable plume of black smoke rising toward the sky. Instinctively, we all looked in the direction of the detonation. It was at the top of the hill, toward the town, just about where the road would be where mamma and nonna could have been. The mushroom cloud of black smoke was rising into the sky as we looked. "O God, don't let it be them, please!" I thought. I should have known better than to think that it might have been mamma and nonna who triggered that explosion. They had left much earlier, and were probably busy moving furniture. But in situations like that, sometimes the most logical conclusions elude the keenest mind, and suddenly I found myself in the grip of a profound, irrepressible anguish.

Having gotten our ball back, we resumed play, but my heart was no longer in it. I gave that ball a couple of distracted kicks, and I walked outside the gates just to do something, sitting on a retaining wall for a while. I even flirted with the idea of actually going into town to look for them. It would have been a crazy thing to do, so I didn't. Shortly afterward my other grandmother called us into the house for lunch. I was grateful. It distracted me for a while. By one o'clock we even learned that the person killed in the explosion was a woman who lived near the outskirts of town. She had ventured into a wooded grove looking for firewood. The area she was canvassing was a mere 300 yards from her house, and she was in a patch of grassy slope that was well off the beaten path. Why it was necessary for the Germans to place a mine there is anybody's guess. That poor lady was the victim of an ignoble act that solved nothing, even as it killed an innocent person. Ironically, her husband, Giuseppe Fantini, better known in town as *Peppe di Mussone*, was one of the men who, being totally illiterate and having never gone to school, had come to America tagging along with my nonno Donato in 1920. He had learned to read a little, though, with the help of a retired teacher whose land he worked. His skill as a reader was good enough so that as they sailed the Atlantic in April of 1920 aboard the transatlantic Roma, every time he had to go to lunch or dinner he had to walk all the way around the outside of the ship in order to bypass the door to the galley, where there was a large can with the word *GRASSO* (grease) written on it. Just the idea of the grease inside that can made him seasick. He had actually spent several years in Norristown, Pa., digging ditches with the Norristown Water Company (now called the Pennsylvania-American Water Company). He returned to Italy in 1924, because his wife was afraid to sail and refused to join him in America. I suppose her destiny called for another, very different pattern. After his wife's death, Peppe was inconsolable, blaming it all to *"il destino,"* (fate). Within a year, however, he had remarried, with "the consent of my son, John," as he told every one. And so, life goes on, thanks be to God.

THE LONG VIGIL AT THE GATES

Having learned that it was not my mother or grandmother who had been killed, my fears were calmed somewhat, but the day had been prescribed since time immemorial as a "heavy duty one" for me. By two o'clock, I began to walk out to our gates to scrutinize the road where mamma and nonna would eventually appear coming home. Even knowing that they would normally come home way past four o'clock, I needed to be out there, as if my presence at the gates hastened their return, perhaps ahead of schedule. I must have made ten trips to the gate, back and forth, all afternoon. At about three o'clock some British soldiers came to the area and started to do target practice on a field diagonally opposite from our gate, using live hand grenades. At least it provided a temporary distraction for me. I started to watch as the soldiers threw those grenades much farther than I thought possible for man to throw an object with his hand and arm. I had seen a soccer ball being kicked two thirds the length of a playing field, but had never beheld the power of a man's arm to do the same (the days when I would reach maximum exhilaration at seeing a quarterback throw a football fifty or sixty yards to score a touchdown were several years into the future). Those British soldiers were throwing their grenades at least forty or even fifty yards, reaching the center of the field where the mines were. Twice, the explosion had been absolutely deafening because the grenades hit a mine and they both exploded at the same time. The soldiers had warned me about the possibility that something like that might happen, and they had asked me to stay behind the brick columns that marked the portals of our property and held its iron gates. Even so, those two larger explosions caused a lot of dirt and stones to fall all around me.

Still, mamma and nonna were nowhere in sight. The sun set beyond the Majella Mountains, casting a giant shadow over the countryside. Soon it would be too dark to spot them as they would walk down from the hill. As daylight began to wane, most of the soldiers left. Three of them stayed behind with mine detectors as a clean-up detail. Thank God they did, because I was about to get myself into serious trouble once again and they were a great help.

Soon it had become so dark that I could barely make out people's shapes in the distance. Nonetheless, I spotted a dark something way up the hill. "It must be them!" I thought, but I couldn't be sure, so I darted up the dirt road toward them. I ran in the middle of the road with the gait of a gazelle, conscious of the fact that every step brought me closer to the moment of truth. There was a beaten path on the left side of the road with a sign in Italian that read, *"Sentiero di sicurezza"* (safety path), but I didn't even see it. Suddenly, I heard my mother's voice scream out: *"Fermati! Fermati!"* (Stop! Stop!) I froze. She told me to stay in that spot and don't move an inch. I didn't. She began to approach me gingerly, as if that would have helped either one of us had she stepped on a mine. Fortunately, the three British soldiers who had been checking the terrain with the mine detectors, heard the commotion, and they came to lend a hand. Hearing my mother's screams, they approached and told her to stop where she was. They were going to use their metal detector and get us both out of there safely. I had ventured right in the middle of a mine field where the mines were placed about ten feet apart in a grid pattern for a distance of about 200 yards of the road and shoulder to shoulder. The British had cleared the left side for a width of about three feet and marked it as a safe way, but I didn't pay any attention to it. It was part of a band of mined land that went from the beaches to the mountains a distance of about 19 miles. I had run smack to the middle of it. Somebody up there was looking out for me.

The soldier with the mine detector came toward me holding the round sensor plate about six inches off the ground. He spanned the terrain from side to side covering an area of about eight feet in width with a set of ear phones on his head, as he listened for the typical sound those machines issued if they detected metal under the earth. He slowly approached me. He was about fifteen feet away from me at my left when he stopped. He shouted something in English to his buddies who immediately went into action with a flurry of activity. He had detected a mine, so he placed a red flag on that spot and continued his approach toward me. I was now about ten feet away from him. Within a minute or two he reached me, put down his machine, took off his earphones, reached out for me and picked me up like a puppet, carrying me to safety. Then he went back for mamma and nonna and led them to safety, as well, guiding them toward the area that had been designated as a mine-free, safe path.

My mother was rough on me that night. There was no way I could have told her that I had had a terrible day, worried sick about their safety, and my dash into the mine field was actually an act of love. The "offense" certainly did not warrant any kind of punishment. But, then, when mamma got mad there was no reasoning with her. Besides, both she and Nonna Concetta were in a state of great agitation. After all, the home Nonno Filippo had built and they had enjoyed for only fourteen years, was about to be blown up by the British, even though it looked to be only superficially damaged, otherwise intact.

Shortly after dinner, I just went to bed, psychologically bruised, perhaps, but happy that the two people I loved the most were safely home; it wasn't even 7:00 P.M. Physically and emotionally drained as I was, I slept the sleep of the just! I didn't wake up for twelve hours, way after mamma and nonna had left on their trek to town. It was to be their last trip, as things turned out.

They had already told me they would not be home at all as they would be spending the night with some relatives of ours. The absence of the male members of our family placed an incredible amount of pressure on them, under the most unusual of circumstances. So, I was shocked when I saw them come home by lunchtime crying inconsolably. The British had already blown up the house and had used its material as fill for the large craters left by the bombers. The soldiers explained that the caterpillar had arrived unexpectedly ahead of time and they couldn't send it away, as there were too many buildings to be torn down. They needed both One Street and Two Street to facilitate the movement of small vehicles such as jeeps and motorcycles. After that, they made One Street unidirectional going north, and Two Street, one way going south. Large military vehicles couldn't pass there, for sure, but they often created a bottleneck situation on the main streets (the original gridlock). However, if small vehicles could have zipped right through the old neighborhoods, they could have bypassed the traffic jams. Those two small alleys are still designated as such today. They were very old, constructed mainly for pedestrian traffic and, at best, a donkey cart or two. Modern day automobile traffic had never been part of their purpose, let alone military vehicles or large trucks. Within a few days, the empty lots created by the destruction of the neighborhood houses provided parking lots for all sorts of military vehicles at night. To conclude the story of that house, it was finally rebuilt in the 1970s with the help of money left over from the Marshall Plan. However, we sold it almost immediately, because we were all living in America, and we couldn't burden anyone to collect rent, or to service it for us. We found a family from Canada that returns to old Fossacesia every year, and sold it to them. The sale underscored in rather dramatic terms the foolish thinking of Nonno Filippo, in 1936, when he left home once again to return to America. Had he sold it then and brought us all with him he would have received a good price for that house and the lands he owned, and that would have allowed us all to buy two beautiful new houses in Norristown, one for us and one for Uncle Nick. And of course, he would have spared us the horrors of the war. A dialect saying goes something like this: *"Ni j'arrivate Sant'Ascanie."* (Saint Ascanius didn't arrive on time). I don't know who St. Ascanius was, but he must have been quite a thinker, because they always blame him for arriving too late whenever people's own thinking powers fail to achieve their normal function. The new home, rebuilt according to modern criteria, has the most modern amenities available and it has been divided into two apartments, one upstairs, the other down, each with its own bathroom and kitchen. Across Two Street, we owned a building and an empty lot. They made it into a garage and a small vegetable garden. I often go back to my old neighborhood and I feel sad every time I pass in front, or in the back of that house, especially as I think about the heartbreak it caused to my mother and grandmother. Mamma always held Mussolini personally responsible for its destruction. I blame the leaders on both sides! At mass we pray, "I confess to Almighty God that I've sinned . . . ," and we ask forgiveness adding, "for what I've done and what I have failed to do." The average person is always aware of the "what I've done," but few people pay much attention to the "what I have failed to do" part. So, I condemn Mussolini for allying himself with Hitler, no question. But, I also condemn the Allies for failing to exhaust all possibility of a diplomatic solution. Thousands of lives could have been saved on both sides but for "what they failed to do."

HERB SPEEDIE OF TORONTO

By the middle of December, a couple of Canadian soldiers began to frequent our home. Having learned that my grandfather spoke English, they would come to our house almost every night. Those young men loved to spend their free evenings in our house. They would talk up a storm over a glass of wine, while munching on roasted *ceci* (pronounced *chey-chee,* chickpeas), or chestnuts. Those evenings were like holidays for me, because I enjoyed the company of the soldiers even though I didn't understand their language. For Nonno Donato, it meant an evening of nostalgia as he retold his American experiences from 1898 to 1926. Not to mention that it gave him a chance to keep his English well lubricated and functioning.

One of the soldiers, Sergeant Herb Speedie of Toronto, Ontario, took a particular interest in me, seeing that I was always with my English book in my hands. He had an uncanny resemblance to Errol Flynn, the actor. He was part of a teamster regiment whose job was to keep the front lines supplied with ammunition. His truck was always loaded with cannon shells, ready for delivery to the front lines on a daily basis.

One evening, a few days before Christmas, 1943, the Canadians had come to the house, as usual. They began their long session of talk, munching and drinking while I was trying to speak English with Herb's help. I had a bit of a problem negotiating certain peculiarities of the English language. I kept confusing 'three' with 'tree,' "How are you" with "How old are you," and I called a sergeant named Hugh, 'Hoog'. That silent 'gh' in particular gave me enough *"acido"* to last me for a month. With Italian being my native tongue, the language that is the glorification of the vowel and leaves nothing unpronounced, English began to appear to me as a strange language indeed. Many years would pass before I would learn to appreciate English for the practical language it is and to value its elegant aspects through the works of Shakespeare, Hawthorne, Hemingway and many others.

One evening, somebody said there would be a mass celebrated in Fossacesia on Christmas day at 10:30 A.M. I expressed the desire to attend that mass. With the Church of San Donato practically destroyed, Monsignor Tozzi had opened the Church of the Holy Rosary for worship. It was small but conveniently located in the center of town, as previously established. It meant, of course, that I would have to walk about two miles from our house in the country to the center of the town, under extremely muddy conditions. By then the dirt road had been closed to traffic altogether because British engineers were trying to clear it of mines once and for all. Even the highway was very muddy, and since I had no shoes and nothing decent to wear, my mother said no. There was no way she would allow me to be seen in town in that condition. I pointed out to her that everybody else in town would be in the same condition. We discussed the situation, and Herb came out with the perfect solution. He would take me to church in his big truck. He would, also, try to get me a decent pair of shoes as well as a suit of clothes, if he could find one at the distribution center. Of course, he had to pull some strings to do that, because the distribution of donated clothes that came from America was under strict supervision of the military. Every family had been given a number and when their turn arrived they would be escorted inside the warehouse where the clothing was displayed. We didn't have a number. Why? Mamma considered it a humiliation, so she didn't even apply. But Herb knew the soldiers in charge of distribution, so he said he would take care of everything.

For the next two days, my mother still insisted that in no way was I to go to town, especially in church, and Herb insisting that it would be OK. Finally, on Thursday night, the day before Christmas Eve, Herb came to the house with a pair of brand new military boots, size 6—the smallest available. I tried them on, and my feet were having a ball moving around inside them. They were too big. Nonno tried to stuff some rags in their toes, and it was decided that I could walk in them, sort of.

The suit was another matter. Nonno Donato, without telling mamma, had been at the distribution center twice and, taking advantage of the fact that he spoke English, was allowed to rummage through what was available. He found nothing. But, Herb wasn't going to be denied. He stood me on a chair, stepped back, and began to look at me in a strange way, sizing me up and down as if I were a suspect in a police lineup. But, that's exactly what he was doing: sizing me up. He decided that, suit wise, I was a size 12. He had a son my age back in Toronto named Douglas. That was his size. The next day he went to Fossacesia and visited the distribution center for the third time, as the stock of donated clothes was constantly being re-supplied thanks to the generosity of the American people. When he came back to Caporale and showed my mother what he had found, she broke out in an unstoppable series of belly laughs that in no time infected the entire family, including Herb, whose laugh sounded more like the bray of a jackass. And he could be heard all the way to downtown Fossacesia, a mile away. So what was so funny? The suit was green—shamrock green. It was a nice enough suit and it actually fit me (although my mother had to shorten the pants by a foot and the sleeves by a good six inches). Also, he had found a shirt that actually fit me very well. It, too, was of a strange color, but it blended in with the suit in an irrational sort of way. When mamma asked him why he had failed to get me a tie, Herb was actually ready to jump on his truck, ammunitions and all, and go back to town to get me a tie, but my mamma stopped him. She said it was not necessary that I wear a tie. Herb, however; the next morning, Christmas Eve, brought me a black tie. He said that it was his Christmas present from his son and he wanted me to have it. This conjured up all kinds of psycho-sociological discomforts. Black, in Italy, at least in those days, was associated only and exclusively with the dead. Mamma did question the reason why his son would send Herb a black tie, and he said that it was part of his dress uniform. So, since Herb had made me a gift of something he cherished so much, coming as it had from his own son in Canada, we accepted the gift, but I have no memory of having worn it at Christmas or at any other time.

My new "wardrobe" was topped by a trench coat—a couple of sizes too big. Mamma didn't have time to shorten the sleeves, which matched the pant legs in length, so to speak, but she was a master in the art of the needle and thread, so she rolled them back inside the sleeve, stitched them several times and pressed the ends. It looked as thought it had been made specifically for me. The khaki trench coat actually did blend with the green suit, but I must have looked very much like Sad Sack, nonetheless.

CHRISTMAS DAY, 1943

Herb had told my mother he would take me to church in his military truck. She agreed without thinking beyond the normal. She didn't know the truck in question was loaded with ammunition, or she would have never given permission for me to make the trip. No one bothered to tell her the details of the situation. After mass Herb had planned to take me home and then proceed to Ortona where the Christmas day battle of that city was in full swing. Very early in the morning he loaded the truck, planning to make his full schedule of three trips.

When we entered the town, suddenly I found myself to be part of the parade of military trucks rolling down our main street headed north. I felt important, so I was hoping to see people I knew, so I could wave at them, but I didn't. As we reached the church Herb asked the MP directing traffic where he could park, and he was directed to make a right at the church. There was a parking lot not far from it. I had the shock of my life when I realized that the parking lot in question was the empty lot resulting from the razing of our elementary school. The Mario Bianco School was no more. The plot of land upon which it was built had been turned into a makeshift parking lot for all sorts of military vehicles. Herb parked the truck there and asked a soldier directing traffic nearby to keep an eye on it, and we walked to the church in the piazza two blocks away.

I enjoyed that mass. It was the first mass I had attended since the one in Signor Moretti's barn for the feast of all Saints Day almost two months before. There were no German soldiers to worry about at this service. For the first time, I heard some of the Christmas carols that were popular only in America, such as Silent Night and Adeste Fideles. Since Christmas in Italy at that time was exclusively a religious holy day, with the festivities limited to one's family, we had but one Christmas carol that everybody sang: St. Alfonsus Liguori's *Pastorale*. So, musically at least, that mass gave me a glimpse of Christmas in America that I was to experience a few years later.

After mass, Herb took me home, and Nonno Donato invited him to stay for dinner. He declined the invitation because he was actually on duty, and had to rejoin his teamster outfit. On the way down to our cottage, Herb had stopped twice to talk with other Canadian soldiers, and was given a bleak picture of the fierce battle going on in Ortona. They were fighting in the streets house to house, he was told, so he suddenly panicked because his comrades needed the ammunition. He gunned the truck and we made it home in no time. He knew then he had better hurry up and make his delivery immediately.

Christmas that year fell on a Saturday, and the soldiers had been complaining for days that a moratorium should have been declared so that both sides could celebrate the universal holy day. Some of the soldiers even suggested that their commanders negotiate a two-day truce, the next day being Sunday. As it turned out, the Canadians were engaged in the fiercest battle of their participation in the war, Christmas or no Christmas. Herb made three trips and then he was ordered to make a fourth trip to deliver medical supplies due to the tremendous number of wounded resulting from the battle of Ortona on Christmas day, as punishment for not being with the rest of the motorcade in the morning. I felt bad when I heard that. Apparently, he had made up a story of having had engine trouble on the way, but had failed to convince his commanding officer, and he had to take the consequences.

The Canadian WW II veterans today, the few who are left, still refer to Ortona as their "Little Stalingrad." 2,605 of their comrades were either killed or wounded at the Battle of Ortona. Their dead are buried in a beautifully kept cemetery atop a hill overlooking the Adriatic Sea, in the area of San Donato, just south of the city (see photo on page 324).

Herb continued to spend evenings at our house and we loved to give him hospitality. On evenings that he and other soldiers did not come, I used to be very sad and disappointed. Nonno Donato said they had orders and were probably on duty. Sometimes they pulled guard duty, or mess hall duty, and sometimes, too, they visited other homes in the area, since they had made other friends among our neighbors, as well. In the process of allowing those young men a little respite from their war duties, I would take advantage of the situation, working on my English pronunciation so the next time they showed up I could impress them, especially Herb, with my progress. I credit him with the fact that, even though I speak English with an unavoidable accent, it is not a heavy one. Some people hear it immediately, but most often people are surprised when I tell them that the English language is not my native tongue. My children, knowing my first real exposure to the English language came from a Canadian soldier, often tease me: "Hey Dad, how come you don't say, "Eh?" Well, maybe I should!

Herb did help me a lot with English. Since he had a son my age, Douglas, I provided him with a surrogate son. My own father was in America, so he fit the father figure for me. Hence, we complemented each other very well and became close friends.

The one thing that disappointed me was that the Canadian soldiers didn't play soccer. I wish they had, for that was my sport. Instead, I used to see them try to hit a small hard ball on the ground, with a bent stick. It got pretty cold in Abruzzo, but not cold enough to freeze solid the small ponds that were in the area, and so, unable to play ice hockey, they played field hockey, instead, on our front lawn which was pretty big. They used to play actual games on it, occasionally entering into fierce arguments.

Herb remained with us until Good Friday, 1944. For the three months that he stayed with us he continued to coach me in the correct pronunciation of the English language. He did not know much grammar, but he was able to make sure that my pronunciation was relatively accent-free. And he insisted on enriching my vocabulary. Each night he would drill me pretty much as Captain Campbell had done a few months before. He also made me pluralize each word, especially the irregular ones such as child/children, man/men woman/ women, etc.

Since Herb had not been able to share our Christmas dinner with us, Nonno Donato invited him to join us for our Easter dinner. He accepted and we were looking forward to it. On Monday of Holy Week, however, his outfit received orders to pull up stakes and hightail it back to England. They would leave at dawn on Good Friday. Nonno decided to have a special dinner for him on Holy Thursday. The one peculiar event I remember about that dinner was that Herb asked for "spaghetti and meatballs." Well, that's an Italian-American specialty, not an Italian one. Still, mamma, who was a great cook besides being a great seamstress, obliged. When we sat at dinner on Holy Thursday, she put on the table a large bowl of *"maccheroni alla chitarra,"* that is, homemade spaghetti made with a sort of stringed gadget which we still today call a guitar. She also arranged a giant pyramid of meatballs impregnated with *sugo,* or tomato sauce (or is it gravy?). Each of us children was given two of those meat balls and were told to make three bites out of each one. This was standard procedure. During the war years we had been indoctrinated that way, and so we began to eat with the three bite method. Herb, however, stuffed those meatballs in his mouth one at a time. When we, the children saw that, we were horrified, but naturally we said nothing. Three-year-old cousin Giuliana, however, being the youngest, began to complain in a loud voice: "How come he can eat one at a time and we have to make three bites?" Of course she said it in Abruzzese dialect. Everyone was horrified that she had said it aloud. Fortunately, Herb didn't understand a thing, so there was no need to explain or apologize.

Herb's outfit left on schedule before dawn on Good Friday. Three years later, I myself left for America, so I thought I would never see him again. However, in 1973, I happened to be in Toronto, and I remembered that it was Herb's hometown. I consulted the biggest telephone book I had ever seen and looked up his name. Sure enough, there he was. He lived in an apartment on Bathurst Street, near Bloor. I called him up. It took a few minutes for him to focus on who I was, but when he did, he practically jumped out of his skin. He invited me to go visit him, which I did, and we had a grand reunion. He no longer looked like Errol Flynn, having lost all his hair. He was still relatively thin, but he had developed a cute little pot belly. He remembered details of the time he spent in Fossacesia and frequented our house on a regular basis, details I myself had forgotten. He remembered my little cousin, Giuliana, who always walked around carrying her pet chicken in her arms. He remembered my mother who used to write interminable letters to my father. I told him of her untimely death not long after we left Italy. He was saddened to hear that. He inquired about my younger brother Filippo. Then he asked me what I did for a living. I told him I was a high school teacher in Norristown. "What do you teach?" he wanted to know. "English, of course. What else?" It blew his mind. But I gave him full credit for having helped me in developing a decent pronunciation that allowed me to teach it without much deviation which might disturb the students. I told him that my mother's death made it impossible for me to go to college, but, at age twenty-seven, after returning to Italy and marrying my childhood sweetheart, with her help and encouragement, I was able to enter Villanova University, where I earned a college degree in night school. After I was hired as an English teacher at Bishop Kenrick High School in Norristown, Pa., I went back to Villanova, where I earned a Master's Degree in English.

In 1969, I started to teach in high school, even though the classroom had never been part of my life's ambition. In order to teach in a Catholic school and survive, I had to hold two full-time jobs, since I also had four children to raise. But everything worked out just fine. The Lord, it seems, wanted me in the classroom in the worst way, so He smoothed my path toward higher academic horizons.

Herb filled me in on what happened to him after he left our area in 1944. He said that his regiment was assigned to a unit in England that was awaiting some sort of major event. After a brief furlough, his regiment joined the forces training for that major event, which of course, turned out to be the landing at Normandy. A month after the landing, he said, as he and his assistant were delivering ammunition to the front lines as part of the usual convoy, they were attacked by the Luftwaffe. As the alert was sounded, all drivers abandoned their vehicles and sought cover. And that's why they survived that attack; because their truck, that very same truck with which Herb had taken me to mass six months earlier, received a direct hit and was literally blown into history.

Giving credit to the mass to which he brought me on Christmas Day, 1943, Herb said he had recently been baptized into the Catholic Church. Well, that, I must confess, pleased me. If I had not mentioned that I wished to go to mass on Christmas Day, this might not have happened. The Lord works, indeed, in mysterious ways.

Two years later, I was in Toronto again. I called Herb just to say hello. He begged me to go see him. His wife had died recently, so he was very lonely and it would have pleased him to see me once again. Unfortunately, I could not do it. I had waited until the last minute of our stay in the city before I called him, and we were ready to depart for home. I begged him to excuse me for this time. Next time, I promised I'd go and really spend some time with him. But, next time never came. For various reasons, I did not return to Toronto for over ten years. By that time, however, Herb's name was no longer listed in the telephone directory. I have a terrible remorse that I didn't go see him. I never saw Herb Speedie again. He was a good man.

THE FRONT STAGNATES

After the Battle of Ortona and its aftermath, the British stopped fighting, waiting for the Americans to resolve their difficulties on the western front. This made it necessary for a group of Italian patriots to organize themselves into a fighting entity and begin combating the Germans themselves. The Majella Brigade was formed. It took quite an effort to convince the British that they could be trusted, but they finally relented and suddenly the German force had a new enemy to contend with. The Majella Brigade appears to be the best organized of the resistance forces operating in central Italy in 1944 and 1945. It would require a great amount of research to ascertain that theory, however, and that's not within my sphere of interest. Suffice it to say that they were well armed by the British, and in the end the Brigade was awarded the Gold Medal for bravery. Unfortunately, their presence caused problems to the civilian population, because for every man they lost after engaging the Majella, the Germans reversed their rage directly upon the civilian population, men, women, children, the elderly, made no difference, as they unleashed a barrage of unabated ferocity, killing hundreds of people especially in the Abruzzo region. So, for every man they lost as a result of an engagement with the Brigade, they made the civilian population pay with their lives.

ITALY'S MINI-HOLOCAUST

Beginning in November, 1943, the Germans conducted a series of massacres upon the Italian population. I call it Italy's mini-holocaust. The first that we in Fossacesia became aware of was the killing of twenty-one men who were rounded up at random in Francavilla al Mare, 15 miles north of Ortona. They were summarily shot in retaliation for the killing of one German soldier. The reason this story made a profound impression in Fossacesia, and especially in our old neighborhood, was that Anna Maria's family were friends with Francavilla's De Medio family who lost their father and a recently wed son in that particular slaughter. The Fantini girls used to spend weekends with the De Medio girls in Francavilla and vice versa, both localities being

Adriatic Sea shore resorts. The De Medio siblings, as children, spent many a weekend in our neighborhood, and so they were an integral part of it. One can imagine the profound dismay the entire town felt when they heard that Giuseppe, the father, and Pietro, his son and soon to be father, were both shot, the innocent victims of a society gone mad.

The German soldier, whose death the retaliatory killing sought to avenge, allegedly had tried to rape a young girl. The death of the twenty-two civilian males could and should have been avoided. Tommaso Tozzi (no relations to Monsignor Tommaso Tozzi, our pastor), a writer from Gessopalena, a mountain town not far from Fossacesia, reported the killings in Francavilla in his book *The Majella Brigade*. The massacre took place on Sunday afternoon, December 26, 1943. A local young woman was being pursued by a German soldier. It has never been established beyond a reasonable doubt whether he was pursuing her with intent to rape, as the tale goes, or whether he was part of a consensual encounter. The fact remains that her father naturally assumed that he had bad intentions in mind, especially after he had killed the Nazi. The daughter ran into the house, so the story goes, followed by the soldier with the father in hot pursuit armed with a shotgun. He fired once, and the young German was dead in a few minutes. After the killing, the father and the entire family ran away, but for some reason, they left the girl's grandfather at home, perhaps because, sick and old as he was, he would have been a hindrance to their flight.

The German reprisal was swift and unmerciful. The first victim was the octogenarian grandfather. The usual rule was that for every German soldier dead, ten civilian males between 14 and 65 would be rounded up and shot. Well, that was done in a matter of a half hour. The grandfather didn't count. They rounded up ten men at random and summarily shot them. In an unexplained misunderstanding, a German marshal arrived on the scene shortly thereafter and, seeing the German soldier lying on the floor dead, either not knowing the ten innocent civilian victims had already been executed, or for sheer meanness, rounded up eleven more males and shot them, too. To further complicate the tragedy was the fact that Pietro De Medio left a young pregnant wife. Early in 1944, she in fact gave birth to a boy whom they called Pietro, in honor of his father. Surviving Giuseppe were his wife, an older son, Ferruccio, and three daughters.

Once, I told a friend that Hitler had saved my life. "How did Hitler save your life?" was his incredulous reaction. I explained that it was by Hitler's direct order that the "head" of the Gustav Line was moved from the Sangro Valley to the Moro Valley, fifteen miles or so to the north. By doing that, the bulk of the German Army stayed north of us. And between November 1943 and June 1944, those marauding German soldiers ran around the entire province of L'Aquila sowing death among the civilian population with reckless abandon. There are many gory stories I could tell here, but I will spare my readers disturbing details. I will, however, tell a few because it is time the rest of the world knew what my people went through in those days.

THE MASSACRE AT GESSOPALENA

From a crossroads known as Sant'Agata, in the municipality of Gessopalena in the mountains of Abruzzo, one can enjoy a breathtaking view of the Majella Mountain in all its majestic beauty. On the morning of Friday, January 21, 1944, before dawn, a squad of about ten or twelve German soldiers pounced upon the area, knocking down doors with unusual ferocity, woke up women, children (even those still in their cradles) and old people, and got them up out of their beds by prodding them with the butts of their rifles. They amassed everyone in a corner of the kitchen in the home of one of the residents. Then the monsters went outside locking all doors, and from a small window that led into the kitchen they threw upon the group several live grenades. After the third bomb exploded, they threw a fourth grenade which resulted in the collapse of the kitchen floor into the basement. All the victims fell into the basement and died horribly disfigured. After a while, the Germans, to make sure that they were all dead, picked up a burning log and put it against the faces of each of the victims. A teen aged girl, Antonella D. L., and her eleven year old brother were not very badly wounded, so they played dead despite the fact that they both lay under a pile of dead bodies, even managing to endure the pain of the fiery log on their faces impassively, and so they survived. As soon as the executioners left, the two children ran through the fields and sought help in the homes of some of their neighbors. After a while, they saw the Germans return with flame throwers and set fire to the house of the mass murder and several others. The total dead in Gessopalena that morning numbered forty-one innocent victims. What was the reason for that massacre? Two of their soldiers had been killed the day before in an armed confrontation with members of the Majella Brigade. It gave reason to the Italian population to wonder what kind of monsters the Germans were. Of course it was easy to blame the whole thing on Hitler, but ultimately, in the words of Giovanni Palatucci, the lawyer-hero: "I reject the concomitant circumstances of causality to diminish the responsibility of the guilty person, because it is still he who renders them operative and effective."

So, all the people who committed acts of war, at any time in the foul, wicked, corrupt history of mankind, and who defended themselves by saying, 'I only followed orders,' should heed Truman's advice (and Palatucci's, too!): "The buck stops here!"

Without going into its bloody details, may I say that in addition to the Gessopalena massacre, the Germans perpetrated murderous slaughters in Pietransieri, Capistrello and other places in the Marsica region of Abruzzo, near Avezzano. In the northern part of central Italy, they went on a rampage on a much grander scale. They burned down the entire city of Marzabotto, province of Bologna, resulting in 1800 dead, while in Tuscany, they burned down Sant'Anna di Stazzema which resulted in 600 dead. And there were many more similar incidents elsewhere in Italy, both north and south.

THE FUTURE BISHOP AT FILETTO

I'm now going to give an account of the last horrible act of incivility the Nazis committed in Filetto di Camarda, a small hamlet of barely five hundred souls located half way up the Gran Sasso d'Italia Mountain, the Apennine's highest mountain (9,000 feet). The town is perched on the western slopes of the mountain, at about 3500 feet above sea level. It is a sheep and goat raising area being the ideal elevation in which to raise ovine. The story is significant because of subsequent historical events that will take place in spite of the crime committed there in 1944. I first read the story in Tommaso Tozzi's book, but later it was confirmed by many articles in Italian and American magazines, including Time Magazine. Now, it is all over the internet.

After the winter lull of 1944, the Germans found themselves in the position of having to confront the Majella Brigade once again. As they retreated toward the north, they would raid all the sheep farms they encountered. By now, the great army of the Third Reich was completely out of food, and survived strictly by raiding whatever they could find in local farms. The shepherds of Filetto were concerned for their own flocks having heard that the Germans were raiding the pens. It must be remembered the *transumanza,* the annual transfer of thousands of sheep to the south of the Italian peninsula, had not taken place that year due to the war emergency. So, the people of Filetto sent a couple of young men up the mountain to ask the members of the Majella Brigade to come down to Filetto and help them discourage the Germans from raiding their sheep herds. But, an unfortunate sequence of events was about to occur: almost simultaneously, a truckload of German soldiers made its way up the mountain to Filetto. By permission of the author, Tommaso

Tozzi, given via telephone in 2004. This is my translation of the story directly from his book, *La Brigata Majella*.

On June 7, 1944, around 1:00 P.M., a young man from Filetto approached major Rasero of the Majella Brigade, and delivered an urgent message to him from the people of Filetto. They asked to send some of his men to Filetto in order to discourage the retreating Germans from raiding not only their sheep, but their homes or destroy anything else they could not load on their trucks. The major refused at first fearing a reprisal of the Germans against the population, but at the insistence of the young man that the message came from the entire population of the little hamlet, he considered his options. The young man showed him several sheets of paper bearing many signatures of the people of Filetto. He also assured the major that there were only two Germans in the town with a small truck. The major relented. He gave orders to a small contingent of partisans to go to the little hamlet. The men grabbed their rifles and proceeded toward Filetto, unaware that the platoon of SS troops was also headed in the same direction. At the confluence of two local roads the two groups ran into each other and there occurred a brief skirmish resulting in the loss of one partisan and one German soldier. Meanwhile, as the truck with the Germans entered the town, they killed two harmless citizens of Filetto and then calmly did the same thing to a man who was just coming out of his house on his way to work. The Commandant of the local police, seeing this execrable act of ferocity, protested vehemently against the attitude of the Germans. They raised their weapons against him and fired, killing him instantly. Today, in Filetto, the Carabiniere killed that day is considered one of the local heroes.

Then the soldiers occupied the town, and toward evening captured seventeen men and put them in a field at the edge of town, while placing their wives and children in another field nearby all under heavy guard. They kept them there all night without food or water. The next day, June 8, 1944, at 1:00 AM, Wehrmacht Capt. Matthias Defregger ordered his soldiers to shoot the seventeen men and burn their bodies. Then they went to the women and told them their "roasts were ready." Defregger's later excuse for the vile act was that he merely passed the order on.

On June 7, 1969, as the people of Filetto gathered in the local church to commemorate the twenty-fifth anniversary of the horrible event, the German magazine Der Spiegel of Hamburg, Germany, published an article that had worldwide reverberation (Time Magazine, August and October, 1969) in which it said that the SS Captain in question was none other than the present Auxiliary Bishop of Munich, the Most Reverend Matthias Defregger.

At this point, following Professor Tozzi's lead, I will not go further into the story. Anyone who may be interested in learning more, can go to the Internet and find all kinds of stories about the man. Times Magazine reported the story on two of its August, 1969, issues. We can assume that after the war was over, Captain Defregger returned to Munich, his hometown and, correctly thinking that the whole world would be after his hide for war crimes, returned to the seminary where he had been studying before the war and very effectively hid there. Who could possibly think of looking for him in a Catholic seminary? And he succeeded. He was ordained a priest in 1949 and made a career in the Church. The pastor of Filetto in 1969, after the Der Spiegel article came out, said, "It is our duty to forgive our enemies. I am sure that God has already forgiven him!" But, one has to wonder what kind of mixed up psyche possesses a man who goes from a Jesuit seminary, into the ranks of Hitler's marauding death squads, and back into the seminary with total impunity? The bishop retired in 1985 and died in 1995. After 1969, some limits were put on him as bishop, but he was never prosecuted for war crimes.

Now, it is easy to blame the Germans for all the excesses perpetrated during that bloody war. The fact is, to some extent, the Allies were guilty of excesses too. Nowhere nearly as many, of course, but their "white hats" were somewhat tarnished as well. Recently, my choir director, Mr. Joseph Verruni, a distinguished gentleman of sterling character typical of the "Greatest Generation," and himself a member of a B-24 ground crew in the Asian theater of World War II, gave me a book by Stephen E. Ambrose entitled, *The Wild Blue* (Simon & Shuster, NY., 2001). It is all about the airmen who flew the Liberators out of Cerignola, about a hundred miles south of Fossacesia on their way to bomb northern targets in Italy, Austria and southern Germany. These were the very men who were inside the waves and waves of bombers that passed over my head twice each day for a year and a half in 1944 and 1945. The key figure in the book is George McGovern (yes, the same Senator George McGovern who ran for President of the United States in 1972 only to lose to Richard Nixon). He was in his early twenties and already a Liberator pilot. There is a very disturbing entry in the book that shocked even me. I'm paraphrasing now:

> There was a club in Cerignola where pilots could unwind after a mission. One night, while visiting the club, McGovern overheard two fighter pilots bragging about the fact they had strafed two Italian men right off a bridge from which they were fishing. "Did you see them "I-ties" drop?", said one, laughing. "Yea", replied the other, "they won't fish again!" That chilled McGovern. "My blood ran cold", said he. "How could they do that to two innocent men who were just fishing? I was embarrassed. That's what Hitler's gang did. They were a disgrace to our country and to humanity."

Well, some Americans were not much better than their Nazi counterparts, obviously. But, then Ambrose made an interesting observation:

> "Yet he (McGovern) was a bomber pilot. Almost certainly he was responsible for more civilian deaths than the two fighter pilots. But, from high up, he couldn't see the direct effect of those explosions, not at all like the pilots who had strafed two Italian fishermen. Besides, he was bombing Germans. He needn't exercise his conscience about it."

As already stated, there is little difference between the pilots who killed eight civilians in Fossacesia on October 1, 1943, McGovern and his crew, the two American fighter pilots who shot the fishermen, a thousand others who threw a million tons of bombs indiscriminately over vast areas of Europe and Asia, and the Germans who shot Tommaso Natale on November 27, or even those who shot Anna Maria's dog on November 9. From a distance of miles above the ground, killing does not engage our consciences especially in the course of a so-called "just war." Those two fighter pilots, however, acted deliberately and intentionally—it was a case of pure murder! Ironically, whereas the Nazis acted with rage, the Americans did so in frivolity bordering on puerility. To some, World War II, the bloodiest war mankind had ever seen up till then, was probably simply the extension of a Coney Island amusement stand conveniently set up for their entertainment and distension. The incident just mentioned is a perfect example of this. Two pilots had just killed two men who were simply fishing, most likely to feed their families. In those days, nobody fished for sport. Their killers found their deaths funny. No wonder McGovern was furious. War is hell, indeed!

LIFE IN THE POST BELLUM ERA

It is strange how, when our lives are threatened, we seem to accept any and all restrictions imposed upon our lifestyles. Imagine a family like Anne Frank's who had to live cooped up in an attic for two years, or even us, living in a small stable for three weeks. I was not bored, even though I had only one book with me. But, now that I was free at last, I was bored. I wished I'd had a soccer ball. We had a rural tool building near the entrance to the property. Nonno Donato used it to shelter things in it like plows, farm tools, scythes, and other farm implements. Some soldiers asked if they could use it as sleeping quarters. Nonno gave them permission, and they erected a tent under the barn roof, which was not exactly rainproof, and there they slept cozy and comfortable. I visited that hut daily, and I used to look at American magazines. I became acquainted with Life, Time, Look, Collier's and the Saturday Evening Post. I did not understand what I read at the time, but I looked at the pictures and I did try to figure out what the caption said, even under those cartoons. I rarely succeeded. I did understand some, though, especially when a magazine carried those spectacular photos of American landscapes: The Grand Canyon, Niagara Falls, the Golden State Bridge, the Statue of Liberty, not to mention buildings of historical significance such as Independence Hall, the White House and the Capitol.

The one thing that disappointed me, however, was that America didn't seem to have the sport of "football" either (of course, I meant soccer). Occasionally the magazines did feature sporting events, but they never involved soccer. I was not at all impressed with pictures of Babe Ruth that showed the superstar dressed in what appeared to be striped flannel pajamas. Of course, the soldiers who were on our side of the Italian boot were British. They didn't care for baseball, either. One of them, seeing me in a puzzled state, twisted his mouth as if to say, "You're right kid!" Later, after a few months in America, I realized that baseball has to grow on you. But, my interest in it is only as a spectator. I could have never played it or basketball either, not to mention American football which requires a person to have leather skin encasing his body. Since I only ever played soccer (mostly with home made balls made of rags), my sporting instincts were concentrated strictly in my legs and feet. The upper part of my body was not developed in such a way to allow me to throw any kind of ball with my arms. I kick things.

Meanwhile, the war continued. Throughout the month of January there was gunfire in the distance all day long, especially after 6:00 P.M. when the big cannons went into operation. I was unable to figure out where they were set up, but the sounds came from beyond the Santa Maria Imbaro Ridge. Every time a cannon was fired, our windows rattled to a point just short of shattering. These were the large caliber guns, probably shooting at areas beyond San Vito, 12 miles away. Our concern, of course, was that the Germans had to answer back sooner or later, and now we would be in the German line of fire. But, they never did. This didn't make any sense to me. If they are fresh out of ammunition, which I kind of suspected remembering the trains all along the Adriatic rail trunk blocked by bombed out bridges, destroyed rails, and even machine personnel who had long ago abandoned locomotive, train and caboose, since September, why don't they surrender? This thought was to bother me until the war was finally over.

MY FIRST JOB

In early January, the British Army set up various work shops in the area in support of the fighting troops, and they hired many civilians in all categories of the labor force. Every carpenter in town was working, as were other skilled people. They also hired non-skilled labor that included young people, even as young as twelve years of age. They even hired me. I had turned 12 years old on January 16, 1944. On March 3rd I started to work. Juvenile labor? Nah! That's a modern American concept. Working gave me a sense of purpose, even as I made a little money to help the family. Dealing as I did with British and Canadian soldiers all day long, I had a chance to practice my English which I had begun to study seriously with the help of those Canadian soldiers who came to our house on selected evenings during the week. My job was to help in the distribution of carpenter materials and tools, and to keep track of the time cards for the civilian workers. Since the cards were written in English, and some of the people could hardly read and write at all, it was my job to make sure they signed and dated the cards in the proper places when they received their pay envelopes.

Another of my "duties" took place every morning at 10:00 A.M. Four of us boys had the duty of going to the mess hall to get breakfast for the troops. We had to walk about three city blocks to reach the area where they had improvised a very active kitchen. Every day, we returned the empty vessels from the day before, and we picked up the full ones for that morning. Danish, coffee and tea was the daily mid-morning snack each soldier enjoyed. The containers of tea and coffee were the heaviest, so we arranged a line with the Danish in the center, and the liquids on either side. The boys in the middle had to carry both the pastries' container in one hand, and one of the liquids in the other. Obviously, the boys at the end only carried the one thing. But the middle positions were actually the best, because although the kettles were heavier, weight was well balanced in both hands so it was easier to proceed with them. I used to fight for one of the middle positions, until somebody figured it out, and eventually a Scottish sergeant who looked more like a caricature than a man, decided it was time we took turns. Nobody balked!

For me, even the consumption of a Danish and tea or even coffee represented a mild culture shock. They were too sweet for our taste. Also, those guys used a mug that appeared to contain a pint of coffee, and then they added milk to it. Cappuccino was not yet invented, but we enjoyed espresso and caffè latte. Very few Italians actually put milk in their coffee. But we soon began to imitate the soldiers, and, after they had their fill, it was our turn to "sacrifice" ourselves and eat the remainder of the stuff. I held my own, I suppose, but some of those guys who lived around the area, most of whom I knew because in a small town it was difficult for anyone to hide, had some prodigious appetites. There was one young man, a couple of years older than I, who could make a half a dozen of those Danish pastries disappear as a start, and then munch on three or four more, before the supply was consumed completely. Yes, we had to eat a lot of biscuits in those days. I suppose that, after having gone without food for such a long time, we felt that we deserved it, after all.

At lunch time I went to the home of my cousin, Mario Sorgini, for lunch. Mario also worked for the British Army. My aunt Antonietta, his mother, would make us some great dinners (in Italy, lunch time is called dinner time, and the dinner usually matches the name), but more than the daily dinners themselves, it was the camaraderie that made it special: I enjoyed their company and their friendship. Besides Mario, and my aunt, there was my Uncle Fioretto, my mother's first cousin for whom she held a great amount of respect, Lilia his eldest daughter and a beauty of unusual radiance, and Donatino, the youngest.

We received a meager wage, and we were paid in "occupation" money every Friday afternoon, which was nothing more than paper money, literally. After a few weeks in circulation, they looked pretty much like used paper napkins. Even in buying power those occupation bills were worth little more than paper napkins. In fact, it was at that point that my mother realized and commented on the disastrous results of an act of personal pride on the part of Mussolini. He had been told that Italy was not ready nor willing to go to war, but it didn't faze him. He was going to resurrect the glory that was Rome. Now, many deaths and much destruction later, we had the added insult of a galloping inflation. She commented that in 1935, when one Italian penny was worth exactly one American penny, a silver five-lire coin was worth five American dollars. Now, it took over six-hundred lire to buy one dollar's worth of merchandise.

After dinner, Mario and I would walk back to our jobs. At four thirty, I used to return to their house and there I invariably found either my mother or grandfather who came all the way into town just to accompany me home. Occasionally, one of the Canadian soldiers I knew would be there to do some errands, and he would take me and whoever came for me, home in a jeep. I used to like that. Some of the adult workers waiting for transportation used to be impressed that I, a twelve year old kid, could manage to speak in such a strange language and get a ride home in the process.

According to what my mother wrote to papà on Nov. 13, 1944, the famous thirty-six-page letter, I worked between March 3 and June 6, 1944. I earned a total of 2,400 lire. It was not a great deal of money, but it helped to defuse a certain amount of tension beginning to emerge subtly in the overcrowded household about who was going to feed whom, the usual picayune concerns of people whose main focus is fundamentally earthbound. When I first read that letter, I was appalled to learn that the people whom I loved so dearly, Nonno Donato especially, should have been reluctant to feed me. Amazing!

Of course, learning of that situation, I was also able to understand the reason why Nonna Concetta began to look for "a room" to rent anywhere in town, preferably in our old neighborhood, so that she could get out of a hostile environment to which she felt totally estranged. She did find it, too: one room! It used to be the living quarters of a very poor woman in our neighborhood who never came back to it. Perhaps she was killed during the bombing raids of November. Could it be that she was killed and nobody noticed? Or was she taken "north," by the Germans and didn't have the means to return to town? Who knows? But, at the time, the single room was vacant. All it needed was a little cleaning up, and some immediate and urgent repairs to keep the wind out. There were many holes along the walls through which winds of every kind blew in unmercifully during winter when we didn't need them, but failed to do so in summer when we did.

THE WINTER AND SPRING OF "44

After the front passed the Sangro River Valley, a parade of airplanes began to pass over Fossacesia beginning around 10:00 A.M. every morning going north, and around 2:00 P.M. they limped their way back south to return to their bases. Filippo and I had become experts in recognizing each type of aircraft because the soldiers used to give us cards with their pictures on them. Each pack of cigarettes they opened contained an airplane card, shown from the front, from the side and from below. We didn't know that they were to be collected and treasured. Today such a collection would probably be worth a small fortune. But the cards helped us familiarize ourselves with the individual crafts that passed overhead every day. The parade of airplanes was to last for another year and a half. As a kid, I was not in a position to figure out where they came from or where they were headed. Occasionally a truck driver would stop for water, or some food, and would conjecture that they came from Africa and were going to bomb Munich. Many years later, I learned that the U. S. 15th Air Force had moved its bases from North Africa to southern Italy, in the Apulia region (the heel of the boot) at the end November, 1943.

Unbeknown to me at the time, there were two distinct dramas unfolding along both sides of the German's Gustav Line: on our side of it, the liberated side, there was the danger of the insidious land mines, ranging from anti-tank, to anti-personnel mines, to attractive gadgets such as fountain pens, pen knives and small radios packed with explosive and upon removing its cap or turning it on, would explode. They rarely killed, but they maimed hands and face, condemning its victim to a lifetime of agony and pain.

On the other side of the Line, the side still under German occupation, there was nothing less than a mini holocaust going on, as already mentioned, in which over 600 civilians lost their lives, including children and old people. Throughout the month of December, 1943, unaware of the fact that the Germans had buried thousands of mines all around the towns where they had planned to establish resistance lines, quite a few farmers were killed as they tried to do farm work that had been left undone because of the war. Depending on the exact area, some farmers did not have time to pick the grapes in their vineyards, nor were they able to climb olive trees to pick olives. Both of these crops, one to make wine with, the other for the production of olive oil, are essential to the cooking needs of the Italian people, especially in the region of Abruzzo whose people have been known for centuries as the chefs of Italy. Naturally, as soon as they returned to their homes, the farmers wanted to go onto the fields and catch up on the work they had been unable to do at the correct time. Many, alas, were not aware of the many mines buried in the most unusual places imaginable. There is a story of the Morrone family whose father, Luigi, one morning in March of '44 attached two oxen to their big cart and made ready to go to the flatlands of Fossacesia to do some farm work. He was accompanied by his son Ernesto, 18, his daughter Laura, and a friend of the family, Angelo Spoleto, 23. Laura had just turned sixteen and was one of the most sought after beauties in town. They started out and had gone no more than a quarter mile when the wheel of the cart rolled over an anti-tank mine and blew up, killing everyone on board, as well as the two oxen, and destroying the cart. Another tragedy compliments of the glorious Third Reich.

There were similar tragedies not only in Fossacesia, but in every town where the Germans buried anti-tank and anti-personnel mines in the fields, and also in places where people wouldn't think there would be any mines, such as on steep hills where no tank would pass. Those Germans were masters of the evil sleight of hand. As the farmers attempted to get back to their work, many people were killed by those mines, precisely because the danger lurked in the most unimaginable places. Many animals were victims of the same fate, too. Mostly, they were large work animals, but also smaller ones like dogs, an occasional fox, and quite a few sheep. I believe they had to weigh at least ten pounds to activate the firing pin. Fortunately, in our area, no children were killed or maimed because they stepped on a mine while at play. The parents were, of course, extremely careful, and kept them within sight of their homes. But, elsewhere, many children were indeed killed at play, or simply because they had been walking in the company of adults who had the misfortune of stepping on a mine. My barber in Norristown was one such victim at the northern end of the bay of Naples. He was only eight years old when he accompanied his older brother on the beach to pick up fish killed by the explosion of hand grenades as American soldiers practiced the art of killing. They were walking along the sandy beach when a friend of theirs who headed the group stepped on a mine. The brother and his friend were literally cut in half and the eight year old Mario Martello, though wounded, survived the ordeal. The presence of mines on that beach was significant. I suppose the Germans thought it would be a good place for the Americans to try to come ashore.

AND THEN MAY 28TH ROLLED AROUND

A website on the Internet describes the Gustav Line as follows:

> The Gustav Line was the most rearward of the three German defensive lines on the Italian peninsula south of Rome. Built along the Garigliano and Rapido rivers it was fortified with gun pits, concrete bunkers, turreted machine gun emplacements, barbed wire and minefields. The Gustav Line was held by 15 divisions

of the German Army under the command of Albert Kesselring. Several attempts were made to breach its western flank during the Anzio invasion (January 22) without success. They succeeded only in late May, 1944.

The above description fails to mention that the Gustav Line had its upper head bastion precisely at the Sangro River Valley, although before the British arrived at the river, Hitler had ordered his troops to retreat to the Moro River, near Ortona. So the German winter line went from Ortona in the north east to Gaeta in the south west. In the final effort to break through the Gustav line, after the Anzio beachhead and the battle of Monte Cassino had taken place, the American Fifth Army made several attempts during the winter months of 1944 to breach it in the southwest, without much success. But, on the 28th of May, 1944, a strange event took place that would gel only six years later in America, when the four principals that were directly or indirectly involved would meet by accident in a Bible study session in Norristown, Pa. On that day in '44, however, they were lined up in a straight geographic array, like four planets of our solar system that occasionally appear to be positioned in a single file with foreboding precision. I was part of it even though I was thirteen years old. We might not have been very precise in alignment, but when the story came out six years later, we were all amazed at the strange sequence of events that led to that day. The alignment was as follows: on both ends of the Gustav Line there was a De Simone: I was at Fossacesia, it's original northeastern terminus, and Corporal Louis De Simone, an American soldier from Bridgeport, Pa. (across the Schuylkill river from Norristown) was working as a translator in the American command headquarters at Sparanise near the city of Caserta, near the southwest terminus of the Line. We were like a pair of parentheses that encompassed a most intense and moving war drama. The protagonists of the drama itself were Sergeant Harry Billela, another American from Norristown, and *Radiotelegrafista Prima Classe,* Luciano De Nardis, an M Battalion volunteer (M for Mussolini) who had regretted several times the spur of the moment decision he had made in 1942 to join up. He migrated to Norristown in 1951 from Italy, via Montreal. On the night between May 27th and 28th, these two were in the same place but on opposite sides of the Line. What followed would be pure fiction except for the fact that it really happened, in all its unimaginable absurdities. The four would eventually come together on a Tuesday night in 1952, in Norristown, Pa. Only then the full story came out. In order to tell the story at this point, I have to do a flash ahead. Stay with me, dear readers, please!

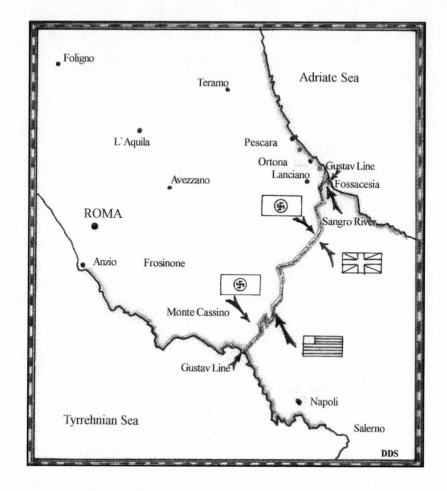

Map of Central Italy under siege

This is a facsimile of a map that appeared in an American newspaper on December 1, 1943, the day after the Battle of the Sangro River. It clearly shows the Gustav Line that bisected the nation after the September 8 armistice. The German winter line ran from the Sangro River Valley in Fossacesia, to the Garigliano River at Gaeta, in the south west. In October, Hitler ordered his army to move the head of the Gustav Line from the Sangro River to the Moro River, just south of Ortona. That was good for us because the Germans held firm for about six months. At that point it should have been clear to them that the game was over, but they became enraged instead, disseminating death and destruction among the civilian population still under their control. Hundreds of people in Abruzzo lost their lives, including children, seniors and the sick. They treated everyone equally, those Nazis!

GEE, THAT STORY SOUNDS AWFULLY FAMILIAR

After my family was finally reunited in America, we joined Holy Saviour Church on the East End of Norristown. I sang in its choir from the very first Sunday in America, June 29, 1947. In the congregation there were many war veterans who had just formed a post of Catholic War Veterans. One of the veterans who took a particular liking to me was Harry Bilella, so we became good friends even though I was 12 years younger. In the fall of 1952, our pastor Monsignor George Delia suggested that we form a Bible study group. We did, and we met every Tuesday night at each member's home.

One Tuesday night, we were in an apartment on East Main Street. We had a special guest that night: the newly ordained Rev. Louis A. DeSimone, who was an expert on the Beatitudes. It was an extraordinary session. The young clergyman that night gave a superior dissertation. I was so impressed that, in an impetus of euphoria, I told him that he was headed straight for the episcopacy, if not the papacy. Well, the papacy did not pan out, but my prediction of his becoming a bishop, given in jest, was absolutely prophetic, for Father De Simone became, indeed, the Most Reverend Louis A. De Simone, Auxiliary Bishop of Philadelphia, in 1981. He is now retired.

When the treatise on the Beatitudes was over, there was the usual question and answer session, and the conversation drifted to include the parable of the Good Samaritan as well. After a few more questions on the subject, the lady of the house invited everyone to the dining room for the usual cake and coffee. The young wives of the men in the group went out of their way to prepare scrumptious sweets for us. The priests and I, not being married, managed to get a free ride. But the guys were very gracious about it. A cup of coffee and a piece of pie was no big deal, they used to say.

That night, I had taken a friend with me, an Italian immigrant whom I had befriended recently at the opera house in Philadelphia, Luciano De Nardis. His brother Tony and I played on the same soccer team at nearby Ambler, Pa. We normally sat randomly around the table. That night, Father Delia sat at the head of the table, I sat to his left and Lou to my left. Directly across from me and at the priest's right sat Harry. Young Father De Simone took his place at the other end, facing the older priest, with the other members in between. After a quick prayer before meals, coffee was served together with the best upside-down pineapple cake I had ever tasted. Since Father De Simone had touched upon the story of the Good Samaritan, taking a cue from the parable, he told us about how his own vocation came about. He said that after the front finally moved to the area of Tuscany, he met a Franciscan priest, Padre

Eustorgio, and it was his inspirational talk at mass one Sunday that slammed home to Sergeant De Simone his decision to become a priest after returning to the United States. He had been considering the priesthood ever since he was at Villanova University before he was called to active duty anyway, but he was somewhat hesitant, until he met Padre Eustorgio, who gave him the right kind of encouragement. He considered the Franciscan monk his Good Samaritan. Upon his return to Bridgeport, Father De Simone discussed the situation with his two brothers, Sal and Russell, and they too decided to enter the seminary, so that their parents, who had only three sons, ended up giving them all to the Lord.

After Father finished to tell his story about his Good Samaritan, he asked each one of us to think back and see if we had a Good Samaritan in our lives. I went first, but I said that my Good Samaritan was not a person at all. It was a dog. So I told the story of my neighbor and future wife's dog, Bricco, who saved our lives by barking in the middle of nowhere one early evening when we were being herded northward by two armed Germans. I considered Bricco my Good Samaritan. Inspired by the priest's story, Harry began to tell a story about his own Good Samaritan that was to have untold reverberations.

He said, that on the night of May 27, 1944, he was leading a patrol of American soldiers in an area near Frosinone. Ten men volunteered, including a lieutenant, as the commanding officer, and Sergeant Billela was the second in command. Normally, those noble warriors who had defeated Hitler and his Nazi machine rarely talked about their war experiences. However, having heard the young priest talking about the Good Samaritan who had inspired him, Harry decided to tell his story so that he might lift once and for all a nagging thought he had about what happened that night. He was asking the advice of both priests on how to resolve his dilemma. It had been eight years, now, and every time he had a chance to talk about it, for some reason, he couldn't. Now, it seemed to be the perfect time to air his tale once and for all. Here is the story he told.

THE MISSION

It was a beautiful, warm spring evening. Above, in the crystal clear Italian sky, there was a mantle of stars like he had never seen before. During the late afternoon each member of the volunteer scout party had slept for about four hours, gone to chow, and the Catholic soldiers had even gone to confession, "just in case!" Actually all but one or two fell into that category. It was 8:00

P.M. when they boarded a military truck that took them to the edge of a hill and deposited them there. They were about a half mile from a creek that marked the dividing line between the German and the American positions. It was still daylight when they began their trek toward the river running at the bottom of the hill. It was just a pleasant walk. When they reached a clump of trees near the creek, they stopped, waiting for total darkness to settle over the land. Their orders specifically said to move out at exactly 22:00 hours, ten o'clock. They had previously synchronized their watches, and at precisely ten o'clock they moved out, their faces darkened, their rifles at the ready, a prayer in the mind of each of them.

They had no trouble crossing the creek. They proceeded along the fields protected by the fairly tall vegetation, mostly wheat which had not been properly cultivated because of the war emergency. It provided enough cover for them, so they proceeded rapidly toward their objective, two miles to the northwest, in the general direction of a small hamlet. All was proceeding normally. They walked through the fields in a sustained yet relaxed pace. Moving in a single file, Harry was the second man behind his commanding officer. They proceeded in silence, but with determination, toward a given rendezvous point. They got there in ten minutes and waited a little more in order to take advantage of a truly dark night. The moon would set soon.

Suddenly, there was a loud explosion. The lieutenant walking in front of Harry had stepped on a mine and was killed instantly, and Harry was badly wounded. They were too far out from their headquarters and in enemy territory, so there was no way they could summon medical help. The men did their best to keep him supplied with morphine. Unfortunately, Harry was a hemophiliac, and they were unable to stop the flow of blood. Unless they were fortunate enough to find help, he would bleed to death by morning. They found a cave large enough to accommodate the whole group, camouflaged the entrance, and tried to stabilize their badly wounded leader. Two of the guys who, like Harry, spoke Italian, approached a farmhouse nearby. There was an elderly couple living there, who gave them some soup and some medical gauze, but they had nothing else. The men returned to the cave with the gauze, but were still unable to stop the bleeding.

At 1:00 A.M., they decided to leave the cave to try to get medical help in the small town they could see about a half mile from their position. That's when they ran directly into a platoon of Germans. *"Halt! Who goes there?"* These and other menacing words were exchanged, and, without a doubt, weapons were raised at each other on both sides. In the German platoon, however, there was a second lieutenant who spoke perfect English. He asked,

"Who is in command?" The Americans identified Staff Sergeant Harry Billela as their commanding officer. They had been so preoccupied about trying to save Harry's life that they had failed to pass the scepter of command to the next in line. That's when the Americans realized that the Germans were also carrying on a makeshift litter their own commanding officer, a first lieutenant, who was badly wounded. The German lieutenant who spoke English was actually a Polish national and an American to boot. His name was Darius. At the urging of the young Polish lieutenant, the two enemy groups decided to stay together, and seek help from the local citizenry.

They were not successful in getting the medical help they needed, but the lady in the farmhouse suggested they could stay in the *tettoia* (utility hut) the usual hangar-like shelter present on most farms whose walls consisted of alternating brick and a hole. It was covered by a tin roof. The night was cool, and the holes in the walls admitted to the interior every slight breath of air and made it sound and feel like an approaching hurricane. Since it was only a shelter for farm machinery, the building was walled only on three sides; the front was completely open. This was good because the barn fronted on a north south roadway and they could see any military vehicles that might approach especially from the south. At least they were covered, and each of the men from both sides found some straw upon which to sleep. By mutual, yet tacit agreement, they placed their weapons on the far side of the building. All went to sleep, except First Lieutenant Darius, who took charge of Sergeant Billela and the other wounded lieutenant. Harry said Lieutenant Darius spoke English because he was actually a Polish-American who grew up in Philadelphia's St. Adalbert's parish. Lt. Darius told one of the American soldiers during their long night vigil over the two wounded soldiers that his family had returned to Poland due to an urgent family problem in 1938. Just before they were to return to Philadelphia, however, the Germans invaded Poland and they were trapped. But, he was planning to return to the United States as soon as the war was over.

Lieutenant Darius continued to care for both wounded men. Unfortunately, shortly after 3:00 A.M., the German lieutenant died. Both American and German soldiers moved the body toward the rear of the barn, and again congregated toward the front part of it. The Americans gave the Germans some American cigarettes, and this sort of broke the ice between the two factions.

When Darius learned the wounded sergeant was from Norristown, Pa., not far from Philadelphia, he actually cried. He continued to care for Harry, staying with him all night long and ministering to him the best he could.

From time to time he gave him a spoonful of soup to keep his energy up, and wet his lips with water when they became parched. All night long, he knelt on the side of Harry's stretcher, never leaving the wounded American for one minute.

At dawn, the young lieutenant was still kneeling by Harry's side, cleaning his face with a wet towel, giving him water from time to time, and reassuring him that help was on the way and they would be rescued soon. Suddenly a shell exploded in the open side of the building, less than ten feet away. Harry, who was lying on the stretcher, was wounded again, but the young lieutenant, who was in a kneeling position beside him, took the brunt of the explosion and was killed instantly.

With the German patrol group, there was a radio man. The other German soldiers had referred to him as Lance. He had made several attempts to call for help ever since the two groups had become one without getting a response. When the shell exploded in the morning, he renewed his efforts, and by 7:00 A.M. he managed to get the medics of the American Fifth Army on the line. He gave them their position, gave directions, described some landmarks, gave a description of the wounded and what it was they needed, and then took off his head gear and walked away. He went behind some bushes, and everyone assumed he went for an urgent call of nature, so no one paid much attention, especially since everyone was very busy, what with a newly wounded sergeant, and another dead lieutenant.

Within the hour three military ambulances arrived, followed by two trucks, in anticipation of having to transport captured prisoners of war as well as the American soldiers not wounded. They captured seven Germans and put them in one of the trucks, under armed guard. The wounded were loaded in one of the ambulances. Two Germans and one American with minor wounds climbed aboard a second ambulance. Some of the German soldiers were directed to place the bodies of the two dead German lieutenants in the third ambulance while the rest of the Americans climbed aboard the second truck. They were making ready to depart, when one of the German soldiers called out for Lance, the radio man. But, Lance was nowhere to be found, so everyone assumed he had managed to escape capture by the Americans and would go back to his outfit to fight one more day for "the glorious Third Reich."

When Harry finished telling his story, everyone was astonished. Coffee and cake were served and the conversation turned to praises for the woman of the house and her prowess in baking pinapple-up-side-down cakes. Then, Harry continued: "That young Polish lieutenant stayed with me all night

long, taking care of me, and he died in the process. I've felt guilty about it
ever since." He added, "If he hadn't been kneeling by my side he would have
been saved. I will always pray for him, the rest of my life. He was definitely
my Good Samaritan."

Father De Simone, with Father Delia echoing his sentiments, reassured
Harry that the night-long vigil the lieutenant spent by his side was his ticket
to heaven. It was the young man's banner of victory. "Pray for and to him, of
course, but don't feel guilty about it." The young curate and future bishop
added, "It wasn't your fault, Harry. It was an act of free will on his part,
prompted by his strong sense of charity for his neighbor. He has already been
rewarded for it, I assure you." From 1951 until his death in 1992, Harry and
I made an annual spiritual retreat together at Malvern, Pa. He never failed
to enter the name of Lt. Darius on all memorial lists that were placed on the
altar at every mass.

Meanwhile, as Harry was telling his story, twice or three times my friend
Luciano had exclaimed, "That sounds like something that happened to me,"
or "I was in a similar situation," and similar statements. Suddenly, Lou became
very tight lipped. He looked a little strange, and soon he gave signs that he
was actually annoyed of the whole story, and wanted to go home. Since I was
the one who drove, he forced me to leave early to take him home. On the
way, Lou revealed his own story to me. Unfortunately, he gave me just enough
information to satisfy my immediate curiosity, but I had to wait several months
to one night, in 1953, when he finally told me the rest of the story.

After making me promise solemnly not to tell anyone what he was about
to reveal to me, he told me the reason why the story was familiar to him was
that he was with the German scout party the morning of May 28, 1944, in
Italy. He was the German radio man. That surprised me immensely, so I said,
"How in the world did you end up in the German Army, Lou?" He assured
me that he would tell me that in due time, but not that night. It was too long
a story. He made me swear again not to speak about it to anyone, and said
that when he was ready he would tell me everything.

THE REST OF THE STORY

On February 3, 1953, Lou and I went to the World Theater in Philadelphia
to see Frank Sinatra's *From Here to Eternity*. When the movie was over, we
stopped for a hamburger and coffee at Nick and Lou's, a favorite after movie
luncheonette across the street from Holy Saviour Church. I don't know if
it was the coffee or the burger or both that inspired him, but suddenly Lou

revealed to me the circumstances whereby he became Lance, the German radio man, in Harry's story. He was the "German" radioman who always had it within his power to call a German ambulance, but if he did the Americans would certainly have been all killed, because those were the days in which the full force of German rage had come to the surface. Besides, the Germans at that point did not have the means to take prisoners. They hardly had enough food for themselves, having been reduced to scrounge around the farms for something to eat, so they would not take on the responsibility of feeding prisoners of war, too. Solution? A quick burst of automatic fire, and that would have been that. It was amazing to realize, Luciano said, that almost every German soldier blamed the Italian population for their lack of military success, citing their non-cooperation. That, they would say, was punishable by death and that is how they appeased their consciences.

Lou continued his side of the story: For the rest of the night, he kept trying to figure out how to get out of this dilemma, but when, at dawn, the shell exploded that killed the young Polish American, Lou quickly moved away from the German soldiers so they would not hear the conversation, and he called the Allied radio band, and asked to speak to an Italian because he spoke no English in those days. He explained the situation in Italian and took off immediately. He was from somewhere around Agnone, and his hometown lay but a scant 30 miles to the southeast, just beyond the mountains. The reason why he didn't want to be captured by the Americans was that, being so close, he wanted to go home, and not be taken prisoner, albeit by the Americans. Besides, he had joined an army which now was an enemy of the Italian nation. He didn't know what to make of that, so he hoped to make it home and then he would see what to do. The first thing he did was reveal his real identity to the old lady in the nearby house. He needed some civilian clothes. In order to convince her, he had to speak in the dialect of his native town. It was like magic: now she believed him, for the dialect was so bad that only a native son could manage to recreate its mysterious dissonance. She hid him for the rest of the day, and gave him some of her husband's clothes, though they were too big. At sundown, he set out on foot and headed toward the town of Castel di Sangro, in Abruzzo, due east, because the mountains are too tall in the area and he would have to go all the way to Venafro to get around them from a southern route. So he went slightly north and east, and from there, he could cross into the British sector at Castel di Sangro. He stopped at a small village where he befriended a man at a bar and from him he bought some decent civilian clothes so he could travel without too much trouble. Finally, he came to a British check point. He had a bit of a problem explaining where he was coming from, but Luciano was possessed with an open, pleasant personality and so was able to persuade the guards to let him pass. He was free. Within the British occupied sector, he was even able to work for the army a few days so that now he had some money in his pocket, besides. By early June, he was home. The puzzling question still remains, of course: what are the odds that two men would meet on the battlefield, fighting on opposite sides, meet up in the middle of the night as enemies, get together because of a common need for help, and then, many years later, they should be sharing Bible stories, cake and coffee, together, as friends in America? Amazing! But then, life, so they say, is stranger than fiction.

FROM RUSSIA WITH HUNGER

But, how did Lou get to serve in the German Army? In a very strange manner, to be sure! Eighteen-year-old Luciano De Nardis, a butcher's apprentice in a small town in the Molise section of the Abruzzi region, high in the Apennine Mountains, decided he wanted to have a little bit of an adventure so he joined the so called "M" Battalion, a crack outfit of the Italian Army named "M" for Mussolini. It was early in 1942. He was sent to several different Italian cities for boot camp and other training purposes and, within a year he ended up in Germany, close to the Russian border. From there, he was sent deep into Russia, traveling by military transport trains, reaching as far as the Don River area. Actually, he never did any real fighting himself, since he had trained in communications, but he saw thousands of Italian soldiers returning from the front lines in tatters, frozen stiff, and hungry as wolves. Train loads of replacements were going the other way to take their places, but they were no longer singing the Fascist songs that, at the beginning of the war, had given them the necessary spirit to nurture the illusion that, *"dulce et decorum est pro patria mori,"* (It is sweet and proper to die for one's country!—Horace). These guys didn't think it was such a great idea to die, for your country or anything else. The M Battalion, being the elite outfit that it was, had been reserved for greater deeds, although no one knew exactly what; they had little ammunition, few cigarettes, and soon even food began to get scarce. A few weeks into the Russian winter of 1942, hunger began to become serious. They were spending the few lire they still had to buy boiled potatoes from local farmers, who didn't even have enough for themselves. And the Russian winters weren't exactly filled with cool breezes and gentle zephyrs, either. They were brutal. The Italians were housed in wooden barracks that were little more than ice boxes. To say it was cold would have been grotesquely inaccurate: the temperature dipped to incredible levels below zero. It was bitter cold. They were hungry, thirsty and tired. The threat of the Russian troops crossing the Don with their tanks was ever present, although the thickness of the ice over the level of the water had been measured at eight inches, not enough to support the weight of the tanks. Several weeks after reaching their destination, their orders were no longer coming from the Italian Army, but they were told to do the bidding of their German comrades. In other words, take their orders from the Germans who despised them and kept them hungry. That did not sit very well with the Italians, especially the members of the M Battalion.

The Germans weren't advancing. Their orders were simply to hold their grounds. At this point, the only thing that helped them hold their grounds was the Don River itself. It was frozen solid. It would have been possible to carry on normal activities over its surface, such as driving automobiles, carts, even trucks to go across it. Tanks were another matter. In order to permit the tanks to cross the iced over surface of the Don, the ice thickness had to be at least ten inches. Occasionally there would be sniper fire reaching them from the Russian side. Lou said that there was a comrade of his named Valerio from Viareggio who had received a letter from his girlfriend for his birthday. Her name was also Valeria. It was a rarity for anyone to receive mail that far away from home. She had put a single cigarette in the envelope, one of those expensive cigarettes with the brand name written in gold and made not round but flat. Valerio was so happy that he lit the cigarette and walked outside to share a puff or two with his captain. He had walked no more than ten paces when he collapsed and died, the cigarette falling in the snow. No one had heard the shot being fired, that's how far they were from the other side of the Don River. Valeria had intended it as a gesture of love for her boyfriend, but it turned into his death sentence.

By mid-January, the ice over the river was expected to reach a thickness of well above ten inches. The Russians tanks would come across, and it would be a disaster. To measure the thickness of the ice, the Italian command sent two "ice experts," a Sicilian and a Florentine, neither one of whom had ever seen an ice covered river in their lives prior to their being called into the army.

The technique for measuring the thickness of the ice was another peculiarity. No, they were not given an electronic device capable of doing the job. They were given the necessary tools, all right, but these consisted of a pick and a long, thin straw, a hollow tube of the cane variety of the rattan plant that grows plentiful along waterways, worldwide. They were to drill a hole in the ice with the pick, then suck up until they drew water. At that point, they would put a nick into the tube and then measure its length from the end of the straw. That crude, certainly unscientific, yet practical method, would give them an approximation of the thickness of the ice. The most challenging part of that operation was avoiding the searchlights that constantly floated over the frozen expanse of the river. They had to wait until the circle of light passed a certain point, then run out and hope to accomplish the mission before the light came around again. Occasionally, snipers would fire at them, too, indiscriminately, hoping to hit something, or at least keeping the "enemy" honest. A sense of hopelessness had begun to snake its way through the ranks of the Italian Army. The promises made to Mussolini that the German Army would provide fuel and ammunitions for the Italians to be able to fight alongside of them, never materialized. If the Italians had failed to engender in their hearts a love for those burly warmongers, the Germans had no problem generating a sense of disdain for their southern would-be comrades, either. There was no love lost between the two "allies." The Germans did not provide anything for the Italians, and all the Italians wanted was to go home.

JOIN THE ARMY OF THE GLORIOUS THIRD REICH

One day, a couple of German officers came to the Italian camp, and asked the commanding officer if they could talk to the entire regiment. After conferring among themselves, the two officers and their aides decided to put the Germans' request in writing and pin the paper on a bulletin board. The request was that, if any Italian soldier wanted to enlist in the "victorious army of the Third Reich," they not only would be welcome, but they would receive a generous pay, warm uniforms and would be treated like a German soldier. "Talk among yourselves and we'll be back tomorrow at noon for your signatures," they said.

Talk among themselves they did, but most of them felt that it would be tantamount to betraying your own country by joining the army of another country, albeit an "ally." Besides, Mussolini may have joined forces with Hitler, but the Italians were too much aware that they had been their enemies a mere twenty-five years before and now they were supposed to join their army? As a result, most of them refused to join. Out of eight-hundred fifty soldiers that made up Luciano's battalion, only nine of them joined up. Among the nine was Luciano. The nine reasoned that they were so far into Russia that the chances of their ever going home was practically nil. So, let's let them take us back westward, and when we get there, we'll make another decision. And, they were right. Among those who did not sign, very few made it back home after the war. Most of them are still listed as missing in action and presumed dead. One of the few who made it back was Gelio Sartini, from Sant'Angelo in Vado, province of Pesaro. Sartini didn't make it home until August, 1946, with his right foot amputated due to severe frost bite he had received in Russia. He wrote a book detailing his prison years in the hands of the Russians (*Campo 160*, Castaldi Editore, Milano). After reading that book, one could plainly see that the few Italians who joined the German Army had made the correct decision.

Lou and his eight buddies after signing up, much to the derision and condemnation of the rest of the Italians present, were put on a German troop train. They traveled for days and days, moving slowly but steadily, at night, but stopping frequently during the day, mainly because, after they entered into German territory, they were subjected to frequent air raids. Most of the German cities through which they passed were nothing but mountains of rubble. Sometimes, even the tracks were interrupted, and the soldiers on the train had to get off and provide the manpower to restore the rails enough so that the train could proceed.

Finally, they reached the city of Dresden. Here they boarded military trucks and were transported to a small town about 30 miles south of the city. They were herded into some barracks. They were outfitted with all new equipment, including a German uniform and helmet. "It felt awfully funny on my head," said Lou when he finally told me the full story. "For the first time, I realized that what my buddies in Russia had said about joining the German army was absolutely true. I felt like a traitor," he said, "but, my reasoning was absolutely correct. They had taken us back to civilization. Immediately, my thoughts went to my former comrades that I had left behind in Russia. I wondered if any of them would ever make it back home."

"The feeling that I had betrayed my own country by wearing a German uniform didn't last long, however," Luciano added. "Not because I had fallen in love with the Germans," he explained later, "for they treated us with total disrespect, but because within a week it began to appear more and more that the nine of us "reprobates," as one of our buddies had put it back in Russia, had indeed made the right decision. All we had to do now was await the right occasion to bolt it and go home, one way or another. We were put on another train. Just prior to boarding that train, they swore us in and read to us a long dissertation about our obligations, or at least so I was told because it was all in German and I didn't understand any of it. Another German soldier tried to relate the speech in very poor Italian. We were reminded of "the great privilege we had received in being permitted to serve the great Führer and the glorious

German Army. Well, it went in our ears and emerged in the form of gas via a very delicate part of the human anatomy!" Lou quipped with sardonic humor. "We just wanted to see where this adventure would eventually lead. And, of course, the next move on my agenda was to bolt it out of there as soon as possible. But, it was absolutely essential to be patient. One false move and it would have been the end of the adventure."

The second train they boarded traveled for three nights. They couldn't travel during the day because it would have meant dodging bombs and bullets as it proceeded. Three times they had to abandon the cars, and at one point a bomb exploded dangerously close to the tracks, but it was determined that the train could proceed. When they finally arrived, the Italians turned Germans could not believe their eyes. They had arrived during the night in total darkness, but when daylight broke, they could see that they were in Verona. They were home. Verona, however, was under German control, so far as they could see. The Italian soldiers in Russia had not been told of what the situation was in the various fronts. The nine Italians, veterans of the Russian campaign from which they brought with them nothing but extreme hunger and thirst, were more than shocked to hear that the Italian cities were the targets of nightly air raids by American heavy bombers. They learned that those planes were based in Benghazi, Libya. Obviously, then, the Italians had been thrown out of North Africa. It took several days, before Lou and the others could focus properly on current events, and figure out what was going on. Of course, now they could buy newspapers written in their own language, and this helped. The Italian soldiers were in a strange predicament: they hated the Germans, but at the same time they felt awkward about losing a war. It just didn't feel right, no matter what the logic of the situation was. The Italian soldier is not the non-hero that most foreigners think he is, but heroism too has to have a purpose, otherwise it is nothing but an exercise in masochistic self immolation. I read a story on *Epoca Magazine* (now defunct), of an Italian bersagliere in North Africa who found himself in a skirmish together with some German soldiers against an attacking British patrol unit. He had no ammunition, so his rifle was useless to him. But, he was reluctant to kill, *anyway,* especially Americans since his father had been in America for a number of years. So he took cover, waiting for the battle to be over. After some shots were fired, however, he noticed that one of the Germans in the group had fallen, so he left his cover and went to his aid. He helped him up, and was trying to get him to take cover with him. The German, however, had other ideas: he turned toward the enemy and fired again. The Italian grabbed him by the waist and tried to pull him to safety, saying as he went:

"No, Camerata. E'pericoloso qui. Andiamo via!" (No, Comrade; it's dangerous here. Let's get away). At that point a volley of bullets mowed down both the German and his Italian would-be rescuer. As I said, heroism has to have a purpose higher than itself.

TO PADUA, FOR SOME R & R

At this point, the situation got a bit comical: the nine Italians were sent to Padua for some R & R. I guess the Germans thought the Italians needed a little relaxation before sending them to the slaughter house. However, they were always under strict surveillance. Lou had already tried to see if there was a way to escape, but security was extremely tight: it would have been suicidal.

After ten days in Padua, they were sent to the upper Po Valley, near Turin, for a two week accelerated combat training, and then they were finally sent to their destination. They traveled southward on trucks for several days. Soon, he began to see signs that said Roma 30 miles, then 25 miles, and finally they drove right through the heart of Rome, Lou was very happy, indeed. Still, escape was impossible. Patience, at this point, was the greater part of valor.

After they arrived in Rome, they were given another three day leave. Still under tight surveillance, but he was able to catch up on the news, and to make several phone calls to friends in Rome. Lou was able, therefore, to send news to his father that he was safe in Rome, for the time being. With God's help, he could be home soon.

While in Rome, the German command found Lou more useful in reading documents, together with a German soldier who had studied in Firenze for two years, back in 1937. They worked in a palazzo near Piazza Barberini. He enjoyed that stay for a few months until the Americans landed at Anzio, then, all hell broke lose.

Luciano, re-baptized Lance by the Germans, had become used to life at the palazzo. Not only his quarters were spacious and quite accommodating, but also he had gotten used to dining at a nearby restaurant off the Corso called *La Vela Azzurra* (The Blue Sail). On Fridays, they served nothing but seafood, splendidly prepared Abruzzese style by their old chef, a middle aged man from the *Alto Vastese* (literally Vasto Heights), called Alfredo Vinciguerra (Vasto is the beautiful city 20 miles south of Fossacesia. It's the city where I would be taking my exams in 1945. It's renowned for its superior ways of preparing seafood). Lou had revealed his real identity to Alfredo. The chef's last name means, literally, "win-the-war." He used to joke about the fact that, due to his old age, he could not go to war, otherwise, he would teach these modern soldiers how to win wars. He had fought the First World War and "We won that one!" he used to quip. Actually, they had not won that war at all, even though Italy had fought on the side of the Allies and lost 600,000 men in the process. At Versailles, Italy fared almost as poorly as the Germans, who were supposed to be the losers. This proved once again that war could forever be avoided if man inserted justice in his dealings with his fellow man, but that has never been the case, and so we are doomed to wage war against one another, forever: *"Lotta continua!"* as the Italian Communists used to boast (Continuous struggle).

Alfredo, also, used to say that it was he who invented fettuccine *"all'Alfredo."* That one was never confirmed, however, so I'm going to table it. Meanwhile, each time Lou saw him, he would burst into Violetta's aria, in Verdi's Traviata: *"Alfredo, Alfredo, di questo cuore."*

Chef Vinciguerra became Lou's friend, confidante, and fellow opera buff. Consequently, he was the only one who knew that Lou was not a German at all, but an Italian, even though Luciano tried to speak Italian with a fake Teutonic accent. He was good at that. He used to sing at the restaurant, too. He had a nice, Sinatra-like baritone voice, and he loved to sing, so he sang an interminable repertoire of Italian songs that astonished his audiences. How can a German know so many songs in Italian? He also used to sing in 'French.' Well, sort of. His French songs sounded genuine, but he actually only made sounds that resembled French—a grunt here, a nasal lamentation there, and, voila, a perfect rendition of *La vie en rose* (no disrespect of the French language intended here). He was often praised on his perfect pronunciation of Italian, and even French, when he sang. The one strange thing about this "German" singing soldier was that he never sang in German—he didn't know how! He could fake French, but not German. Lou always responded to the audiences' sometimes enthusiastic and always polite applause with a shy bow. With a wave of his hand, he thanked everybody, in a sort of distracted way as he quickly walked off the stage and out the door. He never returned to the stage for a second bow: he didn't want to attract attention to himself.

The final leg of Luciano's journey home from Russia took place in January, 1944. Just about the same time the Germans mobilized their 26th Panzer Grenadier Division, as part of the German 10th Army, operating in the vicinity of Frosinone. The American Fifth Army had dug in north of Naples awaiting the spring, and were slowly moving northward with great confidence, not anticipating the tough nut to crack that Montecassino would turn out to be. The Anzio beachhead had taken place with relatively low casualties but, after coming ashore, the Americans stopped for unexplained reasons, giving the Germans time to recover and reinforce. I saw a documentary in which the Germans themselves commented on this, and were grateful for the opportunity to replenish their supplies. The biggest problem the Germans encountered was the daily attacks by American Air Force, which possessed B-24's and B-17's by the thousands and had no plans to save them for future wars, sending them over in wave, after wave, after wave. Then there was the constant barrage of American artillery that pounded them unmercifully from dawn to past midnight. Where did they get all that ammunition? Lou and his comrades were baffled. At this point, Lou realized exactly how insane it had been for Germany, but especially Italy, to go to war against this inexhaustible war machine that spat fire and fury at will.

At the end of the 20th century, with Harry already dead and Lou suffering from Alzheimer's disease, and living in Wisconsin, it is impossible for me to reconstruct their activities, or even to ascertain the dates or the locations, precisely. From what Lou told me that night over sixty years ago, I seem to recall that he went through some tough days during that period. He didn't want to risk receiving a volley of bullets in the back from his "comrades" by attempting to escape. He knew that his hometown was less than fifty miles away, but there were too many dangerous hurdles to be overcome, and so he stayed put, awaiting the right moment to make his final move. He had even been told by his German commanders that he was "a good soldier." Fortunately, being a communications expert, he was not required to shoot anyone, even though he had been given a weapon. So he bid his time and waited for an opportune moment to escape.

It was the 27th of May, 1944, when, in the vicinity of Frosinone, around four in the afternoon his unit was strafed by two American P-51 Mustangs. Whenever Lou told that story, he always made me laugh uncontrollably, as he related the fact that he was down in a small ravine behind a bush that hid him from view, with his pants down taking care of an unavoidable physiological need. He was exercising his mind at the same time working on an Italian crossword puzzle. He was stuck on one word, as he recalled: *o-n-o-r-a-r-i-o*. The clue was: "It is due to professional people." He didn't know then that a lawyer's or a doctor's fee was called *honorarium*, in Latin, becoming *onorario* in Italian. Judging by the one or two letters he already had on the line, he kept thinking "*onori*" which not only didn't fit, but he knew that both doctors and lawyers need to eat and one cannot eat honors.

Suddenly, there was a roar right over his head. That first plane must have passed no more than a few hundred feet above his head. Lou dropped everything, picked up his pants, and ran to take cover. Of course, in retelling the story for the Nth time, Lou accompanied his narrative with the required, appropriate descriptive sounds that kept his audience in stitches throughout. Having reached his defense post, he didn't even know what to do. He was supposed to shoot at the planes with his rifle. But, how, how do you hit an airplane as fast as the P-51 with a rifle? They would pounce on you so fast, and before you raised your rifle, they were gone. Lou fired a few rounds just so he could say that he fought back, but those bullets went for naught. He didn't mind it, though. It was not in his heart to kill anyone. He, like the Italian people in general, was not mad at anyone.

The attack was quick, but devastating. Two of their men were killed, and their commanding officer, a first lieutenant was hit by two bullets, and badly wounded. They called for help, but the German medics did not respond. They tried to get help from a country doctor who tried valiantly to stabilize him, but without success. He had no medical supplies at all. Finally, around midnight, they decided to try to take the wounded officer to a hospital if they could find one. They were trying to reach the highway, about a mile distant, when they ran into a platoon of American soldiers. Both groups raised their weapons toward one another, but their commanding officer, First Lieutenant Darius a Pole, spoke English to the Americans, and was able to defuse a potentially explosive situation. Having a common problem, the two groups decided to stay together. They proceeded to a farmhouse along Highway 7 occupied by an elderly couple. They were actually in bed, but they made enough noise that the lady got up and opened the door. Having been acquainted with the problem, she told them they could stay in the barn. She warmed up some broth she had from the night before and gave them some tincture of iodine knowing how insufficient it was. The men on both sides spread around the barn each trying to find a spot upon which to recline their heads and get some sleep. By order of Lieutenant Darius in agreement with one of the Americans, everyone unloaded their rifles and placed them in the rear of the building.

While all the soldiers went to sleep, Lieutenant Darius placed himself between the two makeshift stretchers upon which the two wounded men lay and began to minister to them. He didn't have much, but he did have the bowl of broth given to them by the lady of the house and a pitcher of water. He also had some morphine volunteered by the men, even though military law prohibited the soldiers to part with it.

At quarter after three, the German Lieutenant died. He had moaned in pain all night and then he stopped. Everyone thought he was resting, but some time between 2:30 and 3:15 A.M. he had expired without anyone noticing. There simply was nothing anyone could have done for him. Some of the men from both groups carried his body to the rear of the barn, they covered his face and went back to sleep. Darius resumed his place at the side of Harry's stretcher and continued to minister to the wounded American soldier.

Suddenly, disaster struck. It was just before seven A.M., most of the soldiers were still asleep when without warning there was a shrill whistle followed by a tremendous roar: a cannon shell of gigantic force exploded about ten feet in front of the hangar. Harry, who was lying down, was wounded again, though not too seriously, but Lieutenant Darius was killed instantly. He was 23 years old. Being in a kneeling position next to the wounded American sergeant, he took the brunt of the explosion. It was a devastating situation. In addition to killing Lieutenant Darius, the explosion also injured several other soldiers, both German and American. Fortunately, they were all asleep on the inside of the barn, so the wounds were superficial for the most part.

After the morning explosion, Lou made the necessary call on the American radio band and waited. When the ambulances arrived, he took advantage of a moment of confusion the rescuers seemed to have, seeing the commingling of Americans and Germans, apparently not in a hostile attitude toward one another, he ran to the house nearby. With the help of the lady in the lone home, in the rural area somewhere south of Rome, Lou was finally free. He dumped his German radio pack down in an overgrown ditch, donned some civilian clothes the lady provided for him and by ten o'clock he was on his way home, on foot.

Eight years later, the now Father and future auxiliary bishop of Philadelphia, Most Reverend Louis A. De Simone, DD, veterans Harry Billela and Lou De Nardis, and I, twenty year old Danny De Simone, a non-combatant war veteran just the same, were sitting around a table in America, drinking coffee, munching on a pineapple upside-down cake, having just discussed the intricacies of the message of the parable of the Good Samaritan. We were the key elements in that strange yet true story that took place the night between May 27 and May 28, 1944.

THE POST-BELLUM ERA

SCHOOL REOPENS—SORT OF!

What does one do after a war passes through his very street destroying everything in sight? Pick up the pieces and keep going. Our lives were scarred, after all, and we had to continue where we left off. For that reason, in January 1944, Monsignor Tozzi announced at mass that there would be some kind of school reopening for the middle grade students on Monday, Jan. 10th. The classes were to be conducted in private homes. Whoever had his home still intact and could spare a room or two was to make it available to the recently organized *DDE (Distretto Didattico d'Emergenza,* or Emergency School District). The teachers were recruited right from town, and invariably they were our old elementary school teachers. There were a few young men in town who had been members of the Italian Army who had been serving in the southern part of the Italian boot whose homes were in the unliberated north. They remained with us until such a time as they could go home. Two of them claimed to be *"professori,"* so they were pressed into service teaching English and math. One such person was the Professor from Rimini; I never did learn his name. He claimed to know English. So, they gave him a class at the home of the local blacksmith which was right up the street from the house where I was born, and I was assigned to it because I needed to learn English, anticipating my eventual emigration to America.

I ran into a problem the very first day: my book, the one I had found in nonno's house on December first, the one that claimed to teach you English in three months without a teacher, didn't please the professor very much (it must be remembered that in Italy, even today, a teacher who teaches the 6th grade and up has the title of professor) I had gone to school with much anticipation figuring that I would be the only student who possessed a book on the English language, only to be told that my book was worthless. That was funny, because it was the only book on the subject in the entire town. So, I went home at noon and told my mother about it, but she didn't know what to make of it. That night, however, Herb Speedie came to our home and I shared my problem with him. He was enraged. Being a truck driver, hence not versed in the intricacies of the world of academia, he could not fathom the idea that a book on any given subject would be declared unfit for that purpose. To him a book was a book, period. He decided that the next morning, on his way to deliver his first load of ammo to the front lines, which by then were in the towns surrounding Ortona, he would take me to school and he would talk to the teacher himself. And so he did. The next day, bright and early, he drove me to town in that same truck full of ammunition with which he had taken me to mass three weeks earlier. He parked it in front of my house, right under the balcony of the room where I was born, and we walked the half block to the Petrosemolo household. The classroom was upstairs. Unfortunately the professor arrived late, and Herb began to get nervous. While waiting, I had an enjoyable time observing Signor Petrosemolo's eldest son, Domenico, "making glasses." With thousands of bombs falling all around the town, anything made of glass had been reduced to a fine powder. The family had nothing with which to drink water or wine. Up to then they had gathered beer bottles discarded by the soldiers and had assigned each member of the family a bottle. His sisters didn't think it was very dignified that they should drink out of a beer bottle, so that day, Domenic had an idea: what if we cut the bottle in half using a diamond glass cutter and smoothing out the edges in the forge fire? It worked. The "glasses" looked awkward and clumsy but they did the job. He had made five glasses already when we got there. He wanted to make ten.

Finally the Rimini professor arrived, and he and Herb had a long conversation in English. The professor seemed to have a good flow of the language. They came to an understanding, at last: I could use the book until something better could be obtained. Three years later, I still had a hard time finding appropriate textbooks for my courses. But, as far as I was concerned, that book was good. The fact was that I had already formed a solid grammatical and syntactical base upon which to take on the study of the English language using that book as a study tool. I actually learned English with it; perhaps not in three months, but certainly without a teacher. That professor left a few weeks later and I never had the opportunity of finding another teacher. When I went to a real school in the city of Chieti, they actually did have one class where they taught English, but it was a very popular course, so by the time my mother had made up her mind to send me there, the class was full, and I had to take French. But, that was good, too, because I was able to learn two languages instead of just one.

For the next two years, we attended school in private homes. There were several families who made rooms available for that purpose, and we the students adapted. But, we had no books, no paper to write on, no pencils and no blackboard, much less a library. As for any sort of science laboratory, we didn't even have those in our regular schools. The only science available to us was seeing chickens being born from their eggshells and raised to chicken adulthood, (which probably few American students, outside of the farm boys and girls, ever witnessed), or planting seeds and seeing green beans, watermelons, or zucchini grow.

WATERMELONS AND REAL BOMBS

Talking about things that grow brings to mind an episode that happened on June 6, 1944. We were still living with Nonno Donato in his small country home at Caporale. That day, nonno decided to plant some watermelon seeds along the back wall of the house. It was a simple enough project. I went with him. He took a hoe and a water sprinkler, which I carried. He began to loosen the soil at the far corner of the house which he considered the best place for watermelons to grow. The location was very near the break in the hedge we had discovered the past October, which by now had been mended with some new hedging plants Nonno Donato had planted there in March. He had just turned over a couple of shovelfuls of earth when he called me, somewhat excited, and beckoned me to run to the house and get everybody out and into the far field, as far as we could. I did, but I failed to convey the intended urgency to the people inside who came out one at a time, slowly and reluctantly. "What's the problem?" Mamma wanted to know. "I don't know," was my reply. Just then, nonno came around to the front of the house and announced that he had just discovered that the house had been mined by the Germans. There was a large box-type mine back there. Now, overcome by panic, everyone began to run toward the little shed we had in the middle of the field. So, that's what the breach in the hedge was that nonno and I had noticed the previous October. They had placed a mine in the corner of our house, a few feet away from the road.

Meanwhile, Nonno Donato headed straight for the field offices of the Canadian Royal Guards, and reported the incident. He had found what looked like a plate of spaghetti coming out of a wooden box. It was, indeed, a mine. Obviously, the Germans had intended to blow up our house, too, just as they had blown up the other houses in the area, but may not have had time to complete the operation. Within a few minutes, a British bomb deactivation team came to our house, evacuated the people from the few houses in the immediate area, and proceeded to remove the detonator before digging up the mine itself from its hole adjacent to the corner wall of the house. We, therefore, had literally sat on a powder keg for six months. Thank God nothing had happened.

I had made it to the age of twelve despite the horrors we had experienced. I had brushed sleeves with Sister Death, as Saint Francis called it, several times and survived. I have often looked back on my life during the past five years, trying to find some sort of logic for all that happened. In the early 70's, a book came out in Italy by Elsa Morante, an Italian Jew from Rome, entitled, *La storia* (History). In it, the author makes an interesting paragon between Hitler and Mussolini. She writes: "Mussolini attached his clown's cart to Hitler's hearse." The paragon couldn't have been more accurate. But, mistakes abounded on both sides. Insanity reigned supreme and there wasn't much that could be said either for the action or the reaction. Hitler was crazy, yes; Mussolini was a charlatan, OK, but when Allied planes hit a sleepy little town killing eight civilians, including five children, one has to marvel at the insanity of war and ask oneself, what is wrong with man that he cannot get along with his fellow man? Who paid the highest price for it, of course, were the children. Theirs was the biggest burden because they had done nothing to deserve the suffering they had to endure. But, they suffered silently and patiently without understanding it, sometimes with an anguished, plaintive lament that tore your heart out, but which you were powerless to alleviate.

SLOWLY, LIFE RETURNS TO NORMAL: OUR FIRST DIAGNOSTIC EXAMS

In June, 1944, the national Ministry of Education, finally communicated with the local school authority. They weren't all killed after all. They ordered diagnostic exams to be given to all Italian students in areas that had been directly affected by the war, especially those where schools had been completely destroyed and student records had been lost. In my case I had to take the sixth grade exams.

The schools in Lanciano were directed to give general diagnostic exams for the entire district. The Fossacesia students were told to report to the

Liceo Vittorio Emanuele II in mid-June. That's the school I had attended with Professor De Benne. Immediately, problems arose: transportation. How are we going to get these kids to Lanciano, our mothers asked, a distance of eight miles, for seven or eight consecutive days? The normal bus routes were inoperative for lack of fuel. There was one bus that had been left in consignment by its owners, the Donato Di Fonzo & Fratelli Transportation Company of Scerni, to the driver, Giovanni Toscano. He was willing to use the bus, but it would be up to us to obtain gasoline. Signor Toscano required two hundred liters of gasoline, or fifty gallons. Where could we get such a great amount of gasoline?

Then our mothers thought of using the old fashion *"diligenza,"* the old horse and buggy coach. There were two or three people left in town that still had a horse or two alive. There was Canzano, who alternated his trips taking people to Lanciano and to the cemetery, and Peca, who went mostly to meet the few passengers who got off an occasional train at our station, two miles away, adjacent to the beaches. This alternative turned out just as problematic: now, we had to provide feed for the horses. One of Peca's sons, whose nephew Michael plays professional hockey in the NHL, just recently recalled that the horse was so weak due to malnutrition that for the occasional trip he took to Lanciano after the war, he would ask the passengers to get off at the bottom of the Saint Ostazio hill and walk behind the coach, otherwise he feared the horse might die on him. Occasionally, some of the men would actually get behind the coach and push it in order to help the horse. The ladies even gave it a try to see if they could come up with some food for the animal as they spent a whole night sifting whole wheat flour in order to obtain the bran for the horse and flour as a fee for the owner so he could feed his family. When they were finished, however, the volume was nowhere near the amount requested as fee for both horses and owner. And they didn't have any more flour to sift. What to do? Our good mothers then called for an emergency council. They met in the church sacristy. They were not able to figure out what to do. Finally, like a voice in the wilderness, one of the ladies had a suggestion: "Why don't we walk them?" The other mothers, stunned, looked at her in disbelief. Yes, most of us in Fossacesia had walked the eight miles to Lanciano at one time or another to go shopping, or for a consultation either with a lawyer or physician. I myself did it a couple of times (it took an average of two hours), but for one day at a time. This would be eight consecutive days, except for Sunday! Mamma provided the answer: "Why not?" Once my mother spoke, everybody listened. And so it was that early in April every student presented his program of studies upon which the exams were to be based then worked like crazy the rest of the time until June 13th. The exams were scheduled from Wednesday, June 14th to Saturday, the 24th. On Wednesday morning, after eating a meager breakfast consisting of coffee with milk and a few chunks of bread, we began the trek westward to Lanciano. It was 5:30 AM. We were to report to the classroom at 8:30 A.M.

We walked along the paved provincial road until we reached the town of Mozzagrogna. There we took a shortcut as we followed the sheep's path during the September *transumanza* (transference of sheep to southern pastures), on which the shepherds of Abruzzo, for centuries, had walked their sheep from the mountains towns high in the Apennines to the Apulia Region, at the heel of the boot, where the sheep and the shepherds would pass the winter. The shortcut saved us a half hour time. By 7:45 AM we would reach the church of St. Anthony, at the entrance to Lanciano and we would stop there to rest a while, and to say a prayer or two that we would be successful in the exams. About a quarter mile before reaching the church, my legs invariably would start to shake, first because I was tired, but mostly because exams always petrified me. I appreciated the fifteen minutes we spent in the church. The school was on Lanciano's main street called *Corso Trento e Trieste,* so there would be another fifteen minutes walk after leaving the church.

When we got to the school the first day, we found masons working to repair the second floor. Two months before, on April 20, 1944, four Luftwaffe fighter-bombers had sneaked behind a group of Spitfires that were returning to their bases after a raid, and penetrated the British defenses. They headed straight for Lanciano where they hit the jackpot: the British had decided to utilize the main plaza, *Piazza Plebiscito,* as a military parking lot and staging area. The planes approached it from the north dropping several bombs while strafing the people, civilian and military, who had gathered to hear a political speech. It was a disaster. Three hundred-and-four military personnel and forty-one civilians lost their lives that day including a pregnant woman who was killed together with her unborn child. I remember that morning in Fossacesia. I was still working for the British when we heard the news. The detail about the woman being pregnant made a profound impression on me. The school was not yet reopened so no students were killed or hurt, but the building was severely damaged. Since the exams had been scheduled for that time by the ministry of education, the school authorities had no choice but to do both at the same time, fix the school and get several hundred students in the building to take the exam. So, they used every bit of space available downstairs, including hallways, storage rooms and even administrative offices in which they could squeeze a student desk.

When we reported for the examinations, the laborers had already started working upstairs and we could hear the noises they made. There was even a singer among them who kept singing in Lancianese dialect. I enjoyed the songs, too, and quickly learned the words to a couple of them. Occasionally the workmen dropped something heavy and the noise was quite distracting.

We were assigned our places in alphabetical order. I ended up in the main corridor, second desk, third row, adjacent to what was left of the corridor. We had to go through the usual barking of the "professors," as they explained procedures. Somehow, they brought to mind those rough German soldiers who used to give us orders in German, knowing that nobody understood a word they said. Of course, the teachers made sure they recited the litany of the dire punishments that awaited the careless students who would be caught cheating. A year in Devil's Island would have been considered a picnic by comparison. Of course, the professors, two at the time, crisscrossed each other walking up and down that corridor watching us like hawks.

THE EFFECTS OF WAR LINGER ON

We began with the *Prova scritta d'italiano* (composition in class). It was the usual convoluted title whose lack of clarity challenged the students more than their interpretation of it. The bell rang. The exams began. I placed both my elbows on the desk, chin squarely resting upon the palm of my hands, and I started to think in imitation of Rodin's *The Thinker*.

Suddenly, I began to hear a noise, faint at first, but getting increasingly louder and louder until I began to panic. It sounded like a formation of B-24 Liberators was approaching from the south coming, perhaps, to "liberate" us again. I had to summon all my reasoning powers to realize that it couldn't be. What made the noise was a worker's cart for the transportation of building material. It probably had metal wheels, and darn if it didn't sound like a storm of bombers approaching with less than peaceful intentions. Even those of us who went through a war have the tendency to think that just because the war did not kill or maim us that, therefore, we came off of it unscathed. Wrong! The effects of war stay with us forever; buried deep in our psyche, perhaps, but there nonetheless.

About five rows behind me a little blond girl suddenly began to scream uncontrollably. She, too, had had the same reaction upon hearing that noise, except that while I was able to reason it out, she went absolutely berserk. They had to stop the exams. The professor in charge told the students who had written anything at all to put their papers upside down, and wait for further instructions. There was no nurse on duty, but they were able to summon a doctor whose office was directly across the street from the school. He came immediately, escorted the girl to his office and I supposed he gave her something to calm her down, because she didn't come back to finish the examination, nor did I see her ever again. Meanwhile, her brother who was seated right behind me explained that they were from Ortona. On Christmas day she had to be rescued from their demolished home. She spent most of Christmas day buried under tons of concrete before they managed to locate her and dig her out. She was saved because she had sought refuge under a heavy work bench her father had built in their cellar. Their mother was killed at the same time. No wonder she got hysterical!

Two years later, I went back to that school and her brother was in my class again. He told me that his sister had been sent home that day by a military ambulance and the school board had recommended institutionalization. Her father decided not to send her to an institution. By then, she had already completed the necessary school years required by State law (5th grade, increased shortly thereafter to the 8th grade), so she could withdraw from further education. She opted, instead to learn a skill and start working. She was happy with the arrangement and never returned to school. The repairs of the building were concluded by July and in the '46-'47 scholastic year, and to my misfortune, I would be returning there for the 10th grade.

THE HOMEWARD WALK

The walk home was a pleasant stroll compared to the morning hike. The road was slightly downhill, hence easier to deal with. Mainly, we were all very young, spring was in full bloom, and love in the air, even if in its early candor, and we boys had a chance to show off for the girls. Anna Maria was in the group, too. We raided every fruit tree we passed in the farms along the way. A few fig trees of the precocious variety had a spring crop whose figs, though not as plentiful, were bigger and juicier than those of the fall crop. We gorged ourselves with them. The good Lord even spared most of us the Italian version of "Montezuma's revenge:" We called it "Mussolini's revenge," which is its close cousin. It included a medium size belly ache or two. A couple of the guys did come down with a mild case of it, but most of us lucked out.

When we got home, we were dead tired, as can be imagined. My mother had prepared two eggs for me with crushed red pepper (not too hot) which was a favorite of mine. I ate, rested for an hour or so, and then I had to hit the books. The next day we had the dreaded Algebra exams.

We did that trek on foot for eight days. The second day it was my mother and another lady who escorted us to the torture chambers. That made the trip even more difficult because, with mamma present, I was not free to be myself. I had to be careful, so I got behind her so that she could not see me, and kept far enough back so that she would not hear me speak. It worked. She got talking with the other mother chaperon as they went, and totally forgot about me. By the time we got to the church of St. Anthony, I'd swear she had forgotten she even had a son in the group. I had no problem with that!

When we got to school, we were told to study until further notice: the exams had not yet arrived to the school from the provincial department of education in Chieti. By the time they arrived, it was almost ten o'clock. We got home well after 6:00 P.M. that day since after the math exams some of us, including me, had a history exam to take. Exams were over at 3:00 P.M. We made it home that day in record time telling tall stories and singing fascist songs (the only thing worth keeping from the twenty years of the regime—they were beautiful!), and laughing as we went.

SEPTEMBER, TIME FOR MAKE UP EXAMS—AGAIN!

After all that, I failed Italian and geometry. Was I stupid or what? Well, many years later, analyzing the situation from an adult and even professional point of view, I concluded that no, I was not stupid; quite the contrary. If anything, it was they, my eminent and distinguished professors who were of questionable cogitative worth. I further realized that I had been caught in the grip of a sociological "paradigm shift": Italian society was finally moving from a feudal system in which the scepter of power was passed from father to son, to the modern idea that all men, and women, too, can aim as high as they wish, and then reach as far as their own mental capacity and personal industry can carry them, an idea suggested originally by the Jeffersonian concept that, "all men are created equal and that they are endowed by their Creator with certain unalienable rights among which are life, liberty, and the pursuit of happiness." *The Declaration of Independence* was not standard reading in Italy during the Fascist era, so the teachers who were making up the exams, being from the old school, had not gotten the message, yet. Had I written a masterpiece that rivaled the great Jeffersonian document (which, many years later, I taught to American students as literature!), there would be somebody in the "examining committee" who would have found fault with it. And, so, in September I had to return to Lanciano and take the geometry and literature exams again, the written one day, and the oral another. This time we didn't have to walk. We went with Canzano's "Pony Express," with Giovanni Canzano himself driving the horses and singing opera to us paraphrasing the real words of Tosca with funny substitutes. At one point, there was a steep hill about a quarter mile long. Canzano asked us to get out of the coach and walk behind it until we got to the top of the ridge. He didn't want his old horse to have a heart attack either.

The oral exam entailed a poem (one of three in the program) chosen at random by the examining professor, and a prose work. All three poems in the program had to be memorized, an activity that I truly hated. The poem the examiner chose was D'Annunzio's *"I pastori"* (The Shepherds), and the prose work was Carducci's *"Il nostro vessillo,"* (Our flag). I was well prepared for both. That morning, as we reached the town of Mozzagrogna, once again we left the highway and started to walk on the grass as usual along the government owned and supported pasture land called, *il pasturo,* the graze land. It was like a grassy highway that went from the mountains of Abruzzo all the way down to the Apulia region at the heel of the boot. D'Annunzio, in that poem, calls it, *"Erbal flume silente,"* (The silent herbal river). Wouldn't you know it? As we approached it, we ran right into a number of such flocks. Of course! We were now in September, the very title of the poem, the time when the *transumanza* begins. There must have been well over a thousand sheep dispersed in three groups, each escorted by three shepherds and two dogs, one on each side of the flock. That's what D'Annunzio's poem was all about, so I mentioned it to the professor who was delighted that I had even noticed, so that part was over in twenty minutes and I did well.

The prose took a little longer as he asked me the significance of each color of the Italian flag. I explained everything to his liking. But then, he challenged me with the following question: "As you know, our country is still a constitutional monarchy; therefore the Sabaudo shield still adorns the white part of the flag (the symbol of the reigning Savoia family). If, however, in the soon to be held plebiscite the Italian people vote the monarchy out and institute a republic, what would you put in place of the Sabaudo shield?" I didn't hesitate for an instant: "I would divide the shield in four parts," I replied, "and replace each quarter with the shield of the four Italian Maritime Republics: Venice, Genoa, Pisa and Amalfi!" The professor didn't like my answer since he thought that the Hammer and Sickle would be more modern, hence a much better choice, didn't I think so. Now, I came dangerously close to disaster, because, as an American, a Catholic and a sympathizer of the Christian Democratic Party, I was diametrically opposed to the hammer and sickle, symbol of the dreaded Communist Party. My mother and I had already participated in several rallies in our brief but highly successful attempt to ward off the arrival of Communism in Italy. Having been primed in my thinking, I was ready for a fight. But, he wasn't. As soon as he got an inkling of that from the tone of my answer, he changed the subject. Thank God, too. For many years afterward, I suspected he had a job to safeguard at a time in which jobs were scarce and difficult to obtain for political reasons, so he must have figured, 'I'd better scoot out of this trap!' Two years later, after the Italian people, indeed, voted the monarchy out and the Italian Republic was born, the insignia that I had suggested that day was one of the choices and almost made it, but since everybody was fighting about it, they decided to leave the white part blank. So, the white field remained plain, but the shade of that green next to the white and red is beautiful. Anyway, he passed me. The next day I took the geometry exam, and then, having passed everything, I was able to enjoy the few weeks of vacation still left.

Vacations over, "private" school started again; private in the sense that the classes were held in private homes, often in the midst of much ruin and debris.

SLOWLY BUT SURELY LIFE RE-ACQUIRES
SOME DEGREE OF NORMALITY

Meanwhile, the war continued, though elsewhere. We no longer heard the roar of the cannon, and as far as we were concerned, war was over. We were more concerned with rebuilding our lives, and perhaps finally rejoining my father in America. The theme of going to America had been the constant refrain of my life ever since I reached the age of awareness at two and a half. That was in the summer of 1934. The town administration had decided to repave the central streets of our town, so a steam roller came to town to do the job. I was so impressed with that noisy contraption that whenever people asked me, "Natù, when are you going to America?" I would invariably reply, *"Domani!"* (Tomorrow"). "And what are you going there with?" *"Col battistrada!"* was my proud choice of transportation. I would have had a difficult time negotiating the great Atlantic Ocean "on a steamroller!" But, it underscores the fact that, for me, America loomed in the distance like Emerald City does to Dorothy and her incomplete companions, as they follow the yellow brick road on their quest to see the Wizard. All throughout the 30's mamma tried to get some action from papà one way or another. "Either we come to America, or you return to Italy, once and for all!" she wrote in one letter. She was right, but, she didn't succeed, and then it was too late, the war came instead!

As a result, my mother had her hands full just to keep food on the table with her dress making activity which should have been lucrative, but people rarely paid her on delivery, and when they finally did, they did so in dribs and drabs so that her income was often ineffectual. Still, she managed to save enough money to make sure that I went to the best schools, once the war was over.

SHARING OUR CLASSROOM WITH
A FEW FURRY FRIENDS

As October, 1944, rolled around, life began to give signs of resurrecting, slowly at first, but with renewed vigor and purpose. The many people in town who had their homes destroyed began to rebuild them. Piles of bricks or cement blocks began to appear in front of the most damaged houses, a sure sign of at least the intention of rebuilding. The new construction was obviously going to be made with modern technology, and many people even suggested that it was a good thing those bombers came and destroyed the ancient, dilapidated hovels most of which had been built over three, four and even five hundred years before. The Marshall Plan gave them the necessary money to do so, and the money came with certain requirements which had to be followed by law, so nobody balked.

Monsignor Tozzi, to his infinite credit, once again went out of his way to requisition a number of rooms from private homes where school could be held. We began school in mid October, and things went smoothly. Again, we had to cross town several times a day to change classes, but that was all right. My Italian and Latin classes were to be held in the home of one of the elementary teachers in our town school, Don Domenico Nicolucci. His home was one of the nicer old homes in town, but it was located just outside the line of fire, so that the bombs had left it upright but damaged. We used to meet in their dining room. The students sat around the dining table with the teacher occupying the head table. From their large picture window we enjoyed a beautiful view of the Majella range. From that window, while waiting for the entire class to show up, we could see all sorts of common sights mixed with strange ones: the rolling hills once again were being prepared by the farmers for the sowing of wheat in the early fall. Later, with the chill already in the air, we could see those same farmers sow the wheat, gather vintage grapes, and, in late November, the gathering of olives. At that time of the year there were distinctive smells coming from the farms mixed with the smoke of burning leaves. The mix invited young minds like ours to begin looking forward to the coziness of the fireplace at home that would bring us to the much awaited Christmas holidays. This was our tradition.

There were some strange sights, as well, which beside being distracting, were also dangerous. We saw many a British fighter plane flying so low that we thought they were coming right through the window. They were beautiful to see, especially for us boys, but they were dangerous because if they crashed, they would have fallen right into the center of our *piazza*. They flew so low, they would not have had the possibility of steering those planes away from the inhabited zone. Monsignor Tozzi complained repeatedly to the AMGOT, (Allied Military Government for Occupied Territory), but without results.

The most unusual thing I remember about that house was that the ceiling had fallen down, and it was not yet repaired by the owners because money was scarce and although they had filed an application to receive reimbursement from the Marshall Plan, they were told that the payments would be at least a year away. The result was that since it was a single story building, with the ceiling gone, the roof was completely exposed. We could see the heavy wooden beams that supported the roof. Much to the surprise of all the students and to the horror of the girls especially, from each beam there hung dozens of sleeping bats, hanging upside-down by their tiny feet. Bats are night predators, so they sleep during the day. The first day of school, the math teacher, Signor Ettore Melatti, said, "If we don't disturb them, they won't bother us." When Monsignor Tozzi visited with us, the teacher made him aware of the situation but all he said was, "Children, be sure you are very, very quiet. Don't wake them!" For the rest of that year, we had the quietest classroom I had ever experienced. After a while, we got used to their presence, although every morning each one of us invariably took a cautious, furtive glance upwards just to make sure that one or two of those critters didn't suffer from insomnia. They were definitely not the best conditions under which to learn, and yet learn we did, don't ask me how! My ancestors, the Romans, were right when they said, *"Ad astra, per aspera!"* (To the stars through adversity!) Perhaps it would be better to say, *"Ad astra propter aspera,"* (To the stars *because* of adversity!) Pain and suffering seem to make the best teachers.

Once again, books were not available, and neither was writing material, but within a month paper mills in Fabriano began to put out notebooks made of some sort of recycled material, and they were cheap. The paper was yellowish in color and resembled pulp paper, but they filled a need and were welcome. They were cut smaller than normal, measuring about 6x8 inches in size, but they were thick. Besides serving my purposes, they came in handy for mamma, as well, who used to pull out the middle pages in order to write to my father since normal stationery was not available in stores. She would buy me several of the notebooks and as I started filling the front pages, she would snap one, two, three pages from the center until my written pages caught up with her snapped out pages, then she would begin to snap the pages of another notebook. Mamma was not a woman of few words, so she tore many pages off my notebooks. The first letter she was able to write to my father, as already noted, dated November 13, 1944, was 36 pages long, neatly written in an even, elegant penmanship, and totally error free. Four days later, she wrote him another letter, only this was a shorty by comparison: it was only 24 pages. How she did it I'll never know. And she only went to the fourth grade.

SPRINGTIME BRINGS ROMANCE
EVEN IN WAR TIME

Fossacesia, which had been turned into a busy work place during the entire year as everybody whose house was destroyed or damaged began to rebuild, was beginning to get back to normal. The British and the Canadians had pulled up stakes and gone somewhere else. In June, the place where I worked also closed and I lost my job, but that was no problem. I needed my time to study. In the place where I worked, the British set up a field hospital under a series of tents. It was called Montgomery Hospital, a name that would become tragically ironic for me a year after our arrival in America. Four years later, my mother would die in Norristown, in a hospital ironically named Montgomery Hospital. In December of '43, the visit to Fossacesia by General Bernard Montgomery had coincided with the opening of the military field hospital. It was the general's last official function prior to his departure for England to begin studies for the invasion of Normandy, so they named the field hospital after him in honor of his visit.

Around March, a soldier named Douglas Angove, was rushed to the field hospital in Fossacesia with a bullet lodged in his right shoulder. The doctors operated on him, and kept him in the hospital tent for several weeks. There was no place else for him to live, anyway, because in the meantime his outfit had left the area and returned to England, just as the General had. So, Douglas was ordered to stay put until his new orders arrived. Weeks passed. After Douglas recovered sufficiently to get his own chow at the military canteen, he began to walk the two blocks that separated the tent from the canteen. He would get his food with a metal tray and return to the tent to consume it. Having his right arm in a cast, he had to negotiate everything with his left hand. Most of the time he had no trouble, but occasionally he had difficulty negotiating the two blocks carrying a loaded tray with only one hand.

One particularly windy day, as he was returning from the canteen with his tray full of food, his left arm lost the control of the tray as a gust of wind literally lifted it from his hand and slammed it to the ground. It happened in front of the glass paneled door of the Lanza family. Inside, working at her knitting machine, was a young lady named Jole (pronounced Yo-lay). She saw the whole thing and not only went out to help him, but she persuaded her mother to ask him inside and invite him to have dinner with them. Her mother was not happy about it: What will people say? Your father is in the war, this and that, and the other thing! But, Jole, who had told Douglas to wait outside for a few minutes, was not to be deterred. She insisted, she wheedled, she cajoled, and ultimately she threatened some unspecified awful consequences, so mamma consented. Jole went outside again. She invited him inside. He accepted. The meal was a happy and enjoyable one for everybody concerned.

The next day, at about the same time, transiting in front of Jole's house carrying several accumulated empty trays that he was returning to the canteen, Douglas "conveniently" dropped them all making quite a racket. Jole, who happened to be "accidentally" on her balcony, started laughing hysterically, and went down to help him again. Again, she persuaded her mother to set a place for him at their table. This time, mamma's objections were rather feeble, and when Douglas entered the house he noticed that the extra plate had already been set up for him, together with the rest of the family. Well, it didn't take long for a new sentiment to bloom between the Italian beauty and the gallant English warrior. The inexorable wheel of life, renewing itself even in the midst of death, was turning and grinding. Love blossomed in all its glory. It was spring, after all!

Now, it was prohibited for British military personnel to fraternize with the local population, especially those of the opposite sex, and so when Douglas' new orders arrived he noticed that they were sending him to France, hoping that distance would conquer love. But it didn't. Late in January, 1945, Douglas returned to Fossacesia ready for the altar. One night, during the summer of 1944, at supper time, again there was a tremendous racket in front of the Lanza home, as if somebody had dropped a stack of trays. And that was exactly what it was. Douglas had obtained a ten day furlough, but instead of returning home to Devon, he hitch-hiked down to Abruzzo. That evening, he excogitated the trick as a signal to his girl that he had returned and was there to stay, or at least to take her with him, and home to his own mamma.

They made arrangements with Monsignor Tozzi for a wedding ceremony to take place early the following year.

On February 10, 1945, they were married in the church of Our Lady of the Rosary in Fossacesia (eleven years later, in 1956, I too would be married to Anna Maria in that very same church). The officiating clergy was Monsignor Tozzi and a British military chaplain. I was scheduled to serve the mass. My recollection of it is vague, though, except for Monsignor Tozzi's sermon which was truly exceptional. He extolled the hope for the future exemplified by these two young people who, out of the midst of death and destruction, brought love and a new sense of life to the world. Even the British chaplain made a notable sermon, or so I was told because his was delivered in English, and I didn't understand it. It would be several decades later that I noticed the date, February 10, 1945, matched that of Giovanni Palatucci's demise. So, while in Fossacesia we were celebrating an event of love, in Dachau the Germans were still dispensing death. Ironically, Palatucci died but two weeks before the camp at Dachau was liberated.

Mr. and Mrs. Douglas Angove managed a few days honeymoon somewhere, before Douglas had to return to his outfit which by now was in Northern Europe. However, the British Army had in place a system whereby war brides could be brought home to mamma right away, and so it was that in November 1945, Jole actually flew to London alone via military personnel service. According to my friend Alberto Nicolucci's book, she had quite an adventurous trip, beginning right in Fossacesia when there was not a square foot of space left in the train cars that took her to Naples. The RAF military airport was located in that city and there was very little time for her to catch the plane. The train engineer, who happened to be from our town, knowing her story and not wanting her to miss the plane, invited her to sit inside the locomotive, in a little cubicle he had set up for himself next to the coal tender. One thing she was not was cold, not inside the business area of the steam engines, but she was not entirely successful in staying separated from all the coal dust. She got to Naples looking more like the antithesis of candor, than the blushing bride she really was.

Douglas and Jole settled in his hometown of Barnstaple, North Devon, England. They had four children, Renato, Francesco, Marilyn and Tina. The extended family still lives there although Douglas passed away in 1997. They had nine grandchildren, and now Jole is the great-grandmother to six great-grandchildren. They represent the fruits of a love story born out of death and desolation. I spoke with Jole several years ago on the telephone. I asked her what the British called her, because her name is unusual, even by Italian standards. She said Yo-lah—close enough, I thought! I've been corresponding with her son Francesco ever since, and he refers to his mother as Yolanda. That's even better. After speaking with her, I concluded that the marriage was a resounding success. After nearly sixty years living there, she is a confirmed British subject. Like me, she enjoys making an occasional trip back to Italy, but she could no longer live there. I also noticed with great delight that not only does she speak English very well, but she does so with an elegant British accent!

Mr. and Mrs. Douglas Angove
Yolanda and Douglas on the day of their wedding in Fossacesia, February 10, 1945. Mr. Angove died in 1997, but his widow still lives in Barnstaple, North Devon, England.

THE CAPTAIN OF THE SOCCER TEAM

During the first four months of 1945, the last four months of the war in Europe, while mamma was trying to figure out what the school system was going to do with us students, I witnessed several incidents that kept me focused on the fact that the war was still a reality for us. Mamma would always asked me to go here and there to do errands for her, or to deliver one or two of her Sorgini originals, on foot and sometimes at great distances. Two things were guaranteed to entertain me during the trip: the parade of thousands of bombers and their fighter escorts would take place every morning and again in the afternoons when the planes made their way back to their bases. And, around 11:00 A.M. a single four engine airplane would fly around covering the entire region at a rather low altitude gathering data for the military meteorological services to determine weather conditions for the next day. It was fun for me to watch that plane going around in circles over land and sea, appearing and disappearing, only to reappear again in another direction a little later.

On March 8th, mamma had to deliver several dresses to the neighborhood of Aunt Florence, at the western end of Fossacesia. She had to do it herself because she needed to see it on the lady in order to make the proper adjustments. They had arranged to meet at our aunt Florence's place, where we spent a few days after the air raid on Fossacesia a year and a half before. She asked me to accompany her. We left at 8:00 A.M. since it was quite a long walk.

As previously mentioned, many Italian soldiers who happened to be serving in the southern part of the peninsula but who hailed from the northern regions of Italy were trying to make their way home following the front. Some stopped in our town and remained there for a while. I already talked about my professor from Rimini who decided to stick around our town, and become a teacher—of English, no less. I took his course, naturally, for one semester.

Another young man, by the name of Antonio Rossi (the Italian equivalent of John Smith), stopped in our town in March or April, 1944, and boarded with one of the families who lived at the center of town. We began to call him Mestre because we didn't know his name then and he was from the town of Mestre, just outside of Venice. He met and fell in love with the daughter of his host family, and in no time at all things got serious and they planned to get married. For that reason, he stayed in town and in order to make some money, he decided to go to work removing the thousands of land mines the Germans had buried in our fields. That had been his expertise in the army: defusing land mines.

Besides being an expert mine sweeper, Mestre was a semi-pro soccer player. Before being drafted into the army, he had played with the city of Venice "farm" team, which operated in the *Serie C* league. He quickly made friends in town, and joined the local soccer team. Because of his prowess in scoring goals, he became a sort of player-coach and was elected to the captaincy of the team. Every kid in town, including me (I was thirteen by then), used to worship the proverbial ground he walked on. To us kids, who had not known any sports figure beyond the local ones, Mestre was like Joe Di Maggio, Joe Montana and the Philly Phanatic, all rolled into one.

That morning, when we reached the corner of our Aunt Anne's property, a half mile or so before reaching our destination, after we passed the crossroads, I saw two men and a boy in the middle of a field involved in an activity that seemed strange at best. The oldest of the three was not known to me, but the younger was Mestre, and the boy was his future brother-in-law, a boy about my age. Since I knew the young man well, I waved. He waved back, and Mestre waved at me, as well. I was thrilled. The captain of the local soccer team had just waved at me, and he had even asked where I was going, thus we had a conversation. Wow! I couldn't wait to go home and tell all of my friends of my good fortune. After exchanging a few words with the men in the field, mamma and I continued on our way. We had another ten minutes or so along the road, and five more of driveway to negotiate uphill, before reaching our relative's house. When we arrived, the clients were already there, so they all went upstairs to do their work, remaining up there for about fifteen minutes. When they came down, Aunt Florence offered us some refreshments, and while we were partaking of it, we heard a loud explosion in the distance. Instinctively I said: "Mestre is gone." Mamma reproached me: "Don't say such a thing." I pointed out to her that, if that had happened, whether I said it or not, it wouldn't change a blessed thing. Still, she didn't want to hear it, my remarks serving only to exacerbate her further.

As we made our way home, when we reached the area where Mestre had been working, we could see Carabinieri police all over the place. There was an ambulance, but its function was not to take Mestre to the hospital to fix him up, but to take the pieces of his body to the morgue. I was told that one of his arms was lodged among the branches of an olive tree. It was a sad, sad day for me especially and for the entire town. I was particularly devastated as I realized that I was the last of his many fans to speak to him. A dubious distinction, at best!

The funeral for Mestre was one of the most impressive in the history of our town. His teammates carried the casket on their shoulders, the mayor as well as provincial authorities participated in full regalia. Even rival soccer teams from the surrounding towns whose teams played in the same league, came to the funeral out of respect for their fallen foe.

Among the most conspicuous of the participants were the farmers whose land Mestre had helped restore to normal use by removing thousands of antitank mines at the real risk of his own life. Many years later, upon reading an article about the famous exploits of three Italian naval officers in the port of Alexandria (Egypt), in 1940. Their mission was so successful that it had practically ended British hegemony in the Mediterranean basin. One of them was captured. As he was being interrogated aboard the British ship to which he had attached an explosive, he waited until ten minutes before the bomb was timed to go off, and then he told the interrogators what he had done. He suggested they get everyone top side. They did, but left the Italian officer down there. Well, he survived and after the war he was decorated by the British government for his humane attitude. The author of the article concluded with the following gem: "One of the rare Italian heroes!" I guess he never heard of Mestre, and many others like him! I repeat, heroism must have a purpose higher and nobler than the dangers it affronts, otherwise it's just a foolish masochistic act.

The amazing thing about Mestre's work was that, being now a civilian, he did not possess any of the sophisticated metal detecting devices with which to look for mines. His only means of finding those mines was an umbrella stick. He would carefully insert the point of the umbrella into the dirt and, having reached a certain depth he would move to another area, no more than ten inches to the left or right and repeat the operation. As soon as he felt resistance, he would kneel down next to the hole made by his umbrella stick, and begin to dig the dirt around it, very gingerly. Being certain that it was a mine, he would then free it completely of the dirt that covered it, and then he would proceed with the delicate operation of defusing the firing pin which makes the mine detonate. Yet, with that crude method, Mestre had cleared dozens of fields of thousands of anti-personnel mines, and even more than that number of anti-tank mines. At the end of each "job," the farmers would invite him to an absolute feast of Abruzzese cooking, in the style of their harvest time. This time, there would be no feast. Ironically, the mine that Mestre had unearthed had been completely defused, but it was booby-trapped to a second mine next to it. Teutonic cruelty in those days knew no bounds and it remains unmatched in the history of mankind.

These fallen heroes are but a few of the hundreds of people who died, after the war had passed. In addition to the farmers who died because they had gone back to work, many children died or were maimed by the explosion of land mines while at play, or going to school in rural areas. Boys will be boys, they say, so it is natural for a boy to do a little exploring on his way to doing an errand, or simply being at play. Several times during the past fifty years, traveling around my native town, I beheld a horrifying sight: boys ten, twelve and even fifteen years old, climbing escarpments along the roads that gird every little hamlet in Italy. In my hometown, the local authorities have permitted some impervious areas to be overrun by wild vegetation, figuring that people won't go there and, therefore they are safe. That's a fool's security, at best. Years from now, people will go there for whatever reason, perhaps to build a shopping center, not knowing that those mines are there, and, boom . . . The inevitable residuum of modern warfare.

MAYDAY! MAYDAY! BOMBER IN TROUBLE!

A month or so after the Mestre tragedy, a full spring day, I witnessed a plane crash. It must have been somewhere in the middle of April judging by the weather which was good and warm enough for short sleeve shirts. For some reason, I didn't have school that day. Around 8:30 A.M. my mother asked me to go to the bakery and buy a loaf of bread. There were at least four bakeries in town, but that morning she specifically directed me to go to the Susi Bakery in Via delle Croci. That bakery was, and still is, located on the southern edge of town across the street from the house where I was born. That neighborhood was the place where I grew up, and in which I lived until I was six. I knew my way around the area, and I enjoyed going there whenever I had the chance.

When I got to the bakery, I learned that the bread was not yet ready because they had had some electrical problems during the night and the ovens didn't warm up sufficiently until 7:00 A.M., so I had to wait a half an hour or so. Well, that was OK. I walked around the neighborhood where I saw a friend or two with whom I had played as a child, and then I made my way to the back of the bakery where there was a beautiful garden with benches. I sat down and proceeded to enjoy the stupendous view that mother nature had bestowed upon the Abruzzo region. Earlier there had been a few high clouds, but now the sun had come out, and its rays, reflecting upon the shimmering wavelets of the Adriatic Sea translated as a myriad of tiny diamonds peeking out of the waters and saying good morning to the land, like a chorus of a million lightning bugs. In the distance immediately in front of me, the river's waters, also, reflected the rays of the sun throughout the remainder of its course as it rushed to meet the sea in the last half mile of its descent from the mountains. Mother Nature was indeed putting on a grand spectacle for me that morning.

And what can be said of the majesty of Mother Majella, whose broad shoulders protect and bless all the Abruzzese people and their descendants, forever? She's the second tallest peak in the Apennine range at better than 9,000 feet. In mid-April she still had a white crown of snow in her higher elevations. The snow reflected the sun's rays in a different way, but it was as brilliant a show as that put on by the shimmering waters of the sea and the river. I sat on one of the benches and enjoyed the display as I waited for the bread to finish its baking process. The parade of the big American bombers was still going on each morning despite the fact that the war in Europe was just about over, and as usual at 10:00 A.M. the first of many formations of B-24 bombers began coming over the Torino di Sangro ridge on their way to bomb southern Germany or Austria. I observed the first storm of twelve planes fly overhead in perfect formation. Flying escort for each bomber squadron were about four fighter planes usually P-38 Lightnings, P-51 Mustangs, or P-40 Tomahawks. These had recently been outfitted with extra fuel tanks so as to extend their range enabling them to provide protection for the bombers all the way to target. Being faster than any other plane in the war, the P-38's were particularly feared by German pilots. They used to call them "the twin tailed devils."

A second wave passed over my head without incident. Obviously, this air armada used the coast line as a visual navigational guide. The third wave came into view, but before I could focus my eyes on them, I noticed that one of the lead bombers had left formation, descending about 500 feet or so below the flight path, and, as the rest of the storm flew over our river, that lone Liberator veered to his left and began to fly westward toward the town of Casoli. I remember thinking a little cynically: "Where is that guy going, to the bathroom?" It was a very unusual maneuver. I kept my eyes on it. After flying for about two miles, it banked its wings left, made a 180° circle, and proceeded to fly eastward toward the sea.

Before continuing this narrative, I believe I should explain that I was at the top of the hill that represents the southern edge of our town. Directly in front of me, at the very bottom of the hill a little over a half mile away, was my country home, the one where I grew up in the summer time, and where we returned on liberation day. Nonno Donato still lived there, as the home in which I was born was not yet repaired of its war damages. The big bomber was now flying eastward in front of me, an angle of no more than fifteen degrees, and passed directly over the southern edge of our property. Both fuselage windows of the big bomber were wide open, and I could see people walking around inside. I also noticed that their number two engine was stopped. I realized for the first time that the B-24's engines had a three blade propeller, and not four as I had previously imagined. This plane had developed serious mechanical problems and was probably looking for a place to land.

On its return from Casoli, after passing in front of me, the plane went out over the sea. I assumed the crew was trying to dump their load of sixteen, 500 pound bombs, and perhaps most of its fuel before attempting a crash landing, after all, their target was probably a thousand miles away, but they had traveled only about one to two hundred miles after take-off. But, they didn't, for I did not hear any explosions. Even if they were not set to explode, I certainly would have seen the splash. There was none. After the plane flew over the sea for a half mile or so, it banked left again and it slowly began to trek its way westward toward the mountain. As it passed in front of me a second time, I suddenly realized that two men had jumped and were now parachuting gracefully toward the earth. Having now focused my eyes on the parachutes, I also noticed that two other men had jumped on the first pass in front of me. Those two had almost reached the ground, so that for a few minutes there were four chutes floating to earth at the same time. Then the plane repeated the first maneuver: it went toward the mountain and turned. Upon their third pass in front of me I noticed that the number one engine was completely stopped, too. The plane was now being flown by the engines of the right wings, and this should have caused a tremendous drag on the rest of the plane. When it reached the drop off point, two more men jumped. I concluded that their intent was to have the men reach the ground as close together as possible and as close to the main highway, so they could be easily picked up by a U.S. Air Force vehicle. The plane once again flew out to sea, still I saw no splash nor did I hear any explosions, although they might have dumped most of the fuel, which would not have been visible to me. Once more it made a wide turn and headed toward us again. When they reached the drop off point a seventh and an eighth parachutist jumped. I observed the last two parachutes open nicely, and I was just trying to focus my eyes on the plane again when suddenly it banked sharply and brusquely to its left. In a few seconds, it disappeared beyond the Torino di Sangro Ridge and exploded into flames. Immediately a huge billow of black smoke rose into the air. At that moment I actually prayed that all the men had made it out of the crippled airplane. Later, however, I learned that a B-24 in full combat readiness carried ten crewmen. I assumed then that the pilot and the co-pilot did not make it. It was further obvious that the intent of the pilot was to reach the Casoli area once again, turn around and head east toward the Adriatic Sea, put the plane on automatic pilot with a slight downward inclination so that it would crash into the sea, and they would have jumped. It made sense to me, but they failed to go much beyond the drop off point before the plane's engines went completely awry. I always pray for those two gallant men who made sure their men jumped to safety before they sacrificed their own lives. And, oh, what I wouldn't give to meet one of the guys who made it to the ground! If there is one or two still alive, they would be well into their nineties.

It's probable that one or two or even three of them might still be alive, living somewhere in the United States. They're my personal heroes!

After the highly unusual drama was over, I returned to the bakery. The sales clerk had put a loaf of bread aside for me. It was a good thing because, absorbed as I was with the crippled bomber, I had forgotten all about the bread, and by then it had almost sold out. I asked her if she had seen anything, and she said no, they were too busy to notice what went on outside. My inquiries in town later that day produced equally negative results. Nobody had seen anything or heard anything, so nobody deigned the story with much importance. We had become accustomed even to death.

EPILOGUE

THE LEGACY OF WAR IS DEATH

In the final analysis, what is the legacy of World War II for a little town like mine? Or for Italy, as a nation? Or for all the belligerents, for that matter, including the victorious one, the so called, "good guys?" Nothing but death! Fossacesia lost over two hundred of its citizens at home, many of them children, not counting those who died fighting a war they did not want to fight. Until July 10, 1943, our town's landscape was completely devoid of any foreign presence (except for the displaced refugees running for their lives). By the time 1944 rolled around, we had enough dead soldiers from England and its Commonwealth nations like Canada, India, New Zealand, Australia, and from the United States as well, to fill three cemeteries in our area alone, two visible, one invisible. Every time I go back to Fossacesia I never fail to visit the war cemeteries. My first visit is to the American "cemetery," the one that's "not there." In fact, you don't see an expanse of white crosses, rusty helmets topping them, or Old Glory waving in the breeze. The view that unfolds before your eyes upon arrival is that of the blue, tranquil waters of the Adriatic Sea (see front cover). The reason for that is, as an obscure poet once put it, you can visit the battle sites at Gettysburg, the Ardennes, Iwo Jima or the beaches of Normandy, but you cannot visit the sites of air or naval battles simply because they disappear within minutes after they are over.

> You can't revisit aerial battlefields. There are no hilltops to climb with your children to show where opposing armies clashed. Battlefields of the air are defined not by terrain, but by longitude, latitude and altitude. No cannon shells are to be found there, no trenches, no memorial plaques. The evidence of air combat—black

321

blossoms of flak, phosphorous tracer trails, the smell of cordite, shouts of crew members on the interphone, the plummet of stricken aircraft, falling airmen hanging on parachutes, the noise of engines and guns, streaking chunks of metal penetrating aluminum skin and human flesh—all of this evidence vanishes with the same suddenness as it appeared. And then the battlefield, the sky, looks just as it did before, as if nothing had happened.

(Courtesy 8th U.S. Air Force Veterans)

The Golfo di Venere, so beautiful, so peaceful, so serene is where I saw those eleven American bombers shot down by German flack fire on December 1, 1943. That means that at least one hundred and ten American airmen lost their lives in those waters on that day. Who knows how many more planes were hit and fell in the gulf once they flew beyond our vision. Considering that those planes conducted raids every morning for the previous eight days, I'd venture to say that many more bombers were hit every day, not just on December 1st. To me, then, that bay represents hallowed waters, even without white crosses marking their graves. I never fail to say a prayer for them every time I visit this beautiful seascape.

I also visit the Canadian cemetery at San Donato, near Ortona, a few miles north of Fossacesia. Located at an elbow of the main north-south route as it begins its descent toward the Moro River, the cemetery is the resting place of the fallen Canadian soldiers who lost their lives at the battle of Ortona on Christmas day, 1943. It is typical of all military cemeteries the world over: artistically designed at its inception, meticulously maintained by local landscapers and financially supported by both governments, the Italian and the Canadian. There are 1,613 graves there, of which 1,375 contain the remains of Canadian soldiers killed in the battle of Ortona, while others were killed in battles nearby. Some were killed by land mines or unexploded projectiles, in the days that preceded or followed the bloody battle. There is a small chapel there, as well.

About three miles south of the Golfo di Venere and a mile or so south of the Sangro River, is the British cemetery. There are over 2,500 fallen heroes buried, most of them killed November 29 and 30 in the Sangro River Battle. I feel a strong kinship with each of those fallen warriors because I was in the area when they were killed. By the grace of God, I was not killed. I was just a kid and not a soldier, but I was there, just the same.

As one approaches the entrance, there is the usual arch with the visitor guest book, the plaque that explains the reasons and the significance of the place, and the admonition that this is sacred ground and that a proper demeanor is expected from all visitors at all times. Unfortunately, as is often the case, young people go there to make out. Respect for the dead seems to be a thing of the past. After recording our visit on the signature album, we proceed inside. Unlike the cemetery in San Donato, which is also on a hill, but on a flat plateau, this one is on a slope that faces the south east. The architect probably designed it with that feature in mind. The various sections of graves are disposed in a semicircle, designed to face the south east, possibly with an eye to accommodate the Christians, the Jewish and the Muslim dead. Since the graves of the Jewish dead must face Jerusalem, and the Muslim dead resting places must face the Mecca, both can do so from that angle. I don't think the arrangement upset the Christian heroes very much, though: they, after all, need only to face up, toward God's heaven, and they could do that no matter how they're positioned.

At the top of the hill, there is a giant cross upon an altar-like structure. Below, the graves are arranged in semicircular sections each containing about fifty graves marked by a flat marble stone, with a rounded top. At the very top of the marker each deceased soldier is identified first with the symbol of his faith: a cross for the Christians, the Star of David for the Jews, the Crescent for the Muslims. Many have no symbol at all, perhaps because no one had been able to determine the faith of the man buried there, or perhaps he had none. Many graves carry no name or other relevant data simply because the remains therein contained had not been identified. In that case, in the place where most of the stones contain a name together with the regiment to which he belonged, the unidentified ones are marked simply: *Known only unto God.*

Most of the stones identify each grave's occupant with rank, name, and military unit, such as Fusilier, Armored Division, Royal Marines or Infantry. Also, the number of the regiment to which he belonged is recorded there. At the very bottom, most of them have an epitaph, usually contributed by a loved one at the time of burial. For the most part they are marked with stock phrases such as, "You will always be in our hearts," or "May God keep you in his arms forever." Some have appropriate Biblical or Shakespearean quotations. A few, however, have some very unique phrases. A friend of mine from Fossacesia, Attilio Piccirilli, one year asked me to accompany him to the cemetery, and translate some of the epitaphs into Italian so he could understand them. The one that impressed him the most was, *"To the world you were just one; to me you were the world."* It was signed, *"Rita,"* probably his wife. Attilio often quotes it in his writings or speeches, especially when he gives eulogies.

But, in 1975, the first time I visited that cemetery, I read a very short epitaph that moved me to tears. It read simply: *"Good night, John! Mum and Dad."* The kid was only eighteen years old.

Such are the wages of war! "It's over: nobody wins!"

The Canadian Cemetery at San Donato near Ortona

The Canadians still call Ortona their Leningrad. On Christmas day they had a terrible hand-to-hand combat right in the city. I remember that day because it was the day Herb Speedie took me to mass with his truck full of ammunition. He delivered his load after he took me home. I think he got in trouble for it, too. Visible in the background is the skyline of the City of Ortona.

The Sangro River Commonwealth Nations' Cemetery
This is the cemetery that contains the remains of the British and
Commonwealth soldiers who died in the battle of the Sangro
River. I feel a close kinship with them because I was there, too,
the day they died. I wasn't fighting, of course, but I was in harm's
way just as much. By the grace of God, I was spared. These soldiers
were not as lucky.

The American cemetery at Neptune

By far the most beautiful of all War cemeteries in Italy are the two American ones, the Sicily-Rome cemetery in Nettuno (35 miles south of Rome), and the Florence American cemetery and Memorial. The Allies lost over 80,000 men in the Italian campaign. If the Italian king, prince, and chief of staff had had one brain among the three of them, those and the other thousands of casualties that occurred in Italy between July 10th and the end of the war, especially the children, could have been avoided. Of course, the brains of the Allied military leaders weren't particularly working at full capacity, either!

POSTSCRIPT: WAR'S POSITIVE ASPECTS?

Some of my friends who have read parts or all of my manuscript suggested to me that the aftermath of the war, about forty pages, "while interesting," did not seem to be part of the war time narrative. They all recommended that I either delete the whole thing, save it for another story, or place it in the back as an afterthought, a postscript, if you will. Trashing the whole thing is out of the question. In the prologue, after all, I have premised that this narrative was to be my memoirs of the first fifteen years of my life, up to the point when I rejoined my father in America. The fact remains the several years that followed the war was a very important period in post-bellum Italy, mainly because there was a major paradigm shift in the life of every Italian. Things changed radically politically, socially, educationally, economically, and even agriculturally. It was almost as if the entire country had been turned upside down and placed on its head. Those who were at the top before the war were now at the bottom, the poor became the rich and vice versa, the political vacuum left by the demise of the fascist regime was replaced by a literal whoosh!, made by a parade of political parties, small and large, good and bad. My mother and grandmother were once again pushed into a position of prominence as the farm people, coming to town to attend mass on Sundays, would stop by our house to ask for advice on how to vote. The Christian Democratic party was known in my house as the party of America and the Communists were known as the red party, the party of Russia, Baffone's party (that's what the anti-communist Italians used to call Stalin, with reference to his big mustaches).

There was also a shift in education from a feudal system upon which our schools were based to a more liberal mentality, one that foresaw the inclusion of a large segment of young people heretofore excluded from going beyond the 5ᵗʰ grade, such as the children of farmers, artisans, and service people. It used to be that the doctor's son became a doctor, the lawyer's son became a lawyer, and the engineer's son became an engineer. Often, their offspring were anything but "a chip off the old block," but a little bribe here, and a little greasing of a palm there, and he would become a professional, too. I was the son of an immigrant, and was expected to depart from the premises as soon as possible, so that I would not be competing for "a piece of bread," as they used to put it, against those who remained in Italy and contributed to the wealth of the nation. That's why I tell about my rejoining the school scene after two and a half years hiatus, during which I had received a makeshift education at best.

It was sociologically significant, too! Before the war began, Mussolini used to tell us that Italy was too small a country to be able to support the Italian population. We needed "a place in the sun." There were simply too many of us. The Italian population was "destined to emigrate and colonize." At a distance of a mere half century, Italy is now one of the countries into which all kinds of people immigrate, mostly illegally. They just appear off shore on rusted out old boats, overloaded with poor people, who had traveled for days in a standing room only arrangement.

Even the farmers got into the act. Within a few years after the war ended, they had gone from total animal power to one hundred percent mechanical power in all phases of farming activity, increasing their production to unheard of levels. The farmers became the new well-to-do segment of the town's population.

So, the post war stories are important, and I will not discard them, although I did streamline them a bit. However, I did accept the suggestion that I place the entire post war section at the end, as a postscript. It's optional for the reader, of course, but important and historically significant. Oh, go ahead and read it. It will only take a few hours! But, first, a few more pictures.

Official Studio Photo of Mr. and Mrs. Nicola De Simone
I think my mother had just spotted my father's white socks with a black suit; that's why she looks so somber. It was February, 1931, but the exact wedding date is unknown. Of course, for the wedding itself, she wore white, because before the war I saw her veil and some silk flowers that adorned her gown, but I never saw a commemorative photo of the wedding.

Anna Maria's First Communion

She was born exactly six months before I made an appearance on the scene (7/16/31 vs. 1/16/32). She received her first Holy Communion on the feast of Corpus Christi, June 11, 1939.

Our honeymoon included a three day visit to Padre Pio da Pietrelcina

This photo shows Anna Maria (black veil) kneeling at Padre Pio's altar. Minutes later I joined my bride as we received a special blessing for newlyweds from the Padre. That same afternoon, at the request of the future saint, we sat at a conference table with him so I could explain the procedure for making the Salk Polio Vaccine, which was my job at the time at the Merck Sharp & Dohme, Inc. plant in West Point, Pa. Padre Pio had just inaugurated his Home for the Relief of Suffering, and therefore was interested in learning about everything related to medicine.

Anna Maria shortly after her arrival in America

It was in November, 1957. I posed her in this fashion by the window of our first home on Haws Avenue, Norristown, Pa. She didn't want to do it. She thought it was not her style. I knew exactly what she meant, but pictures like this serve more to fan a husband's pride than a bride's vanity. Besides, I threatened to divorce her.

Motherhood

Anna Maria with our third child, the newborn Francis. I took this photo about mid-August, 1963, a few days after I brought them home from the hospital. It seems that I caught the very essence of a mother's love. I called it MOTHERHOOD. It's Anna Maria's favorite photo, especially since she's showing off Francis, the charming, the charismatic, the eternal optimist who sees every half-full glass as not only full, but overflowing. Maybe that's why today he is a psychologist.

According to a letter our mayor wrote to the provincial prefect dated 8/19/43, there were a number of refugee families housed in this school. After September 8th, however, the Italian underground must have taken them to safety together with Ninni's family.

The Mario Bianco School in Fossacesia B.B. (before the bombers arrived)
This school, together with the Basilica of St. Donato, was in the bomb sight of the Allied bombers from day one. The church was damaged extensively, but was fixable. The school, however, didn't make it. On Christmas day, 1943, Herb Speedie parked his military truck on this site, now reduced to a parking lot.

Summer of 1947—We finally made it to America

Back row: Aunt Margie (Uncle Nick's wife), me holding my little cousin Theresa, Mamma and Papà.

Front row: My little cousin Concetta, the lady of house in South Philadelphia, Nonna Concetta, my cousin Philip, and my brother Phil holding a canine.

The lady seated in front, next to my grandmother, was her best friend before she came to America in the 20's. During that first summer in America, we traveled to Philadelphia almost every Sunday to have dinner with the friends of my mother's or grandmother's. Besides wanting to see them again, they were anxious to hear about the war in Fossacesia. They found our stories hard to believe.

ITALY EMERGES FROM ITS ASHES

WAR IS OVER, ALL OVER!

On May 3, 1945, at noon, the bells of the churches all over Italy began to ring festively, and they did so for one solid hour. I had not been aware of the reality of the war that was still going on in other parts of Italy, and the world. I read the papers daily, but somehow they failed to convey any kind of immediacy. War, as far as I was concerned, had been over for a year and a half, ever since we had ceased to be its target. As the bells began to peal, we all went outside and everyone was asking what was going on. Within minutes, we heard music. A band had formed. The remnants of the old Fossacesia Musical Society had reconstituted itself and began to play marches. They weren't bad, either. There were only twenty-three musicians, and of course, they had no uniforms. In fact, they were dressed in rags, but they made a convincing racket. A parade was quickly organized and in a few minutes the mystery of the moment was unveiled: the Liberation of Italian territory of all foreign presences, good and bad. Today, they still celebrate Independence Day in Italy, but, for some mysterious reason, they moved it from May 3rd to April 25th.

Earlier in the spring of 1945, the Ministry of Education had decreed that all students take another exam for final placement. The students were to be assigned to a school of the district by lottery. I drew Vasto, a beautiful and picturesque little city on top of a promontory that ends in a wide gulf. It is located about 20 miles south of Fossacesia and easily accessible by train or bus. Mamma accompanied me there on Monday June 11th. She had made arrangements for me to stay with a family that lived in the corner of Via San Pietro as it flows into Piazza San Pietro. Despite its grandiose sounding name, the piazza had nothing to do with its Roman namesake. It was a piazzetta, a small piazza, no bigger than two basketball courts placed side by side. Its name, like its Roman counterpart, was due to the presence there of the ancient church of St. Peter with its impressive Byzantine façade. The church faced west so that its back looked out to the Adriatic Sea. Behind the church was a *lungomare,* a panoramic promenade that ran from Vasto's main piazza, Piazza Rossetti, to the school where I was to give the exams, approximately a quarter mile long. All I had to do to go from the house where I lived to the Lungomare Adriatico was to walk one block alongside the church, and I had the most spectacular view of the Golfo di Vasto, which lay five hundred feet below, with its splendid beaches and the railroad tracks. I loved to watch trains come into and out of the station.

VASTO CHANGED MY LIFE FOREVER

On June 11th, then, we took a train to Vasto. From my window on the sea side of the train I commanded a spectacular view of the Adriatic beaches in full summer array, and pullulating with early bathers. Just offshore sailboats with white, blue and striped sails in full display added a touch of romance to the scene, and an occasional motorboat was showing off in the distance. The right side of the train offered equally spectacular scenery of the majestic profile of the Majella range of the Apennine Mountains, still showing a few traces of late snow in the higher elevations.

We arrived in early afternoon but we found no connecting transportation to go up to the town, so we walked. We found the house without any problem and, since the street that climbed to the town from the marina passed right in front of the school where I was to be examined, my mother took the opportunity to register me, and at the same time asked the clerk for directions to Via San Pietro. We settled everything in no time. The lady of the house had prepared dinner for us and after dinner we spent the rest of the day becoming acquainted with the Vasto's beautiful downtown area.

The next day, mamma returned to Fossacesia very early. She had to be in the main piazza at 6:30 A.M. to catch the Vasto-Lanciano bus, so she didn't wake me when she left. However, it was the first time that we would be apart, and she felt awkward to say goodbye prior to my going to bed. Even I could feel the tension. For some strange reason, my mother never touched me or kissed me. Some people say of others who are not particularly lovable, "He's got the face that only a mother could love!" Well, in my case it was worse than that, for I seem to have the face "not even a mother could love." I don't know why, though. I was cute enough as a kid, or so I was told, and I was congenial, too! I was not rambunctious or repulsive in any way. But, she was strange in that respect. In the morning, before leaving, she did open the door to my room and sneaked a peak. I made believe I was asleep and without her realizing it, I had one eye open, and I saw that she was crying. And when mamma cried, she produced tears the size of the rain drops of an Adriatic summer storm. And, that morning those tears flowed large and copious.

Exams were not scheduled to begin until the following Monday, the 18th, but there was much red tape involved, so each morning I had to go to school and do something such as fill out forms, pick up the exam program, pay a fee, or whatever and these things always involved long waits in line. It was my first taste of Italian bureaucratic red tape and it was nerve-wracking. By noon, however, I was invariably home. Dinner was at one o'clock, and after dinner I loved to go out for an hour or so, admire the view of the gulf, then I'd walk along the parapet to enjoy the view, before turning into Piazza Rossetti, and eventually back home. When I got there, several hours of study awaited me. The lady of the house made sure that I did study as per my mother's request. But, she was more reasonable than mamma ever could be. She did give me some leeway, whereby I could stretch a little and display my innate trustworthiness. My mother never did that.

The exams were tough, but I passed everything except for the *Prova scritta d'italiano,* as usual. I would have to come back in September. Of course, the *prova scritta* (composition) meant that the grade was going to be strictly subjective. If a student had an intelligent teacher with a heart and a lofty view, the student passed. If the teacher was a jerk, not a plain jerk, mind you, but a jerk-jerk, a moron, the student didn't pass. Ironically, had I not been interfered with, I could have passed the toughest exams, provided they were fair, for that was the problem: those professors were anything but fair. So, I prayed some, studied a lot, and hoped for the best. As I have already mentioned, I was caught in the middle of an academic *"paradigm shift."* The attitude of the people was changing, that was certain, and the old teachers did their best to try to maintain the status quo, and deviate the course of progress. In a further ironic twist, after a life time spent in education, I am now a writer, both in Italian and in English.

VASTO CHANGED MY VIEWS ON LIFE, AS WELL

In Vasto, for the first time in my life, I was alone and had to make my own decisions. Left to my own devices, I paced myself properly, I was able to try out my tender wings a little, and I even learned to appreciate opera during those two weeks. The nights of June 12th and the 13th, the vigil and feast of St. Anthony of Padua, there were big celebrations in the main piazza. There were two symphonic bands from the Apulian cities of *Francavilla Fontana* and *Corato*. Each band was a symphony orchestra, composed of between sixty and eighty pieces. I was about to hear some wonderful music for the first time in my life. The war had made sure I didn't get to listen to whatever music was prevalent in our place and time. The musical associations (symphonic bands, including Fossacesia's) that used to entertain us during the summer had ceased to exist because its members were all in the war and many of them never came home. The night of the 12th, I asked the lady if I could go to the piazza and listen to the bands. She said yes, but come home at intermission times and let her know that I was all right. I promised and I maintained the promise. For the first night's concert, *Francavilla Fontana* offered an arrangement of Rossini's *The Barber of Seville,* while *Corato* answered with Verdi's *La Traviata.* I went home after the concerts as the lady wanted me home by 10:00 P.M. I had no problem with that because the house was close enough to Piazza Rossetti so that not only could I still hear the music, but at midnight, from my balcony, I could see the fireworks as well. The next night, the feast day of St. Anthony, I went to mass at twelve, and even joined in the traditional procession after mass.

That night, I went back to the piazza and again I was thrilled with two beautiful arrangements of operatic music. *Corato* regaled us with Donizetti's *Lucia di Lammermoor,* while *Francavilla Fontana* thrilled the enthusiastic crowd with Verdi's *Rigoletto.* I went home even more intoxicated than the night before by those wonderful melodies. At thirteen years of age, my life was changed forever. Five years later, in America, through a series of lucky breaks, I was able to see many an opera at the Academy of Music in Philadelphia. My life was complete. My cultural horizons were about to be expanded exponentially.

THE FIRST SIGN OF THE APPROACHING SPECTER OF COMMUNISM

Sunday morning, June 17, 1945, my landlady, Signora Amalia made sure I got up and properly dressed to go to mass, as per my mother's instructions. After mass, I asked her if I could take a walk to the piazza before dinner. She said yes, but be home by 1:00 P.M. This time I took the more direct route to the piazza and walked along via San Pietro. When I got to the piazza, I turned right and decided to explore some of the stores that had reopened after the war had passed through. Vasto was hardly touched by the bombers which made me think that Fossacesia must have been picked to be bombed mercilessly for spite, and my house for a double spite. But, I didn't begrudge Vasto its good luck, and now I was enjoying looking at its beautifully decorated shop windows which seemed to be asking me, *"War? What war?"* I felt like answering, *"Oh, excuse me. Forget it."*

One shop in particular sparked my interest: a store of musical instruments. It featured a small sized, very green accordion. It was such a pretty green that I was absolutely fascinated and couldn't take my eyes off of it. After that, I kept going back to the store every chance I had and practically made love to that green accordion. Green has been my favorite color ever since. While I was thus absorbed by the bewitching attraction, I heard what seemed to be an angry crowd approaching. The convulsed voices came out of a side street at the far eastern end of Piazza Rossetti. After a minute or so, I saw a group of young men carrying red flags and wearing large red kerchiefs around their necks. It was a mob of communists coming to disrupt the speech of Senator Spadaro, a locally born politician who was scheduled to speak in Piazza Rossetti at four o'clock that afternoon. In true "democratic" fashion, they were determined to prevent him from speaking since he was a member of the Christian Democratic Party. When I heard the mob approach, I got scared, repaired to a side street, and quickly went home. Later, I learned that the senator had had enormous trouble negotiating the trip from Rome, so he didn't arrive to Vasto until late that night. He gave his speech on Monday, instead, while many people were at work and there was nobody there to interrupt him. A few years ago, I returned to Vasto on vacation, and I noticed that on the spot where he had delivered his speech in 1944, now rises a bronze bust of the senator, an honor that tells future generations that he was instrumental in preventing the Communists from forming an effective red wedge into the Italian political fabric. These were the stumbling blocks that confronted the fledgling Italian Republic at the eve of its birth. There were many people at all levels who did their best to prevent the spread of Communism in the post war era, including my mother.

As usual, when the results of the exams were announced, I had not passed *La prova scritta d'italiano*—again! So during the summer, I had to study some more and return to Vasto in the fall to take my make-up exams. In September, since I was only going to be there for a couple of days, mamma took me and stayed with me until exams were over. We returned home three days later by bus in a driving rain storm. But, I passed, thank God, so I was happy. I was glad to be home, too, even though the home in question was nothing but a one room dilapidated hovel.

WE RETURN TO A REAL SCHOOL

At this point, my mother had to make a series of decisions about my next school. She had hoped for the input, or at least the financial support of my father who was still in America. In the final analysis, as for the input, that is his counsel, he had no clue as to what she was talking about. He even complained that her letters were too long. His financial support was reduced to about $50 a month, which was not enough for anything. So, she knew she would be making "Sorgini originals" for quite a while, yet. As for myself, I relaxed through the rest of September, and part of October. I kept my eyes on Anna Maria who had grown up to be quite a pretty young lady. She was fourteen years old by then; I was thirteen and a half. Her father had decided not to send her back to school since she had already completed the sixth grade, as required by State law at the time. The economic situation being what it was, she had to learn a skill to help with the family budget. She decided to become a seamstress like my mother.

But, then, things changed dramatically: mamma decided to send me away to school in the city of Chieti, together with my best buddy, Lino Di Stefano. She soon got busy preparing a sort of "dowry" as required by the rules of admission to the academy. It was a long list of things I needed to be able to spend a year at the school. I was supposed to wear a uniform fashioned after those of the naval cadets at Livorno, but due to the unavailability of material in the post war time, that requirement was waived. Everything had to have my initials embroidered on them, socks, shorts, shirts, and T-shirts, so mamma was very busy for about a month. Actually, school had started on October 1st, but mamma took a long time to decide whether or not she could swing it, and so Lino and I started school almost a month late. I was very excited: it would be the first time in two and a half years that I would see the inside of a real school, one with a blackboard in it and no sleeping bats on its ceiling!

THE GIAMBATTISTA VICO ACADEMY

We departed Fossacesia on Saturday, November 3rd, heading for the City of Chieti about fifty miles to the northwest. The mode of transport was the Di Stefano family's tiny pickup truck for the one hour long trip. Lino's uncle, Giovanni drove, his mother sat up front while he sat between the two adults. My mother and I sat on the floor in the back of the truck together with all the luggage. It was a nightmare but, we made it. Fortunately the truck, little as it was, had a canopy in the back that repaired us from the cold wind.

The school had set up a system of having the senior students greet the new students and their families and help them get situated in their respective squad quarters. Lino and I were assigned to the third squad. After a series of paper signings, fee payments and other preliminaries, we entered into the majestic portals of the *Accademia Nazionale Giambattista Vico,* located on the main street of the city, the Corso Marrucino. The word with which the students were designated was *convittori*. If the word conjures up visions of a convict in chains, it's because it has its roots in the same Latin word for convict. Left to the imagination of a thirteen year old, however, the concept acquires overwhelming proportions. We were invited to enter through a secondary French door which led into a garden atrium. A bell tower greeted us with a large clock and a foreboding sign underneath of it, which proclaimed, *TEMPORIS FUGA IRREPARABILIS,* Latin for, "The flight of time is irretrievable." We turned left onto a dark corridor and, as we immersed ourselves into its mysteries, I was sure that I had read that sign wrong. It probably said, "Abandon all hope, ye who enter here."

Temporis Fuga Irreparabilis
This is the famous clock in the atrium of the Giambattista Vico Academy in Chieti, where I studied in the scholastic year 1945-1946. The year had been shortened to less than six months, because of the lack of everything. There was food at first, but there was no material with which to make required uniforms for the students, no fuel with which to heat the building, and at times even food was rationed. But, what a school! I learned French that year, and I'm still fairly fluent in it. The clock's sober warning reads, "The flight of time is irretrievable!" In other words, wasted time is gone forever!

We climbed a series of steps and entered into the quarter assigned to the third squad. It was a nice suite for about twenty students divided into three sections: a study containing eighteen large study desks on one side of the oversized room, and an empty space reserved for recreational purposes on the other, the dormitory with eighteen beds, and next to it a large bathroom, showers and a grooming area. It was beautiful. All the beds were meticulously made up, except two that showed two skinny mattresses resting on thin bed springs. Those were our beds. At one end of the dorm was a larger bed completely surrounded by a curtain, pretty much like the beds of a hospital room. That was the bed of the squad's guidance counselor, usually a university student who was simply a living quarter supervisor, not a teacher.

By early afternoon we had settled in, and we were given the rest of the afternoon off, in the custody of our parents. We were told to return to the school by five o'clock. We got back on the little truck and we went to the local hospital to visit a friend of both families who had been there for some time, recuperating from the explosion of a mine during the summer. While the adults went to visit the patient, Lino and I waited by the truck. There was a heavy feeling deep in our souls. This was the first time that we were going to be on our own for a long time. To alleviate somewhat the emotional gravity of the moment, Lino's mom bought us each an ice cream cone from a nearby bar. After about twenty minutes, our mothers and Lino's uncle came out of the hospital, and so it was time for them to depart and for us to give the final slash to our mothers' apron strings. As I said goodbye to mamma, we did so from a distance of at least three feet. Once again she shed many very large tears, but no hug, no kiss, no nothing. "Be careful." "I will, don't worry." "Write often, and make sure you study hard!" "O.K. Good bye!" I watched the little truck start out down the incline of via Arniense. I kept staring to the back of the little truck where I knew mamma was sitting crying, even after it had become but a little dark spot, before turning left as it headed toward Francavilla al Mare. This was worse than Vasto, because I knew that I would not get home now until December 23rd, for Christmas vacation, almost two months later.

There would be many things to tell about that "year". In real time, that year turned out to be barely five months long because when Christmas vacations were over and we returned to Chieti, we found the school empty and cold. We were told to go home and await further instructions. There was no fuel available to heat the building, and the food supply had dwindled to practically nothing. So, Christmas vacations were extended until further notice.

When the middle of February rolled around, we finally went back to school, but it was still half empty. Not all the kids in the squad had made it back. Many of them lived in little hamlets spread around the Majella Mountain range, and they were buried in snow. Since the school was not even functioning when we got there, after the "Di Stefano limousine" departed,

Lino and I decided to go to the movies. At the Corso, they were showing *Dagli Appennini alle Ande,* a tear jerker about a young abandoned boy who hopped on a rickety merchant ship headed for South America from Italy to try to find his mother. After much abuse on board a leaky boat, and many adventures later on land, he does manage to find his mother, only to learn that she was dying. We knew the story because it is a classic Italian short story from Edmondo De Amicis' *Cuore,* and we should have stayed clear of it, but we didn't think. We came out of the movie theater feeling like a couple of dish rags: totally dejected and emotionally drained.

School finally started again on Monday, February 18th. Thus began the most intense period of study I had ever experienced. Despite the abbreviated school year, it was the most productive year of my scholastic career. The teachers were tough but fair, even though I did run into one major problem involving a vice principal.

One of the reasons for the school's efficient teaching methods was due to the fact that our time was totally programmed. We got up at 6:30 A.M. with three claps of the counselor's hands. By 7:00 A.M. we had to be all lined up at the foot of our beds for inspection, after having showered, and taken care of our various physiological needs. Even our shoes had to be shined. My particular counselor used to say, and repeated it at nauseam, *"L'eleganza comincia dalle scarpe!"* (Good grooming begins with one's shoes).

After inspection, we would head for the refectory for breakfast. At 7:30 A.M. we would file into the study, and there we would sit at our desks until 8:30. At that point, the counselor would call out the kids whose school was at a walking distance from the living quarters, so they had to leave ahead of time. The last group to go was ours, since Lino and I, together with about a dozen other students, were going to the Liceo Ginnasio which was housed in the same building and was, therefore, an integral part of the Academy. We did not have to leave the building. All we had to do was walk down about ten steps and turn left. An elegant glass door admitted us into the school proper. Lino, who had signed up ahead of time had managed to find a place in the 4th gymnasium (9th grade), section B which studied English as its foreign language. I was assigned to the section C, the French class, an all boys class of twenty-seven students. I was disappointed that I didn't get into the English class, but in the long run it proved to be a blessing because I got to learn French, too. At the same time I continued with the study of Latin and was introduced to classical Greek. And, of course, I had brought my father's book with me, the one that promised to teach me *"English in three months without a teacher,"* and so, in addition to the other languages, I studied English on my own, in my spare time.

School let out at 12:40 P.M. We usually had four sessions per day. We didn't study every subject every day, so the day was unusually short. However, we did have to go to school on Saturday. Dinner was at 1:00 P.M. At 2:00 P.M., each squad lined up two by two, and marched, accompanied by our counselor, to one of about five city locations, usually a *piazza,* or a park, for recreational and exercising purposes. Each day we changed destination. After reaching our destination, we were given a half hour of recreation. This was our exercise hour. One of the episodes I remember vividly was that, as soon as we walked out, more often than not, we ran into a similar squad of girls, approximately our age, from the Orsoline Academy for Girls.

One of our boys, Martin by name, an older student of about sixteen, had fallen madly in love with one of the girls named Luciana. He would wait until the two double lines of students were about to intersect each other, then he would begin to sing as loud as possible, *"Luciana, la mia vita sei tu . . ."* (Luciana, you are my life . . .). Every time that happened, invariably at our reentry, the telephone in the rector's office would ring and the nun in charge of the girls' school would complain that "one of your urchins, insulted our young ladies today . . ." For a time, the rector handled this as a serious matter, and he addressed us severely, but after a while we began to meet the rector at the school's door as we were reentering. He began to take his own afternoon walk, while we could hear from our squad quarters the telephone ringing insistently in his office, with no one there to answer it.

I enjoyed that school. Besides the foreign languages, I solidified the study of Italian, my native tongue to the point that after having lived in America for sixty years, I still remember it all, including the difficult intricacies of its highly structured grammar. I thank God every day for the gift! My homeroom consisted of twenty-seven boys, ranging from brilliant to also-rans. I considered myself comfortably in the middle, constantly trying to stay on the tail end of the first group, yet often finding myself in a struggle against the traditional, medieval school system. An incident that happened one day in March, 1946, is a typical illustration of this.

I had gone through my normal morning routine. I had studied diligently for a classical Greek test we were to take that morning. I was calm, relaxed, confident. As usual, I had gone downstairs to the school's corridor well ahead of the first bell, so I waited outside the classroom which opened into the main hallway. Many of students were outsiders. So, I was standing in the hallway in front of my classroom, serenely awaiting a probably tough classical Greek test. Looking down the hallway to my right, I saw a girl I knew, one of the walkers, coming toward me. Her classroom, the one where they taught English, was in the basement of the building. As she approached me, I noticed that she was having breakfast as she proceeded: she still had about a half dozen dried figs left. She stopped to talk to me because we used to exchange classroom notes. She used to share with me the English exercises that she received as homework which I would then do and afterward she would check mine against hers, this way I would learn and so would she (well, we were serious students then. We had to be, otherwise they would throw you out without mercy)! Laura gave me the exercises she had worked on the night before, and we talked for a few minutes. In the process, she kept eating her dried figs and offered me some. I took two, placing one in my mouth immediately chewing as I talked. Within a couple of minutes, she left as the bell was about to ring, and as I watched her walk past the auditorium and toward the door that led to the stairwell and the basement, I placed the other fig in my mouth and I began to chew.

All of a sudden, there was a commotion coming from the auditorium, like all hell had broken loose. What in the world was going on? I kept on chewing as I noticed the vice principal marching toward me, red in the face with anger. He had been reprimanding a student about some sort of "crime" the kid had committed. Then he spotted me: "And you," he sentenced, "eating in school like a sheep herder. Go to my office, and wait there!" I was as innocent of any crime as the Lamb of God. I had never seen a shepherd in school let alone one who ate while there. Had he arrived to me two seconds later I would have swallowed that damn fig. Besides, I was not in a classroom in session: I would have known better then to put anything in my mouth then. This was in the hallway, BEFORE THE BELL! That non-bell became an obsession with me afterward, and for many years to come. It was the key to my defense.

The infernal vice principal made me wait in his office three quarters of an hour before he showed his still raging face again. Meanwhile, the bell had rung, and my classmates were knocking their brains out on that equally infernal test, and I was waiting in an empty office accused of a stupid non-crime. Incredibly, when he finally showed up, that miscreant attacked me from the minute he stepped into the office, picking the argument up from where he had left off: he re-proposed his paragon to a shepherd who eats in school, adding that I had no manners, and I was a no good something or other, and he suspended me for three days. He sent the janitor to Professor Italia Cieri's 4C classroom, my teacher, to inform her that I, obviously a suspect on the list of the Secret Service's most wanted, had been apprehended, and that she should enter my crime in her register. On his return, the man brought my books to me. This was an unexpected calamity. Mamma is going to kill me, I thought, and there was nothing I could do but to assist in her choice of weapons. And I cried, oh, how I cried. I cried like I hadn't cried since I was a child. I went back to my dorm, sunk on my bed and had a most miserable time for about an hour. Then I calmed down, I made a phone call to Dr. Carusi, my sponsor and official physician to the school, to inform him of the incident. I was really hoping that he would use his influence and get me off the hook, perhaps with a severe talking to. But he did no such thing. He suggested that I use the situation as a learning experience and keep on fighting to achieve perfection. Once again I had to listen to the old Latin adage, *Ad astra per aspera,* (to the stars through adversity), which was popular in those post war years. Yea, yea, yea! It's all right if one wanted to go to the stars, but all I was looking for was a little justice right here on earth.

Suddenly, I got mad. I was as enraged as that moronic vice principal had been. So, I wrote a letter to my mother explaining to her what had happened. I apologized for forcing her to lose a day's work and come to Chieti to bail me out, and promised her that from then on I would refrain from acting like a shepherd in school (actually, I felt like acting in the manner of an avenging angel with a flaming sword as I confronted that vile excuse for an educator!). After that, I decided to enjoy my unexpected vacation. I was given permission to go out to the cathedral of San Giustino to talk to Monsignor Venturi, perhaps confess my innumerable sins and do the appropriate penance. But, as soon as the outside air hit my face, I felt liberated. I started to sing a song, I bought a crossword puzzle magazine, sat down at an outside table of the Caffè Vittoria, and had a giant ice cream cup, *"corretto,"* that is with two or three drops of Punch Abruzzo, a liqueur typical of the area, which turned the ice cream into nothing less than the desserts of the gods on Mount Olympus. Life was good, I decided. Vice principals? What vice principals?

Mamma arrived on the third day with the ten o'clock bus. I said my last prayers just in case. Duly, I saw my whole life pass in front of my eyes, but the entire episode turned out to be just a dress rehearsal for when the real thing comes along, because when mamma saw me she actually smiled. I expected a mini tornado to step off the bus, instead she wasn't even mad. As usual, she didn't hug me or kiss me, but she did put her hand on my blazer's sleeve. *"Come stai?"* she inquired. I knew then that my guardian angel had smoothed things out for me, and my last day on earth had been postponed until further notice. We went to the school. She talked to an assistant, because the tyrant was out of town. She had to sign a paper no doubt admitting that she was raising a juvenile delinquent. Then she went to talk to my teacher who assured her that I was doing very, very well in spite of my suspension. She tried to hide a smile at this, but without succeeding. I could tell that she was very pleased! Then we went to a caffè for lunch during which we spoke of the political situation. I knew she was testing me to see if I was up with current events. We discussed many things, and she was absolutely calm. This reaffirmed my conviction that I was the victim of an *"asino"* of a vice principal (that's a jackass). It even reinforced my hopes that, if I got promoted in June, I would be the proud owner of a brand new soccer ball. I could already smell the acrid, yet delicious scent of new leather. I accompanied her to the bus stop for the return trip, and during the walk, I accidentally on purpose, took the route that passed under Chieti's central mall where the sporting goods store was located. It had a gorgeous yellow leather soccer ball prominently displayed in its window. I sort of suggested that it would make an appropriate gift for an end of the year reward for being promoted in June. She nodded, sort of absentmindedly, but never said yes. That worried me a little, but I figured when the time came she would be happy to get me the ball. She got on board, took a seat and within a minute the bus departed. *"Arrivederci a Giugno, Ma!"* *"Ciao! Non rallentare gli studi, sà!"* (Goodbye, Mom. See you in June! Goodbye, don't slack off on your studies, you hear?) I returned to the academy in time for the study session. But, what a day I had!

That day my suspension expired, and the next day I went back to school. My teacher affronted me with: *"Ti sei fatto sospendere!"* (You had yourself suspended). *"Et tu Brute! Professoressa Cieri,"* I thought to myself, "not you, too!" I said nothing, however. It's better to take another humiliation in silence, and return to normal, I thought. But, then she made me happy: she said that there had been a problem in the classroom and the Greek test had to be given again, so I could take it then.

Once I had experienced a suspension for the first time, however, suddenly I became emboldened. One afternoon, Mario Borrelli and I had a question about a certain Latin project we were to do. Mario was my classmate and protector. So, we decided to sneak into the school hoping that our classroom was open and snoop around the teacher's desk to see if we could find something that might have given us a head start on it, an activity not unlike that of inside trading. Now, that would have been a punishable infraction, but we didn't find anything, so we would have gotten away with it had we simply gone back upstairs to our living quarters. But, no! We decided, instead, to sneak to the outside through the school's front door. We told the doorman that we were from outside. Alas, we failed to convince the old goat. He picked up the phone the minute we stepped off the great portal's step, and called the rector. He described me to a T. *"E' 'nu Miricane,"* he said in dialect. What gave me away as an American was the jacket I was wearing that my father had sent me from America. It had a hood that opened and closed with a zipper at the center of the head. In a zipped up mode it formed a warm hood, great for cold winter wear; unzipped, alas, it fell to the back of the shoulder like a sailor's back flap, and it looked ridiculous. Nobody else had one of those in the city of Chieti. Maybe not even in the entire Italian peninsula. I couldn't hide and we were trapped. But, I didn't know it then. We went to a public telephone cabin intending to call a classmate, the top man in the class. Surely he would know something; he always knew everything. But he didn't. And then we decided to really take advantage of the situation, and we went to the movies. We went to see the movie version of Puccini's opera, *Tosca,* which we both enjoyed immensely. I still have vivid in my memory the scene in the second act when Baron Scarpia, the wicked chief of police, enters the scene. Since it was a movie version, he arrived at Palazzo Farnese in a black, horse-driven cab. As the cab stopped, being a rainy night in Rome, one of his policemen went to him, opened an umbrella and escorted him inside. This, of course, does not happen on stage.

We came out of the movie house at 7:30 P.M. It was dark. Oh, my God, what are we going to do now? We headed straight for the academy hoping to beat the squads to the dining room. As we proceeded, Mario kept singing in my direction: *"L'ora è fuggita, e muoio disperato . . ."* Cavaradossi's lament in the fourth act (The hour is fleeting, and I die a desperate man!). I wanted to laugh, but crying would have come easier, so I did neither. I increased my gait and forced Mario to do the same. But, it was too late. When we got to the academy's imposing portals, we had to sign in. We tried to figure a way to sneak in so that the doorman wouldn't see us, but without success. Oh, well! We will be punished. So be it! Sure enough, the next afternoon during our study period, a messenger came to the door of our study hall and handed a note to the squad mentor. Oh, oh! Here we go. The mentor, who had not said a word throughout the incident, looked at that note for a long time in silence. I think he was trying to let us simmer in our own stew. After all, we were his personal responsibility. We had "sinned" against him personally. Finally, after about ten minutes that seemed like ten hours, he thundered out: "Borrelli and De Simone, you're wanted in the rector's office immediately." So, like two adolescent boys caught with their hands in the loose change jar, we sheepishly walked out of the study under the curious stares of our classmates.

Just before knocking at the dreaded office, Mario stopped in the vestibule and began to invent elaborate excuses to try to get out of a heavy punishment. After a while, I convinced him not to aggravate the situation. "Let's go in, tell the truth, and take our lumps like men. Besides, what we did is not exactly punishable by death, so let's not make it worse than it is!" I didn't wait for his answer. Being near the door, I knocked with authority, just as Mario raised his hand trying to stop me, accompanying his gesture with a pair of wide eyes that reflected shock if not fear. "Let's go," I said.

The eminent, distinguished, esteemed Rector, who was reading something from behind a pair of thick glasses, didn't even look up, or acknowledge our presence. He kept on reading as if he had not even noticed us. We waited a long time before he deigned us with his notice. Then, he got up, assumed a solemn, pontifical pose, and proceeded to give us a lecture on the dangers of the streets, the responsibility the school had to our parents, our own responsibility to the school, followed by a long list of admonitions. Finally, when I was almost asleep on my feet, he warned Mario that one more visit to his office would have meant dismissal (Mario had anticipated this before we went in, but he said that the school needed our money, so it was just a meaningless threat). He gave Mario two weeks in the corridor. Then he turned to me: *"E tu, De Simone!"* A denunciation not unlike the one hurled at Brutus by the dying Julius Caesar, *"Et tu, Brute!"* I hated that. When a teacher called my name like that, that *"mo"* in Simone reached me like a cannon shell that hit me square on the chest filling me with a deep feeling of anguish. Only this time, it made me angry. What do you mean, *E tu, De Simone.* I declaim the right to get in trouble once in a while if I so choose, I thought to myself! I accepted one week in the corridor (since this was my first infraction) not only with resignation, but with a sense of pride.

After another round of warnings, he dismissed us. We "curtsied" and walked out. Just as we reached the door to our third squad quarters, Mario started to laugh for no reason at all, quietly and softly at first, then louder and louder until his laughter became a series of uproarious, clumsy, crude belly laughs. What could I do but to join him? And so we laughed, and laughed, and laughed . . .

YOU WENT WHERE? TO THE OPERA?

All the time, between the time we tried without success to sneak into the dining room without being seen and when we returned to the study hall the next day, eighteen hours, no one had said a word to us. Mario and I knew that the episode was on everyone's mind, and yet no one dared to ask us for an explanation. Not even the counselor who would have had the right to an explanation. After all, he was the one responsible for our welfare, and we were absent without leave from his squad. Still, he kept a most annoying silence. It was totally exasperating. We got back to our desks in the study hall, sat down, got some books out of the deep well in the desk, and made believe we were doing something important, although I had a difficult time concentrating.

After the study period was over, however, suddenly everybody wanted to know what in the world had we done, where had we been, and what dire punishment had we been given. We confessed all! But then other problems arose. Martino Mario, the singer of the serenades to Luciana, said to me: *"Ma dove siete stati?" "All'opera!" "Dove? All'opera?"* Well, I suppose it was a bit strange even then that two teenage boys would even want to go to the opera, let alone get in a heap of trouble doing it. With that revelation, the entire squad roared with laughter. We did all that to go to the opera? It was absolutely embarrassing. I wish we could have said that we had been to visit a house of ill-repute! After all, I was already fourteen! Mario's case was even worse, because he was fifteen and a half, and an established leader. The embarrassment notwithstanding, I enjoyed the movie and that was that. Our classmates crucified us for the next week. However, I began to perceive a subtle, indistinctive, yet undeniable sense that now my classmates held me in higher esteem, now that I was about to experience a week of punishment in the corridor: I finally felt like one of the boys!

Starting the very next day, Mario and I began serving our sentence. The corridor in question was the one running up and down the length of the building from the lobby, passing in front of the administrating offices, and ending at the dispensary. It was illuminated by large globe shaped lamps hanging from the ceiling every ten feet or so: twelve of them. Each day, under everyone of those lamps, a student stood at attention for an hour, while our squad buddies were in the recreation area having fun. Well, so what? It was worth it and the experience made me grow, if not physically, at least in character. The only problem was the Rector's little Pekingese dog that kept barking at us as if to add its own reprimands for our misdeeds. Occasionally, the reprobate students got into a fit of muffled laughter for no reason at all. And it was contagious: one of the *guys* started it and the others followed suite, laughing uncontrollably even while trying to repress it, without even knowing why.

HISTORY WAS ABOUT TO BE MADE

All in all, the year, short as it was, proved to be the most productive of my scholastic career. It reinforced the linguistic base that had been established during my elementary grades, and it gave me a chance to build upon it five languages. Many years later, I figured out that the war had shortchanged us even there. Especially me! I was headed for America where math and science are held in high regard, instead I got a large dose of the language arts. Most of the math and science teachers in provincial small towns were men, and they were still in the army, so we were stuck with the girls even after three years. We didn't mind that so much except that I wanted to be a doctor and math and science were fundamental to that dream.

During the entire month of May things really got interesting. The Italian people were getting ready to hold a national plebiscite to determine whether to keep the monarchic form of government or change over to a republic. One of the poll places was the front corridor of our school. Not only that, but they asked us students to help out. On June 1st and 2nd, 1946, the plebiscite was held throughout the nation, the first free election in over twenty-five years. The students, those who were still in school, were used as "gophers." We were busy all day long helping older folks to understand the voting system, moving boxes of ballot forms from one place to another, going to a nearby store for various items needed by the officials. I liked the latter because it gave me a chance to go out into the town on "official business." School was over by then and many counselors had gone home. Things were very relaxed and we were able to stay out for long periods of time before anyone would be looking for us.

There was a refugee camp still operating in Chieti, long after the war was over, so we visited Carletto, a friend of ours, at the camp once in a while. While there, we rendered a few services for the people such as filling forms since most of the refugees could not read or write Italian. We fetched water from a nearby fountain for an old lady who spoke a very refined Italian with a distinctive Triestine accent. On June 3rd, we even helped Carletto raise the new Italian flag, that is, the Italian tricolor minus the Sabaudo shield, the mark of the Savoia Monarchy, which had been defeated the day before, on June 2nd. It was a historical moment.

On the 3rd of June, the city of Chieti celebrates the feast of its martyred patron, Saint Justin. The Teatine people (the people from Chieti) celebrate the event in a grandiose manner. Lino and I, teenagers full of youthful verve, yet restrained in our behavior, spent the whole day out of the academy. There was nobody around to care one way or another, anyway. Besides, what could they have done to us, the year was over. I had spotted a girl around 10:00 A.M. whose looks intrigued me. I had seen her several times in school, but I didn't even know her name. I followed her at a distance for most of the morning, even into the church for mass, where I lost her. I supposed she went home for dinner. At night, before returning to the academy, I enjoyed a great symphonic concert by the famed Banda di Chieti. I even remember the piece that impressed me the most, Tchaikovsky's *"1812 Overture."*

PROMOTED IN JUNE

The final grades were not going to be announced until June 15th, but since Signor Di Stefano came to pick up Lino, I decided to go home, too. Dr.

Carusi assured me that as soon as the final grades were posted he would send me a telegram with the results and mail me the card by postal service. On June 7th, however, I received a telegram with the announcement that I had been promoted. He was able to use his influence as the physician of the academy and was able to sneak a peek ahead of time. He told me that on a scale of 1 to 10, I had received all 6's, except for history in which I received a 7. What a difference a half century makes! A six was the minimum passing grade. Only the elite few received 7 or 8. A 9 or 10 were practically unheard of. All my 6's and the one 7 in history were the numbers that stood in testimony of an enviable body of knowledge which still serves me today. After I received my rank in class for the year, I was the fifth of only five students promoted in June from in my class. Mario Borrelli was third. In other words, I barely made it. The others placed in various positions, but fifteen students had to take make-up exams in September, while the remaining seven flunked out for the year. Which means that the percentage of students promoted was a mere 18%. It was not exactly a fair distribution of the goods, so to speak, but it proved to be the death rattle of that feudal system which had been in place in Italian schools for the longest time. Within a year, things would begin to change, though not necessarily for the better (pushed in no uncertain terms by the "new leftist powers," the Proletariat, as they called themselves). At a distance of a half a century, schools both in Italy and in the United States would change radically as we entered the TV era, with all its distractions, and as a result, actual knowledge became a commodity that rarely matches the easy promotions, and the inflated grades that are given so freely today even at the college level.

WE MEET THE FUTURE SAINT, PADRE PIO DA PIETRELCINA

When Easter arrived that year, I had gone home for vacation. No sooner had I entered the half ruined single room that the B-24's had relegated us to, I made the announcement that my promotion in June was all but assured. I was finally going to get my soccer ball, or even a bicycle, maybe. I already had picked the ones I wanted in the sporting goods store in Chieti's elegant Corso Marrucino.

Mamma was happy and she said: "If you are promoted, I will take you to see a living saint." "A what?" I exclaimed in disbelief. "Saint, did you say?" And she proceeded to tell me the story of Padre Pio, who was 58 years old at the time. "Well," I thought to myself, "good-bye soccer ball!" And I never did get one. Now, in my old age, I have a brand new soccer ball in my study. It just sits there among my books and records. I keep it there as a trophy to the ball I never had. Every day I bounce it off my carpet, and off my knees from a sitting position, and otherwise make love to it, sort of.

So, in June of 1946, soccer ball-less and bicycle-less, I joined my mother and several of her lady friends, on a trip to the Gargano Mountain area of the Italian peninsula. San Giovanni Rotondo, province of Foggia, had on its mountain slopes, a Franciscan monastery where, since 1912, there lived a friar named Padre Pio da Pietrelcina. In Italy, Franciscan friars are identified by their first name (usually not their given name, but an adopted religious name), plus the city or town where they're from. For example, at one time at the monastery of San Giovanni Rotondo there was a Fr. Bill of Milwaukee. Padre Pio's given name was Francesco, but he took on the name of Pio after Pius IX (Pio Nono, in Italian). Padre Pio's hometown, in the Benevento area, is called Pietrelcina, literally "Little Rock." Padre Pio, was a mystic who had received from Our Lord, the signs of the crucifixion: the stigmata. The first stigmatist was, of course, St Francis of Assisi, but Padre Pio was the first ordained stigmatist. So, he was a priest, where St. Francis was not. It is said that through his intercession, there had been innumerable miracles performed, and that many American servicemen, especially Air Force personnel stationed in the airfields of southern Apulia (the "heel" of the Italian boot), had gone up the mountains of the Gargano peninsula (the spur of the Italian boot), to visit him. Many went home to America with some incredible spiritual experiences.

And so we went. Despite the fact that he had been there, and with the stigmata since 1918, my mother didn't hear of him until after the war, and I knew she could not rest until she had gone down there to see for herself. We lived about 100 miles from San Giovanni.

Traveling by train, in those days, was a traumatic experience in itself. Many Italian soldiers, especially those who had served in Russia and then spent three or four years as prisoners of the Russians, were just then making their way back home (many more never made it back). Trains were few and jammed to the brim with passengers. They even had men riding on the roofs of the cars. Many a young soldier was killed in those days when the train entered a tunnel, and not paying attention, they were swept right off the cars.

We managed to board a train headed for Foggia one day around the twentieth of June. The steam engine was a war survivor, too, and it leaked water from its reservoir like a sieve. The engineer had to stop three times to refill the water tank. As a result we got to Foggia at four in the afternoon, fully an hour after the bus that took pilgrims to San Giovanni Rotondo had left, which meant that we had to wait in the station until the next day. There were no hotels available, even if we could afford to go to one (which we couldn't). Most of the existing ones had been destroyed just three years earlier, and reconstruction was slow and painful. And so, we settled in for the night on some of the wooden benches of the Foggia train station. It was the longest and most tedious twenty four hour period of my life, but we survived. The next day, I washed in a public fountain in the piazza of the station. The ice cold water revived me from the sense of grogginess that a sleepless night normally produces. At the station bar, my mom bought some pastries and I had my very first cappuccino.

The next day, we boarded the bus, but in spite of the fact that we were there already when the bus arrived, I had to ride standing up all the way. It wasn't too bad, though; I happened to be standing next to a girl my age. We struck up a conversation, and that made the time go by faster. At four thirty, we arrived in San Giovanni.

The first item on the agenda was finding a place to stay. There were no hotels there either. We knocked at one of the five or six houses built on the slopes of the mountain. Luckily, we were accepted by the people who lived in the very first house at which we knocked. I don't know what my mom paid the lady of the house, but it couldn't have been too much. We slept on the floor all three nights that we stayed there.

As soon as we were settled in the house, we made our way up to the little church of the monastery. We went in. The church was a tiny little chapel indeed, but, in the subsequent times I went to San Giovanni, it kept getting smaller and smaller in my mind. It was dark, the tiny temple was faintly illuminated only by the rays of the late afternoon sun which, filtering as they did through some small alabaster covered windows high on its ceiling, gave the altar and the statues a subdued, surrealistic glow. Peace reigned supreme at that moment. We sat there for a while, praying and meditating. I have to confess; even there what I prayed for was a soccer ball.

We had been in the chapel about fifteen minutes, when a monk appeared from the little door on the side of the main altar, and slowly made his way down the isle. No one had to tell me who he was. There was a glow about the man that radiated spirituality to all who gazed upon him. His eyes smiled at you and his face reflected the profound inner goodness that permeated his entire being. That's why he was able to endure the incredible sufferings to which he was subjected day and night. Not only did he endure the pains of the crucifixion, but he was visited and beaten nightly by the devil, and was subjected to other indignities that would have floored a much stronger, bigger man. In the three days that we were there, we were able to notice that Padre Pio, despite having those tormented and sleepless nights, also put in a sixteen hour day, mostly in the confessional. Considering his nightly torments, he probably hated to go to sleep! But, then, God picks only those souls capable of untold heroism to do His work on earth.

The next day we got up at four. By four thirty we were at the front door of the church. Mass started at 5:15 A.M. (I never understood why the Catholic Church always started the day at such an ungodly hour). Those who did not get there at least an hour before would not get in, and if they did, they would have to stand in the back of the church for the entire three hours that Padre Pio's masses took, in those days.

Yes, Padre Pio took a full three hours to celebrate a mass that most priests managed to mumble out in a half hour or less. What did he do in all that time? Well, it is difficult to say. Besides reading the prayers in Latin, he would often be absorbed in ecstasy. It was said that, especially at the Consecration, he would contemplate the mystery of the Incarnation, of the Eucharist, of Redemption to such levels of intensity that he would be absorbed into them for the longest periods of time. I was fourteen and a half years old at the time, and one would think at that age I would be bored to death at the prospect of participating at such a mass. But I wasn't. I had served many a mass since I was eight years old. Often, I had been so fidgety that I could not wait till it was over. But that was not the case at Padre Pio's mass. I was totally engrossed in it, and followed his every move. It was awesome! After that first mass, I heard Padre Pio's masses eleven more times between 1946 and 1956.

I went to confession to him also, three times. The first time, I had the feeling that he read my mind. For a while, some people were spreading rumors that he had denied me absolution. I don't know where that story got started, but he did nothing of the kind. That first day, he did encourage me to take a few minutes to remember a certain item that was in my possession that did not belong to me. It was a high quality harmonica that I had "borrowed" from one of my classmates in Chieti, and which I, intentionally, albeit without malice, had not returned to him. I returned a few minutes later, my memory's clarity restored to the crispness of a winter sunset in Pennsylvania, and I was absolved. Needless to say, as soon as I returned home, I made a package and made restitution of the item, helped by the fact that I had received a nasty letter from the owner of the instrument urging immediate restitution of his property. Anna Maria still remembers that once I reached home that year, the first thing I did was try to sell some of my books in order to pay for the postage, without my mother finding out. But I couldn't find any buyers. So I told my mother about the incident and she took care of it. I considered the experience a learning step in my growing up process. Since then, I never took a grain of salt that did not belong to me. I suppose that was Padre Pio's intention all along. Well, it worked.

Padre Pio wore a pair of knitted half gloves of brown wool to cover the wounds on his hands as he went about his daily routine as a priest and Franciscan monk. During the mass, however, he would take them off, and when one received Holy Communion from those pierced hands, one could see a large blotch of dark red blood that covered the entire area of the palm. Over the centuries, the wounds of the crucifixion, like those on Saint Francis of Assisi's hands, for example, have been painted thousands of times by various artists all over the world, as neat, clean slits on the palm of the hand. Padre Pio's were not like that at all. They looked more like a blotch of dark red, raw flesh covered by dried blood. It was not pretty. Once, somebody asked him if the wounds hurt. The good padre answered, "The Lord did not give them to me for decoration." The amazing thing, one that has baffled me since 1968, the year of Padre Pio's death, is that within hours after his death, which took place during the early morning hours of September 23, fifty years to the hour after Padre Pio originally received them, the stigmata totally disappeared. Many theories have been advanced by the skeptics, professional and not, to explain the stigmata themselves. Padre Pio had the wounds on his hands, on his feet and on his side. Most documentation I read usually dealt only with the wounds of his hands. The unbelievers, unable to give a reasonable explanation for the phenomenon, most often theorize that the wounds were due to psychological auto-suggestion. Nonsense! The innumerable medical examinations to which the Church subjected Padre Pio over the years, all indicate that the wounds were not superficial but through and through perforations in both hands and feet. What is most intriguing to me is the gash on the side resulting from the lance of Longinus is the right side of Jesus on the cross. The wound on Padre Pio's side was on his left. This would indicate a direct linear zap originating from Christ's right ribs and hitting Padre Pio's left side. No auto-suggestion on earth can create such a phenomenon. Of course the most intriguing marvel of all is the question of how did the flesh in those hands, feet and side manage to regenerate itself within a few hours after the holy man had already died. In Man's limitations to really understand his own existence, there comes a time, even in these high tech days, in which he has to admit that he cannot explain everything. Padre Pio is a phenomenon for our times, and now he is the saint for the millennium. He brought millions back to the fold, and he touched so many lives that to try to explain him in earthly terms is not only useless, it's a case of outrageous arrogance at its highest degree of insolence. For once, let us realize our limitations, and accept the limitless immensity of God's powers. Padre Pio, even after his death, is one living example of such power. He was a priest, a stigmatist, and now a saint forever. Photos taken within hours after his death show his hands smooth white, completely free of any wounds, or scars; nothing! There is no way to explain that.

AMERICA, HERE WE COME!

In October 1946, Mamma decided, much to my regret, not to send me back to Chieti. It was simply too expensive a proposition for her. Had my father been more cooperative, she might have made it financially, but he had a "public" mentality. To him, public schools were fine, and free. He had no concept of wanting to pay for something that was academically superior, even if public schools were free. I would have wanted to return to Chieti, but I remembered the sacrifices mamma had made the previous year, and I couldn't ask her to continue to do them. So, she decided to let me commute to Lanciano by bus, sending me back to the school where I had been before the war arrived.

Unfortunately, my teachers at Chieti had been as great as those at Lanciano were mediocre, at best. The first impression I had was that this was a hospice for deformed people, no disrespect intended: my titular "professor," Dr. De Mellis, our homeroom teacher, was lame to a significant degree. The French teacher, was a four-foot tall hunchback. It was obvious that these physical traits were congenital, and I would be blameworthy if I were to rebuke them for something over which they had no control. But, they both had severe personality defects, as well, that did not go well with the profession they had chosen. The French teacher taught me nothing. I walked into her classroom with a solid knowledge of French under my belt. It had been inculcated in me by professor Scardapano at Chieti, a beautiful and grand lady, fifty years of age or so, who spent every summer in Paris with her sister. Her French was perfect. At that point I needed either to continue with her, or find an even better French teacher in another school who would take me to the next level. Instead, I found old hunchback (I don't remember her name) who was very active in the PCI (Italian Communist Party). She would miss at least two days of school each week because she had to serve the party by going to the mountain towns to spread the gospel of Communism. Fortunately, I was able to teach myself the French she failed to teach me.

But, De Mellis *"era un altro paio di maniche!"* The phrase literally means "it was another pair of sleeves," an Italian expression similar to our, "Its a different ball game," "A horse of a different color," and the like. He "taught" me classical Greek, Latin, Italian, history and geography (no wonder he was always grumpy!). The first shock I received when I walked into his classroom was that instead of my familiar gray Greek grammar that I had used in Chieti, I had to buy a different grammar—a yellow one. It wouldn't have been so bad if it followed the same teaching pattern as the book I used in Chieti, but this one approached Greek grammar from a completely different angle. Instead of three declensions for nouns and adjectives, this book presented only two, *"squishing"* the third into the second. Talk about confusion, this must have been a situation similar to the one that gave rise to the English expression, "It's Greek to me!" It wasn't just Greek to me; it was chaos!

De Mellis' problems went much deeper than that of the French teacher, however. It was something he did to me in the spring that embittered me to such an extent that I decided never to set foot in his classroom again, and that precipitated our final push to go to America. At that point my mother must have given up on me, even though my encounter with De Mellis had been even worse than the encounter I had the year before with the vice-principal at Chieti.

After struggling with almost everything at Lanciano, given the lousy teachers we were stuck with, I had managed to reach the spring trimester. I wasn't doing too well gradewise, and I didn't know why. I studied hard, I understood everything and I presented my written work on time, and still my marks were below average.

The whole thing came to a head one day in April, 1947, shortly after Easter vacations. De Mellis must have been in the grip of a personal crisis that day and didn't feel like teaching, so he announced a *"compito in classe,"* that is a composition to be written in the classroom. De Mellis was not a very nice man. We, the students, used to call him *"Il professor Sù-e-Giù"* (Professor Up-and-down), a reference to the fact that when he walked he rose a good three inches with each step, and came down by that much when he rested his body on his deformed right foot. It wasn't a very nice thing to do, but students will be students. If he had been a little nicer as a man, perhaps, he probably would have commanded more respect from the young people entrusted to his care, but he wasn't, and so he got stuck with, *"Il professor Sù-e-Giù!"*

The composition was to be completed in class in two hours. It had a most unusual title, as follows:

> *During the long anxious night the heart was sad and despairing, but in the morning, with the rising of the sun, and the ringing of the bells, the soul regained its serenity and a sense of hope.*

This was the tenth grade, to be sure. Our composition themes were well beyond, "What did you do in your summer vacation?" But, this was too much even for us. But, I placed my left elbow on my desk, rested my chin on the palm of my left hand, and began to think deep thoughts just to please Professor Sù-e-Giù.

The first thought that entered my mind was the obvious: a young mother kept vigil all night long over her sick little boy, her heart filled with anguish. But, in the morning with the first rays of the rising sun, and at the first tolls of the church bells, the child felt better, and everything was fine. But I quickly discarded this. I decided it was too simplistic. I was going to develop this narrative "metaphorically." Actually, I had never heard that word before, nor had I read anything that could be considered the "metaphor" of something else. I just acted on impulse even in the absence of the technical mechanism that defined it. I remembered that when two years before, on May 3, 1945, at noon, church bells rang all over Italy and continued to ring for an hour in thanksgiving to God for the end of WWII, the people came out of their homes, hovels as well as villas, with tears in their eyes and they hugged each other in a euphoria of jubilation. The heavy burden of war had been lifted from our entire nation, and the whole world, too . . . well, almost—war in Japan was not over yet: the first atomic bomb over Hiroshima would not be detonated until three months later, on August 6th. But war in Europe was over.

Eureka! That's it! I was going to make our war evacuation period correspond to the night, the rising sun would symbolize the new world peace, and the ringing of the bells would correspond to those that actually rang for an hour announcing the end of WWII. I deemed it perfect. I wrote it down, then edited it and finally recopied it on a clean sheet. I finished ten minutes before the end of the period, and handed it in with a sense of accomplishment in my demeanor. I fully expected it to be considered one of the best, if not *the* best of the lot.

Two weeks went by before Professor Sù-e-Giù got around to returning our papers. One can image my shock and surprise when, instead of the best, he announced to the class that he considered my "masterpiece" to be the absolute worst of the lot. Obviously he didn't understand it. But then, even Dante says that, *"Oft, crass matter is deaf to art's intention!"* (paraphrase from *Paradiso,* I, 127-129). Well, OK, you want to give me a bad mark? You want to throw the whole thing into the wastepaper basket? Fine! But, don't make a fool of me in front of the whole class, which is what he did. After announcing that he was going to read "the worst paper" first, to my great dismay, he called out my name, asked me to stand and remain standing. I did, and as I stood there in great disbelief, he began to read my paper his way, emphasizing the points that did not call for emphasis while reading with barely audible voice the areas that were intended to be emphasized. Not having understood the metaphoric intent of my paper, he read it in his own misguided way. It was a free-for-all. The whole class became a pack of snarling dogs. Even those I had previously considered my friends snickered, sneered, howled, jeered and scoffed on command. That's when I had my first experience with mob mentality. At that point, Professor De Mellis could have asked those kids to go around the school and shoot up the place and they would have done it.

After he finished with my paper, he read the one he considered to be the best composition. It was about a mother staying up all night with her sick child, feeling very sad as she cared for him, but in the morning, as the sun rose, and church bells announced the first mass, the child felt better and everything was *"peachy-keen,"* as the expression goes. It was the paper belonging to the cutest little blond girl from nearby San Vito.

When the reading was over, the professor asked her and me to go to the front of the room to pick up our papers, while he asked two girls to distribute the other papers to the rest of the class. I saw the marks for both: she received a 9 out of 10, a sterling mark. I only received a 3, with 6 being the passing minimum. As he handed my paper to me he sentenced: *"Tu non imparerai mai a scrivere una lettera!"* (You will never learn to write a letter!). So much for the caring and nurturing of young, sensitive souls! On my way back to my desk, I put on the most contemptuous look I could muster. I slowly and deliberately gathered all my things, and with a dramatic gait, walked out the door, even as he called out after me in a threatening voice, considering that there were a good twenty minutes left in the period.

That was the last day of school in Italy for me. The next day *"ho fatto filone,"* (I cut classes). For the first time in my life, I didn't go to school. Instead, I joined the chronic class-cutters as they rented bicycles and rode around the city's park lanes, up the street from the school. I did that for two days. But it was an expensive proposition, and I was not exactly swimming in money. The third day, while sitting at a table at the *Caffè Modernissimo,* sipping a *caffèlatte* and eating a brioche, I overheard a young lawyer sitting at a table next to mine telling his lady friend that he was on his way to the tribunal to defend a case of sheep hustling. Ha-ha! That's where I'm going, I said to myself. So, for the next two days, I sneaked into the courtroom watching the proceedings. Three brothers from Palena, a sheep growing town half way up the Majella Mountains, stood accused of stealing about thirty sheep from a flock belonging to one of their neighbors. The accused brothers claimed that the sheep were rightfully theirs because those animals had wandered into their flock abusively and had grazed on their land for over a year. They were claiming the spirit of a law called *usucapione* (a euphemism for legal larceny). That's when I decided that the law profession was not for me, thank you!

On the third day of the trial, when the judges were going to announce their verdict, I went to a caffè for my usual breakfast, except that I decided to change venues, trying the *Caffè La Fazia* this time, located on the opposite side of the school. I was looking forward to going to the tribunal, anxious to hear the verdict. I had decided that the sheep herders were wrong. If they could prove that the sheep had grazed on their land for a year, they could demand a compensation to be set by the court, but they could not abusively detain the thirty sheep that didn't belong to them. I was curious to know if the judges' verdict agreed with mine. I paid for my breakfast, and after walking out the door I nonchalantly began to walk toward the tribunal. I passed in front of the school, I even greeted the doorkeeper, the rotund and rubicund, *Signor La Rosa.* Immediately after I reached the side street that separates the school from the arches of the shopping mall, I walked past the first two columns of the arcade and then I headed for the opening between the third and the fourth column. That's when my mother confronted me, her eyes spewing fire, flame and fury, as she headed toward me, murder in her heart. And, she attacked me physically hitting me repeatedly in the face, the head, wherever she could find an opening. Only, this time, I wasn't going to take it. There are times in a man's life when a sense of justice demands rebellion, and this was such a time for me! I took off running as fast as I could toward the ancient Roman Bridge which spanned the *Valle di Santa Cecilia* that ran alongside Lanciano's Cathedral, ignoring her warnings of dire consequences when we got home. I dashed across the busy main street nearly getting hit by a motor scooter. As mamma saw me head for the bridge, a well known suicide site, she stopped. I think she was concerned.

The bridge in question is a narrow stone bridge that runs alongside the cathedral a block away and parallel to the city's main drag and shopping mall. At its middle point it is at least 300 feet deep over the exit point of an underground creek. It ends at the front of the cathedral leading onto the piazza. So, running at breakneck speed, crying all the way, I crossed the *Piazza Plebiscito,* and hid behind the monument to Lanciano's fallen heroes of WWI. From there, I could see, without being seen. I sat down on the monument's marble pedestal, and tried to calm down. I had run so fast that there was no way mamma could have imagined that I had reached the monument in less than two minutes. At that moment, my biggest regret was that I didn't get to hear the final verdict of the sheep hustling case.

The city of Lanciano has, even today, a quaint way of announcing to its citizenry that it is high noon: they explode a loud cannon charge from the top of the cathedral's bell tower. It never failed to scare the *heebie-jeebies* out of me (my wife's Aunt Camilla's favorite expression). I sat there for over two hours until the bell tower boomed that it was 12:00 o'clock—high noon. A few minutes later, I cautiously came out into the open. I had seen mamma going crazy looking for me several times. At one point, she even stopped two *Carabinieri* (policemen) as they patrolled the downtown area on bicycles. She talked to them for a few minutes, but they must have told her to wait a little longer before filing a formal missing person request.

I sat on the front of the monument in full view this time and waited for whatever would come my way. The bus would have left Lanciano at 1:00 P.M. And she didn't see me for a long time even though she looked my way at least a half a dozen times. Finally, spotting me, she started to come toward me. So I dashed again, but this time, I headed for the bus, I had my boarding pass. I took a seat in the back with the other students. Then I saw her get on board. She located me, but did not confront me, taking a seat in the center of the bus. Within the hour, we were home. When we got off the bus, we walked home separately, one behind the other, as we covered the three blocks that separated the bus stop from the hovel we called home. No more was said for the rest of the day. At night I tried to explain what happened, but I had that sense of futility common in such cases. The next morning she got my little brother up to go to school in town, but she made me sleep, instead. I think, that at that point mamma gave up on me completely, figuring that once we got to America, she would let my father handle me. All her dreams for me were completely shattered.

Three days later, we both went to Lanciano to speak to *Signor Bellarmino,* the agent who represented the Italian Lines, and we made plans to sail for America. We set our departure date for June 14th. We would leave Fossacesia on the 9th. America, here we come, finally!

OUR SECOND VISIT WITH PADRE PIO

In May, 1947, just before we sailed for America, we returned to San Giovanni Rotondo. This time, train transportation had improved somewhat, and we did not have to wait overnight in the train station. Again we had to knock on doors of private homes to find lodging, and this time it proved a bit tougher, because the fame of Padre Pio had spread all over the world and people were traveling more, especially after the thousands of American GI's who had met him had returned to America. The house in which we had stayed the previous year had been rented out and there was no room at the inn, literally. So, we ended up farther away from the monastery, but it was close enough. We still slept on the floor with barely a couple of blankets under us as mattresses.

Padre Pio's masses were just as long and his joviality still intact. We were told that Beniamino Gigli, the famous opera tenor of the thirties and forties, had been there a few weeks before, and the talk around the monastery was about the night when, in the gardens of the monastery, Gigli asked Padre Pio if he wanted him sing something. Padre Pio requested *Mamma,* a song that the singer had made popular through films just before the war. Gigli sang it, and Padre Pio wept, as he remembered his own mother.

The second day, someone told my mother that the Padre was wont to say a memorable phrase to anyone who was about to undertake a long journey. She told me about it and made me promise to try my luck. I promised, but I was a little intimidated; I wasn't sure I could deliver. So I sat in the sacristy at the point from which a spiral staircase ascended onto the second floor, the floor that housed the monks' tiny cells. Padre Pio's cell was #5. I sat there for almost two hours and no Padre Pio. Meanwhile, darkness began to creep onto the room and I was just about ready to call it quits, when I saw Padre Pio enter. He headed for the spiral stairs and began to climb them. I quickly got behind him. He didn't see me. When we both reached the second floor, I called out to him. "Padre Pio! Padre Pio!" I was fifteen and scared to death, conditioned as I had been all my life to fear all my superiors, including God. We had reached the entrance to cell number 5 when he finally realized that someone was behind him. He stopped and said, *"Beh, che c'è?"* (Well, what is it?). In response to that inquiry I blurted out something about a saying. I told him that we were about ready to sail for America. He asked me where in America I was going, so I told him that my father lived near Philadelphia. He told me that his own father had lived in Philadelphia for a few years. He turned toward me, placed his pierced left hand on my head and blessed me with his right as he wished me, "Buon Viaggio!" He wished me a fair voyage, then added, ". . . e *ricordati di vivere sempre col santo timor di Dio."* (Remember to live always within the holy fear of God). I was ecstatic. Mission accomplished! I kissed his hand and pivoted out of there, jumping down the spiral steps three at a time. I immediately reported to mamma. She was jubilant at my success.

My mother made a valiant attempt to go to confession to him, but to no avail, this time. They had devised a system whereby women had to make a reservation to confess to the very busy stigmatist. I had no problem going to confession to him because I was able to join the men in the sacristy and go to confession face to face. Women, on the other hand, were not even permitted to enter the sanctuary in those days let alone the sacristy, and so she had no choice but to make a reservation. At one point a young woman let go with a demoniacal scream that reverberated throughout the little chapel. In a loud voice, she hollered out that some people were unworthy even to enter the church let alone the sanctuary. Well, in those days that's what the situation was. Mamma's number was called the day we were supposed to depart. Those women must have had a lot of sins to confess that day because mamma judged that each penitent took between ten and fourteen minutes of Padre Pio's time. There was no way that we could have honored the reservation. We had to leave after only three days, and the wait, even with reservation, was already at five days. Still, on the third day of our stay she managed to get in line. She stood there almost two hours until she was only the third in line when Padre Pio closed the little window and left the confessional. She was visibly upset that she had failed to go to confession to the future and present saint, and she took it as a bad omen. When, in 1948, after exactly one year of life in America she died of complications from childbirth, the know-it-alls in town had a field day when they received the shocking news: Padre Pio knew it, they insisted, that's why he didn't hear her confession. My own theory is that, if Padre Pio knew she was going to die, would he not have wanted to confess her all the more? I wonder!

DEPARTURE

We set our departure date from Fossacesia for the morning of June 9th. Since we had several trunks to take with us, Signor Bellarmino had to hire a larger truck to take us and four other people to Naples. Mamma and nonna would ride in the cabin, while Filippo and I together with the others would ride in the back with the trunks and the suitcases. During the time between my last day of school and the date of departure, Mamma sold everything she owned, she visited all our relatives to say goodbye, and she settled all the financial situations, hers and nonna's.

The night before our departure, my friends gave me a farewell party at the home of one of the boys. It was held in an elegant dining room with about twenty invited guests. Anna Maria was there, too. The mothers who volunteered to organize it brought sweets and cakes, and a bottle of Martini and Rossi red sweet Vermouth, an Italian aperitif wine. Italian law does not forbid teenagers from drinking, but I often mentioned that farewell party in my classrooms to illustrate the fact that, while Italian teens had no restrictions on their drinking, they didn't abuse the privilege, either; they enjoy the various potions (mostly wines—no hard liquor!), but they respected them and seldom abused them. When the party was over, all the cakes and cookies had disappeared, all but the crumbs. After everyone had had a half glass of Vermouth to toast my departure and wish me a calm voyage and good luck, there was still about a third of the liquid stuff left in the bottle. Italian kids simply don't make a fuss over liquor, even now. Every one took their half glass, raised a toast in my honor and drank it. The girls didn't even do that, some barely wet their lips. No one reached for the bottle for a refill.

The next morning, as we said goodbye to the crowd of neighbors who had gathered in front of our shack, mamma put on quite a spectacle of emotion. Just as she began to say goodbye, she took one look at the empty lot on which our house had stood four years before, and she completely lost it. She screamed in a disconsolate, desperate, anguished manner. She contorted her whole body in total distress. I have never seen a departure scene quite so intensely impassioned before or since. Some people still alive today remember it vividly and they are certain that it was because she had a premonition of the tragedy that was to overtake her exactly one year later to the day.

The large truck finally departed headed for Lanciano because we had to stop at the travel office and pick up our sailing tickets. It stopped in the middle of Lanciano's piazza and while mamma walked to Bellarmino's one block away north, I walked to my old "watering hole", the Caffè Modernissimo, for breakfast. We had arranged it the night before, so all my friends were there waiting for me and we set up another mini party prior to their going to school. I'll never forget my friend, Filippo Susi, the musician and comic spirit of the group as he, after we all had coffee and a pastry, presented me with a box of cookies, saying as he did in his usual deadpan manner: *"Fije me, quiste ti li migne pi lu vijaje"* (Abruzzese dialect meaning, "My son, this is for you to eat during your journey." Of course everyone laughed. Filippo thought, perhaps, that they didn't feed us aboard ship? But it was just a joke.

NAPOLI, MON AMOUR!

Napoli is my favorite Italian city, crime, pollution and possible volcanic eruptions notwithstanding. It was the first major city I had visited as a child, and I have some indelible memories of the two visits my family made there when I was six, and seven. Also, Napoli is the musical capital of the world, and I love its songs. And, of course, the grandest reason of them all, I've been a fan of its soccer team since the fall of 1945, when I was at school in Chieti. One can't get any more Neapolitan than that! *"Vedi Napoli e po' mori!"* goes the old saying (See Naples and then you can die!). Modern cynics will invariably add: *"di asfissia!"* (of asphyxiation!), with sardonic reference to modern day air and water pollution in that city. Perhaps, but I still love Napoli.

As with our previous stays in the city, we stayed at the Gallozzi Hotel, the classic hotel for departing Abruzzese migrants. I enjoyed our stay there. We took short walks within a block or two of the hotel. Mamma and nonna enjoyed window shopping along the Via Roma, Napoli's première thoroughfare and shopping strip.

Knowing that it was going to be four days before we sailed, mamma decided that we would visit the shrine of Our Lady of the Rosary in Pompeii. We had been there in 1939, and I enjoyed the experience then also. On June 11th, we took the Trans-Vesuviana RR to Pompeii. It was a local two car trolley-like train that connected the city of Sorrento on the southern end of the gulf with the large city of Naples at the other end, while linking other cities and towns such as *Torre del Greco, Torre Annunziata,* and *Castellammare di Stabia* along the way with each other, as well. We visited the shrine, everybody went to confession, we heard mass, mamma bought a few items to bring as gifts to various people in America, and finally we went to a restaurant for dinner. While visiting the gift shop, I took the opportunity to send Anna Maria a "significant" postcard. In 2003, her Aunt Ernestina, at 96 years of age, still recalled that card from Pompei that, in her judgment, was the initial spark that would eventually lead to our marriage. We had time to visit the excavation of the ancient city of Pompeii, the one that was buried by *lapilli* from the eruption of Mount Vesuvius in the year A.D. 79. It was the first time I had ever seen something I had previously studied in school.

WE SAIL THE OCEAN BLUE

At noon, Saturday, June 14th, we consigned our three trunks to the acceptance office to be loaded on board the ship and we carried the four suitcases with us as we boarded. There was much excitement on board. There were many people who spoke a language other than Italian, mostly English but other languages, as well. I learned later that there were many people from eastern European countries sailing with us. Less than two years had passed after the end of World War II, and normal passenger service to New York had not yet been restored in the northern European ports. The only port that was fairly active was that of Naples, so they came from all over the East: Poland, Hungary, Czechoslovakia, the Ukraine and, of course Italy. They were Americans who were trapped by the war after they had returned to their native country for a family visit. They were going home after a seven or eight year absence.

At 6:00 P.M. on the dot, there were three blasts of the ship's fog horn, which, besides scaring the shadow out of everybody on board since the smoke stacks were right above our heads, signaled that the ship was about to leave the port. Within a few minutes the tugboat serving the port had pushed the giant transatlantic liner out on to the bay, and the Saturnia's powerful engines began to churn up the water with those big propellers. The white ship began to move on its own in the Gulf of Naples like a regal swan in the middle of a park pond. Slowly and majestically, she headed toward the open waters of the Mediterranean Sea. The Saturnia had begun its voyage in earnest. Soon, we could see the majestic grandeur of the fabled Gulf of Naples so often extolled in the ever popular Neapolitan songs. It had gotten sufficiently dark so that the entire coastline had come alive with street lights and the hillside had become peppered with myriad points of light. The little orchestra set up on the rear deck which had played Anchors Aweigh as the ship was pulling away from its dock, now was playing the sad, mournful, yet haunting strains of the Neapolitan migrating masses of earlier years, *Santa Lucia luntane*. While it was the classical lament of the Italian migrant masses in the 19th and 20th century, the modern migrant did not escape its heartrending effects. It was a poignant moment; one that sears your soul with an enduring, indelible mark. Will I ever see this magical land again? Someday, perhaps!

Meanwhile, the little orchestra, having played its last piece, pulled up stakes and each of the five members went inside to begin their principal duties such as waiters, technical personnel, laundry personnel and the like. Within a few minutes, a waiter came out onto the rear deck ringing a gong and announcing that supper was about to be served. He made quite a racket as he also announced that all passengers were required to proceed to the dining room, choose first or second turn, choose a table which would then be assigned to each of us for the duration of the voyage, and pick up some forms to be filled out for the benefits of the U. S. Customs when we got to New York. We followed the crowd to the dining room. At the recommendation of Signor Greco, an elderly family friend who was sailing with us, we chose the second dinner turn, so that we could sleep a little later in the morning. *Zi' Mattè* (Uncle Matthew), as we used to call him, was an old "American" who had spent many years, off and on like my own grandfather, in the Detroit area. He was nearly seventy years of age, but decided to return to America just to call his two grandsons to the States and give them a fighting chance. His son, Tommaso, the father of the two boys, had been killed in the November 27, 1943, air raid. Signor Greco had sailed from this very port many times in his lifetime, so he had plenty of traveling experience. Being an early riser, he chose first call. Being sleepy heads, Filippo and I chose the second. We selected a table and dinner was served. We had never had that much food before, superbly prepared, and elegantly served. Filippo and I were particularly impressed by the bread. It was a small roll of Italian bread that was so delicious that one could eat it all by itself. Since we could take as many as we wanted, I stuffed about four of them in my pockets. Hoarding was a remnant of the war years.

The Saturnia and its sister ship, the Vulcania, had been converted to serve as troop carriers during the war. When it was put back into regular civilian passenger service, their owners didn't bother to reconvert it, especially since the demand for passenger transportation to and from America was so great that there wasn't time to do the job. Therefore, instead of cabins, there were bunk beds lined up side by side and head to foot in a large barracks-like room that probably contained a hundred or more two-tiered bunks. After being assigned a double bunk (I still remember their numbers, 48a and 48b), Filippo insisted on taking the upper bunk. I gave him an argument about it just to increase his determination to win his point. I succeeded: I didn't want the upper bunk, anyway!

We found our suitcases under the lower bunk as specified in our boarding procedure manual, but mamma had the keys, so I could not put the pilfered bread rolls in the suitcase. They probably wouldn't have fit, anyway. So I placed them under the pillow. To my shock and dismay, Filippo had taken some rolls, too—a lot more than I. He ended up putting them under his pillow, too. The next morning, after we had slept on those rolls, they had become a pile of crumbs. After the gong called the second group, we went to breakfast. Again we were shocked at the type of food and the vast amount we could have. So, we had our fill. After breakfast, mamma gave me the keys to our suitcases, so that I could get some writing material, and at about 9 o'clock I went to my bunk to open the suitcase. To my dismay, I found that the beds had been made up, but the rolls were nowhere to be found. I looked in the upper bunk and, Filippo's were gone too. A gentleman occupying the bunk next to ours, noticing our dismay at not finding the rolls said that the service ladies had thrown them into the trash. Oh, what a shame, I thought to myself. Not to mention that, as I grew up, it had been inculcated in me that it was a mortal sin to throw food away. But the man told us that it was not necessary to hoard food. The war was over, and there was plenty more rolls available at any time. Not to mention that it was not a very hygienic practice to keep food under one's pillow. Of course, I instantly realized that I knew that, but the war years had blurred my thinking. We did not hoard any more rolls after that.

The rest of the voyage was a splendid experience. The sea was as flat as a table with just enough of a ripple to make it interesting. The June sun shined in all its brilliance over the blue Mediterranean. All day long there wasn't a cloud in the sky. After two days, we reached the Strait of Gibraltar. Having done well in history and geography, I knew all about it. So this is what the rock looks like! In late afternoon, the Saturnia announced its presence with three blasts of its powerful fog horn, then it dropped anchor for a few hours to take on passengers. At dusk, with three more fog horn blasts, the ship began its transatlantic voyage.

The Atlantic was different from the Mediterranean. In the Mediterranean the ship pitched, that is it alternately dipped and rose, bow to stern. The motion was front and back, and it didn't seem to bother anybody. In the ocean, however, the ship rocked and rolled. The motion was from side to side, and a lot of people became seasick, including Nonna Concetta. But the waters were calm, and the malaise didn't last very long.

Once in a while, we would see schools of dolphins as they, in groups, would emerge from the water, and after describing a graceful arc in the air, would dive back into the ocean. Occasionally we crossed paths with another ship, passenger or freight, going in the opposite direction. Once in a while we did see clouds in the sky, especially in the morning, but they were not threatening clouds. The second or third day, we passed the Azores Islands.

One great service the ship provided, at least as far as my mother and I were concerned, was the music that came out of those loudspeakers all day long. They played Italian and Neapolitan songs mostly. This was a first for us. Not having had a radio all our lives, to hear all that lovely music non-stop was an absolute dream come true. I learned a lot of songs during the trip. Sometimes they would interrupt the music to make an announcement or two. At noon they even broadcast international news in Italian, English and French. I didn't understand the English, but I took in both the Italian and French version. This gave me a bit of apprehension: I'm going to have to learn that language. Convinced as I was that I had learned nothing while in school, I was concerned. But, I decided to deal with the problem at the proper time, and went back to enjoy the music.

There were some passengers my age on board too. One young man was headed for Buffalo, New York, one was going to Columbus, Ohio, and one whose destination was Boston, Massachusetts. There was a set of twin girls on board, very pretty. They always dressed alike, but I believe they only had two dresses, a red one with white trimmings; the other, a country-girl style blue and white checkers. They were attractive and I couldn't keep my eyes off of them. But, I wouldn't dare strike up a conversation, not with my mother there watching my every move. Their mother, too, had the demeanor of a *Bersagliere* (Italian specialized troop). I didn't want to be embarrassed.

On Saturday night, June 21st, there was a bevy of activities on board. All U.S. Customs forms had to be collected, all suitcases were to be placed along the external corridors on the starboard side of the ship, and other disembarkation preparations were to be made. Mamma was happy to see me interpret those complicated customs papers written in English. I was happy, too, because it was the first time that I was able to realize that maybe, just maybe, the teachers who maligned me at every turn were wrong, after all. For the first time, I was able to read English and understand the gist of the written word.

Sunday morning, June 22nd, I attended mass in the ship's upper deck. I got to serve it, too. Then we went to breakfast. Once in a while, as stated already, the captain would interrupt the music to make an important announcement. I didn't like that. Couldn't he have waited until the song ended before rudely interfering with it?

HELLO, LADY LIBERTY!

It was 8:30 A.M. There was much to do in preparation for the disembarkation which was supposed to take place around noon. We were just coming out of the dining room when we heard the first announcement by the Captain; *"I Signori Passeggeri . . .*! (The esteemed passengers are advised that at approximately 10:30 A.M. we will pass in front of the Statue of Liberty. Anyone wishing to see it is invited to assemble on deck by ten o'clock. Please maintain order and discipline. It will be an emotional moment and we wish to make it a pleasant experience for everyone. Thank you!"). I looked over the railing and I could see the skyline of New York city in the distance as the M/N Saturnia began the final stage of its voyage, entering majestically into the Hudson River Bay. The atmosphere on board was festive and animated, becoming more and more charged with excitement with each passing moment. After breakfast, we went back to our respective bunkers, picked up our suitcases, placed them outside along the corridor where they could be picked up by the porters, made sure we left nothing behind and by 9:30 returned on deck. Mamma and nonna had been invited by an officer to observe the proceedings from a platform at the second level of the ship, access to which was normally blocked to cabin class passengers (it used to be called third class, but the war put an end to that, too. It was now referred to with a euphemistic name). He brought out four chairs from the dining room so mamma, nonna, Joanne, a friend who was headed for Detroit and her mother were sitting there like the four queens in a deck of cards. They had a completely open view of the statue. Filippo and I also found a place on which to climb, so we had an unobstructed view, as well, otherwise we would have seen nothing because in no time that deck looked like the outside of a sports arena on the day of a championship game. Filippo and I sat on a large box protected by a brown canvas cover, our legs dangling on its side, while a large sign near our feet proclaimed that it was strictly forbidden to sit on the structure. We never read the sign, and we didn't know what the structure was but it appeared solid enough to sustain us without itself or us incurring any sort of harmful effect.

While we were preparing our accommodations, another group of people began to arrange for theirs, too. It was the five gentlemen members of the little orchestra who played at the ship's departures and arrivals. They set up right in front of us but adjacent to the railings, so I was able to observe their entire routine. After taking their places, they tried a couple of marches.

And then we saw her! A tiny white speck at first, then it began to acquire shape and getting larger and larger as the ship got closer and closer. Finally, we passed in front of it, and there she stood in all her glory, Lady Liberty proclaiming hope to the whole world. There was pandemonium on board. People cried, they laughed, they hugged, they kissed, they danced, (some drank too) giving off impassioned hoop-la's and hoot-hoots. Excitement had reached fever pitch: we were home. Someone gave me something to drink in a paper cup. I smelled it and gave it back: it was a horrible alcoholic substance, probably whiskey. I handed it back but not to the same person who gave it to me. He quickly gulped it down without even looking at it, or smelling it. I was amazed.

Shortly after passing in front of the statue, I left our high perch because it had started to get hot while something inside of it began to hum. Now I knew why it was strictly forbidden to sit on it. Besides, it was uncomfortable and my legs had begun to "go to sleep." After jumping off, Filippo and I approached the starboard railings and what a spectacle opened in front of our eyes: the Manhattan skyline loomed magnificent and striking in front of us, resplendent in the June sunlight. As we passed in front of the mouth of the East River, mamma approached and pointing to it, saying, *"Quella città è Broccolino!"* "(That's the city of Brooklyn). How did she know that?

As soon as we passed the Statue of Liberty, the ship, which had reduced its speed considerably from the early hours of the morning, slowed down even more to the point that as it approached an island to our left it stopped all together. It was Ellis Island. On its large front lawn, we could see a large sign written with shrubbery planted and groomed in the form of letters. It read: QUARANTINE. They had closed it, so we didn't have to stop there, but it was evident that it was not a very auspicious place to be greeted by, after the Statue of Liberty's lavish promises.

Within a few minutes after we had become aware that the ship had come to a complete stop, the captain came on the PA system and advised the passengers that, the day being Sunday, the ship could not dock immediately until 8 A.M. Monday morning. The longshoremen did not work on Sundays. Relax and enjoy your first day in America, we were told.

Everyone remained on deck for the rest of the day, looking at this and that, glued to the railings on both sides of the ship, scrutinizing this miracle called America which that day smiled resplendent in the June sunshine looking like the enchanted castle of a fabled realm. Filippo and I kept looking at the many, many cars zipping by on a highway on the Brooklyn side of the river. Wow! They all looked new! "Where are they going," asked my little brother. "I don't know!" said I, a little irritated. "Where could they possibly be going?" was Filippo's constant query for the rest of the afternoon.

ARE THEY GOING TO BOMB US?

We went to dinner when they called for the second turn. We had turkey. I didn't like it. We were told that this was the American thing to do. I ate it, but I determined right there and then that turkey would not be my choice of meats in America: it was too dry and its taste too demanding. No wonder they drowned it in all that brown gravy! Ten years later, after my wife arrived from Italy, we developed our own family tradition for Thanksgiving and Christmas: we celebrate with capon, rather than turkey, a much more savory aliment.

We were also served apple pie. That was OK. "The only "American" thing they didn't serve us," quipped a passenger at our table, "was a nice new Chevrolet car!" The quip didn't mean anything to me that day. It took several years for me to grasp the full significance of that statement.

After dinner, we strolled on deck, the music repeated the same songs we had been listening to since we left the port of Napoli. The twins looked really sharp in their Sunday best: one wore yellow with a blue motif, the other wore blue with a yellow motif. That was different. Still, amidst all the excitement of the first day in America, the afternoon loomed long and tedious.

Suddenly, around 2:00 P.M. there was a lot of excitement on board. We heard airplane engines droning overhead. I looked up, startled. I saw two small planes flying around almost as if they were chasing each other playfully like a couple of squirrels. But, soon, they began to leave a white smoke trail behind them. "Oh, no! Not again!" was my first reaction. Filippo, however, was truly concerned, as he ran to me for reassurance. "Are they going to bomb us?" I calmed him down and told him I didn't think they were going to bomb the port of New York that day. Nonna, too, was somewhat apprehensive at this unexpected turn of events, remembering that day in October of '43 when two similar small planes traced a perfect square in the sky. I calmed her down, as well. By that time, however, as we kept looking up, it became evident that they were writing in the sky. Now I know I'm in America, I remember thinking: these people even write messages in the sky. And what was the message? Welcome to America? Some other expression of lofty sentimentality, perhaps? Not on your life. What they wrote was: PEPSI COLA! They repeated it several times so that for an hour or so, one could see the words Pepsi Cola all over the blue sky, even as the letters began to lose their shapes and finally disappeared all together. That served me as an initial admonition that the business of America is business, as Calvin Coolidge once put it. I asked around on deck: what does Pepsi Cola mean? No one could give me an answer. I had to wait until Monday morning, after we docked and disembarked. I saw my Uncle Nick again after eleven years, and my father for the first time, and all I could say to them was, "What's a Pepsi Cola?" They told me it was a soft drink and we would have some for lunch in a little while. So, Pepsi Cola became my first taste of America.

MY LIFE IN AMERICA

My first five years in America were both gratifying and disastrous. They were gratifying because I had the opportunity to "discover" this great Nation, first at the local level, then as I began school, I learned about the Jeffersonian attestations for all Americans, our constitutional guarantees, and the dignity America bestows on all its citizens, at least in theory. Within a few months I learned of the many opportunities available to me, and over the years, I took advantage of every avenue that opened up along the way. At age 19, I even did some radio work in Italian. It proved to me that in America an ambitious young man can achieve almost anything if he pursues it relentlessly. I dared to ask and it was given unto me. Of course, I pursued other fields as well once I realized that I had little talent for radio work. Though it lasted two years, it added a significant dimension to my cultural experience and I had fun in the process. Most importantly, it opened up my highway to opera, which, over the years, became the sustaining prop of my soul.

There were many boys who came from Italy in those days. We would meet at the bounce of a soccer ball on someone's lawn, in a park, or wherever there was an empty, reasonably flat piece of real estate. All, except one of my new friends were older than I, so they all went to work the very next day after arriving from the old country. Because of my classical training in school, however, there was no doubt that I would be headed for some sort of high school. I did so on Monday morning, September 8, 1947, when I entered the West Philadelphia Catholic High School for Boys, 49th and Chestnut Streets, Philadelphia. I was accepted into the 10th grade. In high school, however, beside the temporary language barrier, I was suddenly confronted with a barrage of social pressures for which I was totally unprepared. I didn't know a prom from Prometheus. In fact, I knew who Prometheus was; I just didn't know what a prom was. Even after it was explained to me it didn't make much sense. On the other hand, my new American friends didn't know Botticelli from vermicelli. Oh, they knew vermicelli, all right, but Sandro Botticelli and his *Primavera, Birth of Venus* or *The Coronation of the Virgin* were totally alien to them, as were the other great artistic masterpieces, visual or otherwise. In Italian schools I had read the classics, often in their original language, whereas my new friends in high school were still reading comic books. Now, I don't mean to imply that they were inferior to me in any way. In fact, they were much more advanced than I was in math and science. It was just that we were orbiting the cultural globe on very different planes. All in all, I had crashed head first into a culture-shock wall. One pleasant surprise awaited me, though: in America there was no school on Saturday, as is the practice in Italian schools even to this day. It was my biggest culture shock, and, at the level of teenage mentality, I considered it a weekly "snow day."

By the time I graduated from high school, in 1950, I realized that I had learned a lot in Italy, despite my misguided professors' dire pronouncements to the contrary. It wasn't true that I would never learn to write a letter. In fact, I spent the rest of my life proving old professor Domenico De Mellis to be totally wrong. Unlike the average immigrant, I came to America with a super education. It should have been an advantage for me, but it turned out to be a nightmare because I didn't find a peer group with whom I could share the finer pathways of knowledge. None of my schoolmates had any knowledge of the things I had mastered, the war notwithstanding, nor did they have any interest in knowing about them. Even sports were beyond my sphere of interests. I loved sports, but I only knew soccer and bicycle racing. My new friends didn't know much about either one, at least at that time.

After dreaming about it all our lives, my brother and I couldn't even buy a soccer ball when we first arrived in Norristown because the only sporting goods store there didn't stock them. Filippo and I settled for a volley ball. After playing with home sewn balls made of rags, this was luxury indeed. It was a little light but we didn't mind.

The social interchange was a point of great discomfort for me, however, and nobody was able even to identify that psychological stumbling block, let alone solve it. One night a few months after I started in high school, I was invited to a party. I had never been to an American party before. Every guest was to bring a record. Everyone brought the usual for those years: Harry James, Tommy Dorsey, Glenn Miller and the like. I brought a record that went over like a thud: Edgardo's final aria from Donizetti's, *Lucia di Lammermoor*. It positively crashed. My friends could not figure out how a boy my age could possibly like "that stuff," as they put it. I couldn't figure out how they could not like it. Weren't their ears the same as mine? Apparently not! One of the girls said: "But you grew up with that kind music!" I opted not to try to explain to her that the only music I grew up with was the roar of B-24 Liberator engines, with thousands of 500 lb. bombs providing the percussion.

I was attracted to some of the girls I met in school, but, for me, it was like being in love with the Mona Lisa; beautiful icons hanging on the wall richly framed, but aloof, distant and lifeless. They reminded me of Sandro Botticelli's *Three Graces*: *Aglaia* (Splendor), *Euphrosyne* (Myrth), and *Thalia* (Good Cheer)—ethereal visions made of gossamer and veils. The woman within the vision totally escaped me. There was one "*Aglaia*" that had me going for a while, but she responded with the enthusiasm of a Calico cat. I was probably looked upon by the girls as some sort of quirk of nature. But, then, how could they possibly even imagine that I had survived the onslaught of a major war whose psychological effects were simply immeasurable? One girl even told me to go back to Italy because I didn't have what it takes to please an American girl. It was such a devastating blow to my psyche that to this day I remember the exact spot at the corner of Main and DeKalb Streets in Norristown where she said it to me. Many years later, I realized this assessment to be absurd, but to a sixteen-year-old immigrant it was a near fatal blow. The psychological damage was immense, and I never really recovered from it.

Now, it wasn't that my new friends in school deliberately set out to make my life miserable. Actually, they all wanted to help me, but they didn't know what to do with me. I, myself, didn't know what my needs were or what to do about them. Everyone assumed that my biggest problem was the English language, "the hardest language in the world," as they often described it. Well, after my initial apprehension, English became as easy to learn as licking an ice cream cone. I learned it and learned it well, to the point that later I was able to teach it to American students at the high school and college levels.

Since I mentioned ice cream, may I add that it, too, was a shock to me: in Italy they filled the cones with a spatula; in America they scooped it in a round ball. An insignificant detail? Perhaps, but it made an impression on me, nonetheless.

In learning a language in those days, there was only one method that was recommended: memorization. It worked for me. When I stepped off that boat in New York, I could rattle off all the principal parts of every irregular verb in the English language. My classmates at West Catholic couldn't do that. However it did take me about a year to put the English I had learned in books to practical use. The following anecdote may serve to illustrate what my problem was with the English language, or any language for that matter. When I was a junior at West Catholic, while walking around campus after lunch one spring day in 1949, in the company of two of my classmates, we stopped to talk with Brother Faber, our homeroom teacher. While we talked, there were some boys playing basketball in the courts adjacent to the exercise track. At one point, the basketball rolled toward me. Without hesitating, I simply kicked it back. Well, why not? I was a soccer player, after all. That started a whole new conversation. Even Brother Faber was unfamiliar with the sport. At some point I asked: "Brother, why can't we have a soccer team here at West?" He said: "You'll need a coach, won't you?" I kind of scratched my head for a moment then replied, "Why can't we take a bus like everybody else?" Brother Faber doubled up with laughter. I didn't know then that the word "coach" meant more than just a rail car, or some other form of transportation, it also meant a person who teaches a sport, or directs a sports team. It takes years of speaking a language to smooth out all the rough edges. It would take me a long time to sort out all the subtle nuances of the English language, but I eventually did. And, by the grace of God, I did not forget my native language, in fact, I was able to improve it. Don't ask me how!

Another problem I had was the English alphabet. I had memorized it in Italy on the very first day of our liberation, but I had a bit of a problem in its practical application, especially when I had to put things in alphabetical order. The Italian alphabet only has twenty-one letters as opposed to twenty-six in English. The position of the extra letters, J-K and W-X-Y, always gave me trouble. But, in 1948 Perry Como came out with the alphabet song: *A, you're adorable, B, you're so beautiful, C, you're a cutie full of charm*, etc. I learned the song and I never had problems afterward.

In my first year at West, the Christian Brothers simply let me slide. After all, *"I didn't speak-a da-English,"* as they used to tease me, though mildly and without malevolence. When I started my junior year, however, the first time I said to one of them, "I don't speak English!" Brother Anselm roared back, "The hell you don't! Get in there and work, like everybody else!" I knew then that the party was over.

Socially, it was a different matter. Even Santa Claus was a brand new concept to me. It took me several years to figure out some of the things that went on in school, such as the spring dance, choosing the school ring, electing the student council, homecoming, etc. None of this happened in Italian schools, even at their best. Under war conditions, they were not even a dream. By the time I figured out one event, it was gone and I was confronted with new, even more baffling challenges. Before I could assimilate them all, graduation arrived and I became an adult, and the promises of youth never materialized for me. So, while I cannot fault my new friends for my being hurt, hurt I was, nonetheless, by the avalanche of challenges coming to a new country poses. I, after all, had come to America at the worst possible time in a boy's development.

Ironically, after graduation, I learned to dance fairly well, although it never came naturally for me. After graduation, I was even invited to three proms by girls who attended other high schools, in 1951 and 1953 at Norristown High School and in 1952 at Philadelphia's Southern High School. For many years I humored myself in the belief that those girls asked me to the prom because they found me irresistible. It was only after I began to teach in a high school myself, where I had the possibility of witnessing the social process of getting asked to the prom or not, that I realized that my three *Cinderella's* had probably asked me simply because nobody from their schools had asked them. Oh, well, at least I *dazzled* them by knowing how to choose wine after the prom—in French and in Italian!

THE DEATH OF THE ROYAL SWAN

At this point, I would be remiss if I left out the story of Alba Celeste. I used to call her, "La Tosca" because she had a beautiful voice and the imposing figure the Puccini heroine is renowned for. She dreamed of being an opera singer. She had an exquisite and powerful *lirico-spinto* voice that simply needed to be trained a little more. We had met at Philadelphia's Academy of Music the evening of January 2, 1952, when the Lyric Opera Co. gave a performance of Verdi's Aida. She was nineteen years old, while I was two weeks away from my twentieth birthday. I was in the dumps that night coming off a particularly devastating rebuff. There weren't many people attending the performance that night, so many seats were empty. I was seated right behind two young ladies who, after the opera started, began to giggle most annoyingly. After admonishing them twice, I succeeded in calming them down.

At the end of the first act, one of them turned to me and apologized profusely for their indiscretion. She introduced herself as Alba Celeste B. The other girl, her cousin, was Maria Christina B. We started to discuss the opera, and I was amazed how perceptive they were not only on the merits of that evening's performance, but on the enchanting characteristics of Italian and French opera in general. It turned out that their fathers were both opera buffs, and they themselves had played in the orchestra of the Hallahan Catholic High School for Girls. Alba Celeste played the flute, Maria Christina, the viola.

After a while, they asked me to sit with them in their row of seats. The entire row was practically empty, so I jumped over the red velvet seats and joined them. We established an instant friendship. Soon, they both became part of my circle of friends from the church choir in which I sang. We used to go bowling every Sunday afternoon. Later in the year, when summer concerts in the park began at the old Robin Hood Dell in Philadelphia, we attended them at least once a week as a group.

One night in late June, 1952, after enjoying an exhilarating performance by none other than the now legendary coloratura soprano, Roberta Peters, we were taking the girls home in the Roxborough section of Philadelphia in my buddy Lou De Nardis' brand new Buick Special. Maria Christina sat up front with Lou, while I sat in the back seat with Tosca. She looked radiant that night in a navy velveteen dress adorned with a fine work of ecru lace appliqué, just as I always envisioned *"la Tosca in teatro"* (Tosca in the theatre). She looked particularly provocative that evening, too, with a subtle mischievous air in her demeanor. Did I dare make a move toward her? I was thinking. Just then, and I still don't know how it happened, she fell into my arms and gave me the most luscious, delectable, sensual kiss ever regaled by woman to any man. Helen's kiss to Paris? It paled by comparison. It dimmed the glow of Cleopatra's smooch to Antony by several hundred candles. It even dulled the luster of Juliet's osculation to her Romeo. It was an Apocalyptic blast that, for a split second, disclosed the wonders of heaven itself to a mere mortal. It was a thunderbolt that zapped me practically out of my shoes. That night, Tosca truly made me feel like a man. *Aglaya?* Never heard of her!

For the next several months Tosca and I sought each other's company every chance we got. For some reason, however, we never had a formal date, spoke of love, marriage or even a steady commitment. We simply failed to fall in love, that's all. We just kissed the summer and fall away, gloriously, with limitless delight, yet always within the parameters of decency. "Propriety at all times," had said Michaeleen in the movie, *The Quiet Man,* a few months earlier. We were waiting for Christmas with unspoken anticipation. Perhaps, Santa Claus would bring us love.

But it was not to be. Shortly after Thanksgiving, her mother was taken seriously ill, and she and her father moved in with her aunt in North Jersey. In February, 1953, her mother died and her small family never returned to Pennsylvania. I learned later that she made a career in nursing and moved out west somewhere.

She died young, Tosca did. She contracted some sort of incurable disease and passed away on Christmas Eve, 1973, age 41, never having achieved her dream of singing at the Metropolitan Opera. When I heard about it, I was extremely sad, needless to say. Life had been less than fair to her. She deserved more, much more. I remembered at that point that one of her favorite pieces of music was Camille Saint-Saens', *Le Cygne,* from *Le Carnaval des Animaux* (The Swan from The Carnival of Animals). How appropriate, I thought. The swan had folded her royal wings, gently laid down her long, lovely neck and was no more. *Le cygne est mort—pauvre petit cygne!*

I always pray for Tosca, especially at the midnight mass every Christmas Eve, the anniversary of her death. Even in the absence of romantic love, she was my *Euphrosyne, Galatea* and *Thais*, all packaged up in satin, chiffon, and veils.

MAMMA'S DEATH

In the fall of 1947, my parents took a trip to Detroit to visit mamma's friend, Nannina, the one who sailed with us on the *Saturnia* (she became Joanne in America). When they returned, West Catholic High held an open house for parents and students. My father was bored by it all. He thought I should have learned to be a cobbler, anyway, because, "my friend, Tom, makes good money fixing shoes!" But, mamma, who had seen the inside of every school I had ever attended in Italy, was not only very excited to visit my new American high school, but she was truly impressed seeing the big library, the auditorium, the cafeteria, and she was completely overwhelmed when she visited the science labs. She knew that in America I was going to make it, whatever field I would have chosen.

Moreover, in November the West Catholic High School for Girls, our school's counterpart for female students located four blocks away, gave a concert. I attended the matinee performance given just for students, and I was totally overpowered seeing the 130 piece orchestra made up of young musicians between the ages of fourteen and eighteen. They made heavenly music. So, I asked mamma to accompany me there on Saturday night. I didn't bother to invite my father, who was probably grateful, anyway. Of course, mamma, who loved music as much as I did, was delighted with the whole experience.

She enjoyed Christmas that year, her first in America, and she loved it. Shortly after she returned from Detroit she had gotten herself a job as a seamstress just a block away from where we lived. That made her truly happy. She was making her own money and didn't have to beg my father for it. She was beginning to chart her future as well as mine and Filippo's within this framework of the many wonders that was America.

But, then, in February, 1948, she announced that she was pregnant, and things went down hill after that. We had a very distinguished looking man as our family doctor, Dr. Stephen Stanford. He was such a fine physician that three quarters of his practice was made up of the Italian people from the east end of Norristown, despite the fact that he was an African American. The walls of his office were covered with the pictures of all the children he had delivered. Three quarters of them were white children, most of them Italians. Dr. Stanford even spoke Italian fairly well having served in Italy during WWII. My father should have taken mamma to him, but no, he listened to his "friends," and took her to an "Italian" doctor who couldn't speak a word of Italian. The new doctor botched the whole thing, and by late May, mamma was rushed to the hospital, with all sorts of complications. I prayed a lot in those days. My uncle and I visited every church in town and nearby communities, made all sorts of vows, and even sent a telegram to Padre Pio to intercede with God and save my mother, but to no avail. On June 3, 1948, mamma gave birth prematurely to my brother, Francesco Pio, better known as Frankie. He weighed less than three pounds.

On June 8th, the last week of school, I took the train in Norristown as usual to go to school in Philadelphia. At about 10:30 A.M. while I was in Brother Faber's geometry class, a messenger came to the room and asked me to report to the office of the vice principle, with all my books. I knew what that meant! Brother John Owens, told me my uncle had called saying that my mother was not doing well and that I should leave school and report directly to Montgomery Hospital in Norristown. I did so immediately, reaching the hospital shortly after noon. Mamma died at 2:30 that afternoon. Irony of ironies! After dodging bullets, bombs, mines fields and the Nazi oppressor, and surviving it all, she comes to America only to die of complications from childbirth, a condition that should have been routine, especially in America, but turned into a tragedy, instead. My mother was 41 years of age.

Spec. 4 Francesco Pio De Simone
Photo taken in Viet Nam when he was with the U. S. Army during the war. He is now 59 years old and has three girls and three granddaughters. He is an electrician. Ironically, he experienced war, too, just as we did, but as a combatant. He and our cousin Johnny Sorgini, our Uncle Nick's fourth son, served in Viet Nam at the same time and together.

SEMPER FIDELIS

Mamma's death placed me and my brother in a very serious situation. Aunt Margie, Uncle Nick's wife, herself pregnant with our cousin Johnny, helped raise our little brother with Nonna Concetta's help. At that point, Phil and I could have easily gone astray. But, with God's help (and a lot of other people's), Phil and I managed to stay with our heads above water. I considered college to be beyond my possibilities at this point. I finished high school and in 1952 I started to work for Sharp & Dohme, which would, in time, become Merck, Inc. & Co. I even improved my social demeanor a little. I learned to roller skate and even to dance, sort of, but the latter did not come natural for me. I did my best.

The early 50's proved to be interesting and fun, but, not having any guidance, I missed several opportunities to go to college, albeit on a part time basis. In the summer of 1950, I spent many hours in the company of Father Delia's brother Joe, a language professor at the U.S. Naval Academy. He begged me to apply at Annapolis for admission. I would have had a free education and the military discipline would have helped me regain my self assurance. But, that was precisely the problem: I had no self assurance, so I did not apply. It was probably not in God's plan for me, either. So, let His will be done!

Then, in 1953, I made two moves that changed my life completely around. First, by a series of unusual events and arcane circumstances that included a reluctant trip to Canada, I reestablished a serious correspondence with my first love in Fossacesia, Anna Maria Fantini. My Uncle Nick wanted to go to visit some of our newly arrived relatives in Toronto. I had just purchased a 1941 Dodge. It ran well, but I wasn't sure it could make a long trip. Besides, I needed tires. So I didn't want to go. He insisted and I finally gave in. After three days in Toronto, suddenly Uncle Nick wanted to go home. It was four o'clock in the afternoon. We would have to travel all night. This time I was the one to insist that we go visit one of my former neighbors from Italy, who had also recently arrived in Canada. I won that argument, however, and we went to visit Elisa Fantini Sisti. I asked how her sister, Anna Maria, was. She said that she was fine, and as a matter of fact she had just received a picture of her, which she promptly showed to me. I took one look at that photo, and the old feelings returned. When I got home I wrote to Anna Maria, asking for a copy of that picture. She sent it to me, and it's still in my wallet after 54 years.

Secondly, that same year, on the spur of the moment, I joined the United States Marine Corps. I reported to Parris Island and took my basic training there. I was a good Marine, too, despite my small stature (and I wasn't the shortest Marine in Platoon 182, either. There were several recruits as short as I, or even a little shorter). I loved the Marine Corps. After boot camp and before I received my first orders, however, the U.S. Navy, routinely going through the background of some of the new recruits, discovered that I had been under heavy bombardments as a boy during World War II. To aggravate matters, within a month's time I had had two bouts with a virus infection, with high fever and some incidents of deliriousness. The Navy brass called me in for an interview. I was drilled at length by a committee of five high ranking naval officers. One of them even asked me if I had collaborated with the enemy. That Lieutenant J. G. must have had a poor sense of time and history, or else he would have figured out that I was eight years old at the time WWII began. Well, in the process, they decided they didn't want to take a chance on me, so they gave me a full discharge under honorable conditions and a very handsome separation pay. Actually, Captain Harper, my commanding officer, suggested that as soon as I arrived in Philadelphia I go directly to the recruiting office and re-enlist. Once I reached Philadelphia, however, I was home and I couldn't resist going all the way home to Norristown. Once home,

my folks persuaded me to take my discharge and count my blessings. I took it
and never regretted it. Still, I often ask myself, what if? I loved the Corps, and
my superiors liked me. Over the years, however, subtle little things happened
to me, especially in my dreams, that gave me the impression the Navy may
have been right, after all. They had more experience in that sort of thing.

Despite the brevity of my military career, the United States Marine Corps
restored my self confidence and made me believe in myself. They inculcated
in me the idea that there was nothing I couldn't do if I wanted to do it badly
enough. I've been a little cyclone ever since. Few are the stones I left unkicked!
Also, they ingrained in me the importance of honor, respect for others and
the merit of never betraying the trust others place in you. If you give your
word, keep it at all costs, they told us; your fellow Marines may depend on
you for their very lives. The value system I took home with me from Parris
Island became the basic platform of my future endeavors.

This was "me," B. M. (Before Marines)
This photo got me in trouble in Parris Island. It was taken at a
party some of my friends game me before I left for the Marine
Corps. A friend of mine had the film developed and sent me the
photos at Parris Island. My D. I. (Drill Instructor) opened my
mail—illegally—saw the shock of wavy hair I was sporting in those
days, and proclaimed, "So, you were a cool cat, weren't you?" And,
with that, he proceeded to beat me up with the broomstick of the
Wicked Witch of the West (I think she was his mother!). He made
me bend over and with all the strength he could muster, delivered

ten well placed swings that numbed my back. I was not able to sit down for the next three days. It was nothing short of assault and battery, and totally unnecessary for the making of a good Marine. About ten of us were subjected to that indignation. If it happened today, I could have that baboon court-martialed. By then, of course, that hair had been unceremoniously and cheerfully shorn off by the Corps' sheep shearer. It never grew back quite the same way.

Finally, after chasing empty dreams for nine years, I decided that the girl who told me to go back to Italy because I wouldn't make it in America was probably right, and so I decided to return to my roots. Besides, I had all but mastered the English language and I felt invincible. It had become clear to me, by then, that there was indeed a place for me in America, but as an Italian American, my place was on one of the lowest rungs of the ladder of success. There was a definite pecking order in this society, and my number was nowhere near the top. I could not accept that. I was too much aware of my cultural heritage to be willing to play second string to a basically unenlightened multitude. So, not having my mother's guiding hand to help me along, I decided to go back where I came from. Surely there would be a job for me in Italy! Still, I had no college education. It would have been a difficult task, but I couldn't see it then. After dreaming about America since my first years of awareness, I was totally disillusioned with its realities. I felt I could never be accepted into its social fabric. I was fascinated by the world I had observed and wanted so much to be a part of it, but I could not find the door, much less the key that might have unlocked its enigmatic, esoteric mysteries.

I sailed from New York aboard the liner *Cristoforo Colombo,* on April 12, 1956, bound for Naples, fully intending to remain in Italy. I had a return trip paid, just in case, but I made arrangements to get my money back should I decide to stay in Italy. When I got there, I learned that Anna Maria Fantini, my first love, the most beautiful girl in town, and the nicest (and what a cook!), was available and willing. After only a few days that I was there, I was all set to go to Rome to start looking for a job possibly with an American firm or agency, when her father, an old American, said to me, "You want my daughter? You can have her with my blessings, but on condition that you go back to America and count your blessings." He convinced me to return to the United States instead of chasing impossible mirages. I had to admit that, eleven years after WWII had ended, things in Italy were still very bad. Remnants of the war were still visible all over town and poverty was running rampant. Money was scarce and people were on the verge of despair.

The Italian ocean liner Andrea Doria on her way to New York, April 16, 1956.

I filmed it from the deck of its sister ship, *Cristoforo Colombo*, in mid-Atlantic Ocean, with the telephoto lens of a personal movie camera. I was able to print the above picture from a 45 year old single 8mm frame. On June 25th, I sailed the *Doria* from Naples back to New York. On July 25th, near the end of her very next trip to America, the *Doria* was speared by the Swedish ship, *Stockholm*, and sank.

Anna Maria and I got married on June 2, 1956. Italy, that day, was all aglow with flags and festoons. I joke about it saying that I thought it was for us, but actually I knew it was the same day the country was celebrating the tenth anniversary of the Republic. I remembered that as a student in Chieti ten years before, I had participated in that historical event. So, on June 24, 1956, as previously planned, I sailed the Andrea Doria back to New York—the trip before she sank.

A year later, on May 11, 1957, Anna Maria joined me in America and we started on the runway of life together. Over the years we have encountered but few bumps along the way. And, why not? We grew up together, went to school together under the most difficult of circumstances (including the experience of the sleeping bats in the classroom), and, above all, we suffered together. We understand each other. We had four children and three grandchildren.

Our family before wedding bells began "breaking it up."
Seated on the floor are my two daughters, Rosanna, in the white dress, and Maria Pia in the sailor outfit, holding the cat, "Poozie." Anna Maria and I are seated on the sofa. Standing top left is Mario, our oldest. He is with the Lord now. Bringing up the rear is Francis. He has since cut his hair and slimmed down somewhat. The photo was taken in our house in May, 1982. In June, we all traveled to Italy for Pia's wedding to the son of one of our former neighbors she'd met while visiting her grandparents. She has two boys.

These are my three grandsons. Maria Pia's two sons hold dual citizenships and are proud to be Americans. Max, at 21, has visited with us in America eleven times already.

Massimiliano Natale, Max, for short, our first grandson. He is studying at the University of Pescara to be an interpreter and hopes to spend some time living and working in the United States.

Lorenzo Natale, a "sinfully" handsome soccer player. He has opted to pursue his studies as a culinary high school student at the famous G. Marchitelli Institute in Villa Santa Maria, one of the most important schools of its kind in Italy.

Anthony Chiaravalloti, Rosanne's boy. At fourteen, he is quite a soccer and ice hockey player. He is a handsome boy with an open personality and pleasant disposition. He will enter Kennedy Kenrick Catholic High School this fall. It's the former Bishop Kenrick H.S. where I taught.

Finally, with Anna Maria's help and devotion (and Merck's financial support), I entered Villanova University's part-time division, in 1961. It took me eight years to earn my degree, but I finally made it. I graduated with the class of 1969. My graduation picture appears in the '69 *The Spires*, Villanova's year book. Together with the photos of the graduates that year, each page contained a picture of a campus scene. In the center left of page 258, they put a picture of a large piece of land the University had recently purchased on the south side of the P&W train tracks, intending to build high rise dorms on it. Over the years they did just that, but then it was nothing but wilderness. So the caption under the photo reads, *The Great Wasteland!* Unfortunately, that caption is also directly above my head. Fortuitous incidents like that tend to keep a man very humble, indeed!

Even that late in my life (I was 36 years old by then), I still held out hope that I could study medicine. But, part-time evening school was at its early stages and the necessary pre-med courses were simply not available, so it didn't work out. After graduation, I even considered entering law school, but I settled for whatever I could get.

My job with Merck put food on my table and a roof over my family's head, and lasted 42 years. However, although they sent me to college, they refused to give me an opportunity for advancement. For many years I held a grudge against the management for denying me the opportunity to exercise the education in which they had invested thousands of dollars, until one day it finally dawned on me: the Lord didn't need another supervisor in that company. What He did need was a teacher, one who understood the way to reach young people effectively and without pressure. Without going into great details of how it happened, let me say that after I received my degree, in May, 1969, I still had not even thought about becoming a teacher. Yet, by September, by a series of arcane incidents, somehow I ended up in a classroom. I started to teach at Bishop Kenrick High School. I felt God's presence there, too. I needed a money job and a psychological job. It would have been nice to have one job that incorporated both, but it was better than nothing. At Merck I applied for the position of lab technician, in the second shift and got it. So, I opted to remain there and teach during the day. The very same day I started at the high school, I also started my new job at Merck. It was supposed to last two years at the most. It lasted nineteen years!

So, here I was, teaching English to Americans in high school. Me! An immigrant who learned English as a teenager! Where, but in America? I taught English and Business Math for a few years until one of my principals discovered I could teach other languages as well. From then on, I taught English, Latin, Italian, French and Spanish, as needed. Providentially, they took math away from me. The first faculty meeting I ever attended at Kenrick, the principal, Father Richard LaHart, encouraged his faculty members to, "Teach values. Regardless of your particular discipline, teach values, first." I took him seriously. Since it was a Catholic school, it was easy to do. So what were my values? The most fundamental value I learned, besides the basic tenets of my religious beliefs, was what I learned in the Marine Corps: "Never betray trust. If you give your word, keep it at all costs!" That wise counsel served me well for the rest of my life, and I hope I was able to pass it on to all my former students.

I returned to Villanova University and in 1975 I earned a Master's degree in English. Later, still, I received another Master's in Romance Languages from Rutgers University, coming within a hair to getting my PhD. But, by then, I was 55 years of age and I had had it with school. In 1988, just before Bishop Kenrick High School merged with another high school to become the Kennedy-Kenrick Catholic High School, I opted to retire, thus avoiding some bitter collisions with other teachers in the system. After that, I taught Italian and English at various colleges in the Philadelphia area as an adjunct professor, while remaining at Merck. I even returned to Villanova University as an adjunct professor of Italian for a number of years.

Finally, in Dante's *Inferno*, Odysseus advises us, *"Considerate la vostra semenza: fatti non foste a viver come bruti, ma per seguir virtute e canoscenza."* ("Consider your seed: you were not made to live as brutes, but to pursue virtue and knowledge." *Inferno, XXVI 118-120*). With the Lord's help and my mother's prodding, I heeded the Divine Poet's advice and sought to widen my cultural horizons. In that respect, I may have imbibed the spirit of the Renaissance with my mother's milk and breathed-in its rich and varied aromas with the salty air of the Adriatic Sea I inhaled as a child. But it was here in America that I found the substance that brought it all to fruition. Here I found the well stocked libraries, great schools and universities, majestic theaters and opera houses, and magnificent museums richly endowed with some of the world's greatest artistic masterpieces. Also, over the years, I purchased books, records, tapes and videos that made the whole package bloom and flourish. It's been an exhilarating roller-coaster, and it rendered my life worth living. Thank you, America!

WAR REMAINS WITH US FOREVER

Recently, I asked my wife if she thought the war had conditioned us. Her answer was an unequivocal yes. Just because we weren't killed or wounded, it doesn't mean that we were able to brush off the nasty experiences we had, for they will stay with us and condition our every move for the rest of our lives. Still, by the grace of God, we survived. The main differences between us and our American friends must be judged against this background. And so, to the most compassionate, caring, considerate, thoughtful and loving person I know, my wife, Anna Maria, I raise a cup of Asti Spumante with a resounding TI VOGLIO BENE! She, after all, rendered my life meaningful.

For us, America is home, but we try to return to Fossacesia every couple of years. For one thing, every time I go back it's like I never left. As soon as word gets around that we're in town, our old friends come around one by one. In no time they get me involved in the socio-cultural programs they have set up during the month of August each year—the famous *Ferragosto*. In 1995, I even got to be a judge in a beauty contest for the preliminaries of Miss Italy. I enjoyed that one very much!

The most important reason, however, is that we have family there. On June 2, 2006, Anna Maria and I celebrated our Golden Jubilee. It's been an uplifting and fabulous trip together. I am what I am because of the woman I married.

**Anna Maria and I celebrating our 50th anniversary
at the Jersey shore**

We gave each other as an anniversary present a ticket to a concert
by André Rieu and his Johan Strauss Orchestra, in Atlantic City,
N.J., (her choice, but one that met with my instant approval). I took
her out to dinner and afterward we took a stroll on the boardwalk
before going to the concert hall. A friend who accompanied us took
this photo. Anna Maria is holding an ice cream cone. Shortly after
the picture was taken, as she has done innumerable times in fifty
years, she handed me the cone asking me to finish it for her. Oh,
the things I won't do for my beautiful lady!

Philip De Simone and Dr. Vincent Sollimo
The photo was taken at Girard College in Philadelphia the evening that my nephew, Dr. Joseph De Simone, Phil's son, received a prestigious award for his chemical research. Along with my brother is our life-long friend, Dr. Vincent Sollimo.

For many years, I had the pleasure of teaching Hawthorne's *The Scarlet Letter* in high school and college. I was always impressed with Hawthorne's personal touch when he, before beginning the narration, plucks a rose from the rosebush that grows next to the prison door and offers it to the reader "to symbolize some sweet moral blossom . . ." Emulating the gesture of my illustrious predecessor, may I offer a similar tribute at the close of this tale of pain and suffering? Not having a rosebush at hand, however, I will conclude this narrative with Aaron's Blessing instead, offered as a token of gratitude and goodwill to all who read this book, with the hope that peace and harmony will soon reign supreme all over the world.

> The Lord bless you and keep you;
> The Lord make His face to shine upon you
> and be gracious to you;
> The Lord turn His face to you and give you peace.

SHALOM!

BIBLIOGRAPHY

Liceo Scientifico "Fermi," *Il sentiero della libertà, memorie di Carlo Azelio Ciampi,* Edizioni Laterza, Roma, 2003.

Ambrose, Stephen E., *The Wild Blue*: The man and boys who flew the B-24's over Germany, Simon and Schuster, New York, 2001.

Di Giorgio, Antonino, *Un 'estate in bicicletta,* Rocco Carabba, Lanciano, 1982.

Di Sante, Costantino, *Ebrei in Abruzzo 1940-44,* download from the Internet.

Fangaresi, Dante, *Dieci settimane a San Sabba,* Diacronia, Vigevano (PV), 1994.

Franceschelli, Max, *La guerra in casa*, Édicola Editrice, Chieti, 2006.

Eisenstein, Maria, *L'internata numero 6,* Tranchedi, Milano, 1994.

Folkel, Ferruccio, *La Risiera di San Sabba,* PCP Libri, Milano, 2000.

Marchione, Sr. Margherita, *Yours is a Precious Witness*, The Paulist Press, Mahwah, N.J., 1997

Nativio, Giovanni, *La guerra in Abruzzo,* Carabba, Lanciano, 1971.

Nicolucci, Alberto, *Guerra e società a Fossacesia,* Editrice Itinerari, Lanciano, 1999.

Orecchioni, Gianni, *I sassi e le ombre,* Edizioni di Storia e Letteratura, Roma, 1999.

Raimo, Goffredo, *A Dachau per amore*, Giovanni Palatucci, Dragonetti, Montella, 1992.

Robuffo, Laurus, *Giovanni Palatucci,* Polizia di Stato, Nuova Grafica, Roma, 2002.

Sartini, Gelio, *Campo 160*, Guastaldi Editore in Milano.

Spartaco-Capogreco, Carlo, *I campi di internamento fascisti per gli Ebrei*, Storia Contemporanea, Marche-Israele, 1991.

Spinosa, Antonio, *L 'Italia liberata,* Storia Illustrata, Arnoldo Mondatori, Milano, 1995.

Tozzi, Tommaso, *La Brigata Majella,* R. Carabba, Lanciano, 1986.

Vallauri, Carlo, *Soldati—Le forze armate italiane dall'armistizio alla Liberazione,* UTET Libreria, Torino, 2003.

Zuccotti, Susan, *The Italians and the Holocaust,* University of Nebraska Press, Lincoln, 1996.

Zuelke, Mark, *Ortona*, Stoddart Publishing Co., Ltd., Toronto, 1999.

Edwards Brothers Malloy
Thorofare, NJ USA
August 20, 2013